Greek Tragedy in a Global Crisis

ALSO AVAILABLE FROM BLOOMSBURY

Classical Greek Tragedy by Judith Fletcher

Queer Euripides: Re-Readings in Greek Tragedy, edited by Sarah Olsen and
Mario Telò

*The Materialities of Greek Tragedy: Objects and Affect in Aeschylus, Sophocles,
and Euripides*, edited by Mario Telò and Melissa Mueller

Greek Tragedy in a Global Crisis

Reading through Pandemic Times

Mario Telò

BLOOMSBURY ACADEMIC
LONDON • NEW YORK • OXFORD • NEW DELHI • SYDNEY

BLOOMSBURY ACADEMIC
Bloomsbury Publishing Plc
50 Bedford Square, London, WC1B 3DP, UK
1385 Broadway, New York, NY 10018, USA
29 Earlsfort Terrace, Dublin 2, Ireland

BLOOMSBURY, BLOOMSBURY ACADEMIC and the Diana logo are trademarks
of Bloomsbury Publishing Plc

First published in Great Britain 2023

A catalogue record for this book is available from the British Library.

A catalog record for this book is available from the Library of Congress.

ISBN: HB: 978-1-3503-4811-0
       PB: 978-1-3503-4812-7
       ePDF: 978-1-3503-4813-4
       eBook: 978-1-3503-4814-1

Typeset by RefineCatch Limited, Bungay, Suffolk
Printed and bound in Great Britain

To find out more about our authors and books visit www.bloomsbury.com
and sign up for our newsletters.

Contents

Figures

Acknowledgments

My deepest thanks to Alice Wright and Lily Mac Mahon for their generous enthusiasm about this project, and to two very supportive anonymous readers. Many thanks also to various friends and colleagues who have provided feedback at various stages: Karen Bassi, Andrew Benjamin, M. M. McCabe, Helen Morales, Tom Phillips, Jim Porter, Victoria Rimell, and Debarati Sanyal. I am deeply grateful to Judith Butler for allowing me to see the proofs of *What World Is This? A Pandemic Phenomenology* (Columbia University Press, 2022) before publication—and for the never-ending inspiration of their work. Heartfelt thanks also to Bonnie Honig for sharing her wonderful article "Toward a Democratic Theory of Contagion" (part of a larger project) and for exciting exchanges during a summer of "pandemic writing." As always, Alex Press is the conditio sine qua non of all I do. Being always together in our Oakland apartment made the 2020 lockdown not simply bearable, but the most intense (and, dare I say it, enjoyable) experience of partnership and shared life. Alex's intellect, kindness, and patience animate the conception and writing of this book much more pervasively than any acknowledgment could do justice to. I am also grateful to Juliet Gardner for her meticulous copy-editing and to the editorial and production staff at the press (Sophie Beardsworth, Merv Honeywood, and Zoe Osman).

With the exception of *Iphigenia in Aulis* in chapter 3, where I follow the edition of Collard and Morwood (2017), the texts of Aeschylus, Sophocles, and Euripides are cited according to the most recent OCT editions—by Page (1972), Lloyd-Jones and Wilson (1990), and Diggle (1981–94), respectively. Unless otherwise indicated, all translations are mine.

Introduction
Reading Greek Tragedy through Pandemic Times

First the images of absence became common place. Pictures were taken of a newly ubiquitous nothing: of no people on city streets, no people in major plazas of the world, no people at rallies, no people in classrooms, no one in abandoned markets, no one in desolate businesses, no one in churches without mourners where closed coffins conveyed the ever-silenced dead into the afterlife. These empty spaces were also quietly reassuring of state-mandated efforts to contain the spread of disease. For the most part these were images of relative silence. Even as these sonic images of silence bore an alarming resemblance to postapocalyptic scenes of mass extinction, these hushed public spaces were almost always paired with images or descriptions of noisy places where essential workers were busy saving everyone else.[1]

In this account of the 2020 lockdown, the apparent end of life at the beginning of the pandemic era ("the Pandemicene")—in which we are all still deeply embedded, despite denials, disavowals, delusions[2]—art historian Hannah Higgins takes on the role of the Messenger in Greek tragedy, the usually unnamed character who, with a voice amplified by a mask, makes the offstage visible, brings into the open impressions of a polluting event whose verbal (re)creation illusorily protects, or immunizes, spectators. The "sonic images"—perceptive flashes arranged in a pristine parataxis of *no*'s; losses; voided, deserted spaces—capture the contradictory sensations left by the pandemic: the frightening yet liberating feeling of reaching the end of the world, imminent extinction—an imminence, however, laden with the chronic exhaustion of ongoing non-eventality—combined with the realization that nothing has changed, that the systemic inequalities structuring the world as we know it, the race-, gender-, and class-based hierarchies constituting the social, have not been interrupted, but heightened. (The "essential workers" cannot, in fact, allow themselves to desert their stations, but are "busy saving everyone else," are cast in a heroic role that legitimizes their immolation.)[3] The tension between a radically disruptive imminence—not only a dystopian annihilation but also a quasi-utopian reinvention of the social—and a suffocating permanence, a preservation and reinscription of the status quo, appears fundamentally "tragic" in the sense of that which cannot be resolved.[4] There is no question that "the virus itself stands in for the hubris of humanity"[5]—for the ecological catastrophe that is humanity[6]—besides laying bare the Western use of "humanity" to dehumanize; the utter incompatibility between capitalism and care for the other; and the persistence of the auto-immunitarian equivalence between whiteness and invulnerability. The virus also "turn[s] us into something like itself: not living but not yet dead,"[7] each term ("living," "dead") encompassing the possibility of radical disruption or prolongation of the status quo. The "stasis of constant crisis"[8] stemming from this simultaneity and interchangeability of life and death burdens the air. Likewise, the formal archive of Greek tragedy diffuses the unruly energy of *lifedeath*[9] through its never fully graspable diction; its richly opaque performative possibilities, enfleshed musically and choreographically; its twisted configurations of the visual, aural, and haptic; its imbrications of closure and openness; and, most crucially, the intimations of social and political re-arrangement, re-distribution, dismantling, abolition.[10]

    While elsewhere I treated Greek tragedy as a contagious affective machine, whose principles I theorized anti-cathartically,[11] in this book I propose a series of experiments in re-reading Greek tragedy at a moment of planetary crisis, of overdetermined, self-renewing stagnation (medical, diplomatic, political, social), at a time that seems to have breached the fourth wall between tragic mimesis, a world of fictional atrocities, and the allegedly safe space of spectators and readers. The mask, the theatrical prosthesis par excellence, has given us quasi-anonymous, de-individualized faces; it has converted readers and spectators into actors. Repurposing Jean Baudrillard's words from his 1989 essay "Anorexic Ruins," written in reference to the Cold War and capitalism, we could say that our current predicament "is no longer a matter of crisis but . . . a catastrophe in slow motion," marked by "the horror and the charm of [an] ice age,"[12] which, in a sense, is what tragedy, in its aesthetic appropriation of the frozen (yet still alive) world of myth, brings to its readers in any moment of its transhistorical reception. The Covid-19 pandemic, like others before it (particularly AIDS), has highlighted the porosity between the metaphoric and the literal in the notions of "contagion," "infection," "pollution," and "toxicity"—the HIV epidemic literalized the homophobic assimilation of homosexuality to a disease; Covid, conversely, made morbid societal phenomena such as racism and neocolonial capitalisms more readily graspable as viral diseases.[13] In our times, the affective power of tragic aesthetics—usually seen as no more than a mild metaphorical contagion, but impossible to circumscribe in its psychic, spatial, and temporal effect—has never felt more overwhelmingly Real.[14] The unsolvable oscillation between literal and figurative that Susan Sontag famously theorized in her HIV-inspired essay on illness is, to an extent, homologous to the confusion of tragic mimesis and "reality" that, as remarked by Jennifer Wallace, turned Sontag's 1993 Sarajevo production of Beckett's *Waiting for Godot* into a major political intervention, a radical gesture of dissensual *poiêsis*.[15] While, in the course of the book, I refer to and discuss contemporary adaptations and productions of Greek tragedy that were published and performed between 2020 and 2022,[16] or just before the outbreak of the pandemic, my goal is to bring the generative, defamiliarizing anachronism of adaptation into the scholarly practice of reading the Greek "original," which can never be separated from its reception, including literary criticism. This interpretive approach entails not simply reading tragedy through the pandemic, reading the pandemic *into* tragedy, heeding the interpretive effects arising from a specific, historically situated experience of tragic textuality, but also using the "stasis of constant crisis"—the defining psychic atmosphere of the moment, the Zeitgeist of no-time or of saturated time—to inhabit the unsettling non-normativity, the queerness of tragic feeling.[17]

I present, in this book, a series of interpretive and affective engagements with Greek tragedy that, in the practice of critical-theoretically informed close reading, programmatically embrace the exceptional circumstances of my own time. Seizing on the anachronism inherent in every act of reading while refusing the dichotomy between ancient text and modern reception, I show how the poetic form of ten emblematic plays of Greek tragedy can speak to us about the pandemic as well as the crises it has aggravated and come to epitomize.[18] The readings proposed here, which I developed between spring 2020 and summer 2022—some of them in the brief period of mandated domestic seclusion and its extended, voluntary afterlife—originate from, and self-consciously reflect, the effort to understand and cope with the temporal and relational conditions imposed by the pandemic. This effort does not only shape, but is, to a degree, thematized in the methodological orientation of each of the chapters, which are grounded in the valorization of extemporaneous impressions; granular analysis; and the suggestive, unsettling, uncanny power of individual, micro- or macro-units of sense or nonsense. It also informs the chapters' specific concerns: achrony, atmospheric saturation, breathlessness, political decision-making, ecological disaster, extinction, forbidden intimacy, relational toxicity, viral solidarity, geological extraction, neocolonial necropolitics, necroresistance, police surveillance, insurrection. We can say that these readings emerge from the encounter, deterritorialization, and intertwining between an interpreting "I" dispossessed by its self-positioning in a moment of global crisis[19]—and furthering this dispossession in the very process of the reading experience—and a textual object that enacts crisis in all the various facets of its formal constitution.[20] While this equal encounter of *object*ivities (rather than *subject*ivities) is, to an extent, integral to any act of reading—notwithstanding self-serving and circular claims of historical accuracy or discursive "purity" and axiologies of plausibility and implausibility— it acquires particular traction as we conceptualize how reading operates at a moment when the interpretive voice that confronts or bonds with the tragic text's formal crisis or form-as-crisis is suspended between radical break (utopian or dystopian) and paralyzing conservation. In re-approaching the masterworks of Greek tragedy, my methodological privileging of affective adjacency and intimate impressionism, of mutual "interobjective" care as an alternative to hierarchical relational bonds or, conversely, to abstract indeterminacy,[21] is also reflected in the essayistic quality of the chapters. Concentrating on selected scenes, on isolated moments separated from the conventional flow of time, as, in different ways, we seemed to be at the outbreak of the pandemic (and, to an extent, we still are, as we struggle to see a clear "after"), my re-readings seek an experiential imbrication (precarious, imperfect, tendentious) between objects. I conceive the interpretive process as an interobjective being-acted upon, in which the notional interpreter lets herself/ itself be undone by the effects of reading that the textual object alluringly, tantalizingly tenders, dissolving the mastery it ostensibly bestows. Such re-readings, I believe, are, as Fred Moten puts it, "reading's condition of possibility." Moten conceives of "re-reading as refusal ... as the degenerative decomposition of readerly anticipation, as the degenerative recomposition of readerly anticipation, as the speculative, disruptive irruption of what is, as 'is' is anoriginally displaced by 'as.'"[22] Reading is, in this view, nothing but the re-reading that transforms the ontological stability of descriptivism ("is") into the figurative multiplicity and imaginative openness of against-the-grain interpretive disruption ("as").[23] As the chapters show, the anachronistic richness or vitality of Greek tragic form emerges from its overdetermination, its twistedness, its susceptibility to overanalysis and against-the-grain readings, all of which make it converge with and enact the counterintuitive, emancipatory modes of thought characteristic of contemporary critical theory.[24] In a recent essay on Aeschylus's *Eumenides*, Judith Butler observes, "We can, and must, read texts against and beyond themselves, so that they can continue to speak to us."[25] This "we" is, for me, the equivalent of the interobjective deterritorialization fostered by overanalysis, an epistemological and affective self-dispossession rather than a performance of mastery.

With disruptive, excessive, radical force, tragic plots and, especially, the overwrought structures and unruly geometries of tragic form—phonetic, morphological, and syntactical, as well as dramaturgical—materialize subliminal images of infected atmospheres, stretched-out temporalities, achronies, anti-hierarchical affective and social bonding, insurrectionary breathlessness, even a world before (or after) human life, while implicitly building a discourse of resistance, disidentification, abolition. The poetic formalisms that I tease out in my experiments in pandemic reading have an unbound, viral force that is co-constitutive of the contagious power of tragic feeling, in keeping with the disavowed insight that "to be human is . . . to be a human/virus hybrid almost from the year we're born."[26] They connect with our affective and cognitive experiences of the virus, with our exertion in trying to formalize it, to give some vicarious graphic shape or structure to the ghostly invisibility that touches us. A return to hyper-formalistic reading that is structured around some of the most iconic plays and characters (Alcestis, Antigone, Hecuba, Iphigenia, Niobe, Oedipus, Prometheus, the suppliant women, the Trojan women, and Teiresias, Cadmus, and Dionysus in *Bacchae*), this book participates in the debates that have emerged as disaster becomes routine in the time-out-of-joint of a pandemic world that desperately seeks to become post-pandemic. Within the four sections ("Air Time Faces," "Communities," "Ruins," "Insurrections"), the chapters bear the names of characters, singular or plural, whose materializations in and as form, when placed in imaginative proximity with a reader of the Pandemicene, intimate how the ancient Greek tragic imaginary visualizes or expresses our time. A temporal expanse that encompasses all pre-existing and future crises, the pandemic coincides with the queer unhistoricism of tragedy, its distinctive collapsing of present, past, and future, which derives from its recontextualization of myth as a notional past in a performative present that is always a potential reperformative future.[27] A hyper-attention to the formalisms of the Greek text can generate productive resonances and wayward hints of convergences, pointing to unexpected critical-theoretical possibilities and to a metapolitical critique that inheres in tragic feeling.

In a *New Yorker* article (September 1, 2020), Elif Batuman discusses the important initiative of Theater of War Productions: Zoom performances of Greek tragedy (including *Oedipus the King, Antigone,* Aeschylus's *Suppliant Women*) with casts consisting of both celebrity actors and ordinary citizens.[28] Noting that "there were no buttons to change between gallery and speaker view" and that "you were in a 'meeting,' but one you were powerless to control, proceeding by itself, with the inexorability of fate," Batuman invites us to see a threefold correspondence between the abstract principle of "fate"—the abyss where, according to a well-established interpretive paradigm, all tragic characters collapse, regardless of their direct responsibilities—the hyperobject of the virus, and the digital Real, the virtual (non-)reality that has become the routine medium of communication.[29] This correspondence, which confronts us with our inability to grasp, comprehend, capture the virus, might provide us with a convenient excuse for evading our responsibilities, for delaying yet again the moment of societal *anagnôrisis* ("recognition"), the no-longer-postponable time of reckoning. Rather than helping us "get through the pandemic," as announced by the article's headline,[30] which presents the current crisis as a circumscribed phenomenon, a parenthesis before the return to the way things were, re-engaging with Greek tragedy now means acknowledging that there is no return or aftermath. What remains is the chronicity of the crisis, not a state of emergency or exception with a perceptible endpoint, but an endless dilation, in which the longing for a status quo ante, with its inherent impossibility, feeds the perverse pleasure of tragic anti-catharsis.[31] If Greek tragedy can help us cope with the pandemic, it may do so by pushing against our disavowal, our pursuit of restoration, our yearning for repair—a yearning that might contribute to preserving rather than dismantling systemic structures of inequality.[32]

The overdetermined crisis that we are facing is troped by its all-encompassing (im)material, spectral container, which figures prominently in the tragic imaginary assembled by this book: an oversaturated atmosphere claustrophobically burdened by an array of toxins as well as symbolic accretions from its discursive presentation as the space of overlapping catastrophes, and of the rebellious responses to them. As Mel Chen has remarked:

> Covid-19 ... and the California seasonal fires, intensified due to human-induced climate change as well as poor fire policy, are two airy phenomena that dance together, aloft, touching. Surely, they make contact in actuality: in one conjuncture, smoky air intermingles with the exhalations of an infected, unmasked pedestrian, creating a doubly potent inhalant for someone else; in the next beat, wildfire smoke is also inhaled into that infected pedestrian's body.[33]

Russian bombardment in Ukraine, which is reviving the ecological and psychological disaster of Chernobyl, should be added to this chorality of airy phenomena, to the exhalations and inhalations that Chen conceptualizes as an intermingling.[34] A similar image, "intertwinement," is employed by Butler to theorize the pivotal ethical issue posed by the pandemic: that is, "global interdependency as a life-or-death matter," the critically phenomenological (that is, experiential and political) understanding of the world "as a way of already and always being implicated in each other's life."[35] As Butler puts it, "We won't be able to understand shared vulnerability and interdependency unless we concede that we pass the air we breathe to one another, that we share the surfaces of the world, and that we cannot touch another without also being touched."[36] This mutual touching of human bodies and of bodies and air also occurs in acts of rebellion, in the insurrectionary exhalations and inhalations of the BLM, feminist, trans[*], and pacifist protests against the social viruses of racism, transphobia, capitalism, extractivism, and colonialism—the ills that have, directly or indirectly, caused our current predicament. Analyzing Max Scheler's essay "On the Phenomenon of the Tragic," Butler draws attention to the fact that, for Scheler, the tragic is the mode—not just aesthetic, but broadly phenomenological—"in which the world exhibits itself," through a "heavy breath."[37] The world manifests itself through the tragic understood as the air exhaled or vocalized in grief, sorrow, anger, insurrection, feelings that we breathe in daily, in the act of living, the substance of an experiential commons that disrupts the notional separation between self and other.[38] "Potential and actual grief is in the air we breathe," Butler observes, just as "the breath is . . . the means of passage for the virus and for the grief that sometimes follows, as well as the life that survives."[39] Re-reading tragedy now—reading pandemically— means interpretively inhabiting this air, cognitively and affectively feeling the accreted breath that interobjectively manifests the world. Reading tragedy pandemically is, ultimately, a way to valorize the conative impetus of intertwined exhalations that rise against every attempt to stifle the right to breathe of some of us, that is, inevitably, all of us.

"The atmosphere in which we live weighs upon everyone with a 20,000 pound force. But do you feel it?"[40] In the first part, "Air Time Faces," I consider three plays that supply inklings of pandemic feelings: sensory and atmospheric oversaturation, achrony, waiting, decisional anxiety, and a longing for proximity and touch both fostered and hindered by the mask, the symbol of Greek tragedy, which has theatricalized our lives, our daily routines. The sensory congestion that we can locate in *Oedipus the King*, the pandemic play par excellence, has a temporal counterpart in the feeling of excessive time in *Bacchae* and *Iphigenia in Aulis*, Euripides' last two plays, which thematize, respectively, the contagion of Dionysian intoxication and the windless air of Aulis before the Trojan expedition. In the first chapter, I consider the textual feel of miasma or contagion in *Oedipus the King*, heeding the ways that formal congestion (alliteration, polyptoton, and other effects of phonetic thickening) figures a saturated atmosphere that registers as a super-sense. Here I mean not just a convergence of touch, smell, and sound but an overdetermined ghostly opacity, a hauntological *aisthêsis* ("sensation, perception") of heaviness that provides another way of conceptualizing the play's themes of invisibility, darkness, and blindness.[41] In pandemic times, the play's formal texture also bears on the nexus of temporality and perception—on the fact that when time seems unable to divide itself or open itself to the event, perception is dulled.[42] (The loss of smell and taste caused in the early days of the pandemic might be regarded as a negative perception or even a mimesis of the enveloping achrony.) In the second chapter, I dwell on the temporality of hesitation as an alternative that Euripides' *Bacchae* offers to the manic claims of decision-making and the future. Instead of focusing on the Maenads's vitalistic rage, I direct my gaze to an ostensibly problematic scene, the enactment of Dionysian transgender rituals in the static antics of the old men Teiresias and Cadmus. While waiting is at once an unwelcome intrusion in the Covid era and the perennial condition of the migrants and refugees denied coevalness, in the context of the play the "arrival" (*venir*) of a "lack" (*a-*) constituted by the act of waiting and the in-decision of the present's immobility has the potential to forestall the deceptively liberating future of ecstatic Dionysian time and the intoxication that is paradoxically a form of "enclosing" decision, replacing it with an extended (differently) Dionysian chronicity. In lieu of *Bacchae*'s actualized catastrophe, I suggest a break from the hyperactivity of crisis, from the insistence that we must move on and reconnect with the orderly flow of doing and time. As an unheard-of, unprecedented "event," which is at the same time one of the most famous in Greek mythology, the sacrifice of Iphigenia prior to the Trojan War brings to mind the fundamental contradiction of the pandemic, which as Peter Szendy puts it, "appeared as the unlikely and startling novelty of something that, after all, had already happened a long time ago."[43] While in the case of Euripides' unfinished, posthumously produced *Iphigenia in Aulis*, critics such as Edward Said have highlighted the play's sense of belatedness, in the third chapter I analyze the sense of arrested time. More specifically, I focus on the ways in which Euripidean form conveys time as not just stretched-out— in line with the stuckness of the Greek army's long wait in Aulis for wind, which the sacrifice of Iphigenia is supposed to solve—but *ana-lyzed* in the etymological sense, decomposed, dissolved into proliferating instants. Before the sacrifice, the anatomization of body parts through tender clinging, a haptic lingering, is not just a ghostly projection of the sacrificial mutilation of Iphigenia—her imagined dismemberment in lieu of a calf—but an anatomization of time and of the formal corpus of the play itself, which in its unfinishedness, its unboundness is also like our own pandemic time. Yet the haptic obsession of the play also draws attention to the mask as a barrier, a hindrance to affective intimacy, an object that protects even as it reinscribes bio- and necropolitical distinctions between self and other, human and animal, animate and inanimate. The putative heroism of Iphigenia's sacrifice invites reflection on the auto-immunitarian dynamics emerging from the idea, somehow legitimized by the pandemic, that some lives can (or should) be immolated for the common good—among these lives there is also that of the animal, symbolized by the deer killed in the play in lieu of, or in addition to, Iphigenia.

The second part ("Communities") explores the consequences of reading tragic relationalities in pandemic times, starting with *Alcestis*, which confronts us again with biopolitical axiologies that establish that certain lives are more valuable than others. *Alcestis* exposes the oscillation between the literal and metaphor in the idea of domestic toxicity. In Jane Ward's view, the pandemic has exacerbated what she calls "the tragedy of heterosexuality":[44] a mutual dislike between men and women and a never-ending threat of sexist violence. Queerly located on the generic border between tragedy and satyr drama, *Alcestis* connects heterosexuality with death, assimilating the former to the latter. Admetus indirectly kills his wife and the resulting sense of guilt is layered, and complicated, by the burden of repressed bonds with Apollo and Heracles, which emerge in the overdetermined shapes of poetic form, in expressive intimations of spectral triangularity. In Euripides' play, Alcestis's death and her playful, satiric rebirth, encapsulated in a backward glance that arrests the imperative of forwardness, of the aftermath, can be read as a figuration of the death of heterosexuality (and of tragedy and even death itself) and its replacement with an expansive form of relationality, with possibilities of intimate unbound bonds, beyond the dyadic and the sexual. In 2020, in the darkest days of the pandemic, the right to grieve one's loved ones was no longer a given—funerals were banned in places of worship, funeral homes were closed, mass graves made a grim comeback (a point of convergence between the pandemic and the Ukrainian occupation), undertakers became closer to the dead than family members. In Euripides' *Suppliant Women*, which is the focus of chapter five, the funeralization of the city orchestrated by the Argive mothers separated from their dead children's bodies reconfigures affective bonds, producing unexpected attachments and unbound intimacies, intimating possibilities of non-hierarchical caregiving and solidarity figured by the adhesive tactility of supplication. Supplication in the play expresses an inoperativity that queers the very idea of relationality, placing it in a liminal space between praxis and non-praxis. As characters appear to envelop each other in supplication and quasi-supplication, the textual opacity of these formal and performative motions, which correspond to multiple levels of "towardness," "aroundness," and "in-betweenness," points to disidentifications; the relational intensities of an all-encompassing sororal intimacy, a kind of viral solidarity, which dislodges the state from its immunitarian invulnerability; and indeed the model of a feminist commons.

"The pandemic has exposed yet another of the fault lines of our moment: the difficulty of imagining ourselves beyond the current worlds in which we live."[45] The third part of the book ("Ruins") is dedicated to the relationship between tragedy and the end of the world, or the end of the human, a prospect that the pandemic and climate change have made palpable. Here I consider Sophocles' *Antigone* and Aeschylus's *Niobe*, two plays that imagine the origin and the future of the world through minerality and stony materiality. The sixth chapter, in which Antigone's cave, her final destination, takes center stage, connects her with geopower, the earth's rebellion against the extractivist dynamics of geology, racialized capitalism, and the commodification of animals, to which the pandemic can be imputed. Re-reading Sophocles' play in light of Saidiya Hartman's "Litany for Grieving Sisters" and W. E. B. Du Bois's short story "The Comet" allows us to see Antigone's attachment to the earth as motivated not simply by her desire to join her brothers in death, but by the possibility of sensual contact with what has been called deep time, the temporality of the rock, and with imaginative forms of being beyond extraction and beyond human extinction. Antigone's cathexis to the cave, a dramaturgy of geopower, draws our attention to forms of horizontal, i.e., reciprocal, care modeled on the earth as a living organism, a breathing ground, a breath-giving support. In the seventh chapter, I construe the condition of Aeschylus's Niobe as a marker of both the end of time and the frozen yet fresh ancestrality of a before-time, existential registers that the pandemic materializes in equal measure, in spite of our desire for an aftermath, for a fresh future. Condemned to endure a "pan-endemic" condition—something like our current state, neither pandemic nor endemic—while perpetually shedding tears, Niobe encapsulates not just maternal caretaking's uninterrupted duration, but also ancestrality's paradox of a non-living life, a life before life, and the ecological "coldness" of nature, enraged by human extractivism. A vision of a world undone by the auto-immunitarian division between livable and non-livable, grievable and non-grievable lives, a glacial blue Banksy Niobe in the midst of the ruins of Gaza visualizes a necropolitical denial of conditions of livability. But she also potentially unsettles ordinary endurance of the status quo, the numbed consciousness of privilege, something heightened by pandemic petrification, the quasi-unconsciousness generated by achrony, in both its acute and chronic forms.

Centered on how tragic form connects with the protest of our day, the fourth part of the book thematizes the relation between breath and insurrection. The authoritarianism of the police and of the state grounds itself in the "preemption, control, or repression of protest as a contradiction with normative principles."[46] The sensation of this "preemption, control, or repression of protest" is captured in the phrase "I can't breathe," spoken by Eric Garner, Elijah McClain, and George Floyd when they were killed by police in 2014, 2019, and

2020, respectively. In the case of Floyd, murdered early in the pandemic, the phrase bespoke a convergence between viral death and chronic necropolitical violence. In chapter eight, I read the formal texture of Aeschylus's *Prometheus Bound* within an interpretive framework that combines the politics of dance, digital theory, and Frantz Fanon's influential reflections on the colonial *durée*. Within this framework, tragic language appears at once as a form of colonial constraint, a pre-programmed informational path, *and* as a space where phonetic structures (like digital bytes) go awry and proliferate, resisting the linguistic (or digital) distribution of the sensible, opening spaces for anti-hierarchical, decolonizing possibilities of reading. Juxtaposing the play with *Xen*, a video of Akram Khan's choreographic performance, I consider how the dancer's vertiginously spinning body, subjected to the technologies of colonial-as-virtual life, creates another circuit, like the sadistic play of expansion and contraction generated by the eagle's daily feasting on Prometheus's liver, or a loop of "on" and "off," a digital lifedeath. Further, disturbing visual intertextualities emerge from David Wojnarowicz's iconic AIDS-era photograph "Untitled (Face in Dirt)" and news images of Ukrainian mass graves.[47] Notwithstanding the Promethean subjection/abjection, in the impression of sprawling duration that is created by the all-encompassing force of Khan's *kinêsis*, in the unruly temporal expansion, we can feel the claim of infinitude. Likewise, in Aeschylus's play, a graphic expansion, a sprawling wave of letters conveying the description of Prometheus's punishment, paradoxically mobilizes him, as it diffuses the Chorus's kinetic breathlessness—an expansive *thumos* demanding, we might say, a deep, unbroken breath. Interrupting the circuit of perpetual surveillance, extractivist violence (metallurgical and somatic), phonemic continuity rebels against the cutting up of bodies and words, generating a relentless motion directed not toward the reparative but toward infinitude in its full being and duration. In chapter nine, on Euripides' *Hecuba*, I tease out the relationship between the human body, the sea, and the air in the context of non-historical, non-hierarchical, non-normative posthuman survival. Through a comparison with Valeria Luiselli's *Lost Children Archive* (2018), Toni Morrison's *Beloved*, and Deborah Paredez's 2013 poem "Hecuba on the Shores of Da Nang, 1965," I dwell on formal survivance at the end of Euripides' play, where Hecuba gradually disappears, then reappears through an intensive surging into language, a kind of insurrection. In this textual moment, it is as though through the breath of Agamemnon, her oppressor, the dispossessed, silent Hecuba were able to appropriate not just language but also its environment: the air denied to her by the prospect of suffocating slavery. In her intermittent, surreptitious intensity, her clinging to the air as well as the water that surrounds her, Hecuba is a force of resistance against the ecocides of our days, of which the pandemic is just one manifestation. In the tenth and final chapter, I recapitulate some of the central themes of the book (air, face/mask, ecology, insurrection) through a reading of Rosanna Bruno and Anne Carson's *The Trojan Women: A Comic*, together with Picasso's *Guernica*, that emphasizes the notion of "death from and in the air"—from the bomb-like news of Astyanax's murder, cast down from Troy's walls, to literal bombardment and the pandemic itself. Carson's transformation of Andromache into a tree and of Hecuba into a trans-species assemblage channels the surging force of a viral pananimism that persists amid aerial violence.

Part One

Air Time Faces

1

Oedipus

In 2020, the Covid-19 pandemic invaded our lives as an odd combination of sensory overload and lack. While it temporarily deprived many of olfactory and gustatory capacities and frustrated our desire to touch each other, it also assaulted us with the visceral sense that being in the world entails self-dispossession through unceasing contact with agents in the atmosphere, inaudible and invisible but potentially life-altering.[1] As Jean-Luc Nancy has put it,

> If in one respect we feel numb, we have also been stimulated, awakened, alerted and mobilized.... What is lacking is not touching, since what is taking place ... is a properly viral proliferation of contacts.[2]

Oedipus the King, the play most frequently invoked during the crisis and notably performed on Zoom,[3] stages the radical disjuncture between the gazing subject and the gazed-at object by which the object—Oedipus's traumatic past as well as the plague afflicting Thebes—balloons into a hyperobject,[4] into the harrowing power of subjection exerted by the epidemic Real through air, "the mediation and medium of life."[5] In this chapter, I will tease out the feeling of the epidemic Real in the play by considering the overlap of sensory overload and lack that is integral to the notion of the atmospheric. Tobias Menely has observed that "air ... is known by ... the always incomplete way in which it is sensorially apprehended."[6] Referring to Derrida's retheorization of ontology as spectrality—or "hauntology"—Michael Buser remarks, "Atmospheres are arguably the prototypical spatial form of hauntology.... Vague, irrational, and indeterminate, they haunt the middle ground between subject and object." As with ghosts, he says, "their ontological status is always insecure."[7]

This idea of the atmospheric bears on the nexus of temporality and perception during a pandemic. Perception can be construed as an event, a marker of time, in that it confers the experience of a distinction between before and after. One could say that perception is dulled by prolonged achrony, when time seems stalled, unable to divide itself, to open itself to the event.[8] The loss of smell and taste caused by the pandemic might be regarded as a negative perception or even a mimesis of the enveloping achrony. This temporal continuum, in which instants and moments fail to appear (or appear in disappearance, felt but not perceived), is the counterpart of the amorphous continuum of the atmosphere, populated by presences that are imperceptible beyond a hazy, if powerful, feeling.[9] In this chapter, I consider formal congestion in *Oedipus the King* as the figure of a saturated atmosphere, by which I mean an experiential excess that yields a no-sense, a ghostly sense, or even, paradoxically, the feel of a non-experience. Focusing on Oedipal congested atmospheres allows us to reconceptualize invisibility, darkness, and blindness not simply as the visual equivalents of non-smell and non-taste but as expressions of a spectral *aisthêsis* ("sensation") of heaviness, a feeling beyond sensory convergence.[10] The political implications of the atmospheric oversaturation that I retrieve as an aesthetic and, more broadly, phenomenological effect of reading pandemically will emerge as the book unfolds—as my formalistic readings engage with the nexus of time, air, community, ecological disaster, and insurrection.

In *Oedipus the King*, congested verbal form figures and configures an obfuscated atmosphere burdened, swollen by contagion—something similar to London's fog or smog in the nineteenth-century novel but also to the unconscious as an accretion of spectral toxins.[11] While Thucydides and Lucretius supply full accounts of the famous Athenian plague (430–427 BCE), enabling critics to connect bodily and stylistic decomposition,[12] in *Oedipus the King* there are only sporadic descriptions of the epidemic.[13] Yet the pestilence, like trauma itself, is in the air while characters speak, while actors pour forth their breath from behind a mask and feel it, like the steam on our glasses in the time of the pandemic.[14]

While in Seneca's version of Sophocles' play we read repeated pleas for the return of clean air into Thebes,[15] in *Oedipus El Rey* by Luis Alfaro—an adaptation of Sophocles' play set in contemporary Los Angeles—an overdetermined shortage of breath reflects an ecological crisis. Oedipus arrives in East Los Angeles after being released from the San Bernardino Valley prison that gained notoriety in 2009 for arsenic contamination in its water. Though the play never refers to the incident, multiple references to suffocation and difficulty breathing create an asphyxiating aura—as though the arsenic in the water has seeped into the East L.A. air and then into the performative/textual space. We read stage directions such as "The Coro let out a big breath"; "Oedipus fumes" ("fumes" is almost a translation of the Greek *thumos*, "incense" or "anger"); "All we can hear is heavy breathing"; "Oedipus ... lunges at Tiresias and begins to choke him"; "Tiresias struggles for breath"; and "[Oedipus] stifles his screams as best he can."[16] T[e]iresias even reduces the father to an oppressive intergenerational circulation of breath: "A father is made of breath—from blowing into your lungs the ideas of life, and gasping in fear at what you'll do with them."[17] With their stifling hold on the present, Oedipal traumas amount to environmental pollution manifested through proliferating suffocation in the ambience of plot and language.

In my reading of Sophocles' play, I will search for the verbal feeling of miasmic congestion. As is well known, *Oedipus the King* demands from the critic an attentive response to what Jonathan Culler has called "the call of the phoneme,"[18] that is, language decomposed and recomposed on the page and in the air. The target of superb examples of deconstructive and psychoanalytic criticism, the rich punning texture is a constant reminder that this is "a play hard to see or read without becoming implicated in its games of knowledge or insight."[19] As Simon Goldhill has pointed out, Oedipus's name is the emblematic signifier, "open[ing] itself to the series of ironic reversals of knowledge and position ... mirror[ing] in its disseminating force the improper generative process of the parents of the play."[20] The often-remarked double resonances of the name—conjuring both *oida* ("I know") and *oideô* ("I am swollen")[21]— invite us to draw connections between knowing and excess, knowing and the wound as lack, *knowing* as such and *knowledge* of having been wounded, etc. Here I want to continue to heed the insistent "call of the phoneme" that characterizes *Oedipus the King*, reconceptualizing its play with the signifier as atmospheric effects while casting *oidêma* ("swelling") as an environmental condition, not just a corporeal one, as well as an aesthetic category—not a turgidity that falls short of sublime heights à la Pseudo-Longinus,[22] but rather the feeling/no-feeling of saturated air.[23] Focusing on the expression "aerial words" (*epea êeria*), which is used to characterize Sappho's poetry on an Attic hydria, Anastasia-Erasmia Peponi has observed that "like air, the verbal fabric of poetry may at times be sensed like a diaphanous layer surrounding, indeed enfolding, the listener."[24] In his 1986 dissertation, Jim Porter draws attention to a remarkable passage of Vitruvius's discussion of theater, in which a concern emerges with building theatrical structures in "healthy" areas, in sites guaranteeing adequate circulation of air, for, in his view, dramatic enjoyment opens the spectators' "pores"; it exposes them to the potential harm of infected breath.[25] As Porter puts it, Vitruvius "literalize[s] and displace[s] the proverbial contagion of the theater, through the interpolation of a chain of physical causes that tie the corpuscles of the theater's locus (the ludic site of the theater) to the corpus of the ravished spectator (the subject of theatrical *jouissance*)." In my reading of formal-as-environmental *oidêma* ("swelling"), I will treat particular phonemes and graphemes in their contagious diffusion as the toxins in the verbal ambience, in the *peri-echon* ("surroundings"), whether it is constituted by the language on the page or the breathy voices released through the double aperture of face and mask.[26] Showing how re-reading Sophocles' play in pandemic times helps us problematize the idea of sensory reading as such, this chapter calls for a consideration of sensuous congestion as a "visceral abstraction," a sensing of no-sense.[27]

At the beginning of the play, this visceral abstraction emerges from words dissolving into "burning vapors . . . ris[ing], spread[ing] through the air," which seems to assimilate Oedipus himself.[28] In Oedipus's opening words, the plague is felt as a saturation both olfactory and auditory: "the city is filled with incense, as well as hymns and groans" (*polis d' homou men thumiamatôn gemei / homou de paianôn te kai stenagmatôn* 4–5). The word *thumiama* ("incense") seems to extend *miasma* ("pollution"), a key term in the play, through a conflation with the root of the equally prominent *thumos* ("smoke" and "anger," as well as "spirit" and "heart"). Presenting the incense, an aromatic antidote, as itself contaminated by the plague, which it, in turn, circulates through the miasmic air,[29] *thu-miamatôn* also points to a kind of formal pollution, language as an aerial expanse where phonetic toxins roam and recombine.[30] In its own texture, this word enacts the phenomenology of olfaction—a "'fleshy sense,'... opposed to representation ... so resistant to thought that it resists signification altogether."[31] The incense is a *pharmakon* (a "drug" that is both poison and antidote), augmenting the pollution it is meant to mitigate as it merges with the smoke of animal bodies, leaving persistent traces of non-human trauma and death in the human body. The atmospheric auto-immunity brought on by animal sacrifice can be linked to Timothy Morton's ecological reading of Oedipus's story—from the piercing that accompanies his exposure to the contagion opening the play.[32] Morton maps this story onto the trajectory of agriculture, a human mutilation of the earth that in the fullness of its development has fueled the pandemic of global warming.[33] In Oedipus's description of Thebes, whose starving inhabitants suffer from the auto-immune rebellion of the mutilated earth, an impression of heaviness, of air made dense by vocal and instrumental echoes[34] and the smoky murk, stems from the three long genitive plurals *thumiamatôn*, *paianôn*, and *stenagmatôn*.[35] There is an opacity, a layer of non-meaning that language as the domain of meaning provisionally actualized in aurality and in the visuality of reading cannot breach. Indeed an inability to accept the collision of vision with the invisible, and of language with the opacity of the inexpressible, constitutes a central element of Oedipus's tragedy, not to mention a missed ethical opportunity.[36] The formal overdeterminacy of Oedipus's language generates an effect of congestion, which swallows Oedipus himself, with his inscrutable past, his overloaded unconscious, making his existential opacity an atmospheric one. In the same context, Oedipus's decision to attend the purificatory rituals and thereby avoid second-hand information, news passed from mouth to mouth (*dikaiôn mê par'angelôn ... / allôn akouein autos hôd' elêlutha* 6–7), pits his physical "presence" (*hôd' elêlutha* "I have come here") as a solid "I" (*autos*) against the circulation of *logoi* in the atmosphere, the proliferation of meaning-bearing breath (*par'angelôn ... allôn akouein* "hearing [the news] from the accounts of others"). However, when he introduces himself, in the following line, as "the one famous to everybody (*ho pasi kleinos*), called Oedipus" (8), he entrusts, and assimilates, his identity to *kleos* ("fame"), that is, to air, to the dispersion of sounds, noise, rumor, speech in the atmosphere. Human breath, the channel of discourse, and the healing/miasmic vapors mentioned in the previous lines blend into each other. In this sense, Oedipus himself may be seen as dissolving into the synesthetic assemblage of sound and smell as an impersonal constituent of a murky atmosphere. The pandemic atmosphere of the texture of *Oedipus the King* brings forth something similar to the effect of the tornado on the filmic medium's surface in *The Wizard of Oz*, where, as noted by Louise Hornby, "the abstract wind and dust threate[n] the legibility and the coherence of the visual field, turning the screen dark, and obliterating the sky altogether."[37]

Just as Covid brought together perceptive lack and achrony, *Oedipus the King* dramatizes an uncanny formal overlap between pollution and duration. Returning to Thebes from Delphi with Apollo's directive, Creon urges Oedipus not to "grow" but rather to "drive out" the plague—"the miasma (*miasma*) nourished (*tethrammenon*) in this soil" (97).[38] Nourished and drawn out like the participle itself (*tethrammenon*), excessive like the alliterative saturation in Oedipus's words, *pleon pherô / to penthos* ("the grief I bear, I bear it more" 93–94), the plague engenders dysphoria—a difficulty in bearing expressed as a proliferation of labial exhalations. An abundance of labials also appears in the stasimon that follows Oedipus's discovery of the truth (1209–11), perversely merging father (*patri*) and son (*paidi*):

> *paidi kai patri*
> *thalamêpolôi pesein,*
> *pôs pote pôs poth' hai patrôi-*
> *ai s' alokes pherein?*

Chorus [The same harbor sufficed] both for father and son, to fall into it as a bridegroom. How, how ever have the paternal furrows [been able to] bear you?

Generating and feeding each other,[39] the labials extend the miasmic sprawl of *tethrammenon* ("nourished"), which itself resumes the stretched-out participle *xum-metroumenon* used by Oedipus: "*As I count* (*xum-metroumenon*) the days, it worries me what Creon is doing; *he is gone beyond* (*pera / apesti*) what is expected, *more (pleiô)* than he needed for the journey" (73–75). The expansive time and form—a drawn-out participle, a triple labial alliteration (*pera / apesti, pleiô*)—assimilate duration to an atmosphere seeded by exhalations, as we also observe in the parodos, in the chiastically alliterative structure of the Chorus's contorting inhabitation of dread (... *tetamai ph ... / ph ... deimati*): "I am stretched out by fear in my terrified soul" (*ek-tetamai phoberan phrena deimati* 153).[40] The twisting expansion of the subject (*ek-tetamai* "I am stretched out") corresponds to fear's contagious movement, accelerated by the diffusion of *phobos* ("fear"), whose *ph* sound, breathily spit out, spreads contagion. Formally picking up on *tethrammenon* ("nourished")—the participle modifying *miasma* in Creon's speech—*ek-tetamai* also evokes the temporal extension of *xum-metroumenon* ("counting"), an exasperating achronic measuring out of no-time.

While time and body are stretched out, the opacity and impenetrability of polluted air seems to emerge from the tangled extensions of *dus-tekmarton* ("hard to make out from signs" 109). In the tense dialogue between Oedipus and Creon that follows the latter's return from Delphi, Oedipus deploys the adjective to refer to "the trace of the ancient cause" (*ichnos palaias ... aitias* 109), that is, the clue about Laius's death buried by temporal and cognitive accretions. Besides intimating the hindrances to Oedipus's epistemological quest,[41] *dus-tekmarton*—a compound of *tekmarton* ("possible to be determined") resonating with *ek-tetamai* ("I am stretched out")—evokes, through its consonantal density, a barrier, an enveloping layer akin to what Joseph Conrad, referring to London's contaminated air in *Heart of Darkness*, calls "a brooding gloom."[42] This formal impression of opacity can be connected with Hades ("the invisible") in one of the few depictions of the plague, offered at the beginning of the play by the priest: "Black Hades / grows rich (*ploutizetai*) in groaning (*stenagmois*) and in lamentation (*goois*)" (29–30). While "the most hateful plague" opens up a void in the city, emptying it of its inhabitants,[43] bringing it closer to a spectral existence, Hades becomes more itself (that is, *Ploutôn*), by acquiring (*ploutizetai*) more immaterial souls, increasing its invisible ontology (or hauntology), enriching its own constitutive void. Yet outside the Underworld, in the world of the barely living, what "grows rich," with the polluted humors of tears and lamenting lips, is the atmosphere, the unseen Real, a domain on the threshold between materiality and immateriality, a spectral receptacle, like Hades and the unconscious, which is its own increasingly burdened hauntological space.

The play is filled with formal intimations of a claustrophobic relationality— multiple traces of self-reflexivity and alterity, which can be regarded as not only incestuous but atmospheric. The polyptotons *astos eis astous* ("a citizen into citizens" 222), *autos kat' autou* ("he against himself" 228), and *allon . . . allês* ("another . . . [from] another land" 230) in Oedipus's anxious speech before the heated confrontation with Teiresias are the tropes of self-incrimination and of incest, a kinship predicated on congested sameness. At the end of a speech dominated by tragically ironic innuendos, the page is burdened by polyptotic triangulations that intimate the too-intimate triangle of son, father, and mother (253–61):[44]

> Oedipus . . . for me, for *the god* (*theou*), and for this land of ours, destroyed *and* blighted, *god-forsaken* (*kai a-theôs*). Even were this no matter of *god's ordinance* (*the-êlaton*), it did not suit you, so let it lie . . . since I now *have* (*echôn*) [Laius's] power, and *have* (*echôn*) the bed and wife that he *had* (*eiche*) before, a *shared* (*koin'*) bed of *shared* (*koinôn*) children, if *to that man* (*keinôi*). . .

In this syntactically tense passage, the repetition of the loaded words "god," "to have," and "shared" renders Oedipus's epistemological itch,[45] a corporeal loop, an obsessive embodied return to his perversely energizing fears: Apollo; the kingdom and wife that he took possession of; and, especially, kinship, a network of unknown biological bonds. Might we read polyptotic and paronomastic density, a formal and sensory overload, not as the claustrophobia of incest but as a materialization of the contagion, the outcome of other perilous contacts, of unwitting intimacies? This interpretive possibility arises at the end of the prologue, where Oedipus's command "Let another assemble the people of Cadmus here" (*allos de Kadmou laon hôd' athroizetô* 144) visualizes the contagious effect of the gathering through the quasi-anagrammatic exchange between *allos* ("another") and *laos* ("people")—an exchange in which the constituents of an individual (*allos*) appear to affect (or infect) a whole community (the group onstage and the Chorus, as well as the theatrical audience, the people assembled "here"), congesting the air physically and formally, as suggested by the verb *athroizetô* ("Let [another] assemble").[46] The *allos / laon* anagram also implicates Laius[47] and his father *Labdacus*, whose name showcases his disability, a limping visualized by the very letter lambda (or *labda*), which resembles someone "whose legs are twisted outwardly askew," as we read in a lexicon.[48]

In the lyric texture of the parodos, the pronominal forms of reciprocal alterity (*allon . . . allai . . . allothen allai*), with their proliferation of lambdas, equally contribute to the sense of contagion, while their constituents fill the textual intervals (175 and 179–86):

> *Chorus* You may see *one here, one there (allon . . . allai)*. . . . The city dies (*polis ollutai*). . . . Among [the people], *wives (alochoi)* and also *grey-haired (poliai)* mothers by the altar's edge . . . *moan (epi-stenachousin)* somewhere, some from some places, *others from other places (allothen allai)*, and the paean *shines (lampei)*, and the *moaning (stonoessa) voice (gêrus)* is *playing along (hom-aulos)*.

There is a disorderly dissemination of *allos* ("one") in *ollutai* ("dies"), *alochoi* ("wives"), *lampei* ("shines"), *hom-aulos* ("playing along"), *polis* ("the city") and *poliai* ("grey-haired"), an adjective that also conjures the swarming multiplicity of *pollai* ("many [wives]"). While setting the scene, lyric language twists or exceeds itself; it becomes an atmosphere in its own right, saturated with phonemes, fragments, in varying aggregations, of an ever-generative and never-normalized disability. It is as though the pandemic, ghostly intensities reflected in the very excess of the linguistic ambience brought about a collective Oedipalization or Labdacization, by which exchanges result in twisted corporealities. The sensory substance emanating from—yet exceeding—the formal abstraction of the lyric language transforms individuals and communities into the intensity of a disability, which permeates the textual atmosphere.

Not just an effect of the enhanced expressivity or poeticity of lyric language, these aesthetic atmospherics are also felt in dialogue, as in the climactic confrontation between Oedipus and the servant originally entrusted by Laius to dispose of his son (1159–62):

Servant I'll die (*di-ollumai*) far worse (*pollôi ... mallon*) if I should tell you. *Oedipus* This man is set on more delays, as it would seem. *Servant* No, no, but (*all'*) I told you *before* (*palai*) that I gave the child away. *Oedipus* Where did you get this child from? Was it your own or did you get it from *another* (*allou*)?

An accumulation of forms and pseudo- or crypto-forms of *allos* (*mallon, all', allou*, as well as *palai, pollôi*, and *di-ollumai*) generates a contagious alterity, as though at a moment of high tension—when the truth about Oedipus and Laius is about to be made tragically visible[49]—the rate of infection increases, with breath moving from one mouth to another and clotting the atmosphere not only with scattered paternities, but also with ancestral disability, which is transferred to other bodies within and outside the text through all the sensory orifices: nostrils, mouths, pores, ears—and also (readers') eyes.[50]

In these lines, a feeling of sensory overload muddles the border between perceiving and perceived bodies, confounding the distribution of the senses and the sensible and turning sensory experience into a sensation of no sense.[51] Together with the cognate adjective *stonoessa* ("moaning" 186), the overstretched compound *epi-stenachousin* ("they moan") captures the duration and accumulation of prayers and lamentations from suppliants and the sick as well as an atmospheric density underscored by the polyptotic sequence *allothen allai* ("other [wives] from other places") and the other crypto-figurations of contagious alterity. In the same passage, *hom-aulos* ("playing along")—the adjective that modifies *gêrus* ("voice") and, as we have seen, spectrally conjures *allos/Laios*—indicates, for Patrick Finglass, "an idea of harmony tragically inappropriate in this context."[52] Yet "harmony"—a gathering together of sorts—could be seen as a darkly ironic cipher for contagion, for the pathogenic ensemble of the epidemic. The disharmonious, overdetermined assemblage of breathing bodies, with a "voice that plays along" (*gêrus hom-aulos*), merges perceiving human and perceived non-human agents (*auloi* "pipes"), generating a congestion that turns harmony (literally, a fitting together of parts) into impenetrable density. Here we see how the pre- or post-linguistic overdeterminacy that emerges when we read tragic form sensorially disidentifies or otherizes language. In this case, congestion disturbs and exceeds sensation, amounting to an omni-sensation that obscures sensation itself.

This hyper-sensation can also be perceived in the formal overlap between congested air and Oedipus's anger, between the atmospheric and the affective. Seeking to appease Apollo, to avert the impending catastrophe precipitated by Oedipus's epistemological death drive, Jocasta arrives onstage with "incense" (*kapi-thumiamata*). The word occupies half of the line with a gaseous expansiveness, hyper-sensory, but also anti-sensory: "[I come] bringing garlands and offerings of incense. / For Oedipus raises his anger upward too much" (*stephê labousêi kai epi-thumiamata. / hupsou gar airei thumon Oidipous agan* 913–14). *Thumiamata* ("incense") is a miniature of the atmosphere, a hyperobject, like an earthquake or the climate, subjecting us to itself, or objectifying us. Even when a hyperobject produces sensory impressions, our sense of it is always of that which is never fully perceptible.[53] In Oedipus's prologic words, as we saw, *thumiamata*—notwithstanding its apparently reparative emanations—cryptically contains *mia(s)ma*, like a Derridean *pharmakon*; here it merges with his anger, his *thumos*, "a *hot mood*," a "swirling sensation in the chest, like hot smoke or smoldering fire."[54] Juxtaposed with the phrase *hupsou ... airei* ("[Oedipus] raises ... upward"), Oedipus's anger manifests the upward movement of smoke, as suggested by *airô* ("to raise"), which is cognate with *aêr* ("air"). Long before Jocasta's intervention, in a tense exchange, the obfuscating effect of Oedipus's rising *thumos* ("smoke, anger") comes through in the proliferation of anger words in Teiresias's challenge (344): *thumou di' orgês hêtis agriôtatê* ("let your temper rage as fiercely as possible"). The superlative *agriôtatê* ("as fiercely as possible"), which modifies *orgê* ("rage"), encompasses the noun's phonemes, gathering the smoky and pungent impressions of an emotion that erupts and lingers as a miasmic vapor, or a "vaporwave."[55] In the same passage, the anger that suffuses Oedipus's paranoid scenarios of Teiresias's collusion (*xum-phuteusai*) congests the formal flow (345–49):

Oedipus The way I stand in *anger* (*orgês*), I will not hold back anything I know. For know that you seem to me to *have conspired* (*xum-phuteusai*) and

to have done the deed too (*tourgon eirgasthai*).... Had you eyes, I would
have said you alone are responsible for *the deed* (*tourgon*).

Circulating within four lines through the repeated contracted noun *tourgon*
("deed") and the figura etymologica (*eirgasthai*), *orgê* ("anger") affectively and
atmospherically snarls the narrow textual space.

Language's disarraying of sensation as such escalates when Teiresias and
Oedipus exchange accusations of physical and cognitive blindness. In these
lines, where Oedipus attacks Teiresias, the formal congestion effected by anger
undoes the borders of sight, meaning, and sound itself (370–71):

> *all'esti, plên soi; soi de tout' ouk est', epei*
> *tuphlos ta t'ôta ton te noun ta t'ommat' ei.*

> *Oedipus* [There] is [strength in truth], but not for you; for you it has no
> strength because you are blind in ears and mind as well as in your eyes.

In line 370, as Oedipus dismisses Teiresias's claim to truth, his *thumos* ("anger")
conflates a double *soi* ("for you"), dulling each word's accusatory pointedness
into a disorienting blur. In the oversaturated line that follows, the formal
rhythm of Oedipus's description of Teiresias's blindness yields the subliminal,
infectious refrain *tatô ... tato ... tato*, which obscures the boundaries of words
and sensory orifices, eyes and ears, through the expansive strain of a crypto
superlative suffix (*tatom*, very close to *taton*). In the stuttering or hiccupping
effect of the refrain we do not simply see the emergence of sound over language
or the dissolution of (notional) sensorial boundaries, but an *ex-cess*—or
undoing—of sensation. The synesthetic catachresis "you are blind in ears" has
been regarded as a symptom of the play's "parallelism between 'blind' language
and blinded vision"—that is to say, of how "its overdetermination of false
sensory perception ... sets off the special nature of a knowledge that can be
spoken only through the distorting mechanisms of language, the processes of
condensation, displacement."[56] Rather than *condensation*, I am proposing
congestion as a sensation undoing itself, or a sensation of no-sense, emanating
from the nonsensical *tatôtato ... tato*. This no-sense—a sensory negativity—
could be seen as reflecting, prospectively, Oedipus's mutilation of his eyes after
his epistemological re-birth and, retrospectively, his post-natal mutilation; in

either case, there is a sensory hauntology, the specter of a lost wholeness, something like an aestheticized phantom limb. A wish for no-sense translates a desire for opacity, even an assertion of a "right to opacity," to self-divestiture and self-eclipse, that accompanies and contradicts Oedipus's ostensible desire for self-discovery and self-revelation.[57] At the same time, if we consider that "the phantom limb is a felt recovery, a felt advance beyond severance and limitation . . . a feeling for what is not *there* that reaches beyond as it calls into question what is,"[58] we can construe the Oedipal no-sense as a contestation of the dichotomies between being and non-being, embodiment and disembodiment, feeling and desensitization, which disability disrupts.

An opaque sensation of no-sense is provoked by a dense, "wild" formal intensity in this striking lyric moment, when the Chorus, commenting on the mystery of Laius's murder, renders the culprit's invisibility (475–78):

phêma Parnasou ton adê-
lon andra pant' ichneuein.
phoitai gar hup' agrian
hulan ana t'antra . . .
petraios ho tauros

Chorus From Parnassus a command [came] for everyone to track down the invisible *man* (*andra*). For he lurks down in the *wild* (*agrian*) forest and *up in* (*ana*) the *caves* (*antra*) . . . the *rocky* (*petraios*) *bull* (*tauros*).

The formal congestion originates from the attraction between the almost homophonic *andra* ("man") and *antra* ("caves"), as well as the stretching of *an* through the sequence *hulan ana t'antra* ("[in] the . . . forest and up in the caves"). This effect concerns not just the impenetrable thickness of the woods (*hulan*) where the culprit hides, but also the recalcitrance of "wild" or "angry" (*agrian*) matter—the aerial substance, an atmospheric hyperobject, enveloping the human (*andra*) and providing the medium of human language[59] or, we could say, "a transhuman world that escapes the apprehension of any single person's eyes."[60] Immobilizing sound, *an-an-an* (*anan . . . an*) is an overextended alpha privative, a deferral of the preposition *ana*—that is, a deferral of a deferral[61]—forming a cloud or a concentration of pollution that defies eyes and ears and thwarts visual, cognitive, and semantic borders. This sensory and cognitive intractability is accentuated by the idea of a "rocky bull" (*petraios . . . tauros*), almost an adynaton or a cyborg merging animal and mineral, in which the phonetic substance of the latter is implicated with the former. When the Chorus laments the enormity of Oedipus's crimes, the pronominal correlative phrase *tosouton hoson* ("[it] is sufficient [to]"), clustered together with *ton son* ("your[s]"), intoned three times, creates an oddly impersonal expanse where what is "yours" is shrouded more than highlighted (1189–96):

> *Chorus* What man, what man gains more happiness than *is sufficient* (*tosouton hoson*) to appear happy and, after appearing so, declines? With *your* (*ton son*) fate as my example, *your* (*ton son*) fate, *yours* (*ton son*), unhappy Oedipus, I say that nothing pertaining to mankind is enviable.

The concentration of *hoson . . . ton son . . . ton son . . . ton son* in a few lines confounds the senses through a formal swelling, an aesthetic enactment of Oedipus's trauma and name (*oidein* "swelling") that causes a deeply felt non-perception.

Oedipus's name is, in fact, the marker of an aesthetic swelling that, as indicated by Pseudo-Longinus's discussion of *oidêma* ("swelling") as a stylistic category, is also specifically atmospheric. In *On the Sublime*, he repeatedly uses the verb *oidein* ("to swell") and the noun *oidêma* ("swelling") to characterize one typology of the failed sublime.[62] Even though, in his view, tragedy is generically predisposed toward *onkos* ("turgidity"), it should avoid inopportune "swelling" (*oidein*), of which the historians Callisthenes and Clitarchus are emblematically guilty. As he puts it, "Certain phrases of Callisthenes . . . are not sublime but *hang in the air* (*meteôra*)," while "Clitarchus *puffs out* (*phusôn*)."[63] Observing that "what is swollen (*to . . . oidoun*) wants to *rise above* (*huper-airein*) the sublime," Pseudo-Longinus casts the materiality of aesthetic *oidêma* ("swelling") as atmospheric, as the upward movement of congested air indicated by the verb *huper-airein*.[64] In Oedipus's tragedy, the tragedy par excellence, the tragedy of a swollen foot, we feel the atmospherics of *oidêma* ("swelling") not as an aesthetic shortcoming or a failed sublime, but as an effect of textual swollenness created by ghostly appearances of *oida* ("I know")/*oideô* ("I'm swelling") in dense anagrammatic and assonant permutations, conveying formalized impressions of the verbal space as an aerial congestion, hindering sensation, provoking no-sense.

Anger surging in the middle of the play generates an upward movement—the "ris[ing] above" (*huper-airein*) theorized by Pseudo-Longinus—in the graphic layout of the lines. In Oedipus's altercation with Creon, after the one with Teiresias, escalating anger is rendered in the disposition of forms of *oida* (569–74):

Kr. *ouk <u>oid</u>'; eph'hois gar mê phronô sigan philô*
Oi. *tosonde g'<u>oistha</u> kai legois an eu phronôn—*
Kr. *poion tod'; ei gar <u>oida</u> g', ouk arnêsomai.*
Oi. *hothounek', ei mê soi xun-êlthe, tas emas*
    ouk an pot' eipe Laiou diaphthoras.
Kr. *ei men legei tad, autos <u>oisth</u>'; egô de sou...*

Creon I don't *know*; I like to be silent on the things that I don't understand.
Oedipus But this much you do *know* and you would say it if you were sane—
Creon What is *this*? For if I *know* it, I will not deny it.
Oedipus That if he hadn't had an agreement with you, Teiresias would not have mentioned my killing of Laius.
Creon If he says this, you *know* it, but I from you...

In these lines, the elided *oida* ("I know") occupying the second metrical position in line 569 moves progressively toward the end of the line—the fourth and fifth position in line 570 (*oistha* "you know"), the sixth and seventh in 571 (*oida* "I know"), the eighth in 574 (*oisth'* "you know"). "Close reading" becomes "close breathing":[65] from the perspective of line 574, we see *oida* ("I know") rising upward in an atmospheric "swelling" (*oidêma*) that spreads spectral traces of Oedipus's wound onto the skin of the Thebans and audiences. We can feel these traces in an intense stichomythia in which the Messenger from Corinth refers to Oedipus's swollen ankles (*arthra* 1032)—an "ancient ... evil" (*archaion ... kakon* 1033), as Oedipus puts it—as "bearing witness" (*marturêseien* 1032) to his exposure on Cithaeron. The verbal substance of *marturêseien* is infected by the phonemes of *arthra*, a "phantom limb," a spectral hapticity. As the Messenger alludes to Laius's piercing iron, Oedipus's response, "Terrifying blame (*deinon ... oneidos*) is what I received as swaddling clothes" (1035), generates a compounded effect of congestion. *Deinon* ("terrifying") is a virtual anagram of *oneidos* ("blame"),[66] and both words are virtual anagrams of *oidein* ("swelling")—the distinctive root of Oedipus's name, which is evoked not only by the previous line, "piercing points on your feet" (*dia-torous podoin akmas* 1034), but also by the following line of the Messenger, "Thus from this condition *you were named* (*ônomasthês*) who you are" (1036). When, in response to Oedipus's swelling curiosity ("Who gave me that name, my mother or father?" 1037), the Messenger proclaims, "I don't know, but he who gave (*ouk oid'; ho dous*) you to me has more knowledge than I" (1038), further punning congestion clusters around his lack of knowledge: juxtaposed with *oid(a)* ("I know"), *ho dous* ("he who gave") reads as *hodous* ("roads"), as many interpreters have noted.[67] But, besides offering an etymological play on Oedipus's name and imputing the swelling of his feet inscribed in it to his perennial wandering, the overdetermination of meaning and sound prompted by the tongue-twisting sequence *ouk oid'; ho dous* ("I don't know, but he who gave") engenders a formal *oidêma* ("swelling"). This effect re-creates the post-mutilation sensory spectrality, the sensuous duration of a loss, imbuing the textual atmosphere with the feeling/no feeling of a bodily part still appearing through its apparent disappearance. In this formal atmosphere of ghostly congestion, the polyptoton of the pronoun *allos*, actual or counterfeit (*allou ... alla ... allos* "from someone else ... but ... another"), figures the contagious transfer of the wounded baby Oedipus from one hand to another, along with the feeling of Labdacid disability (1039–40):

> *Oedipus* You yourself did not find me, then? You took me from *someone else* (*allou*)? *Messenger* No, *but* (*alla*) *another* (*allos*) shepherd gave you to me.

The looping of *allou, alla, allos* figures not just Oedipus's own somatic inflation, which is aggravated by, almost indistinguishable from, his boundless, exhausting, numbing wandering, but the rising, expansion, and opaque transmission of Oedipal pollution to the senses—the pollution of a phantom limb/lambda lingering in the atmosphere.

After Oedipus has punished himself by dashing out his eyes, the pollution, far from abating, abides in the verbal atmosphere through another congested appearance-in-disappearance of *oidein* ("swelling"). In the Chorus's response to news of Jocasta's suicide and Oedipus's self-blinding—*ô deinon idein pathos ... ô deinotaton pantôn* ("O pain terrible to see...! O most terrible of all!" 1297–98)—the boundary between fear (*deinon* "terrible") and sight (*idein* "to see") collapses, while the encrypted *oidein*, the sensation of swelling excess spread in the air, produces a no-feeling that exceeds sight and the other senses. Haunted by *oidein* ("swelling"), the superlative *ô deinotaton* ("O most terrible") suggests, in its own overstretched form, the recalcitrance of the oversaturated atmosphere, as does the formal hauntology perceptible a few lines earlier, at the end of the Messenger's speech. Observing that in one day "happiness" has turned into an asyndetic conglomeration of "crying, ruin, death, shame" (*stenagmos, atê, thanatos, aischunê*), and "all ills for which there are names," with "none ... missing" (*kakôn / hos' esti pantôn onomat', ouden est' ap-on* 1284–85), the Messenger closes with a negated lack, or double negative. Particularly following the evocation of "names" (*onomat'*), the negated *ouden* ("none") can be regarded as a crypt of *oidein*—Oedipus's eponymous swelling—whose ghostly presence increases the congestion, hindering sensation.[68] In the antistrophe of the same choral song, the opaque cloud of Oedipus's troubles seems to become a sensory ambience (1313–18):[69]

> Oedipus Oh, my *cloud* (*nephos*) of darkness *from which one turns away* (*apo-tropon*), assaulting me, *unspeakable* (*a-phaton*), *untameable* (*a-damaton*), and *driven by an unfavorable wind* (*dus-ouriston*). Alas, alas, *again* (*authis*), what (*hoion*) a sting (*oistrêma*) of these goads and what a memory of evils *has come into* me (*eis-edu*)!

The quasi-undifferentiation of the long adjectives following *nephos* ("cloud")— four of which are connected asyndetically—intimates an aerial expansiveness diffusing the sensation of opacity. In the second sentence of the passage, introduced by the marker of repetition *authis* ("again"), the *punctum* of memory, expressed by the aspect of the aorist *eis-edu* ("has come into") and troped as the sting of the goads responsible for Oedipus's infantile mutilation, seems to swell into the amorphous duration, the spectral sensorium of the post-event, as suggested by the appearance-in-disappearance of *oidêma* ("swelling") in *oistrêma* ("a sting") and the anagrammatic encryptment of the phonetic substance of *oidein* ("swelling") in the phrase *hoion eis-edu* ("what has come into").[70]

Its own source of pollution, Oedipus's curse burdens the atmosphere, even when he wishes to purify the city by being driven out of it. In the last moments of the Messenger's account, the effects of Oedipus's curse are encapsulated by an alliterative *figura etymologica* (1290–93):

> *Messenger* He'll cast himself out of the land, he says, and not remain in his house, *a cursed man, since he cursed himself (araios hôs êrasato)....* His sickness is too heavy to bear (*to . . . nosêma meizon ê pherein*).

The phrase *araios . . . êrasato* ("a cursed man . . . cursed himself") makes us feel the reverberation of the curse, whose intergenerational power, temporal density, and hauntological persistence encumber the air with particles of Oedipal pollution. The *ar-* sounds of this *ara* ("curse") contain *aêr* ("air"), as suggested by the resonance with *aras . . . arthra* ("raising [the pins, he hit] his limbs [eyeballs]"), Oedipus's climactic gesture of "raising" (*airô*) Jocasta's pins in the air and striking his eyeballs (1270). Consequently, the unbearable sickness referred to by the Messenger is also the atmospheric burden of the curse, the pain turned into the rising congestion that is intimated at the beginning of his speech: "What pain *will you raise up for yourselves (areisthe)*" (1224–25). Similarly, near the end of the play, when Oedipus asks to be taken away, he calls himself *echthrotaton* ("the most hated") and *kat-aratotaton* ("the most accursed" 1345–46)—a six-syllable adjective containing another *ara* ("curse")—inviting us to think not just of a polluted Oedipus, but of a polluted material expanse (an atmosphere), which is fed by his command *ap-aget' ap-aget'* ("Take me away, take me away" 1340–41), itself haunted by the root of *agos* (the word for impurity or infection later used by Creon). Even Teiresias's earlier phrase *deino-pous* ("terribly-footed curse" 418), which previewed Oedipus's exile, is a breath made tumid by the implication of *oidein* ("swelling") with *deino-* ("terrible"). While seeking to remove the pollution that he embodies—that he is—Oedipus spreads it through his breath, clouding the invisible atmosphere that envelops the play and us, compromising the community's ability to breathe.

Instead of suicide, Oedipus, as we know, chooses self-blinding. As he puts it, upon his return onstage (1386–89):

Oedipus If there were a way to block the flow of sound through my ears, I would not have held back from closing up my wretched body so that I would be blind and hear nothing.

This is a refusal of sensory relationality or, at least, of the kind of relationality grounded in the internalization, incorporation, and introjection intrinsic to all the senses reliant on orifices (sight, hearing, smell, taste)—at the end of the play, Oedipus, in fact, will still look for a haptic connection with his daughters. Filling up the eyes and ears, the formal congestions I have observed in my reading express a felt overload, which anticipates Oedipus's fantasy of no-sense. In Don DeLillo's latest novel, *The Silence*—a powerful rendition of the experience of the pandemic that was written before Covid—characters "look at the blank screen" or "stare into the black screen," "sitting, watching, cursing silently," "immersed in [a] nowhere stare."[71] We also read that "hands stiffe[n]" and "the gaze [seems] to recede" into a "trancelike state," and that a character "wasn't listening to what [his interlocutor] was saying because he knew it was stale air." *Black* and *blank* do not just overlap semantically, even though etymologically opposite; they also blur together formally, straining eyes and ears. For Fred Moten, to feel is "to sense the blur, and not some normative individuation."[72] As one of DeLillo's characters says, "Isn't it strange that certain individuals have seemed to accept the shutdown, the burnout? Is it something that they've always longed for, subliminally, subatomically?" The stretched, strained formal texture disseminating Oedipus's name and trauma creates an atmospheric swollenness that compels—or allows—us to stare into a black or blank screen, to obfuscate our senses in the congested expanse of textual air, in the congested time of these pandemic times.

2

Teiresias Cadmus Dionysus

The current planetary pandemic is an eminently political disaster, harrowingly bringing into the open—and aggravating—unresolved, never buried social and economic inequalities and tensions; fueling collective motions of dissent and protest liable to be violently suppressed by police; and, at a more basic level, demanding a set of responses from the complex of chronically flawed public institutions that we refer to as the state. For Slavoj Žižek, one of the political dangers ignited by the pandemic is, in fact, the complacency conveyed by rushed, forced, inadequate decisions:

> The impossible happened, our world has stopped, and impossible is what we have to do to avoid the worst, which is—what? . . . More than open barbarism, I fear barbarism with a human face—ruthless survivalist measures enforced with regret and even sympathy but legitimized by expert opinions.[1]

Responding to the pandemic's decision-making interpellation, "survivalist" or "emergency" measures more focused on the economy than human life, reinforcing racist and racializing social inequities, heighten the pre-pandemic calcification of democracy, its (auto-)immunitarian self-protection from the anarchic impetus that makes it while unmaking it.[2] In the same special issue of *Critical Inquiry* that hosts Žižek's intervention, Emmanuel Alloa warns:

> Let us be careful not to sacrifice to this pandemic a fundamental value of all democratic life: its share of randomness, its contingency. . . . Let us therefore

take care, in our generalized immunological responses, not to entomb ourselves even more in our certainties but to accept that this contingency can also act as a powerful breach in our imaginaries.[3]

I want to address the question of the political ecology of decision-making in and about disaster, which Covid-19 has traumatically raised, by considering the Dionysian pandemic in *Bacchae* and the achronies it provokes. In an early scene, Cadmus and Teiresias, two ostensibly "minor" characters, become, we might say, icons of the achrony resulting from the disaster of Dionysiac mania. In pandemic time, as Peter Szendy has observed, "nothing has changed, nothing has happened, but everything that seemed unthinkable, incredible, or impossible has now become obvious, madly obvious and yet so banal." In a sense, the "event" of the pandemic "appeared as the unlikely and startling novelty of something that, after all, had already happened a long time ago."[4] Never to experience Pentheus's dismemberment, the separation to come, Teiresias and Cadmus at the beginning of *Bacchae* embody a certain undecidability in their Dionysian gimmicky performance. In this static scene, there is an overdetermined presentness or no-futurity, a productive lack of *de-cision* (also in the etymological sense of "cutting" or "splitting"). The focus of my analysis—the early scene of *Bacchae* together with Agave's arrival later in the play—shows an imminence morphing into a "remaining in," which models an alternative to a decisional regime whose martial urgency in the face of catastrophe does not leave space for a radical rethinking of the political and the social.

Arriving in Thebes, Dionysus, an "an-economic" presence in the house and the state,[5] diffuses contagious breaths of insanity among his recruits, married and unmarried women, but also Pentheus, the apparent enemy, who has decided to imprison and expel the dangerous *xenos*—immediately, instantly, that is, killing the durational time of deliberation, hastening the "event" of resolution. When Dionysus, in the prologue, paints the effects of his arrival—"I stung (*ôistrês*) them away from their homes with manic diseases (*maniais*) and they now inhabit the mountain, *beside their minds* (*para-kopoi phrenôn*)" (32–33)—he evokes for us an "oestro-genic" substance, i.e., estrogen, allowing us to see, from an etymological standpoint, the misogynistic implications of the term, in line with a never fully erased notion of hysteria in medical discourse.[6] While Dionysus uses the first person singular and, thus, personalizes the contagion, in a choral ode his manic and mania-inducing (non-)self manifests itself as something like *the smoke of Syrian incense* (*Surias . . . libanou kapnon* 144–45), an orientalizing image connected to the emanations of the torches brandished by him and his disciples. Therefore, as we hear or read Pentheus's repeated, frantic announcements of his decision to stop the Bacchic frenzy by trapping it in "iron nets" (231), tracking down the "effeminate stranger who instills the novel *disease* (*noson*) in women" (352–54), chaining him (497, etc.), we picture a state caught in a futile game. Pentheus seeks to wage war on the immaterial, to delimit what keeps expanding; he succumbs to the manic contagion as he absurdly strives to immobilize an unbound elementality—air or fire (778–79)—and materialize this delirious fantasy as a determination, a resolution, an official public pronouncement.[7] Pentheus embodies the sadomasochistic delirium of bio- and necropolitical state interventions. In *Global Civil War: Capitalism Post-Pandemic* (2022), William I. Robinson recapitulates the ill-advised decisions of various governments at the beginning of the pandemic, manic responses to a manically declared stage of emergency:

> At the very start of the pandemic in Wuhan, Chinese officials silenced doctors who first raised the alarm. In Egypt, at least twelve doctors were thrown into jail for criticizing the government response to the contagion. . . . The Russian government demanded that the media stop publishing information on the virus that it declared to be false. The governments of Turkey, Montenegro and Serbia carried out arrests and fined people who published information on social media that "provoked panic and jeopardizes public security." . . . In Hungary, the far-right authoritarian prime minister Viktor Orban sought an open-ended state of emergency that would give him powers to bypass parliament and rule by decree. . . . In Great Britain, a coronavirus bill was rushed through parliament that authorized the government to detain and isolate people indefinitely, to ban public gatherings, including protests, and to shut down ports and airports with little oversight. . . . A law passed in New York State gave Governor [Andrew]

Cuomo unlimited authority to rule by executive order and overrule existing regulations during state crises like pandemics and hurricanes.[8]

I quote this passage at length because Robinson's catalog of rushed decisions mimetically captures the viral mania of state actions and reactions.[9] The problem is not just that the measures listed here were objectively bad— symptoms of inveterate post- or anti-democratic global crises; the very act of "deciding" is informed by a pathological or pathogenic feverishness that resembles a viral force in its own right, superseding its purported agents. Among the various maladies brought about by the pandemic, "decision fatigue"—not the inability to decide, but the discomfort in constantly needing to make urgent decisions—undoubtedly occupies a prominent role.[10]

Yet Euripides' play also makes interpretive room for a counter-impetus to the atmosphere of manic decision-making—both the women's abandonment of their homes and Pentheus's panoptic surveillance, each of them suffering from and enjoying Dionysus's imperious viral influence. In my reading of *Bacchae*, I will emphasize the potentiality of immanence and un-experience (or *monia*) in the counterfactual scenario of in-decision spectrally, or anti-representationally, emerging in the account of Dionysian mania and its aftermath. Through waiting, the present's immobility, materializing in this counterfactual as in-decision, is—to reconfigure Jacques Derrida's notion of the future as *à venir* ("to come")[11]—the "arrival" (*venir*) of a "lack" (*a-*), which has the potential to forestall the totalizing, deceptively liberatory future of ecstatic, Dionysian time with a form of extended chronicity that is Dionysian (and viral) in a different sense, as I will explain.[12] I now wish to dwell on the theoretical notion of "disaster" that undergirds my reconsideration of Dionysian mania. Clarifying the meaning and the temporality of what I call "disaster" is the necessary premise for framing my close or too-close reading of select moments of the play in terms of the ecology of in-decision and waiting. Since waiting is at once an unwelcome intrusion in the Covid era and the perennial condition of the migrants and refugees and other dispossessed people denied coevalness[13] as they are subjected to racialized dispossession, the challenge arises of how to turn waiting upside down, to open up spaces of resistance and paradoxical mobility within its apparent immobility.[14]

Disaster, according to Maurice Blanchot, is a matter of "imminence" or "the advent of what doesn't happen, of what would come without arriving . . . and as though by drifting away."[15] With language that could be applied to the Covid virus, Blanchot says that "the disaster . . . has no regard for us,"[16] observing that the temporal marker of disaster is an evanescent "already" (*déjà*), or an "always already."[17] Here he alludes to a specific passage from Derrida's *Glas* (*Clang*), where Derrida refers to "I am" and "I am dead" as "two indistinguishable statements sensewise," adding that "the *déjà* that I am," that is, as a being that has already come into existence, "clangs its own knell" (its own *glas*), "signs its own death warrant."[18] When Blanchot identifies dying with "the imminence of what has always already (*déjà*) come to pass," his *déjà* brings to mind "Derrida, Jacques" as an inverted signature reduced to its edges.[19] Similarly, for Derrida, Blanchot's oracular writing instantiates the *à venir*—a non-hierarchical form of temporality that disrupts the opposition between before and after, between the past and the future, making room for creative, in-comprehensible temporalities always on the threshold, on the shore of becoming:[20] "I would say that never have I imagined him [Blanchot] so far in front of us as I have today. Awaiting us, still to come, to be read, to be reread."[21] "Disjointed present" captures, for Derrida, the lateness of Blanchot's disaster, that is, his notion of "passivity" in relation to the disaster conventionally understood as an event.[22] As the experience of something that has passed and consequently is "in the past, out of date,"[23] passivity can be thought of as the experience of the arrival of a lack, of an alpha privative—that is, a non-experience, or what Derrida calls, in reference to death, "an encounter between what is going to arrive and what has already arrived, between what is on the point of arriving and what has just arrived, between what is going to come and what has just finished coming, between what goes and comes."[24] In such an encounter, Derrida says, "lightness, elation, beatitude remain the only affects that can take the measure of th[e] event as 'an unexperienced experience.'"[25] While Blanchotian disaster, like the Derridean *à venir*, counters the idea of the future present (a future made present), it also unsettles our perception of the Derridean future-to-come— inviting us to view it not as a perennial non-arrival, an always postponed materialization, but rather as the materialization of a non-arrival, experienced, in Blanchot's terms, as a gratifying immanence, the elation of "remaining in."[26]

In an early scene of Euripides' *Bacchae* Dionysian disaster arrives in the mode of Blanchotian disaster through the movements and words of two old men. Coming just after the prologue, where Dionysus the foreigner ominously announces his arrival, and well before the play's climactic bloodbath, the scene, which features the trans* preparation of Cadmus and Teiresias, has been regarded as a tragi-comic aesthetic problem.[27] But before I focus on the scene, I will consider another expression of Blanchotian disaster, alluded to in the parodos, when the Chorus describes Dionysus's queer or wild gestation after his rescue from the catastrophe visited upon his mother, Semele.

Transferring Dionysus from Semele's womb into his own thigh, Zeus distances him from the *astêr* ("star") that is his thunderbolt; he detaches his son from the event, subjecting him to the unexperiential experience of a lack. In this passage, the Chorus describes Dionysus's double gestation and double birth (88–99):

> *Chorus* Once, Dionysus's mother had him *in the parturient necessities of pangs* (*en ôdinôn lochiais anankaisi*), and when the thunder of Zeus flew she gave birth to him, thrown out of her womb prematurely, leaving her *life* (*aiôna*) to the stroke of the thunderbolt; and Zeus, Cronus's son, immediately received him *in the parturient chambers* (*lochiois thalamois*), and covering him in his thigh he closes him in with *golden pins* (*chruseaisin … peronais*), keeping him *hidden* (*krupton*) from Hera. And then *he gave birth* (*eteken*).[28]

Rescued from the thunderbolt, Dionysus experiences a Blanchotian disaster, the gap of lateness, which is captured by Blanchot's hyphenation of *dis-aster*. Zeus's "delivery" (the *lochos* in *lochiais/lochiois*) punningly overlaps, in fact, with the word for "ambush" or "lying-in-wait," the before of a catastrophe, the not-yet-eventful dimension of Blanchotian disaster. While the word *aiôn* in this context is used simply as a synonym for "life," for the life that Semele has been forced to leave, it evokes the time beyond the event and beyond history, which flows from the disastrous non-experience of Dionysus when he was hidden (*krupton*) in Zeus's thigh. Zeus's imposition of dis-aster—a salvation and separation from the catastrophe—is an act of violence, similar to Laius's

symbolic castration of Oedipus, as indicated by the phrase *chruseaisin ...
peronais* ("golden pins" 97–98), an unmistakable evocation of Jocasta's pins—
the instrument of Oedipus's maternal re-enactment of the paternal wounding.[29]
While apparently used to protect the child and bring him to birth, these objects
become the agents of an oppressive closing-in, which we can call hyper-
parentality—an Oedipality both paternal and maternal enacted in Zeus's
transgender gestation. Yet in this queer reproduction, in Dionysus's waiting in
Zeus's thigh, there is a sense of "uncanny futurity" or of a "negative future,"[30]
that is, an anti-hierarchical one, the alreadyness of a prolonged present, an
excess apart from the impending, ecstatic yet hierarchical, Dionysian chaos.

The un-experience caused by Dionysus's prenatal rescue returns in the
Messenger's account of the rituals on Cithaeron—in the "lying-in-ambush" of
Pentheus's men (*ellochizomen* 722), their "hiding" (*krupsantes* 723) and waiting,
as in Wole Soyinka's adaptation ("We hid / Among the undergrowth covered in
leaves. We waited").[31] In the second strophe of the parodos, the Maenads who
wait (*menei*) on the mountain for victims are described as an *ochlos* ("crowd"),
an anagram of *lochos* (114–19):

> *Chorus* The whole land will immediately dance whenever Bromius leads the
> thiasoi to the mountain, to the mountain (*eis oros eis oros*), where the female
> crowd (*ochlos*), stung by Dionysus, away from looms and shuttles, is waiting
> (*menei*).

Constituting another Blanchotian disaster, this waiting for and before the
event (the sparagmatic dissolution of bodies), underscored by the repetition
"to the mountain, to the mountain," overlaps with the waiting for and after the
event (the dissolution of Semele's body) implicated with Dionysus's birth.

The sense of undifferentiated time at the heart of Blanchotian disaster
extends from Dionysus's gestation to the moment when Teiresias and Cadmus
shuffle onto the stage in female attire, in a Dionysian panoply, already infected
by the god, casting themselves, with a polyptotic or quasi-polyptotic insistence,
as a couple of aged bodies—or, more abstractly, a pair of temporal expanses—
leaning into each other. In the last line of the parodos the Chorus envisions a
bacchant "joyously (*hêdomena*) ... mov[ing] her legs, *swift-footed in her
leapings (tachu-poun skirtêmasi*)" (163–69). However, in contrast with bacchic

swiftness, the long, conjoined words *tachu-poun* and *skirtêmasi* decelerate the syntactic flow, anticipating the slow entrance of the would-be-bacchants Cadmus and Teiresias. When the latter, speaking of himself and his companion, says, "*I, an old man, agreed with the old man (xun-ethemên presbus . . . geraiterôi)* to weave (*an-aptein*) thyrsoi and to have (*echein*) fawns' skins and to crown (*stephanoun*) the head with ivy shoots" (175–77), the dative of accompaniment (*geraiterôi*) is a marker not just of the queer attachments enacted in the scene but also of the temporal accumulation of old age. In a perverse *aiôn* ("time"), infinite and finite alike and reflected in the polysyndetic list of present infinitives (*anaptein . . . echein . . . stephanoun*), actions delay the Dionysian event while they ostensibly set it up with its distinctive prostheses. We could also say that the Dionysian pandemic has already seeped in, without having begun, skipping the eventful moment of an outbreak. A polyptoton (*gerôn geronti*) occurs in Cadmus's exhortation, "Be a guide, you for me, an old man for an old man (*gerôn geronti*)" (185–86), which is accompanied by a declaration of futile tenacity, a claim to *jouissance*: "I would never tire of shaking the earth with the thyrsus day and night; *with joy, we have forgotten that we are old (epi-lelêsmeth' hêdeôs / gerontes ontes)*" (187–89). The adverb *hêdeôs* ("with joy") encapsulates the elation of what Derrida calls the "encounter between what is going to arrive" and "what has already arrived," respectively, in this case, the Dionysian slaughter and the initial epiphany of Dionysus himself, disguised as a foreigner.[32] This encounter of temporal registers is dramatized in the texture of the exchange, where Teiresias's response conflates a reference to the past ("So, you are experiencing the same things that I did" 189) and a projection into the future ("I will attempt the dancing" 190), followed by an additional one in Cadmus's intervention ("Won't we head to the mountain in a chariot?" 191). The tirelessness of the Dionysian movements that Cadmus speaks of is conducive to a perpetual alreadyness, a Blanchotian immanence, while the self-forgetting (*epi-lelêsmeth'*), the self-annihilation, the arrival of the disastrous event—all promised by the Dionysian ritual—are held off by the temporality, the continuous present, of the thyrsus-shaking. Three lines later in the same position, parallel to *gerôn geronti*, we read *gerontes ontes* ("being old men"), a rhyming phrase in which the malignant perseverance of *ontes* ("being") delays oblivion, offering, instead of the event, the advent of a lack—a sensation that, in our times, accompanies the realization that there is no *after*, that the end will never arrive.

The continuous alreadyness of disaster emerges from a third instance of polyptotic intimacy, a gathering of old age (*gerôn geronta*), in which the hierarchy of subject/object seems to give way to a sprawling horizontality as two weary bodies burden each other (193–98):

> *Cadmus* I *an old man*, you *an old man* (*gerôn geronta*), I will lead you like a child. *Teiresias* The god will lead us there without toil. *Cadmus* Will we be *the only ones* (*monoi*) in the city for Dionysus? *Teiresias* Yes, we are *the only ones* (*monoi*) to have a sane mind; the others don't. *Cadmus* Delaying is long (*makron to mellein*). But cling to my arm. *Teiresias* Here we go, clasp my hand and make a pair.

Both lines 195 and 196 begin with the word *monoi* ("the only ones"), in the same location as *gerôn* ("old man"), creating a sequence of horizontal and vertical repetitions—*gerôn geronta* and *monoi monoi*.[33] *Monoi* evokes *monê* (noun) and *monia*—or *moniê*, as we find it in Empedocles—derivatives from *menô* ("to wait") meaning some kind of "stillness" or "persistence."[34] While they aspire to rush toward the experience of disaster, the two old men, bodies joined, transing together, express protracted "stillness," prolonged "waiting," through the expansive *m* sounds (*monoi monoi makron ... mellein*), reconfiguring the longed-for experience as a kind of post-evental imminence or anterior alreadyness. In this respect, Teiresias's call for identification, when he distances the singular plurality of himself and Cadmus from the "foolish rest" ("the others"), may constitute *monia*, rather than *mania*.[35] Stillness brings us back to the parodos's image of an *ochlos* ("crowd"), anagrammatically a *lochos* ("ambush"), of Maenads who wait (*menei*), worshippers of Dionysus who, even immersed in the ritualistic madness of Cithaeron, experience the sparagmatic "event" as past-ness, as they will again and again. We might locate the wildness of the play in *monia* as much as its quasi-homonym—*mania*. At the end of the scene, when Teiresias warns Pentheus that he has already been infected by the god he stubbornly rejects—"you are already mad" (*memênas êdê* 359)—the paronomastic resonance of the verbal form *memênas* ("you are mad") with *menô* ("to wait") subliminally yields "you are already waiting." The temporality of the dissonant statement "you are already mad" is thus further confounded or queered, as with Dionysus's interrupted and doubled gestation, in which, removed from his mother, he could be said to have experienced a "waiting for an already"—or the arrival of a lack (like the lack of an ending to the pandemic).

Cadmus and Teiresias's relationship to the play's catastrophic event, like Dionysus's with his gestation, is informed not just by separation and inexperience but by transing. Involving flesh cut and resewn, Dionysus's birth, discussed in the old men's dialogue with Pentheus (243–44 and 286–87), is a somatotechnical procedure, which, in this case, breaks one body and transplants another even before it is fully formed, rupturing time by confusing the before and the after, the beginning and the ending.[36] The biological ontology of birth becomes a hauntology, or a para-ontology—a term that I borrow from trans* studies and critical race theory to locate the inexperience of the event *beside* the event, in the same position as the *a* in relation to *venir* in *à venir*.[37] "Far from referring to a given catastrophic event," Blanchotian disaster is located *beside* (*para*) that event; it "belongs to history only in so far as it exceeds"[38] history, that is, history understood as a meaningful sequence of events. The scene of Cadmus and Teiresias—"an experience without experience"—exceeds the play's story, introducing "an absence of action . . . a hiatus."[39]

In this scene, the sense of Blanchotian disaster—the achronic disaster of the pandemic—recalls the temporality of the "gimmick," which, as Sianne Ngai has observed, "strikes us as technologically backward or just as problematically advanced."[40] For Ngai, "there is . . . a sense in which the gimmick confronts us with a mode of bad contemporaneity akin to the 'elongated present,' 'endless present,' or 'perpetual present.'"[41] This aesthetic temporality corresponds to what Fredric Jameson calls, in reference to action films as well as several high-cultural products, a "singularity," which he defines as a "pure present without a past or a future" characteristic of products of late capitalism meant to be thrown away once the trick—the "singularity" (like the "gimmick")—has been performed.[42] The *Bacchae* scene is unexpected and novel, with no consequences beyond the moment. All the same, the gimmick is a conceit that can be mechanically repeated ad libitum. It is "at once dynamic (like an action) and also inert (like a thing), . . . like a cause but also its effect . . . both a singular event and the proverbial old saw."[43] In Ngai's view, as a "paradoxical unity of discrepant temporalities—instantaneity and duration, disruption and continuity, singularity and repetition—the gimmick embodies one of the most significant contradictions of capitalism: the way in which the movement of time is continually converted into present time."[44] The scene with Teiresias and Cadmus—a couple who amount to a singular plurality—feels both like a one-off and a worn-out gag: both dynamic and inert, it is set in a gimmicky present that impedes the flow of time as well as the future to come. In such a gimmicky present, the *venir* is experienced as an alpha privative—the equivalent non-arrivals of a one-off and an iterable materialization bring about this lack. Like the sense, circulated by the pandemic, of a present with no arrival—both a one-off state of emergency and an achronic duration—the gimmicky present inhabited by Cadmus and Teiresias is an anti-vitalistic, anti-manic waywardness, a *monia*, which may be regarded as a possible response to crisis itself: as a break from the *mania* of the crisis, an evasion of the Symbolic's anxious call for solutions and decisions—and of the frantically proliferating states of emergency[45]—and a valorization of the poietic force of hesitation, of the affectively and cognitively inventive, radical intensity of dwelling *in* or *with*, rather than moving on.[46]

In both Messengers' speeches, dismemberment, the *de-cision* erupting from Dionysian mania, follows a decision—the outcome of collective deliberation or of Pentheus's ostensible volition. In the first Messenger's account, after deliberations[47] of the cowherds and shepherds conclude with the unanimously approved decision to "hunt Pentheus's mother, Agave, from the bacchanals" (719–20), we are told, the Messenger and his group decided to lie in wait, their *lochos* (*ellochizomen* 722) verbally recalling, again, Dionysus's time in Zeus's thigh (*en ôdi- / nôn lochiais anankaisi* 88–89). In quasi-official language, the Messenger reports that the proponent of this action "seemed to us to have spoken well" (*eu d'hêmin legein / edoxe* 721–22)—a phrase split into two parts by an enjambment, which iconically links this decision with the impending *de-cision*, the act captured by the verb *dia-phoreô* (739, 746 "to bring apart") and by the image of "bodily parts thrown up and down" (741).[48] The decision to separate Agave from Dionysus—in effect, to re-enact the separation, the *de-cision*, of Semele from her son—engenders multiple, visceral *de-cisions*. We can say that in making themselves visible by leaving the bushes—a self-disclosure comparable to Dionysus's exit from his second prenatal *lochos*—the Messenger and his cohort cause the vocalic opening of *monia* into *mania*.

In the second Messenger's speech, which details the mechanics of Pentheus's death, we find another lying-in-wait: Pentheus, the disguised Dionysus, and the Messenger initially sit (*hizomen* 1048) in an isolated, silent space where they can see without being seen, while the Maenads are similarly depicted as seated (*kathêntai* 1053), "keeping their hands busy *in delightful occupations* (*en terpnois ponois*)," not differently from the cows peacefully grazing (735) before being attacked by them, as reported in the previous speech. Pentheus's declared decision to climb a tree for a better view is not just escalating hubris and *mania* before the eruption of Maenadic mania, but a *de-cision* from the group prior to his own *de-cision*. Both *de-cisions* are visualized in the vertiginous lines detailing Dionysus's sadistic bending of a branch to accommodate Pentheus's decision and facilitate his downfall: *kat-êgen êgen, êgen es melan pedon* ("he brought it down, brought it, brought it to the black ground" 1065).[49] The shift from the compound *kat-êgen* to the simple *êgen*—a beheaded *kat-êgen*—captures Pentheus's separation from the group while anticipating his decapitation. My emphasis here is not the moralistic notion of punishment for wanting to see too much, for making a *bad* decision, but rather the connection between *mania* and decision as such—understood as an individuation, an exit from the pack and from undifferentiated (or *un-decided*) time, a plunge into the event. Following Kierkegaard, Derrida repeatedly enunciates in his writings an assimilation of "the instant of decision" to "madness."[50] In the Messengers' speeches, we can locate the counterfactual of in-decision, of temporal de-individuation, a prolonging of the wait, a delaying of the birth of the event, as it were.

The *monia* that can be located in *Bacchae* subsists in a space of un-decidability or in-decision that is at the same time a space of possibility. In-decision and un-decidability play a major role in Derrida's theorization of *différance* and deconstruction in general in his early writings as well as in later ones.[51] If decision can be conceptualized, etymologically, as a cutting, an instant, like each sparagmatic separation of Pentheus's limbs, the gimmicky *monia*, the Blanchotian disaster, of Cadmus and Teiresias's scene bespeaks non-instantaneity. For Derrida, because free, genuine decision can emerge only from a space of radical, unrealized possibility, undecidability is not to be thought of as a state of paralysis but as the very condition of possibility for political action.[52] Massimo Cacciari has observed that in the context of the European Union, where decision-making frequently serves to confirm the hegemonic position of some states over others, the stasis of undecidability or hesitation—we could say, *monia*—can become political resistance.[53] Calvin Warren has pointed out that "decision outlaws black being" and, in Heideggerian terms, that indecision is an "*openin[g]* for the unfolding of Being" and "rather than limiting *becoming*, [it is] necessary for it to occur."[54] Drawing out the etymological force of *decision*, Derrida refers to the death penalty as a "*cutting* decision."[55] As he puts it, "What we rebel against when we rebel against the death penalty is not death" but "rather the interruption of the principle of indetermination . . . of the incalculable chance." Such an interruption disavows a living being's imponderable "relation to what comes, to the to-come and thus to some other," whether that other appears "as event, as guest, as *arrivant*."[56] The death penalty is thus a disavowal, on the part of the one who inflicts it, of the finitude of one's agency in the face of the uncertainty defining life—it is a disavowal of the inability to control time. This disavowal is also a rejection of the "undecidability" that comports with this finitude.[57] While Teiresias and Cadmus have made a decision of sorts, to follow Dionysus, their gimmicky present introduces an element of worn-out duration, of non-eventual elation that generates the (alternative/counterfactual) possibility of the plot's deviation from its movement forward, from its decided course, which here coincides with the destructive decision of Pentheus. We can say that this deviation from the decided course is an element of undecidability unsettling the plot.

More than the Dionysian decision of Pentheus and the Maenads, which operates in the tight interval between free will and coercion, it is in-decision that refuses interpellation and the "logic that stages refusal as inactivity, as the absence of a plan and as a mode of stalling real politics."[58] As Stefano Harney and Fred Moten put it in *The Undercommons*:[59]

> We're more than politics, more than settled, more than democratic. We surround democracy's false image in order to unsettle it. Every time it tries to enclose us in a decision, we're undecided.

In their queer kinship, the two old, heavy bodies, accumulations of time, constitute the alpha privative (the *a* in *à venir*), obstructing time, the arrival of the event. Like the "wild" ontology of Dionysus's birth, but unlike the regime of his ritualized worship, this obstruction hinders decision, that is, the emergence of a political determination out of the shapeless, undifferentiated realm of possibility (aesthetic, existential, political). The explosion of Dionysian intoxication has been seen, à la Nietzsche, as a kind of ecstatic liberation, a re-emergence of the primordial joy of being. Bonnie Honig has reoriented this thesis in political terms, seeing the Theban women's abandonment of their homes to follow the Dionysian cult as an act of feminist refusal or even a gynocratic enterprise.[60] Not altogether different from Pentheus's repressive binding, his intoxicated, rushed, autocratic decision-making, Dionysian intoxication is its own form of "enclosing" decision, a biopolitical subjugation to and assimilation into an all-encompassing power, as well as the most brutal expression of a future present.[61]

The enclosure of decision marks the end of *Bacchae*, when Cadmus brings Agave back into consciousness—a restoration of cognition that severs her from her state of *remaining in*, from her absorption in the undifferentiated time of the Dionysian pandemic. When Agave arrives onstage carrying Pentheus's head, she refers to it with an ominous deictic ("this [*tade*] prize" 1238) and mentions hands or arms three times: "having left the distaff by the loom, I have moved on to bigger things, hunting animals with my *hands* (*cheroin*)" (1236–37); "as you see, I carry this prize *in my arms* (*en ôlenaisin*)" (1238–39); "father, please take this in your *hands* (*cheroin*)" (1240). How shall we translate this verbal insistence into haptic persistence, into theatrical effect and affect? Among the various staging possibilities afforded by the wording, we can imagine Agave caressing her son's head, fondling his hair as if it were a leonine mane. The verbal repetition can be read as gestural repetition, continuously touching and being touched in return, a form of *immanence*, affective and temporal, fetishistic and queer. Agave's tactile attachment to what she takes to be an animal trophy, a non-living companion, results in a care relation between human and non-human, a connectivity "across normative categorizations."[62] The interspecies animacy engendered by this bond—in a scene as campy as the one with Teiresias and Cadmus—also crosses (or crips) temporal bounds, confusing the before and the after, opening up a capsule of temporal stasis within the linear mobility of the dialogue.[63]

Petting the head of a dead child/animal shelters Agave in a queer dimension where time is dilated and the event, the dividing line between before and after, is removed from perception, turned into an alpha privative—this is the non-eventality that we feel immersed in despite the "event" of the pandemic. Pentheus's head becomes a "feral child" anchoring Agave within a pre- or post-Symbolic realm whose temporality is at odds with the eruptive ecstasy of the Dionysiac rituals.[64] Agave's *mania* has slipped into a *monia* comparable to the Dionysian preparations of Teiresias and Cadmus. In both of these scenes, which are *para*-ontological in the sense of being *beside* or almost outside the plot, a queer bond blocks the plot's *de-cisive* rhythm, its structural distinction between a before and an after. In forcing Agave to disconnect from a continuous present and acquire awareness of her dead son, Cadmus's command to "look and learn more clearly" (1281)—a version of Aeschylean *pathei mathos* ("learning by suffering") also addressed to the audience—works as the voice of the decision-making Law.[65] Cadmus commits another sparagmatic act, a repetition of Dionysian *de-cision*: he breaks Agave's bond, her fondling of the lion's/child's head and, consequently, her idyll in *unbroken, undifferentiated, un-decided* time. The apparent return to sanity converges, paradoxically, with the loss of it orchestrated by Cadmus's grandson, an enforcer of his own form of Symbolic constriction.[66] *Monia* in *Bacchae* is a rejection of the event as the dividing marker between what came before or after the Dionysian outbreak; as such, it amounts to a "wild" or deeply un-decided or in-decisive mania, a convergence and synchrony of apparently incompatible conditions—a Blanchotian non-experience of ecstatic, anarchical Dionysian hierarchy and a clinging to its consequences when one is pushed to move on. Especially in the outbreak of the pandemic, urgent decision making aimed to protect the economy more than human lives, enforcing the imperative to move on, to return to the status quo ante, to stop the interruption of life as it (always) was.[67]

With his arrival in Thebes, disguised as an emissary, Dionysus, the absolute foreigner, promises or threatens a messianic arrival, but the gimmicky aesthetics, the non-experience, at the beginning of *Bacchae* suggests the arrival of a lack, of a disjointed present. In his recent re-evaluation of "negation" for the purposes of what he calls "an affirmative philosophy," Roberto Esposito observes that "the negative is . . . the forewarning of a lack . . . the empty point that . . . pushes the present beyond itself, towards the eternally eluded promise of the origin . . . the inactual that continues to disrupt our actuality."[68] This notion of the "negative" converges with Judith Butler's critique of "realizability," a critique that is not "a cynical or defeatist attenuation of struggle" but rather "an unceasing engagement with a desire for the political, sustained by its ultimate unattainability."[69] The gimmick of Teiresias and Cadmus fecklessly adorned as Maenads models the infinite possibility that is undecidability—a resistance to the normative mania of re-solution, to the fantasized return to the status quo ante, that is embodied in the very yoking of the old men's bodies, in Agave's tactile attachment to (in)animate kin. The Dionysian *à venir*, the arrival of a lack, at the margins of the Euripidean plot invites us to shift our attention from *mania* to *monia* as the stilling wherein "the potential to be otherwise" is contained.[70] For Rebecca Sheldon, "The future is . . . in dynamic torsion with the present as a series of feedback loops . . . the give and take of a future neither wholly determined by the present nor mystically sealed by the carapace of chance."[71] In the encounter of tragic bodies, human and no-longer human, filling the interval between before and after, contorting decision through the anti-kinetic agency of slowness and repetition, we see the materialization of an affirmative negative, which might partially mitigate the decision-making hysteria (or even the Schmittian decisionism) of our times, a hysteria shaping even the more recent, sudden decision (of the media, of the capitalized state) that the pandemic is over.

Decision in pandemic times has, predictably, coincided with the rhetoric of war,[72] which also shapes Pentheus's conduct in the play, as he is repeatedly said to be "fighting against the god," *theo-macheô* (45, 325, 636, 1255), that is, waging a war against Dionysus's contagious influence. Joseph Osmundson has demonstrated that, in the United States, the motto "We will win this war," in this case against the virus, legitimizes the death of health care workers by turning them into "heroes" while they are, in effect, otherized, targeted in an auto-immunitarian response that leaves the virus unscathed.[73] Reinscribing the equation of health and capital ("It is virtuous . . . to be healthy, just as it's virtuous, in America, to be rich"),[74] the state's immunological *theomachy*—no matter whether the invisible lethal entity materializes as HIV or Covid—ends up targeting and blaming the victims.[75] As Osmundson puts it, "If we *are* to imagine ourselves as a national body—even a global body—this is a virus we need to listen to, not fight."[76]

Listening can perhaps help us reconceptualize "decisions" from quasi-martial measures into "community acts of care," into opportunities for "*rethink[ing]* systems that have been failing for decades, systems whose deadly consequences are too often made invisible."[77] Decisions need to make space for the intervals opened up by "hesitation," the conditio sine qua non of "rethinking," a zone of indetermination, a phenomenological *durée* that intensively extends the pressure of an unresolved past onto a present frantically tending toward a future.[78] This hesitation (from the Latin verb *haereo*) is a practice of care because it etymologically entails a clinging to each other, a sticking together, an attachment—temporal, affective, cognitive, *and* deliberative—even when we need to be in quarantine, understood as a "social act, not a personal sacrifice."[79] By curtailing the ostensibly liberating and ecstatic but totalizing cutting of Dionysian mania, the gimmicky *à venir*, the arrival of an alpha privative, of a moment of hesitation, creates an *un-de-cided* space of possibility as we sever ourselves from political homogenization and still bond together, waiting and rethinking.

3

Iphigenia

In this chapter I want to linger on the feel of pandemic waiting by considering the relation between time, interrupted or limited affective physicality, and the tactile icon of our times and of theatrical performance: the mask. In *Iphigenia in Aulis*, we experience the alienating feeling of never getting to a destination, of never being already there. Even when the Greeks, freed from a paralyzing lack of air, are finally able to depart for Troy, the murderous act that dislodges the army (the sacrifice of Iphigenia, the deer, or both) continues to affect and infect us.[1] We are induced to believe that there never will be an end of the crisis or, to render this point in language that has become tragically familiar, "we will remain in a viral world continually threatened by epidemics and environmental disturbances."[2] For Habiba Ibrahim and Badia Ahad, 2020 was marked by "(simultaneous) expansion and compression, felt through the slow time of monotony, the racing time of anxiety, the cyclical time of mourning."[3] The pressure of time, of time that presses upon us, invisible, untouchable, (im)materially weighs us down, yielding unrelenting weariness.[4] In my re-reading of the play, I explore the dual pressure of time and the mask, which in our recent lives, as in the world of Greek theater, has been our face. At least for the privileged among us, during the unfillable time of lockdown, connecting with a limited number of our closest human (and non-human) companions, affectively lingering on their bodies, wallowing in protracted physical (re) apprehension of and attachment to corporeal surfaces, contours, and parts appear to be the only ways to break up an all-encompassing temporal totality. Yet in Euripides' play this haptic lingering imagistically overlaps with a cutting-up of human and non-human life, inviting us to reflect on the disavowed (in)animate and interspecies proximities and entanglements that are bound up in the air.

Euripides' *Iphigenia in Aulis* is a play about air, waiting, and indecision—it is, thus, thematically of a piece with *Oedipus the King* and *Bacchae*, a play that was part of the same tragic trilogy, produced posthumously in 405.[5] The Greeks gathered in Aulis are waiting for the arrival of wind—for air that is no longer paralyzed or paralyzing. The metaphorical impossibility of breathing—and getting unstuck—manifests itself in epistemic modes conditioned by thinking through air. Even the desire of Helen (inseparable from the desire *for* Helen) is presented as air: *pnoai ... Aphroditês philai* ("the dear breaths of Aphrodite" 69). At the beginning of the play, Agamemnon expresses the army's waiting as "using" (more idiomatically, "enduring") a pair of lacks marked with alpha privatives, a paradoxical instrumentalization, prior to Calchas's presentation of the harrowingly liberating solution of sacrificing Iphigenia (87–89): "With the army all gathered and assembled (*êthroismenou de kai xun-estôtos stratou*), we sit in Aulis *using* (*chrômenoi*) the *lack of sailing* (*a-ploiai*). As we were using (*kechrêmenois*) our *lack of a path* (*a-poriai*) Calchas the seer [revealed to us ...]."[6] The very fact of assembling—a political ritual at the service of action—emphasizes the waiting, the negation of action.[7] Through a reduplication of the alpha privative in "lack of sailing" (*a-ploia*) and "lack of a path" (*a-poria*), the sequence of parallel phrases (*a-ploiai chrômenoi / a-poriai kechrêmenois*) channels an insistence on the useless effort to use—to exert control over—what eludes control and instrumentalization: the Real of windless stillness, but also, more pregnantly, of the wind itself, taunting the waiting soldiers, making itself felt in the articulatory hissing of accumulated sibilants and aspirates (*êthroismenou de kai xun-estôtos stratou*). In a later choral ode, the same rhetoric of negative use yields ironic effects as it is applied to the lack of (erotic) wind. When the Chorus praises the blessed few who are able to enjoy the pleasures of Aphrodite in moderation, "using windlessness (i.e., calm) apart from crazy frenzies" (*galaneiai chrêsamenoi / mainomenôn oistrôn* 546–47a), the current lack of wind aligns with an overdetermined, affective deprivation: both the negation of *erôs*, what we may call asexuality, and *erôs* itself—the deprivation brought about by a never controllable, never containable feeling. Circulating in the air, *erôs* and its denial—two viral forces equally present and barely distinguishable in this play where Achilles and Iphigenia's marriage is done and undone—impose inaction, endless waiting, paranoiac dallying, a sense of breathlessness, the various inflections of the pressure exerted by an invisible and (im)material agent.

Such pressure is felt in the emotional *aporia* of Agamemnon, who at night ties *and* unties, seals *and* unseals the tablet meant to deliver a deceptive message to Clytemnestra—asking her to bring Iphigenia, the designated sacrificial victim, to Aulis under the pretext of marrying her off to Achilles. The death-driven *fort* and *da* between the two actions—one following the other, but, in a sense, also co-implicated and contemporaneous—problematizes the multiple dualities in the first part of the play, structured around two prologues, two brothers (Agamemnon and Menelaus), two letters, two opposite messages. When Agamemnon hands to his servant the message that undoes the earlier one, the tablet—a grammatically feminine object—meant to erase or archive his sacrificial plan, he casts the expected replacement as a juxtaposition, a coexistence: *pempô soi pros tais prosthen / deltous* ("I send you, [Clytemnestra], this tablet in addition to the earlier one" 115–16). This coexistence of opposites prefigures the co-presence—in the textual, dramatic, and mythical imaginary of this play with two finales—of a sacrificed Iphigenia and a rescued one.[8] The destabilization of the border between realized and unrealized possibilities, doing and undoing, event and non-event—the *aporia* that is "not so much a *failure* of agency but the only mode of agency"[9]—reduces time to a thin, barely visible interval, the continuously shifting line between virtuality and actuality. When Menelaus reproaches Agamemnon for his prolonged hesitation—"You think wandering thoughts, some in the present, some in the distant past, some in the future" (*plagia gar phroneis, ta men nun, ta de palai, ta d'autika* 332)[10]— the chopped-up verbal form construes time as a decomposed entity, whose constituents, singular moments, sites of anxious, protracted, imaginary lingering, are parts refusing to be folded into a notional unity. Later in the play, in a tense encounter with her husband, Clytemnestra, deploying a rhetorical topos ("Which one of my troubles shall I mention first?"), claims to have lost her sense of what comes first, last, and in the middle (*hapasi gar prôtoisi chrêsasthai para / kan hustatoisi kan mesoisi pantachou* 1125–26)—an apparent unity, as underscored by the double polysyndeton (*kan*), constituted by the anamorphic confusion of temporal registers, of discrete portions in the expanse of time that become indistinct, barely recognizable in the experience of waiting.

The anamorphic time of *Iphigenia in Aulis* seeps into discourse—into the play's baroque language (spoken and lyric), an instantiation of what Edward Said calls "late style."[11] Emblematic of this overwrought diction is Agamemnon's initial revelation of his secret plan, which I will translate literally, remaining faithful to the awkward density of the original: "To that one [Achilles] I promised my child, that into bridal beds of embraces I would give her out in nuptials" (*keinôi paid' ep-ephêmisa / numpheious eis ankônôn / eunas ek-dôsein lektrois* 130–32). It is as though voyeuristic embarrassment (layered with repressed desire) manifested itself as a surplus of form, an excessive lingering (verbal as well as tactile), which distorts time through overdetermination, through ongoing—and uncontrolled—addition. The accumulation suggests a wish never to interrupt the (last) embrace between father and daughter—while allegedly announcing her marriage, the ultimate separation between them. Instead of biographically or axiologically imputing the "late style" of lines like this to effete decline, a decadent running out of steam induced by old age, or a turn toward the melodramatic or "new musical,"[12] I suggest that such language is inflected by the play's temporal and environmental atmosphere, the windlessness that feels like a catastrophe. The chronic stalling of time, the atmospheric stuckness, extends to, inflects or even infects, the overextended style, which is caught between doing and undoing, a dramatization of waiting.

Catalog, in this play, is the discursive mode of non-doing, of not being able to act, and of being transformed from subject to object—to the plaything of the atmospheric Real, which, like the pandemic, frustrates but never fully removes our illusion of subjecthood. Transferred into the meta-tragic space of choral spectatorship, the traditional catalog of ships gives way to catalogic aporia, encompassing an inventory of idle occupations, precarious means of filling the unfillable time of waiting (194–200):[13]

Prô-
tesilaon t'epi thakois
pessôn hêdomenous mor-
phaisi poluplokois

Palamêdea th', hon teke pais ho Poseidanos,
Diomêdea th' hêdonais
   diskou kecharêmenon

Chorus ... [I saw] Protesilaus and Palamedes, whom Poseidon's child fathered, seated, enjoying the *intricate shapes* (*morphaisi poluplokois*) of *draughts* (*pessôn*), and Diomedes relishing the joys of the discus...

A meta-indication of performative and verbal tangles—of interweavings of hands, arms, feet, phonemes, words—the multiplicity of shapes signaled by the phrase *morphaisi polu-plokois* ("intricate shapes") also reads as an effort to diversify time, to impart distinct contours, or diverse inflections to it, to break a smooth surface of monotony into the textured structure crafted by the unpredictable cuts and ruptures of the event. While Palamedes and Protesilaus queerly bond over the quasi-masturbatory game of draughts (*pessoi*),[14] Diomedes connects with the *di*scus in a space of *jouissant* interobjectivity, embracing the timelessness of circular time. In the following strophe of the choral ode, entering the plane of ecphrastic discourse outfitted with compound epithets, Achilles—"*equal to wind* (*is-anemon*) in his feet and *light-running* (*laipsêro-dromon* 206–7)"—is contending with a chariot, whose driver is initially anonymous, a four-wheeled wooden and metallic cyborgic counterpart. *Laipsêro-dromon* ("light-running") assimilates Achilles to the animals, animal parts, or commodities (chariot, bridles, etc.) that in this strophe are the only other recipients of elevated epithets.[15] This ontological transformation unfolding through the female Chorus's curious, eroticized gaze fixes Achilles, like the other catalogic heroes, in the miniature scale of a trinket.[16] An army eager to spring into action is frozen in a tableau, martial turmoil stylized as ludic gestures, agonistic postures, vicarious motions. In the encounter with the hyperobject of atmospheric stuckness, the subject discovers itself as a micro-object, even as it attempts to affirm its power of subjection. Achilles is no longer a soldier in an epic catalog but a precious ornament in a collection of verbal props, epic relics converted into amusements for a queer time of waiting—like Diomedes' discus, or Palamedes' and Protesilaus's draughts (or Laura's glass statuettes in Tennessee Williams' *The Glass Menagerie*).[17] Depicted as equal to wind, Achilles figures the hubristic aspiration to match or subjugate the hyperobject, the elemental outside—whether it is a chronic lack of wind or a pandemic. The "late" formal saturation reflected in the Chorus's desire to "fill" (*plêsaimi* 233–34) their eyes with Iliadic content—parallel to the army's viral craving for the sight of Iphigenia (427–28)—prevents language from flowing, from moving, ginning up a hyper-visual blockage that replicates the blocked atmosphere of Aulis's asphyxiating calm.

The play seems to make space for amusement scenes—or dramatized pastimes—fillers of unfillable time. When Agamemnon tells Clytemnestra the name of Iphigenia's promised husband—Achilles—an extended back and forth ensues concerning his identity and pedigree, something like a guessing game (691–715).[18] Why do we find a mini-*Achilleid* in the middle of the play? Who needs an extended mythological digression on the best-known Greek hero? Instead of postulating an interpolation or imputing this scene to decadent aesthetics,[19] I am proposing a hyper-mimetic reading, construing this moment as another dramatization of unfillable time—as though the environmental immobility that sets the plot in motion, or rather arrests it, is felt through and dictates the aesthetic *poiêsis* of its representational medium (of the medium that fictionally produces the windlessness), reversing, once again, hierarchies of subject and object, joining (or even replacing) the authorial function, impersonally generating textuality.[20]

The early phase of the Covid-19 pandemic brought to the fore phrases such as *unstructured leisure*, *structural leisure*, *slow leisure*, and *enforced leisure*, referring to a condition imposed both on the privileged ones "forced" to work at home and the unprivileged ones forced out of their jobs, who experienced capital's capacity for manipulating time—compressing or expanding it—like those whose working hours were, instead, limitlessly extended.[21] Clytemnestra's guessing game, which could be interpreted as a meta-generic gesture of characteristically Euripidean irreverence, a comic incursion into tragic territory, can also be attributed, hyper-mimetically, to *enforced leisure*, the "logical" consequence of the *unstructured* temporality looming over the Greek camp. Clytemnestra and Agamemnon enact a conjugal version of the game of draughts played by Palamedes and Protesilaus. Later, enraged by the discovery of Agamemnon's murderous designs, Clytemnestra prefaces her lengthy reprimand with the striking statement "We will no longer use riddling hints" (*kouketi par-ôidois chrêsomesth' ainigmasin* 1147). The shock of seeing the adjective (*par-ôidois*) cognate with the word for "parody"—in the etymological sense of "additional," "marginal," "tacked on"[22]—embedded within the micro-fabric of the tragic dialogue is matched by the paradox of Clytemnestra's opening speech. Here she concocts a bewildering plot complication, an unheard-of trauma in her past: a marriage with an otherwise unknown Tantalus—a name evoking the remote ancestrality of her husband's great-grandfather—with whom she had a baby, later killed by Agamemnon together with the father.[23] Clytemnestra's (ironic) promise to stick to clarity and linearity is belied by a tale that is both *beside* and *beyond* the point. Juxtapositional, paratactical, the enactment of the oppressive parataxis resulting from disjointed time, this impromptu exercise in mythological revision reads as idle entertainment within the *unstructured/structural leisure* afflicting a military camp in a state of dyspnea or apnea.

This situation corresponds to the "bad leisure" (*kako-scholia*), a consequence of a kind of "homogeneous empty time,"[24] that we see lyrically theorized in the reference to Aulis in the parodos of Aeschylus's *Agamemnon* (192–98):

> *Chorus* Winds (*pnoai*) coming from the Strymon, *bringing bad leisure* (*kako-scholoi*), provoking hunger, making the anchorage difficult, causing mortals to wonder, unsparing of ships and ropes, rendering time (*chronon*) *doubly long* (*palim-mêkê*), *wore down* (*kat-exainon*) the bloom (*anthos*) of the Achaeans with *delay* (*tribôi*).

Instilling a sensation of melan*cholic* apathy (for *kako-scholoi* can be broken into *kakos-choloi*), the lack of occupation that comes from feeling environmentally un-occupied, from failing to feel the breath of air on our bodies, goes along with the wear and tear of time—the "turbulent flows forming eddies, circling back around ... reconfiguring what might yet have been"[25]— captured by the hapax *palim-mêkê* ("doubly long"), time that consumes the Achaeans as well as Iphigenia herself with the "destructive attrition"[26] of void continuity. In *Iphigenia in Aulis*, the Big Other of atmospheric time, a hyperobject with hyper-mimetic capacity, claims possession of the characters themselves. In a time with no possibility of *lusis*, with no end in sight, *enforced leisure* bodies forth an aesthetic and existential para-lysis or over-analysis—a "form of excessive, unproductive, and paralyzing intellection,"[27] an extended sparagmatic rending of time (and discourse), not unlike Iphigenia's sacrificial dismemberment, which hinders easy reparation and teleological resolution. Clytemnestra's narrative "parody" operates alongside atmospheric stuckness as an instrument for delaying the "solution" of the sacrifice, which epitomizes the desire to exit immobility at any cost; her scandalous deviation functions like the argument for slowed-down thinking and life,[28] for rejecting the rush toward the well-known path of normality.

The first instantiation of the *ana-lyzable* time of atmospheric immobility— time broken into dragged-out moments, its imaginary constituents—is Clytemnestra and Iphigenia's arrival, with its decelerated dramaturgy. Even outside the space of choral song, the hyperform of the play breaks unmarked, inert time into distinct moments, into the singular, (im)material instants through which a kinetic posture or gesture unfolds, unrealistically—or hyper-realistically—dilating mundane motions, dwelling on the apparently irrelevant, fragmenting the undivided corpus of silent doings into sayable, visible, and tactile objects,[29] recording the mechanics of "supremely tiny acts" (arriving, disembarking, unloading the chariot, sitting, etc.)[30] with an insistence that goes much beyond theatrical deixis (610–29):[31]

> *Clytemnestra* Now, take the dowry that I bring for my girl, and take it inside, being careful. And you, my daughter, leave the horse-driven vehicle, safely placing your soft foot on the ground. And you, young women, take her in your arms and lift her out of the chariot. And someone give me the support of a hand, so that I can decorously leave the seat of the chariot. And you, other young women, stand in the front of the horses' yoke; for a horse appears frightened in its face when it lacks soothing consolation. And take this child, the son of Agamemnon, Orestes.... Son, are you sleeping, made docile by the chariot? Wake up for the wedding of your sister.... Sit here by my foot, child; Iphigenia, stand near me, your mother, and make me happy for these foreign women.

The operational variety and intensity of these lines reads as a performance of the frenzy arising from a desperate desire or need to fill time that does not achieve actual movement, as we feel if we linger on the ends of lines 613–20, dominated by the phrase meaning "horse vehicle" (*pôlikous ochous* 613), which recurs in multiple shapes.[32] These repetitions have the effect of caressing the horse, who appears to be conflated with the child Orestes.[33] It is as though, prescient of Agamemnon's murderous intentions, Clytemnestra does not wish to, or simply cannot, leave the chariot at all or, differently put, her movement (from vehicle to ground) has a rebellious backward impetus that would affix the subject to the object she apparently seeks to leave: a chariot like the one that was Achilles' non-human target and implicit alter ego in the parodos. The hyper-temporality of Clytemnestra's arrival dramatizes extended, exhausted chronicity ("long time," "long distance"), a meta-fixation in the initial dialogue between Agamemnon and Iphigenia, which itself conjures breath made stale by (scripted) time and time made stagnant by the lack of air (640, 651, 664, 660):

> *Iphigenia* Father, I gladly see you *after a long time* (*pollôi chronôi*). . . .
>
> *Agamemnon* The impending separation between us will be *long* (*makra*). . . .
>
> *Iphigenia* You are sailing *a long way* (*makran*), father, leaving me. . . .
>
> *Iphigenia* How *long* (*polun . . . chronon*) you have been away in the recesses of Aulis!

*Poly-chron*icity here stands in for breathlessness, for deferred exhalation, the somatized pressure of temporal dilation, or paralyzed time.

A deceptive turning point, the arrival of Achilles figures perennial *midst-ness*, a limbo state that makes one despair of a beginning as much as an ending. No sooner does Achilles materialize in a much-awaited epiphany than the evental force peters out, assimilated into the undifferentiation of waiting, the idle counting out of time. The unwitting would-be bridegroom in the Iphigenia wedding plot, Achilles, ironically pointing out that the two camps of soldiers, married and unmarried, do not wait (*menomen*) on equal terms, launches into a punning tirade (812–18):

> *Achilles* After leaving the land of Pharsalus and Peleus, *I wait* (*menô*) by these light breezes of the river Euripus, holding the Myrmidons; and they, always coming upon me, say: "Achilles, why *are we waiting* (*menomen*)?

How much time do we still have to *count out* (*ek-metrêsai*) before the
expedition to Ilion? If you are going to do something, do it, or otherwise
take the army back home *without abiding the delays of the Atreidae* (*ta tôn
Atreidôn mê menôn mellêmata*).

In this speech, Achilles' disorientation is caught in the accumulation and
confusion of "waiting" (*menô*), "delays" (*mellêmata*) and "counting"
(*ek-metrêsai*), but also in the objectification of the ego (*me*) shared by these
three activities, even by the one, "counting," that seems to place the subject in a
position of sovereignty. In the last line, the subject is dilated—nearly annihilated
(*me* "me"/ *mê* "not")—in a monosyllabic hiccupping sequence (*mê . . . me . . .
me*), appearing through disappearance, a micro-presence between other words,
in a condition of continual midstness (Greek *me-son*). Achilles is besieged—
caught in the middle—by the Atreidae (*tôn Atreidôn*) and their ghostly
epiphany in the sequence *menônmellêmata*, which patently encrypts the name
Menelaus, meaning "the hero who withstands (*menei*) a host." Exhausted by his
brother's ambivalence, Menelaus, in this play, embodies the exhausted waiting
(*menein*) of the whole community (*laon*).[34] Achilles is the necessary
intermediary, or a mere instrument, for Agamemnon and Menelaus, a double
of the slave who delivers the deceitful messages that set the plot within the plot
in motion. The initial dialogue between Achilles and Clytemnestra—the two
pawns in Agamemnon's plan—is interrupted by the (semi-)appearance of this
slave on the threshold, in the middle of the scene, in a spatial middle between
outside and inside, outsiders and insiders, marked by a return of the verb *menô*
("to wait"): "Stranger, offspring of Aeacus, wait (*meinon*)!" (855). In a play with
two beginnings (a double prologue) and two endings, the slave's position—like
Achilles' figurations of an encircled subject—tropes the impossibility of clearly
recognizing the edges of the plot, which display an inward orientation,
seemingly projected toward the inside rather than the outside. The first
prologue, Agamemnon's dialogue with his servant (1–48), is strikingly *in
medias res*, while the second, more conventional one (49–114) reads like a
beginning absorbed into the middle. Likewise, the first ending, the mere
announcement of Iphigenia's movement toward the site of sacrifice, has
indistinct contours, appearing incapable of fully separating itself out of the

middle, while even the second ending, in which the Messenger relays at length the substitution of a deer for Iphigenia, leaves the audience breathless in a tangle of narrative details that pass with little in the way of a closural response on the part of Clytemnestra and Agamemnon, both of them immersed in an overdetermined, present and futural, midstness.

In one of the many interventions in the emerging field of pandemic studies, we read:

> As the life of the virus began as a gigantic, distributed hyperobject with amorphous boundaries, a narrative also commenced that focused on identifying its origin in order to be able to mark a beginning (with a host of ensuing conspiracy theories), a middle (long and winding, unfolding exponentially, and bifurcating in various regions of the world), and an end (the form of which at the time of writing is still located in a realm of anticipation and which may continue for a long time).[35]

The narrative described here can never, in fact, come together. While we can heuristically locate the "origin" of the pandemic, its deeper origins (animal exploitation, ecological extractivism, etc.) date back to an indeterminate past and extend into an equally indeterminate future. Far from being isolable and circumscribable in the past, separable from present and future, these origins are *mixed* into them, constituting a perennial middle ("long and winding, unfolding exponentially") that forecloses the very possibility of an ending. Being *en me-sôi* ("in the middle"), *beforeafter*,[36] is the temporal condition made tragically perceptible during the pandemic and in this play, which folds the quintessentially pandemic conditions of *me-nô* ("I wait"), *me-llô* ("I delay"), *me-trêo* ("I count") into the middle (*me-son*) of an excruciatingly dilated and delayed (that is, etymologically, "diluted" or "mixed") subjecthood (*me*). As we will see later, the disavowal of our atmospherically intermingled demi-subjecthood renders the end, the "solution," in the play and in our current lives, nothing but a *pharmakon* that steeps us in the midstness of our (a)chronic predicaments.

This temporal midstness has a troubling affective counterpart in the compulsive haptic aesthetics of this play—its "touch hunger," to use an expression popularized in the pandemic.[37] In her study on physical contact in Greek tragedy, Maarit Kaimio labels this play "a tragedy of manners," using a term (from *manuarius* "of the hand") that encodes the nexus between tactility and social being and becoming.[38] *Iphigenia in Aulis*'s "mannered" aesthetics—its affective dwelling on encounters of corporeal postures, leanings, lines, and shapes—are epitomized by overlapping moments of embrace and supplication. Iphigenia's emergence into the theatrical dialogue happens through her wish to cleave to Agamemnon, which she expresses by placing her father at the center of the line, and by envisioning an eerie contact of chest to chest, suggesting, through the overlap of sound, an identification of intimate "towardness" (*pros*) with paternity (*patros*) as such while concomitantly evoking the frontality of the mask (*pros-ôpon*):[39] *pros sterna patros sterna tama prosbalô* (632). In the rendition of the embrace, Agamemnon's anatomical catalog ("O chests and cheeks, O golden hair" *ô sterna kai parêides, ô xanthai komai* 681)—like Clytemnestra's later supplication of Achilles ("by your chin, by your right hand" *pros geneiados <se>, pros se dexias* 909)—hauntologically previews Iphigenia's sacrifice and the dismemberment of the sacrificial victim as such. Yet this is also an anatomization of time, or a figuration of *ana-lyzed* time, which conjures another resonance with pandemic achrony, as those who sheltered in place lingered—physically or imaginatively—on the cheeks, faces, arms, and hands of the loved ones with whom they shared domestic spaces or whom they were separated from against their will, losing themselves in a plethora of instants. This anatomization of time—cutting time in order to make it perceptible (visible and touchable) when it risks becoming unbound, ungovernable, simultaneously immaterial and too material—dramatizes the idea of the gesture as "the exhibition of a mediality ... the process of making a *means* visible as such."[40] Agamemnon's gesture, in its mediality, or *means*-ness, is the corporeal expression of a *midstness* without end. What I am suggesting is that, in the play, the temporal texture of atmospheric stuckness is allegorized by the processual *means*-ness of touching—which Judith Butler theorizes by commenting on the form of one of the pivotal, syntactically unwieldy sentences of Merleau-Ponty's essay "The Intertwining":[41] "It is a long sentence, and it coils back, refusing to end, touching its own grammatical moments, refusing to let any of them pose as final."[42]

The peaks of the play's haptic imaginary, Clytemnestra's supplication of Achilles and Iphigenia's of Agamemnon, stage unrequited, broken, or hindered touch, inviting us to read for the theatrical mask and reflect on its implications in our own mask-wearing times.[43] In response to Clytemnestra's supplication and her request that he lay his hand on hers (*cheir' huper-teinai* 916), Achilles promises to protect Iphigenia, acquiescing while rejecting physical contact, metaphorizing her embodied language: "I will protect you by *placing* such pity *around* you" (*peri-balôn* 934); "I will not give my body to your husband for him to *interweave* his plots (*em-plekein plokas* 936–37)." Refusing to be entrapped in Agamemnon's plan, Achilles is also evading Clytemnestra's grip, stuckness in a weave of hands, in a tangle of obligations. Achilles seems inclined to separate himself from a gestural reflex of the play's atmospheric aporia, the paralysis oppressing the army. The figura etymologica in *em-plekein plokas*—a linguistic assimilation evocative of supplication's assimilating logic—suggests a fear of contagion in his gentle rebuff of Clytemnestra's invitation of a haptic ratification of their alliance, which he leaves dangling. Achilles is aware that "the moment of touch is the one in which something comes apart . . . and the notion of substance does not. . . .hold";[44] but in his being touched, even without actively touching, his desire to preserve the position of the sovereign subject, with its illusory autonomy and distance, falls apart, as it has in our own times, amid the impossible politics of social distancing guidelines.[45] "Iphigenia's supplication," as Nancy Worman has remarked, "choreographs a singular familial assemblage, as sister and . . . baby brother cling to the body of their father."[46] While pleading with her father for mercy, Iphigenia urges him to direct his eyes toward her, to show her his face and give her a kiss (*blepson pros hêmas omma dos philêma te* 1238)—a striving for contact, dialogic and physical, encompassing the Levinasian command not to kill:

> The face is the other who asks me not to let him alone, as if to do so were to become an accomplice in his death. . . . My ethical relation of love for the other stems from the fact that the self cannot survive by itself alone. . . . To expose myself to the vulnerability of the face is to put my ontological right to existence into question. In ethics, the other's right to exist has primacy over my own, a primacy epitomized in the ethical edict: you shall not kill, you shall not jeopardize the life of the other.[47]

While the pandemic reversed this logic, impelling us to cover our faces in order to save not just ourselves, but, first and foremost, the other, the mask that became the necessary intermediary of our daily social interactions re-materialized ethical opacity and anonymity, sharpening racialized hierarchies and stereotyping along with "face hunger."[48] It has been said that "the mask covers an expressive part of the face, making communication difficult: it muffles sounds and hides facial expressions, creating a sense of anonymity"; it can also be viewed as "a way of separating the body from the world, creating borders."[49] Writer and painter Riva Lehrer has described her experience complying with mask mandates as a disabled person whose body "has been reshaped by countless doctors," suddenly losing the polymorphic expressive capabilities of the face—a mask in its own right, far from transparent or straightforwardly legible:[50] "No one could hear me. Nobody could see my expressions. I was reduced to just a body. . . . We were just muffled."[51] I suggest that we read in Iphigenia's plea to her father a double meta-performative layer of meaning: not just an invitation to turn *toward* her, but also an expression of her "face hunger," a complaint about the intrusion into the affective and ethical space of familial intimacy, the material border thrown up by the theatrical mask (hers and her father's), which, in this play about deception, indecision, and the impossibility of unmediated relationality, becomes the fetishized object of ongoing, aestheticized referencing.[52] The mask already shields Agamemnon from a full display and perhaps the full affective force of his emotions, while safeguarding him, like an executioner, from the miasmic contamination of sacrificial bloodshed (in fact, he will be reported to have covered his eyes with his robe in the climactic moment of the sacrifice in the second ending, at lines 1549–50).[53] In seeking to make Agamemnon a full participant in the familial menagerie that she arranges by holding Orestes in her hands, Iphigenia is revolting against the fantasy of ethical purity and self-protection symbolized by the mask. She is not simply pursuing intimate contact, but conveying an affective contagion in her recollection of past intimacies between father and daughter (1226–30):

> *Iphigenia* This (*hod'*) was, in turn, my speech (*logos*) *while I was hanging near your chin* (*peri son ex-artômenês / geneion*), which I now touch with my hand: ". . . *Will I receive* (*es-dexomai / *) you, when you are old, *in the dear*

welcoming of my house (/ emôn philaisin hupo-dochais domôn), O father, paying you back nurse-like nourishments for your labor?"

Marked by the deictic (*hod'*), *logos* is not just speech, but the material substance of the ethical address, an atmospheric layer pressing upon the skin, like the hand that Iphigenia places on her father's masked chin. Suspended around Agamemnon's chin, hanging near it, Iphigenia is the agent of the participle *ex-artômenês*—a compound derived from the verb *aeirô* ("raise") that separates the possessive *son* ("your") from the noun *geneion* ("chin"), enacting, through enjambment, the corporeal dispossession of the subject in the encounter with the other. She is an aerial force (the *aêr* contained in *aeirô*), which spreads upward, clinging to Agamemnon's face—on and underneath the mask—its contagion troped by the *figura etymologica es-dexomai . . . hupo-dochais* ("I will receive . . . in the welcoming" 1228–29). Through the physicality of supplication, Iphigenia—the *pharmakon* against the lack of winds—is an aerial hindrance that infiltrates a paternal Symbolic masking itself as inert and inept, filling the fissures of a mask of (violent) weakness and cowardice.

Iphigenia's final gesture, her sudden acquiescence to the patriarchal solution, sacrificing herself for the community—whether fulfilled or forestalled at the last moment—aligns itself with the bio- and necropolitical discourse on the disposability of certain lives that became shockingly explicit at the outbreak of the pandemic.[54] Writing about the return of the Euripidean character in the jazz opera of Wayne Shorter and esperanza spalding's . . . *(Iphigenia)*, which toured through the United States in spring 2022, Debarati Sanyal observes:

Iphigenia is the archetype of virgin sacrifice, a daughter dispossessed of her voice and body, killed for the gods, the father and the nation. From Euripides to Racine, from Gluck's opera to Cacoyannis's film, across time and media, Iphigenia has embodied the paradox of a voice that emerges as the condition of its annihilation. Hers is a choiceless choice: to consent to her sacrifice with varying degrees of fervor and possible rationales, to submit to an economy the terms of which are set by capricious gods, a reckless king, a pusillanimous father, and a masculine military baying for blood. The daughter embraces her death so that the father's reputation remains intact, so that no more lives are lost in vain, so that the Barbarians do not invade.[55]

Sanyal's description sounds eerily familiar amid vast death inequality—the preponderance of Covid victims among the disadvantaged, the dispossessed, and, especially, communities of color—and public statements that some lives can and should be heroically sacrificed for the common good (the elderly, nurses, caretakers, essential workers operating in conditions of chronic, high-risk precarity, and other unseen people, such as migrants and refugees).[56]

At the beginning of the pandemic, the words of Texas lieutenant governor Dan Patrick caused much outrage, but also a certain measure of silent approval. "There are more important things than living. And that's saving this country for my children and my grandchildren and saving this country for all of us," Patrick said, adding, "I don't want to die, nobody wants to die, but man we've got to take some risks and get back in the game and get this country back up and running." When we re-read this statement alongside Sanyal's reference to the "economy the terms of which are set by . . . a pusillanimous father, and a masculine military baying for blood," the nature of the "game"—the capitalistic economy that subsumes all other manifestations of the paternal Symbolic—is laid bare. The game of capital—a quest for "ugly freedom"[57] not unlike the colonial enterprise congealed into the fiction of the Trojan war—is perversely regarded as the primary form of life, though it is a depersonalized, purely abstract life-killing impetus, which forces many of us to stand up and never stop moving, as though we were active players and not merely playthings. Iphigenia's individual death is the Real loss enabling yet exposing the ideology of unconditional, all-encompassing biopower that erects the militaristic or capitalistic state. Cast as an unconditional commitment to the production of life rather than life itself, the fetishization of this upright position sounds like a legitimization of what Butler calls "the radically unequal distribution of grievability"[58] and an indirect insult against or profanation of the corpse, the (in)animate remainder of *zôê* that lies on the ground, embracing its disavowed earthly vulnerability.[59]

When Iphigenia announces her intention to face self-sacrifice voluntarily, proudly, fearlessly—in language that interpreters usually characterize as an appropriation of or a complicity with a heroic code[60]—she speaks as culprit and victim alike, ventriloquizing the utilitarian biopolitical economy of masculinist militarism, masking the abjection of her impending reduction to disposable flesh through narcissistic sublimation (1375–81):

Iphigenia I have decided to die; I wish to do this *gloriously* (*eu-kleôs*), placing *lack of nobility* (*dus-genes*) *out of the way* (*ek-podôn*). Now, mother, consider here with us, how well I am positioned. *Toward me* (*eis em'*), *Greece* (*Hellas*), *the greatest* (*hê megistê*), all of it, now directs its gaze; *on me* (*kan emoi*), the ships' crossing and the destruction of the Trojans depend, as does not letting barbarians abduct future women from happy Greece.

Here and elsewhere in her speech, Iphigenia uses the language of impediment (*ek-podôn* 1376; "will I, being mortal, become an *impediment* [*em-podôn*] for the goddess?" 1396), assimilating her young body to an inanimate obstacle, a stone; her corpse to a path-clearing opening. Living, she occupies the street— just as the windless air encumbers the camp and paralyzes the army— preventing the community's movement from here to there, blocking the rush toward the army's destination: colonial conquest (its sexualized implications glibly projected onto the enemy); survival in memorial language (*eu-kleôs* "gloriously"); and reproduction (*-genes*). The insistence on the "I," which occurs at the beginning of consecutive sentences (*eis em'*; *kan emoi*) as a pounding refrain, shows that, as Parama Roy has written in relation to a different cultural context, "we would be mistaken . . . in imagining that an openness to thinking of one's flesh as meat for consumption guarantees a divestiture or even an unsettling of one's human or superhuman ascendancy or autonomy."[61] Rather, it is clear that presenting herself as sacrificial matter, "paradoxically distances [her] from the precarious status of mortal flesh and blood, signaling [her] mastery over the vulnerability of the flesh and over death."[62] Yet the reduction of Iphigenia to one or two syllables (*em'*; *emoi*) or just one letter—"You, [mother,] have given birth to *me* (*m'*) as a *common* (*koinon*) property for all the Greeks" (1386)—in sentences that place her in threatening proximity to the "whole" of Greece or a complex of military actions figures her as cannibalistic prey or, rather, as the corporeal "part" involved in an act of autophagy. Sacrificing a part of itself, an individual, or the familial unit, the state is eating itself like a uroboros—in the immediate moment or in an indeterminate future. Commenting on Shorter and spalding's opera, Butler observes:

So one undergoes a devastating loss, or one enacts a devastating sacrifice for the nation, but the nation at that moment also does violence against itself.

So it is the self-devouring character of the nation and the nation-state understood as a military state that comes to the fore. The nation-state will be a place of infinite grieving. The nation-state will be a place where people destroy what is most important to them for the purposes of the state.[63]

In the elision that we note in line 1378 (*eis em' Hellas*) the blending of the elided *e* in the personal pronoun *eme* ("me") into the initial *e* of the noun *Hellas* ("Greece") visualizes a formalistic effect of autophagy, or even of mutual cannibalism. A graphic "shimmer seeming to bask in leakage, in air's propensity to escape or to be taken away,"[64] this elision brings forth the unrealized capacity or even the desire of Iphigenia—reduced to a minimal expenditure of human breath—to "game" the system, to drag down the nation with herself, by becoming the immolated part that cannot be fully severed from the whole.

Circling back to, and renewing, the trauma of the origin, the deer that, in one version of the finale, is sacrificed in lieu of Iphigenia, the apparent instrument of the play's dramatic and environmental resolution, invites a comparison with the chronic, intensifying abuse and consumption of non-human animals, to which the current, zoonotic pandemic, as well as future ones, is to be attributed. As Achille Mbembe has observed, the pandemic is precisely the consequence of the human refusal to allow the non-human to breathe, to take in vital air, to participate equally in the experience of life.[65] Among the various causes of the atmospheric stuckness afflicting the Greeks, the tradition includes the killing of a deer sacred to Artemis, struck down before the beginning of the war by Agamemnon, who boasted of being a better hunter than Artemis herself.[66] Since the first deer too is the surrogate or equivalent of Iphigenia, we can say that, in cutting down Artemis's deer, Agamemnon is already killing his daughter, alongside the intimacy between the goddess and her wild, feminine pet. The "original sin" that freezes the Greeks is thus an interruption of a certain kind of queer, interspecies love. The appearance of the later deer in the second finale of the play reads as a return of the repressed animal, of the inhuman constituting human corporeality, disavowed along with the inhuman *inside* our bodies.[67] Although the second deer frees the Greeks, liberating the air, she hearkens back to the originary misdeed.[68] Reading this deer as reparation for the one snatched away from

Artemis excludes the animal herself from the economy of relations delineated by the narrative, reducing her as before to a token in a human-divine transaction, to the dispossessed, depersonalized third element in a dyadic reconciliation. Creating the interpretive conditions for returning full grievability—the right to be mourned but also to release anger, *thumos*, projectively, posthumously[69]—to the killed deer entails pursuing what some would call a suspicious or paranoid reading of the second finale of the play. Such a reading can also allow us to heed the non-hierarchical intra-action of material being, to honor the imbrication of the (in)animate (human, animal, and elemental) beyond the facile prospect of a reconciliation. Despite our immunitarian fantasies, our deluded attempts to "defeat" the virus and to reinscribe conventional hierarchies of being, the current pandemic—the zoonotic or, better, anthropo-zoonotic outcome of animal exploitation[70]— continues to provide us with striking demonstrations of the interdependencies that make up the "fabric of natureculture."[71] In the words of one pandemic expert, "The coronavirus pandemic is a result of our gross maltreatment of animals. . . . In the future, we should fully expect our maltreatment of animals to wreak havoc on our own species."[72] Viral "havoc" seems to be prophesied at the end of the Messenger's account of the sacrifice (1601–3):

> . . . *hapan*
> *kat-ênthrakôthê thum' en Hêphaistou phlogi*
> *ta prosphor' êuxath', hôs tuchoi nostou stratos.*

Messenger [When] the whole *sacrifice* (*thuma*) had been fully burnt (*kat-ênthrakôthê*) in the fire of Hephaestus, [Calchas] made the appropriate prayer, so that the army could obtain *nostos*.

The verb *kat-ênthrakôthê* ("had been fully burnt") announces the destructive survival of the killed animal as smoke, conventionally presented as the aromatic delight of humans and gods, but, from a different perspective, a dispersal of toxins, lingering in the space of interspecies co-dependencies, of intermingling elementalities and animalities that we name the environment (the verb *kat-ênthrakôthê* derives from *anthrax*, the Greek word for "coal," which, of course, has the additional semantic baggage in English of a frightening bacterial disease). Tasked with cleansing or mobilizing the paralyzed atmosphere, the sacrifice is an act of autophagy, burdening the air with residues, which, through the very act of breathing, of inhaling, become an ingested form of atmospheric flesh or meat.[73]

As Mel Chen has eloquently written, commenting on another atmospheric catastrophe of our times—the Northern California sky reddened, wounded, infested by wildfires, by air that was "something like meat":[74]

> Meat and air meet in all the other ways that animal substances travel into the air, or in the ways that air recirculates into settled substance to be absorbed, managed, and sometimes kept by the human and nonhuman animal bodies that breathe or otherwise receive, that are porous to the world around them, which is everyone and everything.[75]

When the Messenger uses the word *nostos* to refer to the impending journey to Troy, the mind inevitably moves ahead in time in the storyworld (or backward intertextually) to the disastrous return of the Greeks—served up to voracious waters by stormy air.[76] In this perspective, *thuma*, the word for "sacrifice," signposts the arousal and dispersion of the enraged, aggrieved breath of the killed animal, a kind of pandemic efflux, or "saturation," informed by the double valence of "smoke" and "anger" of the cognate word *thumos*, as we saw in *Oedipus the King*.[77] Such efflux expresses the deer's right to grievability, liberating the air for the moment, but potentially immobilizing colonial thanatopolitics through its heavy persistence, an impersonal and all-too-personal protest, a multi-species, oversaturated density, precisely the atmospherics of the stormy *nostos*.[78]

As we, living in the never-arriving aftermath of the pandemic, finish re-reading Euripides' second Iphigenia play, we are left with the unsettling image of the agony of the animal, not the inflicter but rather the primary victim of the anthropo-zoonotic disaster (1587–89):

> *elaphos gar aspairous' ekeit' epi chthoni*
> *idein megistê diaprepês te tên thean*
> *hês haimati bômos erainet' ardên tês theou*

> *Messenger* Gasping, *the deer* (*elaphos*) lay on the ground, *greatest* (*megistê*) to see and a beautiful *sight* (*théan*), whose blood spattered the altar of the goddess.

The initial metrical resolution that forces the voice to linger on the deer (*elaphos*), the very first word, mimetically prolongs her gasps, contagiously confounding our body with hers. Iphigenia's absorption into the masculinist militarism of the heroic sacrifice is reflected yet undone in the grammatical transgenderism of the deer,[79] which underscores the "gender trouble" caused by her very presence. (Her arrival with Clytemnestra—each played by a male actor—cracks the male homosocial order.) More to the point, the grammatical transgenderism, as the intimation of an ontological *ex-cess* (that is, a "self-exit" from fixed boundaries of being, from hierarchical gendered positions of subject and object), is also visible in the punning confusion caused by a shift of breath between *théan*, the "sight" that belongs to humans, gods, and animals, and *theá*, "goddess": there is an instability between subject and object such that the goddess, the presumed subject, is gazed at, while the animal becomes the sovereign goddess as an object of aesthetic reverence.[80] What, in this passage, remains fixed—on the ground—is not just the deer, but, prospectively, Greece itself, which is destined for the catastrophe of its leaders' thwarted return.[81] The phrase *ela-phos . . . megistê* recalls *Hellas . . . megistê* ("Greece, the greatest" 1378), which Iphigenia deploys in her farewell speech. *Ela-phos* fragments and hybridizes the nation, contagiously, virally mixing human bodies—sublimated in the abstract fetish of the citizen body[82]—with the corpse of the animal, pointing, like the Iphigenia-like hare devoured in the parodos of Aeschylus's *Agamemnon*, to humananimal, (in)animate vulnerabilities.[83] While an animal's death for the sake of a state anxious to get unstuck is sadistically celebrated, a broken breath connects the corpse of Greece with its sacrificial object, no mere hero or victim but an aggrieved and grievable life, perversely prolific and virally rebellious.

Part Two

Communities

4

Alcestis

Texas lieutenant governor Dan Patrick, as we saw in the last chapter, declared, at the beginning of the pandemic, that the economy must keep moving, even if some lives had to be immolated on the altar of the capitalist state.[1] In a Fox News interview, Patrick volunteered the elderly for his sacrificial plan, disingenuously including himself:

> You know . . . no one reached out to me and said, "As a senior citizen, are you willing to take a chance on your survival in exchange for keeping the America that all America loves for your children and grandchildren?" And if that's the exchange, I'm all in. That doesn't make me noble or brave or anything like that. I just think there are lots of grandparents out there in this country like me.[2]

Patrick's vision of "eldercide"[3] brings to mind Admetus's outraged (and outrageous) rebuke of his father for declining to die in his stead, in Euripides' *Alcestis* (642–50)—a play that apparently celebrates a wife's self-sacrifice for her husband (though it is undone, in the end, by a fairy-tale return from the Underworld):

> *Admetus* You certainly stand out among everyone for your *lack of courage* (*a-psuchiai*), since being this old and having come to the end of your life, you did not want—nor did you have the courage—to die for your son. . . . You could have participated in a beautiful contest if you had died for your son; in any case, the time that remains for you to live is short.

Although a few critics have surprisingly found merit in Admetus's argument,[4] ironic self-undermining looms large in this speech, where the word *a-psuchia* ("cowardice," but also "soullessness" or "lifelessness") boomerangs back at the accuser while assimilating his survival at the price of Alcestis's life to death or a heightened kind of lifedeath. While Admetus's self-preservation, his desire for life, bespeaks a biopolitical apportionment of death that is shared by Patrick and Agamemnon, re-reading *Alcestis* in our pandemic times uncovers another familiar dynamic—an oscillation of toxicity between the literal and the metaphoric.[5] In "'Toxins in the Atmosphere': Reanimating the Feminist *Poison*," Jess Issacharoff observes that the death of one of the female protagonists in Todd Haynes's 1991 film "is neither purely symbolic of the gay male experience of AIDS nor individualized, but rather representative of the death of a victim" of the "toxic domesticity" of suburban heterosexual life.[6] In Euripides' play, though Alcestis is escorted to the Underworld by Death (Thanatos), her passing is also dramatized as the outcome of a mysterious disease, whose provenance may have something to do with the upright posture that her husband insists on even as she is about to fall to the ground—a posture epitomizing the controlling pedestal of the conjugal bond.[7] This disease is an embodiment of "toxic domesticity," as I argue in this chapter, an encapsulation of "the tragedy of heterosexuality," to borrow the title of Jane Ward's 2020 book.[8] In an interview, Ward provocatively observes, "In some ways, the pandemic is revealing the tragedy of heterosexuality to people who might not have otherwise paid attention to it. It really looks like straight men and women don't like each other very much.... From an LGBT perspective, [being straight] looks actually very tragic."[9] Though, unsurprisingly, "the response by lawmakers to the pandemic employ[s] a homonormative economic frame to justify policy proposals,"[10] *Alcestis* alerts us to the ways that romantic fairy tales reinscribe never fully de-naturalized, right-killing hierarchies, especially in times of chronically extended crisis.[11]

In this chapter, I wish to read *Alcestis* as a drama of heterosexist toxicity by placing it alongside Robert Browning's translation/adaptation of Euripides' play in his 1871 poem *Balaustion's Adventure*. As Dolores O'Higgins observes, "Alcestis . . . is not exempt from the petrifying effects of marriage, the process of transformation of living flesh to inanimate substitute, of natural creature to cultural possession. Her *actual* death corresponds to the metaphorical de-vitalization undergone by all women in marriage."[12] Re-reading the play during and through our experience of the pandemic allows us to view it not just as a dramatization of the violent "traffic in women"[13] and of masculine callousness in antiquity and modernity (or in the Victorians' modern antiquity), but emblematic of the "tragedy of heterosexuality" in Ward's sense. The complex of relationships underlying Browning's poem—a triangle with indeterminate erotic and affective contours (heterosexual, homosexual, pan- or a-sexual)— can help us locate the tragedy of heterosexuality in the Euripidean dramaturgy, to interpret Alcestis's vaguely drawn disease as the outcome of an overdetermined toxicity, literal and metaphorical, and to observe how dramatic form opens up suggestions of alternatives to the couple form.[14]

Commissioned by Katrine Cecilia Countess Cowper, *Balaustion's Adventure* generates—and is generated by—a triangle, involving another potential Alcestis, Elizabeth Barrett Browning, besides the Countess, whose identification with the Euripidean heroine, which we see in one of her letters,[15] is doubled by the internal narrator, the deliverer of the translation, the titular Balaustion, a young Rhodian woman onomastically evoking a "wild pomegranate flower." In this triangle, Alcestis potentially slips from an object of identification into an object of erotic cathexis. But the plot thickens, for, as we read in the poem itself and as Lady Cowper dismissively indicates in a letter,[16] an additional source of inspiration for Browning is a strikingly queer painting by Frederick Leighton, *Hercules Wrestling with Death for the Body of Alcestis* (Figure 1). Browning and

Figure 1 *Strikingly queer: Frederick Leighton,* Hercules Wrestling with Death for the Body of Alcestis *(c. 1869–71). Wadsworth Atheneum, Hartford, CT.*

Leighton, whose homosexuality was an open secret, had first met in 1853, and, as Catherine Maxwell observes, "were on terms of some intimacy by 1859";[17] then, in that year, Browning wrote a poem as an epigraph of Leighton's painting for the Royal Academy Exhibition—a painting (Figure 2) that showcases an Orpheus whose averted gaze patently rejects Eurydice's persistent pursuit verbalized, in Browning's poem, as "But give them me, the mouth, the eyes, the

Figure 2 *Forbidden* jouissance: *Frederick Leighton,* Orpheus and Eurydice *(1864). Leighton House Museum, London.*

brow!"[18] Orpheus's denial of his face reads as a rejection of the "tragedy of heterosexuality," which is obviously influenced by the tradition of his tragically turning his erotic gaze from the female to the male after the loss of Eurydice.[19]

The starting point for my analysis, which interweaves Euripides' play with Browning's translation and Leighton's paintings, is Admetus's homoeroticism, which I track by way of his attachments to Apollo and Heracles, a marginal, un-tragic figure in the play, whose aggressive, sexual energy, in Leighton's depiction, queerly attracts panoptic and pangender attention. Thanatos in the painting resembles the Grim Reaper, who figures deadly contagion in otherizing, marginalizing representations of the AIDS crisis as a lethal threat to the heterosexual family.[20] Juxtaposed with the main scene of Alcestis's death and funeral, the hero's bare-buttocked, quasi-pornographic match with Death contagiously triggers a series of contortions; positioned in the margins, the scene aligns itself with the paratextual space of the Euripidean prologue, the quintessential locus of dramaturgical "besideness," in which Apollo, who has already negotiated with the Fates an exchange that will allow his protégé Admetus to escape death, ends up wrangling with Thanatos, scolding him for not sparing Alcestis.[21] In using the word "protégé," I wish to stress the queer opacity of the bond between Apollo and Admetus—who is, for the god, not just a *xenos* and a *philos*, but also a master, a friend, and an object of erotic cathexis, as Callimachus explicitly reveals.[22] When, in his exchange with Thanatos, Apollo curtly says, referring to Alcestis, "Go take her (*labôn ithi* 48)" (in Browning's translation), Eve Sedgwick's triangle makes a ghostly epiphany,[23] for, though Admetus appears to be concerned for Alcestis, preparing her and himself for her "beautiful death," even clinging to her, Apollo seems inclined to hasten her disappearance and enable the return of the homoerotic dyad that his grappling with Death intimates while also previewing the sexualized Heraclean match captured by Leighton. And while Heracles is, for Admetus, a substitute for Apollo and Alcestis as well, Apollo, as he confesses in the prologue, had to "serve" Admetus to atone for having killed the Cyclopes, the makers and perhaps maintainers of Zeus's thunderbolt, an attempt, we might say, to castrate the father of the gods (1–9).[24] This divine servitude (or service) replicates Heracles' labors, which here include rescuing Alcestis from the Underworld. In the letter to Lady Cowper that opens *Balaustion's Adventure*,

Browning reveals that the composition of the poem was similarly "imposed" by her on him "as a task," casting himself as Apollo and Heracles, who was requisitioned to perform services for Eurystheus and Queen Omphale (heroic and otherwise).[25] As Alcestis, Cowper is replacing Admetus with Heracles, but she is also Admetus, upper-crust, self-absorbed, devoted to the joys of poetry and music, and employing the services of Apollo/Heracles. That Heracles' Apollinean labor may be construed as "wifely" is suggested by his arrival, in Euripides' play, just after Alcestis's exit—a sequence that smacks of substitution[26]—but also by the marked transferral of the ethical and aesthetic primacy of Alcestis, obsessively and somewhat condescendingly depicted as the "best" wife (*aristê*), to Heracles (*aristou . . . xenou* "[of] the best guest" 559). When Admetus asks one of his servants to accompany Heracles to the guests' quarters (*xenônas*)—a space homologous to the gynaeceum just vacated by Alcestis, which the widowed master wants to be locked properly, ostensibly to protect Heracles and his partying fellows from being disturbed by the lamentations for Alcestis—we are primed to read this wing of the house as a "closet" (546–50):

> *Admetus* Lead this guest to the *out-of-sight* (*ex-ôpious*) *guest quarters* (*xenônas*) of the house, opening them, and tell the guardians to provide an abundance of food; but *lock* (*klêisate*) the doors inside, for it is not *proper* (*prepei*) for people who are carousing to hear *laments* (*stenagmôn*) nor for guests *to feel pain* (*lupeisthai*).

Unheimlich (at once "familiar" and "unfamiliar"), the hidden quarters where Heraclean rowdiness is consummated archive, store away, the loss that is queerness, the otherized *jouissance* of the Real ostensibly excluded from the heterosexual consensus figured by the very structure of the house where both Admetus and Alcestis are trapped, forbidden from accessing "the most inward safe . . . the outcast . . . the outside."[27] The inaccessible closet, exceptionally occupied by Heracles, becomes a pocket, circumscribed and limited, of both visibility and opacity, which ruptures the noxiously homogenizing unity of the house. While, in Admetus's command, the word *stenagmôn* ("laments") can be interpreted as a metonym of tragedy, which itself contains the comic or satyric crypt embodied by Heracles' Rabelaisian, voracious and pansexual, corporeality,[28] it also designates the somber, monotonous hum of "the tragedy of heterosexuality," that is, the heterosexuality that underpins this tragedy, at once the destination of its restorative, romantic movement and precisely what makes it tragic (by fully reintroducing that which is painful and distressing). Just before Alcestis's arrival onstage, the Chorus proclaims, in Browning's translation, "Never will we affirm there's more of joy than grief in marriage" (*oupote phêsô gamon euphrainein / pleon ê lupein* 238–39), foreshadowing the diction of Admetus's command, which seems to establish hierarchies of pleasure and pain, to lay down a distribution of the sensible.[29] In Heracles' criticism of the dejected and gloomy faces he observes in his host's house we can proleptically perceive the boredom, the sadness, the misery that, as documented by Ward, is widely attributed to heterosexual life by both queer and non-queer people;[30] the fastidiously sigmatic solemnity emanating from his description of the mourners' downcast, perturbed, grimacing masked faces (773, 797, 800)[31] is reminiscent of Judith Butler's notion of "heterosexual melancholy," which Ward calls "straight people's displaced and unmournable grief," "too heavy an emotional burden to bear."[32] Heracles' guestroom is the fantasized "safe,"[33] a space of immunity from domestic toxicity, from the "tragedy of heterosexuality," that tantalizes Alcestis and Admetus with the possibility of reconfiguring the conjugal bond: not through the non-relationality imposed by a pandemic, but, as we will see, through a stretching of the couple form into an intensified yet unbound intimacy between sexual and asexual.

Not only Admetus's decadent aestheticism, but also his expressed kinship with Orpheus reveals that the tragicomedy generically engineered in this play aligns with the collapse of tragic heterosexuality.[34] In a famous speech (343–62), Admetus vows that, after Alcestis's death, parties, sympotic gatherings, wreaths, and the barbiton, a lyre that as such is an Apollinean prop, will be banned from the house, for, as he says to his wife, "You took away all the joy of life" (*su gar mou terpsin ex-eilou biou* 347), a line in which the past tense ("you took away" *ex-eilou*) is ambiguous: is Admetus simply talking about Alcestis's life-saving death, which has not occurred yet, but which he perceives as already past? Or is he also looking back at their marriage? The promised elimination of all manner of queer pleasure can equally be retrojected to their time as a married couple. In the lines that follow (348–54), Admetus appears, in the manner of a Victorian aesthete, to savor the delight of fetishistic attachment, of an intense if "cold" (*psuchran* 353) embrace of a statue that is also the materialization of an absent deity (who else if not Apollo?) and of the Lacanian phallus—"*even though I have not,* I shall seem to *have*" (*ouk echôn echein* 352).[35] Rather than a monument to heterosexuality, the statue seems precisely the instrument of anarchivic excess, the prosthesis that, even before being built, supplements yet unsettles the normative conjugality it is meant to preserve or immortalize. A few lines later (357–62), when Admetus bursts into an adynaton, "I wish I had (*par-ên*) the *tongue* (*glôssa*) and song (*melos*) of Orpheus" (357), with the apparent intention to bring Alcestis, Eurydice's dead ringer, back to life,[36] the evocation of the mythical singer—in a sexualized confusion between "being" and "having," identification and cathected possession[37]—uncannily conjures, once again, an Apollo-like figure. Yet it also points to an anti-relational, self-absorbed engrossment in the world of *melos* ("song," but also "limb"), a departure from domesticity's space of overdetermined loss, toward a radical fantasy of otherworldliness (of inhabiting or possessing a different body). The Orpheus narcissistically invoked by Admetus is the same one whom, in Leighton's painting, we see rebuffing Eurydice, preferring the light-wood frame of the lyre—a solid fount of atmospheric pleasure, of contagious melody—to her pale arms, withdrawing into an obscure space of pained ecstasy, of forbidden *jouissance* shielded from the constraining embrace of heterosexuality. (Leighton's Orpheus is the androgynous singer who, even in his encounter with Eurydice, displays the discomfort with heterosexuality that will ultimately cause his sparagmatic death at the hands of the Thracian women.)[38]

Alcestis displays her own chronic discomfort with heterosexuality, which is figured by—and, in a sense, provokes—her death. All that we hear throughout the play is that she is the best wife: *aristê aristê aristê* is the monotonous refrain that puts her on a pedestal even before she becomes a statue,[39] immobilizing her, desexualizing her, numbing her, assimilating her to a fantasized idea of male equanimity,[40] as we infer from the masculine-appearing adjectives *a-klautos a-stenaktos* ("without a tear, without a groan"), which apparently celebrate her courage in facing death and preventing, as we are told, the disease from altering her appearance (173–74). The *aristê* refrain functions not just as a description but as a heterosexist interpellation, a *command* to be the best, whose iterations in the text preempt any sense of exhaustion that might result from always standing, remaining upright or "straight"—a point embedded in the superlative itself through the ending *-istê*, which corresponds to the imperative *histê* ("Straighten!"). The injunction to Alcestis also becomes fetishistically and projectively self-referential, with an implicit assimilation of the wife to the husband's penis, the appendix that heterosexist reproduction always wants to remain erect.[41] *Ar-istê* thus encodes the labor of rectitude, not only moral but also postural, with which conventional heterosexuality aligns itself, disavowing its own inclination ("leaning over"), its bodily dispossession, its constitutive reliance on the possibility of losing balance,[42] thereby legitimizing, "naturalizing" its own boredom and fatigue, which it affectively spreads into the (social) atmosphere.[43] In the female servant's account of Alcestis's last moments, we notice a vague reference to Alcestis's "disease" (*nosos*), which I read as the infirmity of heterosexual assimilation (201–4):[44]

> *Female Servant* He cries holding his dear wife *in his arms* (*en cheroin*), and *begs* (*lissetai*) her not to *leave* (*pro-dounai*) him, seeking the impossible; for she is perishing and *is being consumed* (*marainetai*) *by the disease* (*nosôi*), *exhausted* (*par-eimenê*), *a wretched burden of the arm* (*cheiros athlion baros*).

As though issuing the interpellation encoded in *ar-istê*, asphyxiating her with the arms that ostensibly hold her, Admetus persistently exhorts her not to collapse, not to fall, to stay up (up-right, up-beat, etc.), as we see in the ensuing lyric dialogue between Admetus and Alcestis—a dramatization of what the female servant had previously described—in which he commands her to "raise herself up,"[45] to maintain a statue-like, Apollonian, self-annihilating composure, and thus to keep dying while living. The condition that is debilitating Alcestis, slowly eroding her physical stability, is precisely the injunction not to fall, to always be *ar-istê*, to force herself to remain "straight." Her experience of heterosexuality is a self-condemnation to the weariness of persistent disavowal—a chronic fatigue (something like what has been called "long Covid"), which is dissensually visualized by Alcestis's reduction to a depersonalized corporeal mass attracted downward, a heaviness (*baros*) encumbering her as much as her husband's arm.[46] Previously, as relayed by the female servant, she had fallen on her bed, engendering a quasi-collapse of word-boundaries in the line, encumbered by the flood of tears she was shedding—"the whole bed / *she drenches with an eye-wetting flood* (*ophthalmo-tenktôi deuetai plêmmuridi* 184)." "Slumping forward" (*pronôpês* 186),[47] we are told, "she threw herself again onto the bed once more" (*karrips**en hautên** **auth**is es koitên palin* 188), succumbing to exhaustion—all in a line in which the annihilation of the female subject in the repetition of heterosexual habituation, as suggested by the proximity and resonance between *hautên* ("herself") and *authis* ("again"), is broken, however, by the hiccup of the contiguously recurrent syllables *en au, ên au,* which configure the possibility of an alternative word division beyond signification. The weariness inflicted by chronic heterosexuality, occluded by the self-serving imputation of exemplary womanhood, can be lethal, according to the female servant, who, in fact, wonders, "How could a woman demonstrate her respect for her husband more than by wanting to die for him?" (154–55). If we deconstructively press this rhetorical question, we are drawn to the conclusion that the only way that the wife's willingness to die for her husband—that is, the best possible enactment of heterosexual commitment—can realize itself is by way of death. Through a viral axiology, a toxic "best-ness," an enervating rectilinearity (both vertical and horizontal), there is a flattening out under the pressure of the heteronormative atmosphere. Heterosexuality is tragic here because its entelechy resides precisely in its rupture, in the dissolution of the bond itself. When Alcestis laments Death's delay ("Why are you tarrying? Hurry!" 255–56), she is keenly acting out her prescribed role, sacrificing herself with a "straight" face,[48] that is, showing no hesitation about dying for her husband while continuing to speak, remaining upright. At the same time, she is hastening her exit from the conjugal bond.

An unpredictable possibility of exit from the conjugal bond can emerge, paradoxically, from the apparent restoration of such a bond in the finale. The Euripidean ending presents us with a trio of characters—Admetus, Heracles, and Alcestis, who, however, appears this time not as one of the three speaking actors, but as a mute extra, placed by Heracles in Admetus's hands, precariously restored to the conjugal realm, the world of patriarchal possession. Feminist readings have rightly underscored the homosocial instrumentalization of Alcestis, demoted to a prosthesis, a silent bodily part regained, or a domestic accessory returned to its owner.[49] As Victoria Wohl notes:

> The "new" relationship with Heracles will define Admetus as a subject through a homosocial mirroring.... It is through this relationship that Admetus emerges from the shadow of his lost object, breaks free of the maternal cathexis, and lays claim to his prerogatives as a subject, a man, and a king.... The relationship between Admetus and Heracles is Oedipal as well as mirroring, restoring in new form the patrilineal bond that is broken in the *agôn* between Admetus and Pheres.... Oedipal antagonism is transformed into a shared authority (and a sharing of the maternal body).[50]

This reading is predicated on a relational geometry that, duly emphasizing the sexist hierarchy of the encounter, pits a pair of male friends (Admetus and Heracles) against an objectified female singularity (Alcestis). If we assume, as most critics do, that, within the horizon of the three-actor rule, Heracles is played in this scene by the actor who previously played Alcestis,[51] this geometry becomes more complicated, as Alcestis is reduplicated as a revenant of her former performative self through Heracles and as an extra—an apparent stranger explicitly assimilated by Admetus to a ghost (*phasma* 1127), while evoking, for some readers, his previously fantasized statue.[52] Among the multiple ironies activated by this scene, which has been viewed as a pseudo-wedding scene, we can include the fact that Admetus remarries (a new) Alcestis and marries Heracles as a specter of (the old) Alcestis.[53] After Admetus's *echô s'aelptôs* ("I have you unexpectedly" 1134), Heracles' formulaic response *echeis* ("you have" 1135) presupposes "her" but also "me" as an object ("you have *me*"), for in similar scenes it is pronounced by lovers who find each other again.[54] In other words, the expected "me" is replaced, imaginatively, not just by "her," but, in a sense, also by "me as her" so that the marriage celebrated here is between Admetus, on the one hand, and Alcestis and Heracles/Alcestis, on the other. In uttering the customary *echeis* ("you have [me]"), Heracles is hauntologically speaking as Alcestis, complicating the dyadic structure of the re-enacted marriage ceremony. We could say that Alcestis is afforded a presence beyond language that disrupts the heterosexual Symbolic with a non-verbal

Real, just like the reanimated lion's face that peeks out, eluding the instrumentalizing grip of Heracles, but also the oppressive constraint of the erotic or hostile bond between Heracles and Death in Leighton's painting. The geometry of this artwork encompasses a triptych of couples—unified by the dead Alcestis in the center—of which the two on the left look toward the third one, Heracles and Death. In each of these couples (female-female, male-female, male-male), one member hides their face, physically twisting the couple form by turning away—in a sense, by becoming the Euripidean Alcestis, veiled (double-masked, as it were) and mute, but also Admetus, who, in the play, is urged by Heracles to stretch out his hand to take back his wife, and does so while turning away, like Perseus, as though his wife might petrify him, like a leonine Gorgon (1117–18):[55]

> *Heracles* Have the courage to stretch your hand and touch the foreign woman.
> *Admetus* Here I stretch my hand, as though I were killing the Gorgon.

The gestural implication of the Perseus reference—which acts as both "a desexing and a decapitation of the mother" and an instrument for "killing off the woman, only to revive her . . . silenced . . . at the heart of the new order"[56]—conjures, again, the assimilation of Admetus to the queer Orpheus, with his heterophobic averted glance, if we compare two images of Perseus and Medusa, one ancient and one modern (Figures 3 and 4), and, in turn, juxtapose the modern one with Leighton's painting of Orpheus.[57] In the Leighton Alcestis, as well as in Euripides' play, where Alcestis vocally haunts Heracles' cisgender identity, she is the third party curtailing dyadic immobilization, the hierarchy of subject and object that, to an extent, is enforced by the couple, whether heterosexual or homosexual. An equivalent of the mask—the Other affixed onto the notional self of the face, like the facial prosthesis of our pandemic lives, which depersonalizes or anonymizes us—the Gorgon that Alcestis becomes is the anomic beyondness deforming the couple, defacing it, or twisting it into a grimace in a moment of self-reflection.[58] Alcestis is a line of flight, reclaiming attention from the homoerotic encounter of Heracles and Death that engrosses all viewers, inside and outside the painting, initially distracting them from her death. In Euripides' play, the exclusionary dyad of

Figure 3 *Killing the Gorgon: Red-figured hydria, Perseus fleeing after cutting off Medusa's head* (c. 460 BCE). *British Museum, London.*

Figure 4 *Averted gaze: Francesco Maffei,* Perseo e Medusa *(c. 1650). Gallerie dell'Accademia, Venice.*

the homosocial alliance or the homoerotic bond between Heracles and Admetus cannot cancel out the triangular form of the scene, its tripartite visuality, which, as we have seen, unsettles pronominal objects and the conventional dichotomy of possessor and possessed posited by *echô* ("I have").[59]

"The tragedy of heterosexuality" contested by the Euripidean throuple and the Victorian triangularities we have observed, may be, after all, a question not (or not only) of gender preferences and identifications, but of a stifling enforcement of self-possession in striving to possess a singular other—not unlike our erotic aspiration to bind the virus (to our needs, desires, and decisions) even as we bind ourselves. Looking forward means looking straight ahead; the backward gaze of Admetus (and Orpheus) allows the emergence of disorienting possibilities.[60] Rather than a repetition that brings about a new beginning,[61] this backwardness, which symbolically assimilates Admetus's exit from dialogic contact with Heracles to Alcestis's silence, the possessor to the possessed, is the beginning of a dynamic resembling "recursion." As theorized by Tavia Nyong'o, recursion is a troubling of the visual field that "splits the subject, not only by denying it the fantasy of a stable vantage point and perspective, but further by extending the promise that there is a way out of its maze, provided only that one invests in its logic long enough to perpetuate its effects."[62] Soon after, Admetus seems to be reintegrated into the scene, following Heracles' script in spite of his disorientation, persevering in the unsettling dimension of looking both backward at his lost wife and forward toward the remarriage. But the outcome is an unexpected "way out," not remarriage as such but novel arrangements beyond the dyad that await, and still disorient, the gazer. Even though the pandemic has been an aggravator of the "tragedy of heterosexuality," its distinctive temporal regime—a backward glance indistinguishable from facile hope of an aftermath—can help us imagine disidentificatory relational modes even within an oppressive social atmosphere. Writing "at this Covid-19 pandemic moment" while also looking at HIV/AIDS, Marlon Bailey speaks of "continu[ing] to explore what kinds of experiences of pleasure are possible now, and what are the sources of these pleasures," asking, "What kind of relationships can I forge and nurture?" For Bailey, "the most erotic and emotionally pleasurable experiences ... do not happen ... in the sexual realm"; rather, as he puts it, "the pleasure I experience is emotionally erotic and sensual—it is deep intimacy."[63] The backwardness in the finale of *Alcestis*, which contributes to confirming yet shaking "the tragedy of heterosexuality" through "recursion," need not be seen as merely a melancholic gesture. Rather, it could point us toward a Heraclean desirous profuseness, both tragic and anti-tragic, even in times of isolation, a keen, self-dissolving openness to unbound bonds—not excluding serendipitous interventions of disruptive third or fourth parties (anonymous in a mask or veil)[64]—and to the intrinsic queerness of indeterminate intimate relationalities, in all their gradations, expansions, and compressions: sexual; non-sexual; sexual *and* non-sexual; dispossessively dyadic or non-dyadic; sexual *and* erotic; asexual yet erotic(ized).

5

The Suppliant Women

In "Feminists Theorize Covid-19," a special issue of the journal *Signs*, Miriam Ticktin observes that Covid "has generated the need for new relationships with friends, comrades, neighbors, coparents, lovers and ex-lovers." While attempting to cope with prohibitions or limitations of sociality and various regimes of mask-wearing, we have sought to maintain or reproduce relations as we have always known them while also, willingly or not, altering the texture of togetherness in its many inflections.[1] In particular, Ticktin has argued that "Covid-19 has enhanced experiments in . . . a burgeoning feminist commons"— germane to what Stefano Harney and Fred Moten call "the undercommons"[2]—"a struggle," as she puts it, "against enclosures, against the privatization of spaces of freedom, against exclusion" for the sake of "social relations built on reciprocity, respect, mutuality, and responsibility."[3]

In this chapter, I re-read Euripides' *Suppliant Women* as an experiment in maternal activism[4] by taking as a starting point the obvious resonance of the devaluation or desecration of the corpse in pandemic times with the play's thematic premise—the forced separation of the Argive mothers from the unburied bodies of their warrior sons. Shocked by the images of the Bucha massacre and of mass graves in Ukraine, we remain unable to shed the recollection of the time in 2020 when the rites of mourning were no longer a given. In Italy, funerals in church were banned and funeral homes were shut down.[5] Undertakers replaced kin as the only ones granted proximity to the dead, attending to the care of corpses through the mediating agents of masks, gloves, visors, and hazmat suits. The very rituality of mourning was altered: touching supplanted by the vicarious hapticities of voice and digital sight;

consoling embraces by solemn bowing. Lamenting, contemplating, staring were all from a distance. In "The Return of Antigone: Burial Rites in Pandemic Times," Néstor Braunstein describes the emergency of burials and funerals in Latin America—a crisis reminiscent of the loss of funerary *kosmos* lamented by Thucydides in his account of the Athenian plague:[6]

> Due to the pandemic and fear of infection, the time allowed for a deceased body to be present before it reaches its destination has accelerated: it must be disposed of quickly and as soon as possible.... There are not enough coffins and the dead are often buried in cardboard boxes or plastic bags, such as those thrown into the garbage bins found in the corners of larger cities.... The coffins must be closed. The contact with the diseased's body or clothing is prohibited, as are thanatoesthetics and lustral washes, the cleansing of the dead.[7]

In re-reading *Suppliant Women*, I am concerned with the rearticulation of affective and social bonds and the stretching of proxemic configurations arising from forbidden mourning, from the play's aesthetic and dramaturgical attachments to the corpse, whether absent or present onstage. In this play, the Argive mothers, deprived of the bodies of their sons, stripped of the right to mourn them, arrive in Athens as guests and suppliants, asking Theseus for an intervention, using Adrastus, the old king of Argos, and Aethra, Theseus's old mother, as intermediaries. Their maternal activism effects a "funeralization of the city," to borrow the term that Elva Orozco Mendoza coined in reference to protests of mothers in Chihuahua and Ciudad Juárez against femicide and "the state's role in the production of disposable life through a combination of neglect, criminalization, and abandonment."[8] When Theseus spots the Argive women occupying the site of Demeter and Persephone's temple with their supplicatory paraphernalia, he objects to their shorn hair and gloomy robes (97),[9] materializations of loss, displays of death *in* or *as* life, which, like the "memorial objects that bear witness to repeated episodes of sexual violence, enforced disappearance, and murder of women in northern Mexico," confront the nation state with its complicitous neutrality or inaction, with its neglect of the corpse, with the institutionalization of the principle that, after individual deaths, life must (quickly) go on.[10] As funeralizations of cities aim to demonstrate, the state is responsible for the desecration, mutilation, or neglect of the corpse that Banu Bargu has identified with necropolitical violence as such[11]—"not the reduction of the living to 'the status of *living dead*,' but . . . the dishonoring, disciplining, and punishment of the living through the utilization of the dead as postmortem objects and sites of violence." In *Suppliant Women*, the imputation of inertia to the corpse by necropolitical power is thrown back at the state itself while the affective intensities and embodied bonds generated by the mothers' funeralization of the city intimate queer configurations of feminist commons through the interwoven aroundness, the contagious necroresistance, of their hands.[12]

At the beginning of *Suppliant Women*, the funeralization of Athens saturates ground and air, as well as the senses, making uncannily concrete the epidemiological imagery of affect.[13] "The servants' hands resound" (*achousi prospolôn cheres* 72), sings the Chorus of suppliant Argive mothers; in the atmosphere of the play, characters breathe air accreted with the acrid sound of pain[14] raised by grieving and aggrieved bodies. This distributed pain emerges as the product of the "labor" (*ponos*) of mourning—an unceasing or "insatiable" (*a-plêstos* 79) doing or making (*polu-ponos* 80; *epi-ponon* 84), comparable to childbirth, governing, and war, as we will see. The "work of mourning," performed by a choreographic assembly line of grieving mothers in a factory of endemic pain, kinetically releases fumes into the environment.[15] This funeralization of the city shakes up the state, as we see when Theseus arrives onstage, lamenting the persistent "echo" of pain. His confession of fear manifests itself in a proliferation of *m* sounds birthed by *mêtêr* ("mother"), as though sung maternal grief permeating the air has leaked, emotionally reconfigured, into the flow of his speech, finding in his breath an additional channel of diffusion: "The fear shakes me *lest my mother, whom I look for on foot* (*mê moi ti mêtêr hên metasteichô*), who has been away from home for a long time, have some novel trouble" (89–91). The maternal sound of Theseus's fear anticipates the Chorus's self-referential address, "Wretched women, mothers of wretched generals" (*ô meleai meleôn materes lochagôn* 598), in which the triple continuity of *m* words is enhanced by the punning overlap between the feminine singular *meléa* ("wretched") and the neuter plural *mélea* ("limbs")—the unburied remnants to which the generals have been reduced, all that remains to materialize their mothers' emotional loss.[16] Even before hearing the mothers' demands and deciding how to respond, Theseus is affected by the sonic toxins that the unburied corpses continue to emanate through the mothers' mourning voices, through their "wretched" corporealities—although later, speaking to the Theban herald, he denies the corpses agency, casting them as inert ("Are you afraid of the corpses . . .? What may happen? That, after they have been buried they may destroy your land? Or that they may give birth to children in the recesses of the earth?" 543–46). The funeralization of the city entails a political contagion, which causes Theseus to sound like the mothers, whose mourning, whose inhabitation of their misery in song (*melos*), makes them vibrate with the intensities of the neglected corpses—a resonance that transcends kinship.

The political effect of the suppliant women's funeralization of the city—the delineation of a proto-feminist commons—is encapsulated in the introduction of a recumbent Adrastus, who, as Aethra puts it, carries "the *burden* (*phorton*) of my need in *common* (*koinon*) with these women" (20). The metaphorical burden points to the heap of ashes that will be brought to the stage later in the play, enacting the corpse's function—"a counterforce that defie[s] what states and other biopolitical forces tell it that it is"[17]—and its power to generate multiple bonds (in this case, between Adrastus and Aethra, between the Argive mothers and Adrastus, and between Aethra and the mothers). The heap of ashes is the bond or a *koinon*, solidarity or a political alliance conceived here as an affective connection with grievable (in)animate matter.[18] Not just Adrastus, as we will see, but the members of the Chorus identify with—or even replicate— the missing corpses, in ways that go beyond their lying on the ground, their occupation of the soil. The ambiguity between *melea* ("wretched") and *melea* ("limbs"), in fact, links the Chorus as a performative *koinon* with the unbound whole formed collectively by the bodily remains, the "wandering, unburied bodies" (*sômat' alainont' a-tapha* 62). The restoration, albeit partial, of the right of grievability in the play opens up a space for imagining commons or undercommons beyond or beside the state, beyond or beside reproduction.[19] We may find a name for this commons when Aethra speaks of the supplicatory branches in her hand as an "unbound bond" (*desmon . . . a-desmon* 32).[20] If we consider that the play is a confrontation between the *polis* and a group of "childless," "gray-haired" (*polias* 35) mothers, we can discern the model of a supplementary, expansive, open, feminine (and feminist) *polity*: a *poli-as*, instead of a *polis*. Rather than replicating Athena's patriarchal submission— her epithet is the homophonic adjective *Polias* ("protectress of the city")—this *poli-as* enacts a pluralistic space of political lifedeath (un)grounded in the antifoundational foundation of grievability, in the radicality of the (in)animacy of the corpse. Such radicality goes along with the reinvention of maternity as the creative generation of unpredictable relational intensities, of unstructured yet tight solidarities, and, in particular, non-reproductive, "strange intimacies" (in the phrase of Jennifer Nash and Samantha Pinto) that deterritorialize or (m)otherize the nation state.[21] At the beginning of the play, when the supplicating mothers ask Aethra, the intermediary mother, to beg Theseus to place their children's bodies in their hands (*eman t' es chera theinai nekuôn . . . sômat'* 61–62; cf. 69), they visualize a double level of haptic interweaving—the transfer of corpses into the mothers' arms reproducing supplicatory enfoldings. Through the mimetic power of supplication and the consequent abjection of handling corpses, the state is dislodged from its privileged position of all-encompassing, abstract authority, pulled into the minoritarian realm of ordinary gesturality, of affectively charged yet mundane bodily transactions, of fleshy contagion. The state is confronted with its own permeability,[22] the failure of its immunitarian delusions: it becomes infected, implicated in life's constitutive "intertwinement."[23] Supplication is the literalization of bodily "implication" (etymologically meaning, "enfolding," "interweaving").[24] Rather than bringing the anti-political into the *polis*—what mourning may achieve, according to a line of interpretation[25]—this political infection reduces the gap between those in charge and, in Rancierean terms, those who have no part, imposing a shared ground of horizontal interaction, laying the foundation for a transition from the *polis* to the commons of the *polias*. (As Jean Baudrillard put it, "Revolution can only consist in the abolition of the separation from death").[26] When the Chorus entreats Athens to accept their request for help— "Defend a mother, city . . . of Pallas, so that you do not contaminate the laws of mortals" (*amune matri polis . . . Pallados / nomous brotôn mê miainein* 377–78)—the non-grammatical proximity between *matri* ("[to] a mother") and *polis* ("city") visualizes the possibility of contact in the thin interval between words, a contamination, or a felicitous *miasma*, that, in raising the specter of a compound like *matropolis*, dispossesses the city of its illusion of impermeability and insinuates maternal solidarity (*poli-as*) in patriarchal sovereignty (what the unmaternal Pallas, Athena Polias, stands for), substituting the equality of the commons for the mere concession or dispensation of rights.

As an accessory of the funeralization of the city, embodying the unmarked inertia of the corpse while contagiously spreading his onomastic "non-doing," Adrastus exposes the complacent inertia of the Athenian state, its reluctance to intervene even after it has apparently committed to doing so. Euripides' *Suppliant Women* is a play that, while apparently celebrating Athenian devotion to political and military labor (*ponos*)—a pervasive word in the text— aestheticizes the inefficacy of Adrastus, his being *a-drastos*.[27] The first time that Adrastus presses Theseus to take on the "labor" of rescuing the Argive bodies at Thebes (185 and 189), *ponos*, appearing twice at the end of a line,[28] draws attention to Adrastus's name, haunted by an alpha privative that casts him as constitutionally "ineffective, inert, lazy" (*a-drastêrios*).[29] However, Adrastus is not simply suffering from the exhaustion of old age (166), but enacting, through his own living body, the ontology of the corpse, the (in)animate presence, the inert agency that the state is seeking to erase. Theseus hastens to echo Adrastus's praise of his characteristically Athenian energy—"I labored (*eponês'*) in arguing with others" (195)—signaling an anxiety to measure up to the demands of the political Symbolic, to the Athenian rhetoric of hospitality and Pan-Hellenic "civilizing" benefaction. The lack contained in Adrastus's name comes out in the same scene, when, to flatter his would-be benefactor, he says that "many cities have been ruined *for want* (*en-deeis*) of a leader" (192), an ironic allusion on one level. Adrastus's onomastically reflected inactivity charges the play with a negative fixation that emerges every time an alpha privative is used, as when, in her own plea to Theseus to intervene on behalf of the Argives, Aethra remarks that it is "useless" (*a-chreion* 299) for women to give good advice, destined to go unheeded, and criticizes "indecisive" (*a-boulos* 321) governance. Through the alpha privatives of these adjectives, Aethra—a name evocative of *aithêr* ("air")—reaches beyond the hierarchy of subject and object, power and powerlessness, presupposed by conventional notions of host and guest, insinuating the threat of becoming useless, of being infected by the

ostensible inertia of womanhood, or of the corpse.[30] In the meantime, Adrastus
is lexicalized in a rhetorical strategy that is ironized when Aethra tells Theseus,
"Son ... *don't do these things* (*mê ... drasêis tade* 320)": in this prohibition the
deictic ("these things") signifies hesitation and delay that she codes as inertia
or "cowardice," failed masculinity, *an-andria* (314), a word also conjuring
A-drastus. But in urging her son *not* to do "these things," that is, not to act
like Adrastus, not to succumb to the stereotyped notion of womanhood,
Aethra in effect tells him to *be* A-drastus (a "not-doer"), and, through
Adrastus, to assimilate himself to the supplicating mothers—and, by extension,
the (in)animate corpse, which, like them, lies on the ground. The irony of
Theseus's fixation on doing things—reminiscent of the auto-immunitarian
"overdoing" of Pentheus[31]—is intensified by repetition and chiasmus in the
lines that formalize his commitment to the Argive cause (339–46):

> *Theseus Having done* (*drasas*) many noble things, I set this example for the
> Greeks.... Therefore it isn't possible to refuse *labors* (*ponous*). For what will
> my enemies say of me when the woman who gave birth to me and *is afraid
> on my behalf* (*huper-orrhôdous'*) is the first one to command me to take on
> this *labor* (*ponon*)? *I'll do* (*drasô*) this.

The freezing fear that Theseus projectively attributes to his mother—*huper-
orrhôdous'* (344)—is enacted in the formal immobility conveyed by the chiastic
repetition (*drasas ... ponous / ponon ... drasô*) but also in the rhetoric that
follows. While the Athenian army is sitting (*thassei* 391), about to spring into
action, Theseus declares, once again, that his city is eager to undertake this
"labor" (*ponon* 394). However, seeing the Theban emissary approach, he holds
back his herald, just in case this unexpected arrival might spare Athens the
"labor" (*ponos* 397) of intervening. A timely bit of news may bathetically
obviate the muscular doing touted in Theseus's lofty rhetoric, disclosing the
temptation of complicitous neutrality, of lingering in the intervals of political
zeal, of humanitarian (un)doing. When, as "gray-haired" Adrastus lies on the
ground in tears surrounded by the Argive mothers and a secondary Chorus of
children, Theseus asks him to uncover his face and speak (110–12), he acts as
the Law of the Father interpellating the child, removing him from his *in-fancy*
(in the etymological sense), objectifying him while pretending to confer

subjectivity upon him, turning him from a non-speaking object into a speaking one. However, when Adrastus apostrophizes the Theban herald with "You, most evil man!" (513), Theseus shuts him down ("Silence, Adrastus, quiet!" 513), denying him syntax, reducing his speaking role to a fragmented cry lost in Theseus's extended monologue, demoting him to the role of an extra—a quasi-corpse or, from the women's perspective, an instrument of the funeralization of the city, which Theseus may also turn into by contagion.

Interpellated by the maternal alliance, Theseus draws attention to another ambiguity surrounding *ponos* in the play: the overlap between productive and reproductive labor as well as between reproduction and non-reproduction. Waiting for the return of their dead children, the Chorus of Argive mothers lyrically laments the vanity of reproduction, a laborious doing undone by men's *ponoi* (918–24):

> *Chorus* Child, I raised you, wretched one. I carried you under the liver, bearing *labors (ponous) in birth pangs (en ôdisi)*. And now Hades has my *labor (mochthon)*, wretched that I am. Having given birth to a child, I don't have anyone who can take care of me when I am old, poor me.

Ponos aligns, or identifies, Theseus with the Argive mothers even as the lack of it aligns Adrastus with them, both as "passive" women and as old women subject to an infertility elaborated by a series of alpha privatives (*a-paidian* 170; *a-gamon* 786; *a-pais a-teknos* 966), which underscore their affective kinship to the corpses as corpses (not as just relics of the sons whom they are prevented from mourning).[32] This double alignment of the Argive women and, by extension, of reproduction as such brings together *ponos* and non-*ponos*, Theseus's (re)productive labor and Adrastus's not-doing or un(re)productive labor. Indeed, when Theseus announces, "I'll bury the corpses, taking them out of the land of Asopus. . . . I've endured many other *labors (ponous)* for others" (571–73), an alternative parturition is imagined in which (with obvious Oedipal undertones) dead children are placed in the earth. As we have already seen, Theseus challenges the Theban herald, "Are you afraid . . . that after having been buried . . . they may beget children in the recesses of the earth?" (543–46). By the time we get to Adrastus's comment on Theseus's successful enterprise (951–54)—"Stop, and having ceased the *labors (ponôn)*, guard your cities. . . .

The affair of life is brief; one should get through it as easily as possible and not *with labors* (*sun ponois*)"—we may wonder whether Adrastus is, in a sense, recapitulating the mothers' disillusionment with their own *ponoi* ("What was the use of children for me?" 789). When Evadne, the wife of Capaneus, one of the heroes who had fallen in Thebes, announces that she seeks "the same pyre and tomb" as her husband—a dissolution into Hades of "toilsome (*em-mochthon*) life ... and life's *labors* (*ponous*)" (1003–5)—the duplicity of *ponos*, "(re)productive labor," turns Evadne's suicide, a regressive impetus toward the lack of "toil" of pre-organic (non-)life, into a rejection of reprofuturity, the loop of which is formally suggested by *em-mochthon* and *ponous* at the beginning and at the end of the line respectively. Evadne's declaration can thus be read as a restatement of the anti-reproductive position of the Chorus, a proto-feminist questioning of maternity as a subjection to the masculine state's demand for disposable bodies to use in war—for bodies, like Iphigenia's, to sacrifice for the common cause. The rejection of reproduction is even queerly colored with the suggestion of a retrospective rebuff of heterosexuality as such: "If only my body had never been yoked into a man's bed" (*emon de mêpot' ezugê / demas es andros eunan* 822–23). In Evadne's dialogue with her father, Iphis, she seems even to mock the play's ongoing concern with decision and (over)activity—and the state's fear of inaction—by exploiting his naïveté and tardy understanding of her suicidal intentions: "You would get angry if you heard about my *decisions* (*bouleumatôn*)" (1050); "We have prepared ourselves for some novel *action* (*pragma*)" (1057). The hyper-maternity of the play is predicated on an *ex-cess* ("self-exit"), which unfolds as motherly mourning that can never stop ("I will always drench the fold of my robes with tears" 978–79) but also in a stepping away from conventional motherhood, from the very idea of reproduction. This anti-reproductive stance is an integral part of the play's dramaturgy of necroresistance—the rejection of the state's sovereign determination of the border between life and death, its pitting of the baby against the corpse and, more to the point, the baby against the mother.[33]

The maternal funeralization of the city supplants reproduction with adhesion—a contagious extension of mourning proxemics, intimacy with corpses (and their surrogates), to the very form of political relationality.

Onstage, supplication (*hikesia*)—a social, religious, political practice of physical connection—hermeneutically sways between touch and non-touch, between the literal and the figurative, between doing and not-doing, alternations that are integral to the play's political thematics and to the irony around Adrastus's name.[34] When the Chorus of Argive women first supplicate Aethra with "I beseech you, falling *at your knee* (*pros gonu*)," (42) and, later, Theseus, with "I beg you, by your beard, . . . falling *around* (*amphi*) your knee and hand" (277–79), the question arises of whether the whole Chorus (or just the Chorus leader) touches or simply moves toward them. Does Theseus recoil, keeping himself at a safe distance, rejecting the assimilating force, or the contagious power, of the supplication, taking advantage of the mask's protection, seeking to keep the illusory distinction between "self" and "other" that touch, contact, contamination break down? Staging, of course, operates in the virtual space of a perennially creative flux and is differently actualized in plural historical contexts and in multiple imaginative arrangements. What we can say is that, in the Chorus's supplications, the correspondence, or lack of correspondence, between word and action, between performative utterance and the expected embodied counterpart, is self-reflexively problematized. The Chorus's first supplication fails to persuade Theseus to act, as does that of Adrastus, whose words enact his onomastic inactivity, or non-agentic agency: "I am ashamed to fall to the ground to embrace your knee with my hands" (164–65). Even when the Chorus succeeds in its second attempt, supplication—physical? figurative? a hybrid?—amounts to a form of weak, hesitant, interrupted hapticity. This (non-)touch exemplifies the gesture as potentiality. The gestural captures "the dimension in which works—linguistic and bodily, material and immaterial, biological and social—are deactivated and contemplated as such in order to liberate the inoperativity that has been imprisoned in them."[35] Supplication, in the play, expresses an anomic "inoperativity"—an affirmation of helplessness, of the inability to act, expressed in the interval between touching and non-touching, between embodied word and figurative action, which is, to an extent, an appropriation and extension of the (in)animate ontology of the corpse, of its acting by apparently remaining inactive.[36] This inoperativity queers the very idea of relationality, placing it in a liminal space between praxis and non-praxis. The proximity of Adrastus to the mothers allows us to draw out the affective and political implications of supplicatory (non-)touch, the radical possibilities of feminist adhesion. Adrastus is not so much a protector or an ally of the mothers, also including Aethra, as he is almost one of them, in that he displays a cathexis to them, an intimacy with their homosocial intimacy.[37] In a game of parallel verbal-proxemic circularities, just as the Argive mothers encircle (*en kuklôi* 103) Aethra, looking, like children, for care, the sons of the dead Argives place themselves *around* (*amphi* 106) Adrastus, looking for a surrogate father or mother. As he is about to supplicate Theseus— to re-enact the Argive mothers' supplication—Adrastus first presents himself as a "gray-haired man" (*polios anêr* 166) and then ascribes to them a sterile, "gray-haired (*polion*) old age" (170).[38] The contagious queerness of supplication emerges from the multiplicity and opacity of the levels of desired "aroundness" and "towardness"—the spatial and affective projection distinctive of this play, which is animated by a proliferation of the preposition *pros*, the Greek equivalent of *ad* in "adhesion." In a sense, the first two lines of the play—"De-meter (*Dê-mêter*), guardian of this land of Eleusis, / and those men who occupy the temples, the goddess's *servants* (*pros-poloi*)"—epitomize Adrastus's *pros*imity (*pros*) to the mothers, even if it does not translate into physical clinging. Adrastus is a prosthetic object fastened onto the mothers' bodies—as they wish the corpses to be. In the interplay of closeness and distance, intimacy and detachment, touch and non-touch, supplication's haptic formalism tropes the opaque spectrum of Adrastus's sororal proximities—or approximations— to female intimacy, his participation in or, better, adhesion to the *poli-as*, the supplemented *polis*, a feminist commons.

Alongside Adrastus's emotional adhesions, the Chorus's supplication of Aethra generates queer intimacies through which homoeroticism and parental/ filial bonds mingle and defamilarize each other. After the initial ritual language—"*Old woman* (*geraia*), I beseech you *from my old mouth* (*geraiôn ek stomatôn*), falling to your knees*" (42)—the Chorus continues (60–61 and 69–70):

Chorus Please persuade your son, I supplicate you, to go to Ismenos and place *into my hand* (*eman t' es chera*) the bodies of our valiant dead.... I supplicate your son to place my dead son *in my wretched hand* (*talainai ' n cheri*) so that I can *embrace* (*amphi-balein*) the baneful *limbs* (*melê*) of my son.

While looking ahead to the mothers' imagined reunion with their sons' bodies, the hands mentioned here index Aethra's arms, touched figuratively or otherwise, in the act of supplication evoked by the quasi-technical verb *amphi-balein*, a circular adhesion. The overdetermined performative language of the supplication is thus laden with the hyper-intimacy of the mother-child attachment that informs the later scene in which the Argive mothers lament over their children's ashes. In another gesture of necropolitical domination, of devaluation of the corpse cast as a protective measure, Theseus has, in fact, forbidden them to see and touch the bodies before they reach the pyre because, as he claims, "the mothers would die if they saw them disfigured" (944): he has denied them the "pantomimic" sensuousness of mourning a corpse, the pleasure-in-pain of touching the perceived fullness of an inherently lacking presence.[39] Here mourning veers into necrophilia,[40] but also into the *jouissance* of animacy—of human bodies striving to connect with, or adhere to, urns as surrogate corpses, another expression of the funeralization.[41] This aspirational bonding stretches into the indeterminacy of syntactical bonds in a mother's aggrieved response (1134–37) to one of the surviving children, who laments that he will never be "*in the hands* (*en chersi*) of [his] father":

> *Chorus* Where is the *labor* (*ponos*) of my children? Where are the *gift* (*charis*) of childbirth and the *nourishment* (*trophai*) of the mother and the eyes' sleepless duties and the *loving* (*philiai*) *pressures* (*pros-bolai*) of the *faces* (*pros-ôpôn*)?

Subliminally associating the giftless labor *of* childbirth, which brought the young soldiers to life, with their battlefield labor,[42] the ambiguous genitive (objective/subjective) exceeds its immediate referents, troping the ambiguity of relationships that occupy the unseen, repressed areas where kinship and the erotic are mutually contagious—as they become in an Argive mother's quasi-*figura etymologica* (*philan philêma*) imagining a phantasmic father placing a kiss on the "dear" cheek of the surviving son (1153). The queer excess of these liminal bonds, or forbidden contacts, which emerge in response to Theseus's prohibition, expresses "the pressure both alien and internal to the logic of the Symbolic,"[43] but also the emergence of a socio-political possibility beyond individuation, something that the pandemic has made especially pressing. The antidote to "normative individuation," which Moten calls "the incarceration of difference . . . a regulative concept, a concept of law enforcement," is the "blur" as "a queer phenomenology of perception."[44] The "blur" of two instances of the same prefix *pros* in line 1137 (*pros-bolai pros-ôpôn*) formally conveys relational excess, which reflects back, as it were, on the Argive women's supplication of Aethra, a different yet similar haptic configuration of the towardness of *pros*. A paramorous mother-son intimacy is channeled through the shared caressing of an urn of a husband/father's ashes, a gesture that brings us back to the spectral queerness of the pressing (metaphorical or not) of the Argive women's hands and mouths against Aethra's body (*geraia geraiôn ek stomatôn* 42), of filial mothers leaning into their surrogate mother, in an inexpressible, non-hierarchical continuum of similarity and difference. The polyptotic convergence of *geraia geraiôn*, comparable to the formal rubbing against each other of *pros-bolai* and *pros-ôpôn* (a term meaning both "face" and "mask"), suggests a homoerotic juxtaposition or contagious adhesion, or a homo-kinship, a form of kinship generated without and against reproduction.[45] *Ponos* seems to take on the additional meaning of the handmade labor—formal as well as physical—necessary for crafting "strange intimacies," for building the non-individuated relationalities of the commons. This political non-individuation is sustained by and identified with the air itself: when the mothers, lamenting the loss of their labor, say that the "air (*aithêr*) has them" (1139), the resonance of *aithêr* with Aethra assimilates the chief mother to an embracing atmospheric force that includes and fosters mutual, unpredictable, unbound relations in an open space, never turning the commons into a hierarchy.[46]

The city's funeralization continues to enable Theseus's and the state's contagious implication in the maternal commons, even after the time of supplication is over. Theseus commits to helping the Argive mothers in a speech whose nervous texture, as we have seen, exhibits the *ponos* of decision-making, the pleasure-in-pain of hesitation, curtailed by the solemn performative futures "I will do [it]" (*drasô* 346) and "I will come" (*hêxô* 357), each at the beginning of the line, followed by end punctuation. These formal breaks set a boundary on the commitment, a barrier between host and guest. The futures appear to mark a climactic moment after the back-and-forth or in-and-out of his decision-making. The end of the transaction—political as well as crypto-sexual—is signaled by Theseus's command (359–61): "Old women, remove the holy wreaths from my mother, so that *attaching her dear hand to* mine (*philên pros-apsas cheira*) I may bring her to the house of Aegeus." Theseus is seeking to separate himself from the polluted guest or the migrant, to keep apart "seemingly opposed orders—refugee/citizen, non-nation/ nation,"[47] as well as impure/pure, unhealthy/healthy. As Judith Butler reminds us, "At the outset of the pandemic, the virus was figured by media reports as coming from . . . a 'foreign' place . . . and described as an unwanted immigrant, imported without papers into the body politic."[48] That the polarities in Theseus's order are blurred is shown by the language of adhesion that he appropriates. It as though the refugees' diction adhered to the host's, and Athenian language, stripped of the illusion of self-possession and self-sufficiency, became suddenly inf(l)ected with the accent of the stranger. What formally adheres to this language is the gestural adhesion of the female suppliants and by extension Adrastus's queer proximity to the old women, the women's own homo-kinship, and their attachment *around* and *toward* their sons, which saturates these lines: "Give the children's bodies to me so that I may place them in my arms, *attaching my hands in embracings (peri-ptuchaisi . . . cheras pros-armosasa)*" (815–16). In Theseus's speech, *pros-apsas* ("attaching") queers his enforcement of hospitality as a goal-centered and thus temporally contained transaction. An effort to restrict hospitality, then, paradoxically expresses a non-reproductive hapticity which, in its lack of teleology, is homologous to what Jacques Derrida would call unconditional hospitality.[49] The co-presence of *aroundness* (*peri*) and *towardness* (*pros*) gives the sense of corporeal burdening of the supplicated, who is almost besieged. In a sense, this bodily heaviness produced by the gesturality of supplication for the sake of unburied bodies—trespassing individuation, weaving the commons—replicates the heaviness, the hindrance of the corpse itself, or the "burden" (*baros*) of the ashes.[50] The dramaturgy of supplication—with its interweaving of bodies in line with the community's spread of funeralization—valorizes adhesive juxtapositions; it de-verticalizes the state, enveloping it in the affective circuit of maternal queerness. In defending the corpse, horizontal bonding and non-hierarchical forms of caregiving and solidarity appropriate its invisible agency, its viral expansiveness—physical, symbolic, ideological.

The funeralization of the city makes us think of the feminist commons expressed in the coming together of the protest as a practice of "comradeship,"[51] a political contagion. The BLM protests in the first summer of the pandemic "enacted new forms of connection and structural care," with social distancing and the anonymity of wear-masking not hindering, but enhancing the experience of the commons, extending it beyond the logics of identity, recognition, and sentimentality.[52] The defense of the corpse reconnects the generative power of maternity to the lifedeath of childbirth—a bodily dispossession, an ecstatic self-undoing or self-breaking in the act of life-making,[53] which locates motherhood, in Jennifer Nash's words, in "a form of care that alters the self by linking it to an Other."[54] In her discussion of the corpse as the primary target of necropolitical violence, Bargu asks, "Can we look beyond the politics of mourning ... to create an alternative where the 'common wealth' is really held, shared, experienced, produced, and consumed in common, where this commonality leads us to reconfigure our modes of political engagement and togetherness?"[55] In Euripides' *Suppliant Women*, maternal supplication, with its proliferation of hands not simply touching each other, but creating unpredictable bonds beyond the division of state and individual, beyond individuated (abstract or concrete) subjectivities, expresses a viral solidarity that "could replace the exclusionary format of nation-states and borders with capacious structures and infrastructures of political care"[56] and the infectious equality afforded by being and becoming not just *with* others, but also *around, by,* and *beside* them.[57]

Part Three

Ruins

6

Antigone

In a study published in the journal *Nature* in the first year of the pandemic, we read that the lockdown might, at least momentarily, have done some good to the earth:

> The coronavirus pandemic has brought chaos to lives and economies around the world. But efforts to curb the spread of the virus might mean that the planet itself is moving a little less. Researchers who study Earth's movement are reporting a drop in seismic noise—the hum of vibrations in the planet's crust—that could be the result of transport networks and other human activities being shut down. They say this could allow detectors to spot smaller earthquakes and boost efforts to monitor volcanic activity and other seismic events.[1]

Though the pandemic might have heightened consciousness of the entanglement of the "now of human history" with "the long 'now' of geological and biological timescales,"[2] the desire to go back to normal, to restore life as it was, to return to a complacent and narcissistic status quo ante—an undisturbed Anthropocene—has meant an eager resumption of the extractivist dynamics to which the Covid crisis may be imputed, dynamics that, if allowed to continue, will complete the sixth great extinction in the not-too-distant future.[3] What is conventionally called geology—the epistemological, scientific ally of technologies of subjugation of Gaia[4]—cannot be divorced from the biopolitical divisions between human and non-human, life and non-life, that underpin ongoing practices of neocolonial racialization.[5] Reading Sophocles' *Antigone* in these times—apparently so close to the end of times—may alert us to the play's resonance with, and even possible participation in, debates on the current condition of Gaia and our own approaches (epistemological, political, and affective) to it. Creon's view of the cave where Antigone will die as a prison, a stage for his punitive reduction of her to an inert corpse, the tool of his thanatopolitical designs, denies symbolic power and agency not just to "the dead below," the inhabitants of the subterranean realm of the Underworld, but also to the earth as such—"the world *upon which* we live," as Arthur Conan Doyle put it, "itself a living organism, endowed ... with a circulation, a respiration, and a nervous system of its own."[6] Creon's act can be called *terr*oristic—to borrow a pun used by Salar Mameni to conceptualize the terroristic wars on the earth (*terra*) that neocolonialisms never cease waging.[7] The notion of living, breathing land contests the instrumentalization of the earth, the taken-for-granted setting of human life, and, in this case, Creon's distinction between life (that which is above the earth) and non-life (that which is below it).[8]

The image of Polynices lying unburied on the ground offers an opportunity to shift the notion of Gaia from mere setting to *support*, the surface without which we cannot move or even breathe. Implicitly revealing the disavowed vulnerability behind geological extractivism while theorizing our dependence on basic infrastructures (the floor, the street, etc.), Judith Butler has observed that "when those environments start to fall apart or are emphatically *unsupportive*, we are left to 'fall' . . . and our very capacity to exercise most basic rights is imperiled."[9] As I approach *Antigone* in this global crisis, I am drawn to reading in(to) Antigone's funerary reparation for her brother an attachment to Gaia as the supporting surface, or her own becoming ground or Gaia, both as instrumentalized base and basic environmental support.[10] In my close engagement with the textures of selected passages of the play, I thus want to heed Antigone's attraction to—and her own embodiment of—*geopower*. In the words of Elizabeth Grosz, while biopower is "the power over life that regulates it from outside," geopower "has no outside, no 'place' or 'time' before or beyond it." It is "the force, the forces, of the earth itself: forces which we as technical humans have tried to organize, render consistent and predictable," but which we can never fully master, since "the earth remains the *literal ground* and condition for every human, and non-human, action."[11]

In reconsidering Antigone through geopower, I am also inspired by Saidiya Hartman's poignant "Litany for Grieving Sisters" (2022), in which an "Antigone of the 'black morning' and of Black mourning . . . roams through a city in ruins, clutching a child she could not save from death, in search of a brother who might no longer be alive."[12] Walking in a deserted Harlem, Hartman's Antigone, who "is not the last sister on earth," though "this is how it feels," brings to mind Jim, the protagonist of W. E. B. Du Bois's short story "The Comet" (1920)— written in the wake of the Great Influenza epidemic—in which Jim's return upward, to above-ground New York City, after a descent underground at the bank where he works, results in the discovery that the world has come to an end, that he is the only surviving human.[13] Engaging, in 2020, in the early days of the Covid pandemic, with this work of speculative fiction, isolated in Du Bois's corpus, Hartman draws attention to the epiphany of a surviving female figure—perhaps Jim's lover, partner, wife, or sister—at the end of the story: "A *brown, small and toil-worn woman* makes her way through the crowd with the corpse of a dark baby in her arms."[14] This character is none other than the Antigone in Hartman's "Litany for Grieving Sisters." Retelling Du Bois's story in her 2020 article, Hartman writes:

> The destruction of the world will afford the chance for him to be human like other men. . . . The paradox is that human extinction provides the answer and the corrective to the modern project of whiteness, which Du Bois defines as *the ownership of the earth forever and ever*, the possessive claim of the universe itself. The stranglehold of white supremacy appears so unconquerable, so eternal that its only certain defeat is the end of the world, the death of Man. . . . In the wake of the disaster . . . the last black man on earth . . . will be permitted to live as a human for the first time. "I am alive, I am alive," he could shout in the streets of Manhattan. . . . He is alive because the world is dead.[15]

At the end of the world, in a situation of desolate solitude—the atmosphere of the lockdown—the Black man and the earth, targets of extractivist predation, feel liberated. Both are alive, as though for the first time—rescued from those who have relegated them to non-life, non-being. In Du Bois's "The Comet" and Sophocles' *Antigone*, Jim's and Antigone's departure from an above-ground existence to embrace the earth (rather than excavating or extracting it)[16] has a contagious effect: the survivors, Jim and Creon, return upward to find themselves alone, forced to live in a desolate world, inviting us "to think beyond our own experience of the 'world' in order to think about deep, planetary history."[17] In a move of abolitionist ecology, the world, in Du Bois's story and in Sophocles', is dismantled (or destroyed) to be built anew. In Hartman's "Litany for Grieving Sisters"—which is composed of references to Sophocles' play and Butler's *Antigone's Claim* but also imbued with the speculative atmosphere of "The Comet"—I am struck by the paratactical description of Antigone in the finale:

> The no-longer mother, the not-wife, the kinless sister, the lost daughter, the not-woman, the not-man, the nobody, the cipher, the *matrix*—she is still here.[18]

The persistence of the matrix suggests an assimilation of Antigone to the primary matrix that is Gaia[19]—or geopower and, as the ongoingness of asyndeton intimates, "the abyss of deep geological time."[20] This persistence is shared by the buildings that witness Antigone's desolate walk—supporting infrastructure surrounding her, foundations and enclosures, "untouched, indifferent, and stolid, as if waiting for new occupants,"[21] which allow us to see her as the ground, a platform of stillness, the ecological matrix of care subjected yet resistant to extraction, the surface pressed-upon or put-upon by human life.

My first impression of Antigone's entanglement with geopower comes from re-reading the initial scene of Sophocles' play—the sororal debate on the forbidden burial of Polynices—in light of the forbidden funerals of the early pandemic (65–78):[22]

Ismene

> While asking those under the *earth* (*chthonos*)   65
> to be forgiving—for I'm forced to do this—
> I'll obey those who are in charge, for
> acting excessively does not have any sense.

Antigone

> Dear [to him], I will lie with him, with the one who is dear [to me]
> (*philê met'autou keisomai, philou meta*)   73

after having misbehaved piously, for greater is the *time* (*chronos*)
in which I must please those underneath rather than those
   who are here.   75
For I will lie there forever. But you, if it seems good to you,
(*ekei gar aiei keisomai. su d'ei dokei*)
just dishonor what the gods honor.

These lines stage the rift between Antigone and Ismene, the tragic plot's building block, which Bonnie Honig has famously problematized in *Antigone, Interrupted*—a title whose comma breaks, suspends, or "stills" Antigone's heroic individuality, her exceptional singularity, multiplying it into the plurality of sisterly intimacy and solidarity.[23] Indeed, an inter-linear echo seems, unexpectedly, to connect the sisters even at this tense juncture of the sibling conflict through the formal proximity of two principles, both material and immaterial, both personal and impersonal—"earth" (*chthonos* 65) and "time" (*chronos* 74), which both occur on the edge: at the end of their respective lines. In the context of a durational, expansive *chronos* beyond Symbolic time, a time beyond her life or beyond human life as such, Antigone brings together formally confusing "thereness" (*ekei*) and "recumbency" (*keisomai*)—her own, matching her brother's. In this line, the elsewhere of the Underworld and a kind of horizontality of being are confounded (*ekei gar aiei keisomai. su d'ei dokei* 76), as though the eternity of subterranean life, of time beyond time, were materialized in a prolonged cadence (*kei . . . ei kei . . . ei . . . kei*), figuring the collapse of human vertical ontology.[24] "Lying there" for Antigone does not mean simply residing or reposing within the earth together with her brother, but becoming earth-like, or the earth itself[25]—embracing and inhabiting the horizontality of the ground, enacting a "refusal of standing."[26] Antigone's chthonic *chronos* is thus a prospective embodiment of Ismene's *chthonos*. When, in lines 441–42, Creon asks Antigone, "You, you who are *bowing* (*neuousan*) your head *toward the ground* (*es pedon*), are you admitting it, or do you deny having done it?"—burying her brother—her orientation toward the ground, toward *chthôn*, coincides with the undifferentiated, deep time of silence, *chronos*.[27] In line 73, *keisomai* ("I will lie"), situated in the center, mediates, as it were, between the two overlapping phrases *philê met'autou* ("Dear [to him] with him") and *philou meta* ("with him dear [to me]")—charting, for Antigone, a transition from familial possession to self-dispossession (the referent of the feminine adjective *philê*, she disappears in the prepositional phrase *philou meta*).[28] Yet rather than a disappearance of the female subject (*philê*) or an incorporation into the masculine grammatical realm (*philou*), this syntactical transition suggests a non-hierarchical joining *with* the other—as indicated by the reciprocal elision of personal pronouns, first of "to him" and then "to me." This joining, a juxtaposition of horizontalities, is like contact with the ground, earth as a supporting structure; it is the coming together of two (in)animate horizontalities, togetherness in an encounter of surfaces.

To continue this line of thought, I wish to dwell on the words of the Guard when he reports to Creon that someone has buried Polynices, implicitly— unwittingly—emphasizing a notion of "on-ness," a desire, as I see it, to rest one's body on another: "I'll tell you—someone just now / departed after having buried the corpse of [Polynices], sprinkling *on its skin* (*kapi chrôti*) thirsty (*dipsian*) / dust (*konin*) and *performing all the rites* (*kaphagisteusas*) that are necessary" (245–47). The guilty action is encapsulated by a double *epi*—the preposition that expresses the sprinkling of dust, in the feminine gender, on the body of Polynices (*kapi chrôti*) and the prefix in *kaphagisteusas*, the participle for administering funerary rituals.[29] We can say that *epi* ("on"), occurring in the same metrical position in two consecutive lines, becomes the ground for identifying the mysterious agent with a subject manifesting itself, and its feminine gender, as granular matter poured on a body, the metonymic substance of the ground, which is the support for and of all, the surface that both presses and is pressed upon. In his account of the illegal burial, the Guard reiterates the image of "light dust," or "a thin [layer of] dust" (*leptê ... konis*),[30] placed *on* the body of the enemy Polynices, locating the two elements of this phrase at the opposite edges of the line, crafting an iconic effect of both distance and closeness: *leptê d'agos pheugontos hôs ep-ên konis* ("Light dust lay on [the body] as though [somebody] had wanted to avoid pollution" 256). Divided in two (like brother and sister), the feminine dust supports a textual middle marked by a para-grammatical masculine semblance (the *-os* endings), which suggests Polynices' own on-ness, his corpse reposing on (*ep-ên*) the layer of dust, the ground, offered by Antigone.

Antigone's kinship with geopower, her "on-ness," is also relevant to the Guard's descriptive dwelling on the earth's recalcitrance, on its hard refusal to reveal the identity of the "wrongdoer," as emerges from an accumulation of stiff, harsh sounds (249–52):

> *Guard* ... there was no wounding of an ax, nor *a mattock's excavation* (*dikellês ek-bolê*), but the earth was hard (*stuphlos*) and dry (*chersos*), unbroken (*ar-rhôx*), and *not trodden* (*oud' epêmaxeumenê*) by wheels (*trochoisin*).

The sexualized language of this passage calls forth the virgin Antigone, tying a bond between her name, "the one who is against birth"—in which the prefix *anti* equals an alpha privative—and the adjective *a-rrhôx*, "unbroken" or "unbreakable," which brings out the resistant force of the ground.[31] Later, accompanying Antigone to the cave, "the recess of the dead" (*keuthos nekuôn* 818), the Chorus observes that she is descending to the Underworld without having been violated by a sword or "struck by destructive diseases" (*phthinasin plêgeisa nosois* 819)—that is, she is untouched by vehicles of harm, just as, at the site of Polynices' furtive burial rite, the ground remains untouched by any ground-breaking tool or vehicle (*oud' epêmaxeumenê / trochoisin* 251–52). In the same choral passage, not just Antigone's solitude but her solidity is emphasized by the play between *autonomos* and *monê*, two adjectives that, together, conjure an earth-like remaining-in-place, the stillness of a substrate or a support.[32] Beyond the negative prefix, the Antigonean ground's resistance is expressively conveyed by the sound of brokenness or of that which would break it, in *a-rrhôx* (251) and the nearby *t-rochoisin* ("wheels" 252), a sound that phonesthetically recalls the English word *rock*, in its double connotation of hardness and shaking. As a result of the resonance between *chersos* ("dry") and *dus-cheres* ("unpleasant")—the adjective qualifying the astonishment of the Guard and his cohort at the discovery of Polynices' burial (*pasi thauma dus-cheres parên* "an unpleasant wonder was on everyone's face" 254)—the earth's dryness or barrenness is transferred to the faces of the observers: numbed, hardened into an expression of shock and stupor. *Stuphlos*, a synonym of *sklêros* (cf. English *sclerosis*, *sclerotic*), which qualifies *gê* as a "hard" surface, appears strikingly Antigonean if we read it in light of Creon's later rebuke of her for rigidity: "Know that too-*hard* (*sklêra*) temperaments / are the ones that mostly fall, and that *the strongest* (*en-kratestaton*) / iron, baked by fire so as to become *hard* (*peri-skelê*), / is the one that you would see is most frequently broken and *shattered* (*rhagenta*)" (473–76). Speaking against their speaker, beyond dramatic irony, these lines suggest that the iron maintains its recalcitrant hardness (*en-kratestaton*)—phonically, if not semantically—even when broken (*rhagenta*). We could say that, similarly, the dust—which Creon's men "sweep away" (*sêrantes*) as they drag Antigone offstage (409)[33]—remains an agent of geopower, the matter of the supporting ground, the constituent of the dry surface of the earth. Additionally, *stuphlos* makes the earth Antigonean by containing, and sibilantly supplementing, *tuphlos* ("blind"), an adjective that unmistakably identifies Oedipus (it is the second word of *Oedipus at Colonus*). The morphologically transgender phrase *s-tuphlos* ... *gê* assimilates the ground—the environmental support figured by Antigone—to the bodily and familial assemblage of father and daughter that is the affective and dramaturgical symbol of *Oedipus at Colonus*, a play postdating this one, but preceding it in mythical time. In that play, Antigone is not just a surrogate foot, a prosthesis, but also the human support who doubles the maternal ground of Colonus by offering Oedipus a rest, by seating, positioning, and stationing him.[34]

In the Guard's account of the environmental turmoil that followed the removal of Antigone's dust from Polynices, an atmospheric rage shakes up textual form, precipitating the epiphany of the enjambed juxtaposition *chthonos* / *tuphôs* ("a whirlwind from [of] the earth" 417–18), which seems to re-create the subliminal image of Antigone-as-(Oedipal)-earth behind *s-tuphlos gê*. The paragrammatical attraction of the genitive *chthonos* and the nominative *tuphôs*, confounding cause and effect, earth and its liquid-aerial manifestation, invites us to see the atmospheric protest against the violence of the Law as a manifestation of geopower, realized in a striking alliteration (417–20):

> *Guard* And then suddenly from the *earth* (*chthonos*)
> a *whirlwind* (*tuphôs*), gathering a storm, a pain of the sky,
> fills the plain, harming all the foliage
> (*pimplêsi pedion, pasan aikizôn phobên*)
> of the woods of the plain (*hulês pediados*) ...

In line 419, *pedion*, the ostensible object, appears to fill the line with *p*'s, a labial accretion that enacts the expansiveness of geopower, as though the earth were overstepping elemental boundaries, filling the atmosphere—or time itself—with traces or layers of itself, transferring the subterranean sameness of deep time upward and outward into the air.[35] In these lines, we can read a dramatization of what Kathryn Yusoff has called the "immersion of humanity into geologic time," or the geologization, we might say, the (re)mineralization of *anthrôpos*, which implies "a shift in the human timescale from biological life course to that of epoch and species life."[36] The protesting geopower materialized in the Guard's account proclaims that "being is always tied into being toward the geologic, conceptually, ontologically, and materially,"[37] but it may threaten something more ominous—a burial and destruction of the upper world, as we may infer from the ecocritical implications of the choral announcement (or prophecy) that "the bloody *dust* (*konis*) of the Underworld is burying [the house of Oedipus] again" (601–2).[38]

A different yet related aspect of geopower in *Antigone* is the impression that reconnecting physically with family members in the Underworld entails an intimate encounter with mineral sensuality, a contact with rocky subterranean surfaces as animated dwellings or embodiments of lost loved ones, "geologic subjects."[39] I wish to read in Antigone's speech before she is taken offstage into her prison cave an expressive emergence of prospective and projective "geosocialities"[40] that disrupts the divide between human and non-human objects of cathexis and haptic bonding (891–920):

> *Antigone* O grave, O bridal chamber, O subterranean
> (*ô tumbos, ô numpheion, ô kata-skaphês*)
> *abode that will be forever guarded* (*oikêsis aei-phrouros*), where I march
>   toward my dear ones . . .
> I nourish the hope that when I get there
> I will become *dear* (*philê*) to my father, *closely dear* (*pros-philês*) to you,
> mother, and *dear* (*philê*) to you, my brother;
> for when you all died I washed you *with my hands* (*auto-cheir*),
> and adorned you and poured funerary libations;
> and now, Polynices, for *covering* (*peri-stellousa*) your body I get this . . . .

If I had lost a husband I could have had another one,

and I could have had a child from another man, if I had lost it,

but with my father and mother buried in Hades,

there is no way that a brother could be born for me;

honoring you in the name of this law,

I have been judged by Creon to have erred

and to have dared terrible things, O brother.

Now he drags me, having seized me like this

through his hands—me, *with no bed* (*a-lektron*),

with no husband (*an-humenaion*), *having no part* (*oute . . . lachousan*)

in any marriage nor in the rearing of children.

But living like this, deprived of *dear ones* (*philôn*)—poor me—

I go into the *subterranean depths* (*kata-skaphas*) *of the dead* (*tôn thanontôn*).

This speech is organized around tripartite overdeterminacies, as indicated, almost programmatically, by Antigone's initial "tricolon crescendo with anaphora,"[41] her triple address to the cave, her "forever guarded" home. The ur-triad is, however, the familial one of father, mother, and brother—all of whom receive the adjective *philos*, a marker of affective self-projection, a self-dispossessive fantasy of intimate possession. This demand for closeness and tactile rejoining—which is implicit in the repetition of the possessive adjective *philos*—is complicated, in the last part of the speech, by the reference to the hands of Creon's guards, to their participation in an assault or an act of physical appropriation, which engenders another triad, a series of negative expressions channeling Antigone's devotion to the possession of loss: "with no bed" (*a-lektron*); "with no husband" (*an-humenaion*); and "having no part" (*oute . . . lachousan*).[42] In using negative adjectives that amount to reflections of her name, Antigone is reclaiming the dispossession foisted upon her by hostile hands, seizing it from the state's biopolitical grip. Semantically reconfigured, coopted into her own sphere of being, the punitive touch is shadowed by the ghostly feel of the desired reunion with her father, her mother, and the brother who is invoked just before Antigone deictically directs attention to Creon's violence. The formal proximity between "*O brother*" (*ô kasignêton kara*) and "Now he [Creon] drags me," where the subject of the verb is left indefinite, facilitates imaginative proximities between tactile sensations, wanted and unwanted, tender and aggressive, hauntologically past (and future) and intrusively present. By the same logic of projective and prospective confusion of sensations, we can say that the initial triad, "O grave, O bridal chamber, O subterranean [abode]" (*ô tumbos, ô numpheion, ô kata-skaphês*), overlays geology onto the biology of father, mother, and brother, and thus inorganic onto organic, human onto non-human rocky flesh. Harking back to Creon's instructions to his guards—"Enclose her in the grave that is covered over (*katêrephei / tumbôi peri-ptuxantes*) and then leave her alone (885–86)"— Antigone's words, "covering (*peri-stellousa*) your body, brother," invite us to see an embracing, intimate bond between her and the rock.[43] What I am suggesting is that we cannot interpretively sever Antigone's longed-for re-attachments, the intensity of her prospective reconnections with her *philoi*, from an exposure to geological sensuality. We could conceive of this sensuality as a non-extractivist experience of lithic closeness and affection. As Sarah Cant writes:

> The body relates to the textures of caves in particular ways, sensual engagement supplements spatial dimensions; relations between cave and body fluctuate between patterns of contact and non-contact as the caver moves *through* the space of [a] cave.... Cave systems are known as the caver's body moves through the cave, a defining presence constructing an intimate physical geography of spaces, surfaces and sensations as it makes contact with a physical geography.[44]

Embracing Polynices again means dwelling on and in an intimate affinity with the structure of the cave—which Indigenous studies have taught us to think of as an "earth-being."[45] It means playing with the texture of craggy surfaces as a way to access stratified time,[46] to sample, through impressions of the rock's formation, the rough edges of past familial dramas, even to find and caress the bodies of the dead in stony shapes—in the fortuitous drawings traced by erosion, in silhouettes and profiles, broken lines and contours that the mind is affectively drawn to, tricked into recognizing as familiar in the natural sculptures of the subterranean landscape.

   At the end of the play, the Messenger's account to Eurydice of his journey with Creon, who has had second thoughts, to the subterranean prison where

Antigone and her betrothed Haemon, Creon's son, have already taken their lives, seems to delineate a movement not toward, but within the cave. The abundance of rough compounds, of groups of hard consonants—epitomized by the phrase *katôruchos stegês* ("excavated abode" 1100)—conveys an encounter with the pointed surfaces of the cave; it reflects uncertain movements through narrow karstic passageways, contorted tours of labyrinthine corridors and chasms, contact with agglomerates, with geological asperities, threatening yet alluring products of geopower (1196–1216):[47]

> *Messenger* I escorted your husband on foot
> to the edge of the plain, where the unpitied
> body of Polynices, *dismembered by dogs* (*kuno-sparakton*), still was
>   lying . . .   1198
> after having heaped a high-headed mound of familial earth,   1203
> (*kai tumbon ortho-kranon oikeias chthonos*)
> we entered the virgin's hollow, stone-floored bridal chamber of Hades
> (*chôsantes authis pros litho-strôton korês*
> *numpheion Haidou koilon eis-ebainomen*)   1204–5
> . . . groaning, Creon utters the
> *most lugubrious* (*dus-thrênêton*) word ". . . am I going along *the*
>   *most wretched* (*dus-tuchestatên*)
> path among the roads of the past?
> My child's sound fawns upon me, but, attendants,
> come near quickly, and standing by the tomb, look
> entering a fissure in the heap made by the tearing away of stones."
> (. . . *agmon chômatos litho-spadê / duntes . . .*)   1216

The compound that indicates a coming apart, the formation of a fissure, *litho-spadê* is preceded, impeded by the collision of jagged consonants (*agmon chômatos litho-spadê* 1216).[48] Modified by the epithet *kuno-sparakton* ("dismembered by dogs" 1198), the body of Polynices is assimilated to a scratchy accreted formation that attracts yet repels the touch. In the description of Antigone's bridal chamber in line 1204, the compound *litho-strôton* ("stone-floored") bumps up against the velar genitive *korês* ("of the virgin"), suggesting the intimate contact of human flesh with a rocky surface, as well as the discomfiting allure of deep time's materiality at the end of times. The syntactical parallelism between *litho-strôton korês / numpheion* (1204–5) and *tumbon ortho-kranon oikeias chthonos* (1203)—noun, adjectival compound (*litho-strôton/ ortho-kranon*), genitive (*korês/chthonos*)—once again assimilates Antigone (*korês*) and the earth or the ground itself (*chthonos*); entering the cavernous crypt, Antigone becomes what, in a sense, she already is. In this perspective, Antigone looks ahead to Audre Lorde, who, in her poem "Coal," breaks the sovereign "I" on the blank page into geopower's plurality, into a fragmented, dusty telluric emergence, "refus[ing] the inhuman codified as property to embrace the collective subject of Blackness that has been gathered into categories of earth" (1–7):[49]

> I
> Is the total black, being spoken
> From the earth's inside.
> There are many kinds of open.
> How a diamond comes into a knot of flame
> How a sound comes into a word, coloured
> By who pays what for speaking.

In the Messenger's speech, the concentration of the compounds *litho-strôton, ortho-kranon, kuno-sparakton, dus-thrênêton, dus-tuchestatên,* and *litho-spadê* suggests a sprawling, hard horizontality, an Antigonean "refusal of standing," which places her in a "trans-material" relation—of affinity or identification— with Gaia as the ground.[50] The temporal correlate of this horizontality—the inhuman, repetitious continuity of deep time—attaches itself to Creon's reference to the cave when he lays out Antigone's punishment (773–80):

> *Creon* Taking her to the place where there is a path untrodden by men, I will hide her alive in a rocky cave.... And there she will either ask Hades (*Haidên*) not to die and obtain it from him, the only god *she worships (sebei)*, or she will finally realize that it is wasted labor to *worship what is in Hades (tan Haidou sebein)*.

The repetitious cadence (*Haidên . . . sebei* 777 / *tan Haidou sebein* 780) enacts the temporality of Sisyphus's futile labor, implying that Antigone will become

Sisyphus too, as soon as she enters the cave and partakes of the rocky matter of a subterranean Real. At the same time, the mention of the "rocky cave" initiates a Sisyphean circularity in Creon's discourse, mimetically precipitating him into his own futile labor, into a continuous confusion of "then" and "now," the synchronicity of deep time.

The finale of *Antigone* brings us back to the pandemic extinction of Du Bois's "The Comet" by presenting Creon as the sole survivor of a disaster that he has brought upon himself by disdaining not just the dead or the gods of the Underworld, but the support provided to "those above," as the Greek idiom puts it, by ground itself. Concerning the beginning of "The Comet"—where we read that Jim's bosses "wanted *him* to go down to the lower vaults," for "it was too dangerous for more valuable men" to reach "down to the dark basement beneath, down into the blackness and silence beneath that lowest cavern"[51]— Saidiya Hartman observes that Jim is "relegated ... to the lower depths, as nothing, as nobody," and Blackness is equated to the "bowels of the earth," the target, we might say, of extractivist predation.[52] In Du Bois's story, the "death of the world"—the extinction provoked by the poisonous effluvia released into the atmosphere by the comet—"creates an opening," Hartman says, "that might allow [Jim] to breathe inside his skin and be released from the enclosure of nothing"; similarly, it might rescue beneath-the-earth darkness (the geological counterpart of Blackness) from the position of abused support, instrumentalized non-being. In *Antigone*, the sense of desolate, almost apocalyptic solitude that crushes Creon results in an imagistic and dramaturgical atmosphere of telluric requital. Holding the body of his son (1258), a horizontal burden, in his arms, he becomes human ground, an encumbered or broken base, like the earthly support that opens itself into the cave.[53] When he says, "the god struck me with a great weight" (1273–74), we perceive his earthward precipitation, perhaps into "the bowels of the earth." In the same lines, the use of the verb *eseisen* ("he [the god] shook [me]") adds a seismic movement—the quintessential expression of geopower. In accusing the god of trampling on his happiness, of treading on it like the ground below (*lakpatêton an-trepôn charan* 1275), Creon feels reduced to something like the "dark basement beneath," to the underground he has disdained. His solitude, visualized by his moving between and around the corpses of his son and wife, resembles the outcome of an ecological disaster—the revolt of the extracted earth, which is also the source of the aerial pollution diffused by Du Bois's comet. As he laments the cumulative effect of one death (Haemon) piled upon another (Eurydice, his wife), one corpse beside or upon the other—while Antigone's body significantly remains below in the cave[54]—he describes himself as pressed upon, the object of an oppressive "on-ness" marked by the prefix *ep(i)* in *ep-exeirgasô* ("Hades, *you did me in again* already a dead man" 1288) and *sphagion ep' olethrôi* ("a bloody death piled *upon* death" 1291). In facing the two bodies, he appears to grope for missing ground, for lost material support, for the base that he has broken and lost while serving as ground in spite of himself: "I don't know which one to look toward, where to lean" (*oud' echô / pros poteron idô, pai klithô* 1344).

Antigone may be read as a speculative allegory of extinction,[55] a sudden collapse of the ground under our feet, a reversal of the positional hierarchy between a human "above" and an inhuman "below."[56] The tone of "The Comet" and the collection it belongs to "oscillates between rage and despair," as Hartman writes, adding: "Some might even describe it as an ur-text of afropessimism, but its mood is more tragic; its bright moments are colored by a desire for a Messianic cessation of the given, stoked by a vision of the end of the world, welcoming the gift of chance and accident."[57] What Hartman says of white supremacy—"its stranglehold ... appears so unconquerable, so eternal that its only certain defeat is the end of the world, the death of Man"—can be extended to our trampling, literally and metaphorically, on the earth, to our reliance on technologies of geological extraction that are always enmeshed with racism and racializing logics. Human life as we know it, when qualified as "human," always implicates dehumanization. In *Antigone*, the unburied corpse of Polynices and, later, of Antigone figures not only a denied burial, but a refusal of burial—as a practice that enacts the power of the state by establishing clear boundaries of life and death. It can be read as a refusal to "fold death back into ordinary life—to make death bearable and understandable, which is what funerals and other forms of ritual regulation of corpses purport to do."[58] According or denying, as we have seen during the pandemic, the right of burial is, ultimately, a manifestation of the state's biopolitical power, its alleged capacity for discerning what is possible and what is not, what ought or ought not to be done, who is entitled to a right and who is not. I suggest that, as we read the play today, we shift our critical attention from the corpse to the cave as a locus of intimate contact with the most literal foundation of life itself (human and non-human), which is in itself non-foundational, developing minoritarian forms of affective relationality *with* the inside of the earth, rather than merely dwelling *on* or extracting *from* it. The disavowed or suppressed life of the underground that protects us from extinction, insofar as we leave it as and where it is, can be a site for recovering and re-imagining, through the pre- or posthuman world of deep time, the very possibility of a world while we face the ever-imminent collapse of this one.[59]

Looking at the cave—one of the symbols of Antigone—during the pandemic may perhaps enable us to view *emergency* as *emergence*. In his treatment of the Popol Vuh, the K'iche' Mayan story of creation, Edgar Garcia observes:

Cave-beings emerg[e] from another side of time in the earth's depths, hidden from the casual disappearances and erasures of history. . . . [Caves] . . . could eat you up, transport you to another world, take you to the moment of creation. . . . They are the birthing places of clouds, rain, stars, and the sprouted seed. But they are also involved with the historical matters of the world above. They send forth their strange-bodied creatures to challenge our sense of continuity. They break the world open to close it again in chthonic cycles.[60]

When, at the end of the play, the body of Haemon—metonymous of Polynices' and Antigone's unseen dead bodies—is brought onstage, followed by Eurydice's, the cave or the very inside of the earth tantalizingly emerges. What the cave carries politically is the scenario of a queer ecology, which Yusoff sees as one where "subjects emerge as a constellation between inhuman time, nonhuman force, and geologic materialities."[61] I see this ecology as grounded in a horizontality encapsulated by the fallenness of the corpse—an image of extinction and devastation, but also of the possibility of a reorientation of relationality (spatial, familial, political, ecological) that consists in the juxtaposition, the adjacency of equally supporting entities, of mutually sustaining earth-like structures, human and non-human, micro-*terra*'s, as it were, instead of *anthrôpoi*.[62] In Du Bois's fantasia of pandemic destruction, the final image of a dead baby in the arms of the woman who will become

Hartman's own Antigone curtails the idea of a lineage—a vertical, genealogical line—a "hope about the future," denying "closure or resolution," even while "offer[ing] a glimmer of relation in the wake of devastation."[63] The bond of Creon with Haemon's corpse—supporting arms carrying a body that is in the same horizontal position as the supporting ground—refashions the vertical relationality of (re)productive hierarchy through what Stefano Harney and Fred Moten call a "refusal of standing," of the posture that, for them, epitomizes modernity's "Socioecological Disaster" as constituted by "the transatlantic slave trade, settler colonialism and capital's emergence in and with the state."[64] Sensually bonding with "the blackness and silence beneath [the] lowest cavern"[65] and embodying the fallenness of supporting ground (in a deeply non-human sense) are means for thinking, through the very possibility of extinction, of a different world beyond and against extraction.[66]

7

Niobe

In one of the short stories of Haruki Murakami's collection *After the Quake*—a narrative reflection on the earthquake that hit Japan in 1995—Junko, a young survivor of the catastrophe, develops a perverse attachment to a refrigerator, from which the hands of imaginary corpses emerge, threatening, or rather promising, to drag her in.[1] The fantasy of being sealed in this container, of being locked down or sheltering in place in it, renders the sense of guilt of the survivor (like Murakami himself) as a death-in-survival—more like embalming than hibernation. In Junko's imaginings, this refrigerator, whose opening is a seismic chasm, alternates with the snowy Alaskan landscape where Jack London seeks to build a fire in the famous story that Junko reads "again and again." In this chapter, I consider Niobe, transformed into ever-weeping stone after Apollo and Artemis killed all twelve of her children, as the tragic icon of a grieving survivor in relation to frozen spaces broadly conceived: the Aeschylean stage (re)constructed in Aristophanes' *Frogs*; the Eurasian steppe, the setting of both Ovid's exile and Sacher-Masoch's novels; the glacial *pastfutures* posited by speculative ecology; the broken landscape of Israel/Palestine; and the wintry border between Iran and Turkey. In her adaptation of Ovid's account of the tragic character, Phillis Wheatley entrusts the sense of Niobe's lithic transformation to these lines:

> The queen of all her family bereft,
> without or husband, son, or daughter left,
> grew stupid at the shock. The passing air
> made no impression on her stiff'ning hair.[2]

In the image of *air* unable to make itself felt on *hair*, to lend its elemental motion to, and blend into, a supplemented, "aspirated," version of itself, Wheatley reads Niobe's petrification as an interruption of the contact between the human and the non-human externality that we may call nature or environment. It is this interruption, in its multiple implications, turns, and contradictions, that I want to tease out in my reading of the tragic Niobe, Aeschylean and Aristophanic, through Ovid's exilic persona, Gilles Deleuze's mother of the steppe, Quentin Meillassoux's glacial ancestrality, and Banksy's depiction of her in contemporary Palestine. Exploring pandemic fantasies of a world without humans or an end of the world—coming back but also already or still present—I treat the grieving survivor or the aggrieved nature embodied by Niobe as a figuration of life ensconced in its end or denial, dwelling in and flowing out of its solid annihilation. In this chapter, the anger of hurt nature takes center stage; as we will ultimately see, Niobe, paralyzed yet still weeping, allegorizes the durational temporality of maternal care, as well as the care that nature bestows upon us, while issuing an urgent, enraged call for attention and intervention through the shocking power of a frozen life in ancient tragedy as well as in the cold ruins of our time.

Analyzed together, the portraits of Niobe in Aristophanes' *Frogs* and Ovid's *Metamorphoses* make us see her notorious, prolonged silence after her losses as enacting the seriality of those losses, the duration of pitiless repetitious punishment. In *Frogs*, where we find the most extensive, albeit mocking, testimony on Aeschylus's eponymous fragmentary play, Niobe is tendentiously cast as a symbol of the deceptiveness and smugness of her author and his tragic mode. In Aeschylus's play, the best-known dramatic rendition, Niobe, stripped of her many children one after another in retaliation for her blasphemous boasting, initially appeared as seated, immobile, silent, hiding her face. As we can infer from one of many depictions in vase paintings, where the folds of her robes, more sculptural than painterly, commingle with the stone she sits on, Niobe may have seemed like a rock even before becoming one.[3] According to Aristophanes' Euripides, the aesthetic effect of this iconic posture was that the spectator "sat waiting and waiting" (*pros-dokôn kathêito* 919) for Niobe to "utter something" (920), while the play "went on and on." In Ovid's *Metamorphoses*, at the moment of Niobe's transformation, her petrification is

marked by indications of a body and a tongue immobilized as cold rock
(6.301–9):

> orba resedit
> exanimes inter natos natasque virumque
> *deriguit*que malis. Nullos movet aura capillos,
> in vultu color est sine sanguine, lumina maestis
> stant immota genis; nihil est in imagine vivum.   305
> Ipsa quoque interius cum duro lingua palato
> *congelat*, et venae desistunt posse moveri;
> nec flecti cervix nec bracchia reddere motus
> nec pes ire potest; intra quoque viscera saxum est.

The mother sat down childless among her lifeless sons and daughters, and
her husband, and *became rigid (deriguitque)* because of her *pains (malis)*.
Air does not move her hair; on her face the complexion is bloodless; her
eyes stand immobile on her sad cheeks. Nothing is alive in the picture. Her
tongue, too, inside *becomes frozen (congelat)* together with her hard palate,
and her veins can no longer be moved; her neck cannot be bent, nor can her
arms respond with movements, nor can her foot go. Inside, too, her vitals
are stone.

In these lines, two metrical and syntactical breaks, after *deriguitque malis*
and the dactylic sequence of *congelat*, translate Niobe's frozenness into an
affective intensity, into the feel of formal and bodily interruption. The
interruption of the articulatory breath in the flow of language looks ahead
to stuck air, air incapable of moving her hair, as Phillis Wheatley underscores.
Before the polysyndetic syntax of lines 307–9, a conglomeration of foreclosed
corporeal movements, the verb *con-gelat*—a combination of the prefix *con-*
("with") and *gelu* ("frost")—marks a congealing of poetic form. It is as though
this word, which encapsulates the outcome of Niobe's travails, preemptively
gathers together the individual effects of immobility that she undergoes and
turns them into a conglomerate of frozenness. These effects re-enact the
multiple, tormenting losses, each chilling blow immobilizing Niobe, killing
her without killing her, reducing her to a stony/frosty presence. Returning to

the Aristophanic scene, we could say that the excruciating wait imposed by the grieving Niobe on spectators, the targets of her displaced, unwitting revenge, is a slow, prolonged accumulation of moments reflecting the seriality of her losses, of parts petrified one after another.[4]

In a moment of Ovid's *Tristia* ("Sorrows"), the frozen landscape of Tomis, the poet's place of exile, chillingly echoes with a self-citation from the Niobe episode. In 3.10, where Tomis is depicted as "disturbing and war-torn,"[5] the same rare verb *congelo* that we saw in the Niobe passage renders the freezing of the Danube (*Hister congelat* 29–30) amid stiffening winds (*ventis . . . durantibus* 29).[6] When a few lines earlier Ovid introduces the rigors of his prison on the Black sea with a *praeteritio*—"Why should I speak of how rivers grow, bound by cold, and brittle waters are dug out of the lake?" (25–26)—he seems to dramatize the silencing power of the cold air blowing over the textual surface, felt through *f* and *fr* sounds (*frigore rivi . . . fragiles effodiantur*). As Victoria Rimell has observed, "In the *Tristia* . . . we . . . find many references to blocked or pierced throats and stifled voices, images which evoke not just the political censorship of subversive books, but more broadly what the trauma of exile does to the poetic voice."[7] Silencing himself, rhetorically re-imposing Augustus's violence, projecting the cruelty of his (semi-)divine punisher—a castrating, unnamed yet ever-present emperor—onto the "cutting" atmospherics reflected in the very name Tomis, Ovid becomes Niobe, who is explicitly evoked twice in his exile elegies as a model of infinite lamentation.[8] But there is also a sense in which the frozen landscape, where even air feels solid, is Niobe herself. Covering the ground with a permafrost, the perpetual winter of the Black Sea region blocks time (15–18). Ovid depicts hair rattling with hanging ice, *glacie pendente* (21), a phrase in which the sound *gl* could be said to express a "vocal contortion,"[9] the sense of a broken vocality mimetically (or contagiously) transmitted by a wasteland that passes its own loss and desolation on to the human mouth and throat. Ovid observes that the outcome of this frozen time or perennial winter is frost accreted on the face, a mouth hemmed in by a gleaming, white beard (*nitet . . . candida barba* 22). In this description, the beard, with its gleam of vitality, is a temporal hybrid—an index of old age as shiny and uncontaminated. It is a marker of an end of time (as well as of language), which coincides with the fresh, animated ancestrality of a before-time.[10]

Ovid's self-citation enables us to perceive a cold—not simply stony—Niobe and to characterize her relationship with the tragic audience as a circulation of chilly affect, of an aestheticized glaciality that can be associated with the condition of the Deleuzian mother of the steppe. Niobe's birthplace is Phrygia, an arid region with hot summers and cold winters, which, in spite of its etymological connection with "roasting" (*phrugô*), phonetically exudes the chills of Latin *frigus* (Greek *rhigos*),[11] detectable both in the Ovidian narrative of Niobe (*deriguit*) and in the no man's land of Tomis (*frigore rivi . . . fragiles* 25–26). Cold *Phrygia* also overlaps with *phrixas* (822), used by the Aristophanic Chorus to depict Aeschylus's "bristling" style.[12] This toponomastic coldness is enacted in Niobe's "iciness" on the Aeschylean stage, as misogynistically re-created by Aristophanes. Having seen her many children killed one by one despite her desperate prayers to the gods, the grieving and aggrieved Niobe mimetically subjects the audience to unyielding indifference—not speaking, rejecting contact, becoming an incomprehensible Other, the "disaster" that refuses to be grasped, an aloof object.[13] The audience is placed in the position of the mortal woman supplicating indifferent gods, but, as a multitude fixated on her mouth, it also resembles Niobe's children, once dependent on her care, her words, their serial deaths reflected in the seriality of dead moments that constitute the current waiting. We can say that, in her silence, Niobe at the beginning of Aeschylus's play is made to exemplify the severe, "icy" mother figure, corresponding, in Deleuzian terms, to a female partner dominant over a male sexual partner who acts as a child masochistically caught in fetishistic disavowal, in the illusion of the maternal phallus, in fantasies of non-Oedipal or pre-Oedipal sexuality or of asexuality.[14] In resorting to this Deleuzian figure, I do not intend to rehash or validate the sexist and racist opposition of "hot" and "cool" mothers; rather, I use this concept as a heuristic conceit for framing the interpretive possibility of a nexus between Niobe and frozen, aggrieved nature (or ancestral nature as an icescape) and for drawing out intimations of resistant readings (ecological, psychological, political) for our times.[15] Deleuze extrapolates the model of the "mother of the steppe" from the novels and short stories of Leopold von Sacher-Masoch. In Deleuze's own description of the quasi-maternal agent who provokes the masochistic "supersensuality" of "waiting and suspense," "an indefinite awaiting of pleasure,"[16] phonetic chills shiver through an accumulation of *f*s and *r*'s as we see, in particular, in this passage:

> *L'idéal masochiste a pour fonction de faire triompher la sentimentalité dans la glace et par le froid. . . . Le froid masochiste est un point de congélation, de transmutation (dialectique). Divine latence qui correspond à la catastrophe glaciaire. Ce qui subsiste sous le froid, c'est une sentimentalité suprasensuelle, entourée de glace et protégée par la fourrure.*[17]

The function of the masochistic ideal is to ensure the triumph of ice-cold sentimentality by dint of coldness. . . . Masochistic coldness represents the freezing point, the point of dialectical transmutation, a divine latency corresponding to the catastrophe of the Ice Age. But under the cold remains a supersensual sentimentality buried under the ice and protected by fur.

The "freezing point" of "masochistic coldness" is expressed by *congélation*, a term that brings us back to the Ovidian *congelare*. Like Niobe, punished because of her "excessive" words, the mother of the steppe theorized by Deleuze is both "oral" (that is, loquacious) and taciturn, falling into sudden, tomb-like silence.[18] Furthermore, the Masochian steppe that grounds the Deleuzian oral mother is in Galicia, now part of Poland and Ukraine, from a global perspective not very distant from Tomis (in Romania). The cold air of Tomis/Galicia affects the Deleuzian page; the accreted *f* words circulate impressions of the grassy fur and whipping wind tendered by the desolate landscape of the steppe.

In Ovid's aesthetico-political world, Niobe may be read as figuring Augustus, the ever-present if often unnamed addressee, not just as a castrating father, Laius or the Lacanian law,[19] but as "the oral mother."[20] As Andrew Feldherr reminds us, "Niobe is the daughter of Dione, the Homeric mother of Venus, making her Aeneas's [aunt]."[21] In addition, Niobe's desire to supplant Latona, to become a goddess herself "connects her to the problems of self-definition faced by Rome's *princeps* at this stage in his career."[22] Referring to the ideological importance of what we might call reproductive futurism in Augustus's political propaganda, Feldherr points out that "in his *Res Gestae*, Augustus's description of his own personal loss, *filios meos, quos iuvenes mi eripuit Fortuna* ("my children, whom Fate stole from me when they were young"), is given in language similar to what Niobe will use to predict the impossibility of hers: *maior sum quam cui possit Fortuna nocere, / multaque ut eripiat, multo mihi plura relinquet* ("I am too great for Fortune to harm; though she should snatch away many things, she will leave me many more").[23] A descendant, but also, in a sense, a double of Venus, Augustus acts as a Venus in Fur, identifying with the grandiose monumentality of Rome's imperial architecture in all its seductive stoniness, its (re)productive coldness. While rendering the Emperor's apparently masculine power as a fetish, this cold monumentality, a maternal phallus, drives the citizens, the *pater patriae*'s children, to submit, to "remai[n] suspended or neutralized in the idea"—the all-consuming belief in what is taken to be an anatomical impossibility—"the better to shield ... against the painful awareness of reality."[24] The wasteland of Tomis's steppe is, paradoxically, similar to monumental Rome.[25] The beard, whose frozenness yields a castrating speechlessness, is as "shiny" (*nitet ... candida*) as majestic white marble. Furthermore, while promising to reset the clock, to re-create a new, pure linearity and to reconstruct psychological or moral integrity or solidity, the palingenesis of Augustan propaganda, which is physically advertised in the enticing severity of its marmoreal constructions and in its fertile artistic re-production, imbues the experience of time, individual and collective, with a sense of stuckness—like the landscape of Tomis, located spatially and temporally at the edge of the world. The phrase *candida ... gelu*, applied to the frozen beard of Tomis's inhabitants (3.10.22), also refers to the earth, a mother frozen like a statue: *terraque marmoreo est candida facta gelu* ("the earth was made white by marmoreal frost" 3.10.10). In the insistent images of "waves immobilized by frost" (*undas / frigore concretas* 31–32), of "frozen waters" (*inmotas ... aquas* 38; *rigidas ... aquas* 48), and of "a sea blocked" (*ingentem ... consistere pontum* 37), as well as of ships congealed in marble (*stabunt in marmore puppes* 47) and fish imprisoned in ice (*in glacie pisces ... ligatos* 49), we see the raging tristesse, the wrathful grieving, but also the nausea and tedium of the exiled Ovid. He appeals to but, to an extent, also attacks the Emperor, allegorically depicting the temporal and psychological consequences of the so-called Pax Augusta:[26] a generalized sense of suspension, of arrested development, of attraction and assimilation to a Niobe-like mother nature that seems to act as a Venus in fur or "marble body" or "Venus of ice."[27] The ships in the sentence *stabunt in marmore puppes*—almost a formal preview of *stabat mater*—resemble majestic objects, marmoreal receptacles, similar to Roman monuments celebrating imperial stasis. In an elegiac collection that claims to have come to life without a mother (*de me sine matre creata / carmina* 3.14.13–14),[28] the charged language of these female containers immobilized in marble-like ice points to cryoaesthetics that we can observe, for example, in the monumental, gelidly receptive Ara Pacis.[29] The repetitive rhythm of Ovid's description in this poem exudes a temporality moving toward the "freezing point,"[30] while the cutting, evental force of the Augustan father seems to give way to the timeless eternity induced by the cathexis to the maternal phallus, the "ideal" that we can read into the line *terraque marmoreo est candida facta gelu*, where *marmoreo . . . gelu* ("marmoreal frost") functions syntactically as a cold supplement to the body of the maternal earth, as a fetishistic appendage somewhere between materiality and immateriality.[31]

Niobe can also be considered an image of nature as an inhuman force, as theorized in dark ecology. Using Deleuze's words, we could say that as a mother of the steppe Niobe embodies "the catastrophe of the glacial epoch" and reveals "the secret of Nature"—that is, that "Nature ... herself is cold, maternal, and severe,"[32] recoiling, recusing herself in response to or anticipation of our attacks, our depletion of her nourishing maternity. In his 2009 book *Cold World*, Dominic Fox theorizes the "dejection" stemming from the perception that nature "has a way of existing ... indifferent to our aesthetic and moral values."[33] In this perspective, nature would be the object of an "unrequited longing,"[34] as Timothy Morton calls it in his theorization of dark ecology as a form of melancholic ethics. "By setting up nature as an object 'over there'—a pristine wilderness beyond all trace of human contact," ecology "re-establishes the very separation it seeks to abolish,"[35] while dark ecology urges us to accept and, to an extent, embrace this separation, one that we experience in the environmental overexposure of pandemic times as we insistently and vainly seek to bend the virus to our desires and needs. This view of "nature as an ideal world apart," as "an external, foreign, unknown ... unknowable space" or a wild oppositional space has feminist and queer potential, as Stacy Alaimo has shown, inasmuch as it troubles the hierarchy of the subject-object/culture-nature binary.[36] While the pandemic dissolves us into the environment, merging our allegedly bounded selves into a viral elementality, impelling us to build a social *pan*,[37] it also forces us to look, as in a mirror, at our own self-positioning and (lack of) responsibility toward an enraged and afflicted externality—a hyperobject or nature itself. Imagining nature as a radical alterity may induce us to think of time beyond the present and look at the present "as suspended between prehistorical catastrophe and anticipated extinction,"[38] which may appear as impending—terrifyingly or comfortingly close. Providing an ecocritical (or eco-eschatological) interpretation of Jacques Derrida's *à venir*, Ted Toadvine has suggested that "our awareness of an ancient geological past that precedes us opens our imaginations to an indefinitely distant future after us."[39] This future corresponds to an exteriority not different from a stone, which, in an eco-deconstructive perspective, is always from another time, "like a meteor, a fossil, or a glacial erratic."[40] The nature theorized by Morton corresponds to a notion of the earth as a realm that "must be ambiguously read as beyond the *ends* of the human, as it is irreducible to any anthropological subject, egological consciousness, or *Dasein*."[41] We could say that the impression of nature's or the earth's refusal of a bridge between humans and itself, even while it caringly affects or touches us, transforms it, to our narcissistic eyes, into an inhuman Deleuzian mother of the steppe, separated from the human child by "an infinite difference."

The ancient geological past referred to by Toadvine can be linked with Quentin Meillassoux's notion of ancestrality, which addresses the question of life before organic life, ever-more pressing as we start thinking about what is beyond us or beyond the world.[42] Meillassoux offers ancestrality as a response, in the mode of speculative realism, to the erasure of the non-human world that arises from the Kantian and post-Kantian theorization of the inaccessibility of the object in itself to the human subject. For Meillassoux, ancestrality is associated with an epoch of the world that precedes consciousness broadly conceived—an age of inanimate life before the emergence of organic life.[43] This ancestrality is impressed upon the *arche-fossil*—in Meillassoux's words, "a material indicating traces of 'ancestral' phenomena anterior even to the emergence of organic life."[44] The idea of ancestrality restores the full alienness of the stone by locating it in a world without subjects, that is to say, an external frame of being chronologically and ontologically anterior to and severed from consciousness. In a complementary, though reversed, perspective, the fossil is for Lynn Huffer "a strange time-twisting mirro[r] of 'the ends of man,'" that is, "a proleptic trac[e] of our own extinction"—the projection of a world without us, or even without organic life.[45] Similar to ancentrality, the "cold earth" posited by Herschel Farbman "is [a] kind of substrate of life"—an image of the world without us that will survive us after our extinction. As he puts it, "We may die of the heat we create in our environment, but the earth to which we return in dying will always be cold."[46]

The pre-organic life of ancestrality is an *archê*, an imagined point of origin that constitutes the goal of the Freudian death drive, an inanimate destination symbolized, for Lacan, by the petrified Niobe. In *The Ethics of Psychoanalysis*, during his famous discussion of Antigone, Lacan explicitly connects Sophocles' (and Ovid's?) Niobe with Freud's theorization of the death drive, the regressive rushing perversely energizing each human organism from the beginning of consciousness:[47]

> In effect, Antigone herself has been declaring from the beginning: "I am dead, and I desire death." When Antigone depicts herself as a Niobe becoming petrified, what is she identifying with, if it isn't that inanimate condition in which Freud taught us to recognize the form in which the death instinct is manifested?[48]

In the lyric song from Sophocles' *Antigone* referenced here (823–33), Niobe is not simply petrified while continuing to shed tears. She also seems to be turned into something literally frozen, as suggested by the formal parallelism between *petraia blasta* ("stony growth") and *chiôn* ("snow"), two complementary yet distinct materialities that effect her non-human transition.[49] In their long wait, Aristophanes' Aeschylean spectators experience the death drive in a Lacanian register: as *jouissance*, the pleasure in pain of an endless, futile circling around.[50] The seemingly endless deferral is generated by Niobe's quasi-death, which is fashioned as non-life projected toward life or, more precisely, toward the Symbolic—that is, toward the emergence of language (in her case, a re-emergence), a moment in which she "says something." The audience—in effect, her children—are in a similar state: forbidden to move by the "law" of theatrical seeing, frozen in their seats but also animated by a kind of fervor, ardent for movement and relationality, the markers of life that are captured by the *towardness* of the prefix *pros* in the participle *pros-dokôn* "waiting" (in the present tense and, therefore, incomplete). We could also say that through this waiting, that is, through the temporality of fetishistic idealization, the spectators of Niobe trespass into a glacial present, something like the ancestrality posited by Meillassoux—or the spatial and temporal frozenness of the pre-social shelters that our homes became in the outbreak of the pandemic. While Niobe may embody "being in life without wanting the world,"[51] the spectators are like the privileged ones among us who, from within such shelters, faced the novel reality of being in life without being able to access the world.[52]

Niobe's glacial ancestrality confuses the boundary between immortality and the pre- or post-life or deferred life of hibernation, leading us from Meillassoux to our pandemic times through the interpretive mediation of *Citizen Kane*. Tracy McNulty identifies Meillassoux's "glacial world" with the Freudian "pre-organic," the state of originary non-life towards which the death drive pushes the organism (human or non-human) as soon as life begins. For McNulty, "fetishism *is* a speculative realism"—it creates a kind of speculative ontology through a psychological condition that brings glacial ancestrality into post-ancestral life, spectrally importing the pre-organic state pursued by the Freudian death drive.[53] In post-ancestral life, this haunting ancestrality approximates nature in its radical alterity, nature as the pre- or extra-human externality of a non-human world whose ontological distance correlates, psychologically, with the unfillable gap opened by the maternal phallus, the anatomical fantasy generative of the fetish. The material hardness (stony, marmoreal) of the fetishistic object models the fetishist's masochistic hardening into illusion and into ancestrality itself—a further hardening of nature, of the impenetrable (in)difference that exceeds the human subject. The audience waiting for Aeschylus's Niobe to break her silence—and, by implication, for nature to overcome her grief and forgive us—is itself mimetically in the sway of her coldness, not unlike Charles Foster Kane in Orson Welles's *Citizen Kane* (1941). Kane's "mother of the steppe"—contained in a snowy crystal ball but also containing her son in it—affectively haunts the wintry childhood landscape that constitutes the film's leitmotif. Sending young Charles away forever, in the midst of a snowstorm, Mrs. Kane engenders his hoarding of marble Venus statues, and fetishistic attachment to his childhood sled ("Rosebud"), the maternal phallus he had used to strike his designated father, Mr. Thatcher.[54] The drifting snowflakes that pixellate the surface in several key moments materialize fetishistic coldness, freezing the film as it keeps rolling (Figure 5). Bursting forth from the snow globe, which also contains the cottage of Kane's primordial trauma, the snowflakes identify the very materiality of the film with the frozenness of nature while evoking the texture of a glacial ancestrality. The frozen *jouissance* of Aristophanes' Aeschylean spectators reflects the condition of Dionysus himself, the protagonist of *Frogs*, the spectator par excellence. Arguably jealous of the mother-son intimacy between Pentheus and Agave and of their shared mortality, the Dionysus of Euripides' *Bacchae* could be said to experience immortality as his own glacial state, an unravished plenitude of time, a life that, in excluding death, becomes non-life, an eternal separation from his dead mother.[55] The god of liquid frenzy inhabits a block of ice, which, in its fixity, is the counterpart of Aeschylus's overwrought, verbal compounds, his *rhêmata gompho-pagê* ("words fixed with a nail" 824).[56] The Niobe-like glacial time experienced by Dionysus is a frozen achronic expanse; in *Citizen Kane*, the heap of temporal sheets, of "non-chronological

Figure 5 *Fetishistic coldness: Screenshot from* Citizen Kane *(1941).*

co-existences" that Deleuze sees in the film's crystal formal structure congeals in the opening sequence, at the end of Kane's life, in the quasi-frosted, Tomis-like beard constraining his iconic lips (Figure 6).[57] Frozen time materializes as an encrusted layer on his skin, morphing into a facial cover, a white mask, perhaps like that of the Aeschylean Niobe herself,[58] impelling us to conceive of our own masks (the fetishes of our pandemic lives) as the visual markers of our (semi-)hibernation, as images of the secluded ancestrality—the petrifying blank slate of what can be construed as a before-life—foisted upon our minds and bodies, or even as prosthetic guardians delaying the infliction of language on our mouths.

On the Aeschylean stage, Niobe is subjected to a treatment on the threshold between taxidermy and necropolitics—an endemic endurance—which is illuminated by her uncanny appearance in Gaza. Taxidermy is a practice that works through death while apparently keeping the non-human other alive; for Achille Mbembe necropolitics is, on the other hand, the exercise of a colonial state's power to maim, to inflict a mutilated life, killing the other by denying them death, subjecting them to what Rob Nixon has called "glacial" violence, forcing

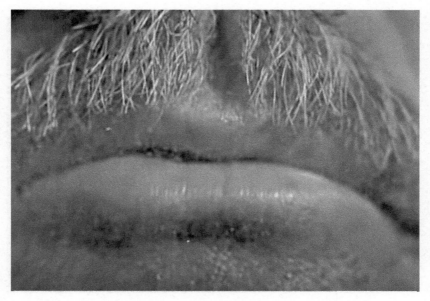

Figure 6 *Iconic lips: Screenshot from* Citizen Kane *(1941).*

them to endure.[59] Discussing Israel's policy of "shooting to cripple" (rather than kill) in both Gaza and the West Bank, Jasbir Puar has described the results as "the stretching of the horizon of life . . . and the finality of death into perverted versions of life [that] seem and feel like neither life nor death."[60] This stretching of the vital spark into a continuity that dulls or freezes it is embodied in Niobe's theatrical epiphany as well as in her metamorphosis into an ever-weeping stone. The appearance of a glacial blue Banksy Niobe in the midst of Gaza ruins visualizes a denial of annihilation—as well as of conditions of livability. In one photograph of the mural (Figure 7), a Palestinian woman (a mother?) whose face is not revealed, stops in front of it, performing her affinity with Niobe in the very act of looking at her, mirroring herself, even though her face remains invisible, in the aggrieved, fasting ancient mother enveloped by ruins. At the same time, the image is a proleptic vision of the end of the world, of a world undone by the auto-immunitarian division between livable and non-livable, grievable and non-grievable lives.[61] Yet through the image of Niobe, the state is also confronted with its "wounded attachment"[62] to rubble, its inhabitation of destruction, its

Figure 7 *Uncanny epiphany: Banksy Niobe mural in Gaza (2015). Photograph by Mohammed Saber/EPA/Shutterstock.*

dwelling in ruination, a kind of perverse *en-durance*—or an *endemic*.[63] The ruins in the picture are, in a sense, fragmented or pulverized replicas of frozen Niobe herself—a crying stone, a screaming rock—extending their own contradictory ontology, their broken, wounded and wounding, solidity to the state that installed itself in them.[64] "As Jewish Israelis, we learned to feel at home in Palestinian ruins," says Hagar Kotef.[65] Making a home in a present of and in ruins means living frozen, inhabiting a glacier, an "assertive materiality" made precarious by the flow of tears.[66] While for some living endemically is received as liberation from the pandemic, for others, subject every day to practices of neocolonialism, it means enduring, that is, being ensconced, entrapped in an arche-fossil, in a cold shell— that is, becoming glacial. Enduring and breaking her endurance with tears, Niobe embraces yet refuses glaciality, which we might construe as abstract life, life without living[67]—the latent, virtual life of ancestrality, vaguely glimpsable in the current "pan-endemic," despite assurances that the worst is over, that we have already gone or are soon going back to "normal."[68]

Niobe's glaciality vibrates in the very form of Aeschylean versification, liberating an impression of the living flow held within the endemic icescape. In one of the surviving lines of Aeschylus's *Niobe*, which drags down the poetic scales of *Frogs*—the instrument ostensibly measuring his and Euripides' value—the "weight" of verbal texture, of crafted *poiêsis*, is felt in the seamless succession of assonant nouns and adjectives describing *thanatos* ("death"): *monos theôn gar Thanatos ou dôrôn erai* ("Alone among the gods, Death does not love gifts").[69] Like Niobe's death-like silence, the rigid, heavy, cold blocks delay the emergence of verbal action till the end (*erai* "it/he loves"). The verbal spark kindled by the bisyllabic *erai*—akin to Niobe's flickering into language, into speaking life before her final petrification—interrupts the formal solipsism of nominalization, if only partially (for desire as such encompasses immobility as well as mobility, coldness as well as hotness). The rigid opacity of nominalization is unsettled by a trickling of (non-)vital sensation. This emergence tropes Niobe's frozen suspension between silence and speech, solidity and liquidity, not just life and death, but experienced living and abstract life, a suspension analogous to the flickering coexistence of actual and virtual underlying Deleuze's "crystal image"—"crystal" being "the perpetual foundation of . . . non-chronological time" and "the powerful, non-organic life which grips the world."[70] The brief glimpse of an action in the bisyllabic ending is the unexpected, sudden, provisional irruption of something more than virtuality—the intensity of a motion that, like Niobe's tears, disturbs endurance and the achrony of an apparent hoarding of time.[71]

In January 2022, a photo of an Afghan mother who had frozen to death while saving her two children on the border between Iran and Turkey broke through the news, disturbed apathy, becoming viral on social media, as reported by Abdullah Ayasun:[72]

> The residents of the Azvek village in the Özalp district of Turkey's eastern Van province on the border with Iran were startled by an unanticipated visit from two young Afghan boys who were seemingly lost in the wilderness in the midst of a bone-chilling blizzard. . . . How they survived the storm . . . was beyond comprehension. . . . After tending to the boys, the villagers went on a frenzied search to locate the unfortunate mother. They found the mother. Dead. Frozen. The sight was to chill and shudder even the most non-sentimental people. . . . To protect them from the punishing cold, the mother slipped off her socks and covered the hands of the boys.

For Ayasun, this emblematic episode of the ordinary thanatopolitical neglect of refugees "represents the death of humanity," stuck in coldness and cruelty. Dwelling in a wasteland between borders, the mother's dead body violates the *Markstein der Grenze*, the border stone with which Walter Benjamin identifies Niobe.[73] The frozen mother, a Niobe herself, transgresses the border that, for Benjamin, Niobe has been instrumentalized to announce. Reified by the media, her death has become a shock that crosses but also challenges geographical and visual borders, just as the exchange of feet for hands that delivered her children breaches the border between lower and upper body, the corporeal distribution of the sensible. Rematerializing and reversing a well-worn affective metaphor, the coldness that killed the Afghan mother affectively expands in space and time, enwrapping beholders in a futile desire to know what happened—a cognitive death drive—generating a bond through distance. Virally diffusing a sense of the end of humanity (or of the cruelty behind the very idea of humanity)—in a subversion of the photograph's documentarian, representational capture—the image of the Afghan mother emanates an impetus against the violence of individuation, toward ancestral (or futural?) de-individuation.[74] This impetus toward de-individuation is both cold and warm, undesired and desired (like our own situatedness in the world).[75] In that respect, it feels something like what Lauren Berlant has called "inconvenience," the "overcloseness, the ongoing pressure" of social coexistence, which initially disturbs us but gets under our skin and which we cannot let go of (as suggested, I would add, by the mismatch of the negativity of *in* and the proximity of *con*).[76] The irruption of the mother's plural singularity into the cold steppes of our lives has a Niobe-like force, interpellating us, asking us to attend and tend to the other, plunging the viewer into a version of maternal caretaking's warm-cold duration—a continuing commitment to warmth and warmth-giving that isolates and depletes motherhood even as its care never peters out. Dwelling in her own ruins, glacialized, both deeply immersed in and removed from time, close and distant, Niobe emanates the gelid air of an ancestral future. Even if, like her, we remain—pan-endemically—petrified, we might feel, if only for a moment, a dissolution of our endemic habituation (to singularity, complacency, indifference), as though the status quo of ordinary endurance could be disarrayed by a flow of tears.

Part Four

Insurrections

8

Prometheus

Insurrection in these pandemic times has the sound of George Floyd's "I can't breathe" in the excruciatingly long nine minutes of his murder. A repetition of Eric Garner's last words (reiterated eleven times) and of Elijah McClain's in similar episodes of state-authorized lynching,[1] Floyd's rebellious cry "intertwines the history of the coronavirus with the history of racially inflected police violence."[2] Clinging to a never fully guaranteed right to life, this cry voices a protest against the police's perverse *jouissance*, against the endlessly repeated fatal game that instrumentalizes Black bodies as fetish objects for sadistic enjoyment, which, as Calvin Warren has observed, is nothing but a feeble, if murderous, cover-up of the Law's intrinsic impotence.[3] "I can't breathe," in fact, shouts out that "breathing is not just a sign of life but … an irreducibly irruptive critique of the normative world"[4] or "a resource from which to perform the resistance that is prior to power."[5] In this chapter, on Aeschylus's *Prometheus Bound,* and in the next two, I consider tragic inflections of breathing and insurrection, furthering a preoccupation with non-hierarchical temporality, de-individuation, and anti-extractivism that has sustained the earlier sections of the book.[6]

The metaphor or, rather, matterphor[7] of police violence against Black lives as an endemic (or "pan-endemic")—the most toxic expression of institutional thanatopolitics, an asphyxiating technology of death—has gained new traction as a result of its concomitance with the respiratory crises inflicted by Covid-19.[8] The virus collaborated with police and capital—allies, stifling para-states— in targeting people of color, in jeopardizing or removing altogether their right to breathe.[9] In Jean-Luc Nancy's formulation, "the Covid-19 pandemic is merely the symptom of a more serious illness, which touches humanity in its very ability to breathe,"[10] the word "humanity" underscores, with bitter irony, the fact that the very constituencies whose "ability to breathe" is most at risk are the ones who have been perennially denied full membership in the category of the "human." In gathering thousands of people while upholding distance and mask guidelines and avoiding an increase in the number of infections, the many BLM protests in 2020 demonstrated that "white supremacy and police brutality" are "a much greater public health crisis than Covid can ever be."[11] As Brett Bowman puts it, "It is precisely [in the] juxtaposition of transmission risk for a respiratory disease through protest against the suffocating effects of police violence that the full force of the brutally racialized social determinants of violence and vulnerability to the communicable disease ... is starkly apparent."[12]

In late spring 2020, when I started writing this chapter, sequestered inside, I kept watching the moving video "WE. DANCE.," put together by the Alvin Ailey American Dance Theater, in response to the murder of George Floyd.[13] In this black-and-white video, the performers release, through their bodies' convulsive motions, the *kinêsis* of anger—"a sense of injustice akin to ... *thumos* ... [a] swirling sensation in the chest, like hot smoke or smoldering fire"[14]—while the narrator's voice says:

> Our mission is to push, to learn, to lift, to teach, to encourage, to build, to carry, to support, to bridge, to raise our communities ... Yes, we are exhausted. Our hearts are tired now, weary and worn ... we persevere always moving, loving, creating even with our heavy hearts ... Our voices ring loudly through our body's language, our voices ring loudly through our body's language ... when our hearts break, we stand up and when our hearts break, we dance. We dance. We dance. We dance. We dance. We dance.

The exhaustion of continuously dancing bodies, which never stop spinning, protesting, insisting, or simply existing, manifests itself in the breathlessness conveyed by verbal repetition, and, especially, by the striking piling up of infinitives ("to ... to ... to ... to ..."). Such breathlessness—a performance of "the precariousness of breath" or of "radical pneumaticism," in the words of Nathaniel Mackey[15]—shows that "dance is the risk of movement" or a "movement at risk," which, as Fred Moten remarks, exudes the "push and pull" between "openness to being affected" and "resistance to being affected," between "the careless negation of what we are" and "the careful affirmation of what we are."[16] On the threshold between negation and affirmation, the accumulation of non-finite verbs—vehicles of indefinite temporal duration, of a present projected into a continuing, never-silent future, of an intensity spilling over into the moment's aftermath—serves to hamper the grammatical period, the punctuation marker that, in signaling the end, imposing provisional finitude through a graphic wound, introduces a deceptive break, a relief from panting, in order for the constraining chain of language to resume after a brief interruption. Just like the persistent *kinêsis* of the peacefully protesting bodies, verbal form, prosaic yet lyrical, seeks to reduce itself to infinite (grammatical) infinity, or infinitude, as it were, turning the breathy intensity of *anger*, of *thumos*, insurrectionary air, into an unstoppable expansion, an unbreakable continuum. This expansion is a reproduction and subversion, or subversive repetition, of the painful length of the video that recorded the murder of Floyd and widely circulated online, exposing voyeuristic watchers—all equally guilty of "a libidinal investment in the spectacle of Black death"[17]—to a temporal dilation overlapping with pandemic achrony, the colonial *durée*, and the slow death to which Black lives have been subjected through centuries of oppression.[18] There is a sense in which pandemic achrony becomes both the outcome and the figuration of the slow death imposed by racial capitalism, an ongoing, protracted extraction of bodies and resources, mimetically reflected in the perceived time of Floyd's digitally recorded execution, time that is, in turn, subverted by the infinite dancing and breathless movement of the "WE. DANCE." performers. Their kinaesthetics of emotional and physical expansion—a panting that keeps them alive, blocking any attempt to make them exhale their last breath—can also be read as an aesthetic response to what Frantz Fanon sees as the social feel of Blackness: a violent pressure on the flesh, or on the throat, a constant effort, in his words, to "contract my infinitude."[19] The digital, which Achille Mbembe calls "the new gaping hole exploding Earth,"[20] is another extractive force, complicitous in the threat to breathing posed by the baleful synergy of capital, police violence, and pandemic.[21]

In this chapter, building upon the radical, abolitionist thought tradition of the Black Prometheus, which includes the interventions of, among others, Frederick Douglass and W. E. B. Du Bois,[22] I read Prometheus as a figure of the *colonisé* stripped of the right to breathe by a necropolitical police state, living in an atmosphere in which respiration has been obstructed by the polluted air of colonization.[23] More specifically, considering Prometheus in the Aeschylean tragedy and a videotaped choreographic performance it inspired, I will connect the somatic "infinitude" of kinetic spinning with modes of recalcitrant expansion, continuity, and infinitude in tragic language as well as in the digital medium, in this case a representational container that (an)archivally documents neocolonial violence. Through punctuation, word division, syntactical break, language exerts haptic violence, a kind of cutting that "contracts infinitude," seeks to arrest the flowing continuum of resistant being. This partitioning (a literal distribution of the sensible) parallels the discreteness of the digital—"a data technology that uses … discontinuous values to represent, store, and manage information."[24] Privileging the discrete over the continuum, digital techno-formalization enforces, for Gilles Deleuze, a representational determinism that kills "the lines of flight" of sensation.[25] Some studies in media theory have, however, looked at digital coding as a perpetual flux, with "a pre-representational status that always breaks away from rational synthesis and logocentric descriptions."[26] Another possibility for positing a continuous, restless sensation within electronic discrete formalization is by seeing the digital as an archival medium, "embedded in architectures of software and in the political economy of social media platforms."[27] What I propose in this chapter is an analysis of the complexities and contradictions raised by re-reading in the *now* a play about the continuing torture of the inventor of technology, of *technai* meant to preserve or enhance mortals' lives. This re-reading is concerned with digital technology as, in a sense, a continuation of the Promethean legacy, which is complicitous in the modern refashionings of necropolitical suffocation but, despite itself, offers possibilities of infinite *thumos*.

The digital exemplifies the idea, formulated by Elizabeth Povinelli, that "the archive is a kind of Lacanian desire, always dissatisfied with its object … the thrill of discovery quickly giving over to the anomie of lack, propelling the archivist into more and more collections."[28] The digital archive multiplies this desire, for "the software itself depends on a vast network of state and capital infrastructures," that is, on a swarm of archontic powers, which aim to archive, that is, immobilize, us, within their vulnerable systems of impression and recording while deluding us with the fantasy of free access and a sempiternal, always "refreshed," survival. In *Xen*, an eight-minute video of Akram Khan's Kathak dance performance in which he channels Prometheus in the guise of a colonial soldier, the dancer's whirling movements destabilize the digital medium's archival aspiration by exposing its "anomie of lack," and embracing this "anomie" as a corporeal contortion, which besieges petrifying colonial power by persistently spinning around it. The digital is (an)archival like the air that enables the dancer's motions—recording, that is, providing the necessary medium for sounds, vibrations, motions to turn into percepts and affects while, in a sense, altering their materiality in the very moment, the event, of their emissions, articulations, and production through the body machine.

The dancer's dizzying movement bodies forth the ever-endangered "infinitude" of the colonized, caught in a bodily spasm, in an unruly contortion between life and death—the two inseparable directions of the archive, digital or otherwise, with its constitutive (in)animation.[29] In the Aeschylean *Prometheus*, poetic form is likewise caught in a circuit between two conations—a phonemic "infinitude" sprawling beyond syntactical partitioning and language's cutting impetus, its urge to break a free, unsignifying flow of letters into discrete units of meaning. Aeschylean letters resemble digital data, the bytes similarly caught in a spiraling double bind—assembling into a discrete informational sequence, a recording unit, and yet flowing rebelliously, rejecting the discontinuity of electromagnetic signification. This spiraling is reflected in the pirouettes of the soldier/performer that are placed before our eyes by *Xen*'s video technology. What we can call the digital "anarchivic"[30] converges with the colonial soldier's spasms, which bring out the electric waves of a swirling *thumos* unsettling archival enclosures and networks as well as colonial petrification. This anger, the manifestation of a continuous spiraling between life and death, conveys the affective "infinitude" that shatters the opposition between *bios* and *zôê* through which colonial, thanatopolitical sovereignty establishes who has the right to rights and who does not, who has part and who has no part. The ultimate payoff of this affective infinitude is not the notion of the tragic Prometheus, ancient or modern, as a cyber-subject. It is, rather, an invitation to rethink the temporality of insurrection, to consider ways for theorizing a continuous moment, for stretching the intensity of political rupture, for extending a disruptive point in time through ever-spinning circles.

Xenos, the solo dancing performance digitally archived in *Xen*, is the last choreographic project of Akram Khan, the artist whom *The Guardian* called "the master mover who redefined dance." In the live performance, which premiered in Athens in 2018, Khan placed himself as a Promethean soldier on the battlefield of World War I, standing for the millions of Indian soldiers enlisted in the British Army from 1914 to 1918. The performer moves amid manufactured objects (ropes) and the technology of a gramophone in a setting of primordial, burning, non-human desolation. Khan's declaration that he is "fighting against time" can perhaps be understood to express an aspiration not just to overcome temporal perishability but to attain, kinetically, a sort of achronicity, or a non-linear chronic continuity—the (a)temporal dimension suggested by the materiality of the setting, the Promethean solitude of the performer, and the formal rigidity of the Aeschylean play itself. (In wishing to restore chronological time, pretending that the pandemic is "almost" or "basically" over, we may facilitate a return to the status quo ante, which would amount to a reconstitution of the conditions of "slow death.") Siobhan Burke, who reviewed the show for *The New York Times*, suggested that, while "whirl[ing] in breath-takingly rapid circles," the performer "seems to be cycling through memories of a bygone life" and asks "Is there any escape? Any return to what came before?"[31] As I will argue, looping around and through soil, a rope, and a gramophone to the point of exhaustion, the Promethean soldier in *Xen* experiences traumatic memory—the tragedy of a plural singularity—in an imaginary thin zone between before and after the beginning of life, a flickering space similar to the one where the digital medium dizzily spins, with its colonizing coercion disguised as global freedom.

Merging the two Greek prepositions *en* and *ex*, the title of this digital Prometheus (*Xen*) folds together *entrance* and *exit*, *insider* and *outsider*, *birth* and *death*, the boundaries that are constantly confounded in the whirling movements of Kathak dancing, which causes a solo male performer to *enter* and *exit*, inhabit and disinhabit, multiple roles, identities, and genders.[32] In the film, the appearance of the Prometheus figure is visualized as an *exit* from an undifferentiated material expanse, a heap of dirt and dust under which he is buried. A fracture in the earth appears as a hand emerges, then a body from a boundless mass. Looking at stills of the video now (Figure 8), our mind's eye may well turn to the images of hands, feet, and shoes peeking out of the heaped soil of the mass grave in Bucha where Ukrainian civilians were (un)buried, victims of a drive to reduce them to the very soil that Russian nationalism lays claim to, made perversely abstract. Amid gut-wrenching scenes of gatherings, consignations of corpses supervised by workers in hazmat suits, which summon up grim tableaux from the outbreak of the pandemic,[33] the epiphany of colored prostheses—a red glove, a purple slipper, blue nails—ruptures the homogeneity of the dirt. It is as though the dead bodies were groping for air, propelled by an upward impetus to seek out an exit, or reclaim a right to appearance.[34] As we watch, handing ourselves over to visual overload, with its overlapping triggers, another image comes to mind: a photograph by artist and ACT UP activist David Wojnarowicz, "Untitled (Face in Dirt)," in which closed eyes, a chin, a nose drawing in air emerge from and against the soil, revolting against a viral homophobia disintegrating the skin into gravel—a fleeting release from the continuing, asphyxiating pressure of a pandemic that has curtailed the breathless infinity of queer sex, formally figured, in his "Being Queer in America: A Journal of Disintegration," by a two-page paragraph with no punctuation closed by "I breathe."[35] Similarly, the reawakened body of Khan's Prometheus opens a breach for itself through spasms, the movements of a newborn or of a dying man, the almost indistinguishable agonies of beginning and ending life, of starting to breathe and exhaling the last breath. With dirt adhering to his clothes and skin, the reborn or newborn subject touches the flesh of the earth, feels the viscosity of the continuum of life and death that is the soil. He is extracted from, yet still pulled into, what land artist Richard Smithson would call a "geological miasma"[36]—that is, the matter of geological extraction. Blended with the soil, Prometheus, the "technologist" or the master technician, becomes the very target or the prey of extractivist operations, projects of consumption, uncannily converging, in ancient and

Figure 8 *(Un)buried: Screenshot from* Xen, *Akram Khan Company.*

modern exploitative systems, around the metallurgical treasure of Scythia/ Ukraine—the region where the Aeschylean character is chained to a rock.[37]

Evoking the cinders of post-war destruction, the fragments of bodies, the archive of dirt figures the paradoxical entry-as-exit of the colonized soldier— *en*listed, taken or let *in*, afforded a deceitful sense of inclusion, just to be *ex*terminated. But it also tropes the opposite dynamic—the soldier's exit-as-entrance, an apparent sense of perverse, hyper-accelerated *ec-stasy* indistinguishable from *en*trapment in the stifling *en*tropy of what Fanon calls "the motionless, petrified world of colonization,"[38] no matter whether we visualize it as a monolith or a granular accretion. As Karl Britto has observed in reference to the Indochinese soldiers enlisted in the French army of World War I, "The proper value of the soldier's body lies precisely in its capacity, through mutilation or death, to offer partial repayment for the successful passage of the colonized subject into the incorporeal realm of civilization."[39] The colonized soldier's instrumentalization as bare matter by the realm calling itself civilization—perched on the pedestal of self-styled incorporeality— makes him undead, places him outside the domain of the living just as the imperative of never ceasing to serve it traps him in, prevents him from actually exiting, or from breathing without feeling the grip of perpetual surveillance.[40]

When we tune in with our computer screens to watch the mutilated life gasping in *Xen*, the sudden fissure surrounding birth/rebirth that initiates the film appears like the trembling fault line of an earthquake, breaking the heap of war's own ruins and launching the tragic rhythm of life as death, or lifedeath. When we click on the switch of our computer and on the "play" (or "rewind") button, making the show begin (again), we simultaneously open a breach in the mass of dust, turning on the machinic soldier—reduced to a robot more than a cyborg—thus activating the digital mechanism that sets him in motion for endless iterations of his gyrations, just like the colonial power, a necropolitical state, serially enlists him for one war after another, without ever letting him breathe, or embrace again the primordial, breathless rest. As Judith Butler puts it, "Colonization is the deadening of sense, the establishment of the body in social death, as one that lives and breathes its potentiality as death."[41] For the colonized, as David Marriott observes, the "black void," the ontological emptiness in which Black lives are constitutionally placed, can be reclaimed or reshaped as "a beyond," or "a fall from [the] inexistence" that is life "into a salvific power that is infinite."[42] While the digital automatism driving the cheoreographic swirls makes the viewer complicitous in a surveillance system and in the violence that locates the colonized soldier in a "black void," it also displays its homology and subjection to the loop of lifedeath. Speaking of photography, Roland Barthes noted, "*Life /Death*: the paradigm is reduced to a simple click."[43] But, as Scott Curtis noticed, the idea of the cine loop is essential to "any sequence of digitized movement that has been set to repeat." As he puts it:

> Edison's Kinetoscope contained a looped filmed sequence that would repeat with every nickel. The content of the scenes filmed for these machines matched the form: a group of blacksmiths hammering rhythmically, a somersaulting dog, circular dances.[44]

Khan's "circular dance" can thus be seen as a metaphor of any cine loop, of the archival circuit of lifedeath that links together Edison's Kinetoscope and the techniques of the digital cyberspace.

The wasteland of Khan's Prometheus—a kind of achronic cyberspace in itself—entrusts his mutilated subjectivity to the energies, of birth and destruction alike, that spring forth from potential enfoldings, from movements toward or away from non-human objects, and from influences and affections stemming from them. In *Xen*, the Prometheus figure experiences his precarity relationally—through an inter-body encounter with a rope, the equivalent of the chains that appear as ankle-bells in the performed show and that imprison his immortal counterpart in the ancient play (Figure 9). In the moving account of *Black Skin, White Masks*, Fanon observes:

> I am being dissected under white eyes, the only real eyes. I am *fixed*. Having adjusted their microtomes, they objectively cut away slices of my reality. . . . In the white world the *man of color* encounters difficulties in the development of *his* bodily schema. Consciousness of the body is solely a negating activity. . . . The body is surrounded by an atmosphere of certain uncertainty.[45]

As Anjali Prabhu comments, for Fanon "the assertion of the individual's subjecthood is a point from where to re-know itself against colonial stereotyping through its body's interaction with the world."[46] Life reduced to purely digital existence aggravates the position of the colonial performer of Khan's *Xen*, his precarious search for a relational (pseudo-)subjectivity. This search for him passes first and foremost through the encounter with a rope, an obvious sign of his constitutive enchainment to the Big Other of colonization, to the signifier as the primary manifestation of an enslaving, inherently colonialist Symbolic.[47] This object externalizes the foreigner's desire to bond

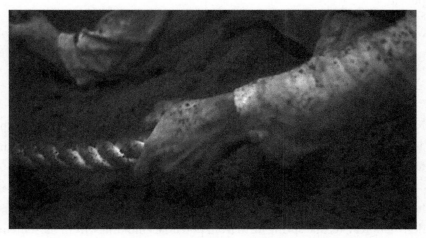

Figure 9 *The knot of lifedeath: Screenshot from* Xen, *Akram Khan Company.*

and connect, but also the inevitable constriction of this desire in the grip of sovereign power. The soldier's contact with the tensile properties of the woven fiber delivers what Eve Sedgwick, reflecting on her dedication to crocheting at the time of her terminal illness, called "the rub of reality."[48] The outcome of this mutual influencing—of skin and fabric—is a bond or meta-bond in which the colonized soldier's erased subjectivity is cast as a web of interobjective affections and his human objectality is recognized in the very pliancy of the cord, itself an instantiation of the fact that "the object resists, the commodity shrieks,"[49] or, we can say, breathes. As Fanon puts it:

> I came into the world imbued with the will to find a meaning in things, my spirit filled with desire to attain to the source of the world, and then I found that I was an object in the midst of other objects.[50]

Like the cord, the human body of the colonized subject can be pulled back—down into the earthen pile—or pulled apart in the very act of resistance. "Life and death are knotted in a thread / the hanged man's rope, and the umbilical cord," says Chilean artist Cecilia Vicuña, whose textile art Julia Bryan-Wilson refers to as threads of protest, peaceful and enraged—what Khan's Prometheus also spins around, with his body reaching out to, and becoming the rope.[51] He becomes the Real, the excess of non-meaning, that the colonized, in a sense, always is—for "the colonized ... has a designated place, but in that place [he] experiences a void of no identity."[52] More importantly, the knot of lifedeath, an untying and re-tying, materialized by the solo performer as he spins and trembles, affords him a special power, similar to that of the earth itself, which trembles while giving birth to life through its own fracturing.[53] This spinning expresses lifedeath not as a cycle or a blurred confusion but as a source of *jouissance*—"a radical expenditure without subject or recuperation"[54]—which also involves the perverse joy of material in its own giddy fraying: fabric as well as bundles of electromagnetic energy and the metallic supports of digital archivization (Figures 10 and 11). Also evoking lifedeath, the gramophone, the sound object that acts as the rope's companion onstage, iteratively emits the impression of a live vocal event as disembodied sensory matter at once alive and dead. Its central aperture suggests another *xen* (that is, an *ex* and an *en*), an endless passage in and out of intensities or relational vibrations.[55] But as we

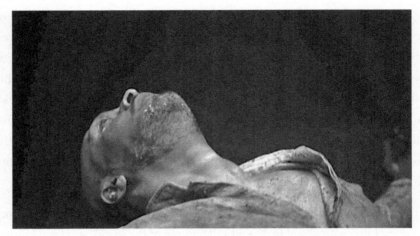

Figure 10 *Giddy fraying: Screenshot from* Xen, *Akram Khan Company.*

Figure 11 *Relational precarity: Screenshot from* Xen, *Akram Khan Company.*

feel—sympoietically—the synergic spinning of texture, flesh, and of the digital medium itself, we are also impelled to circle back to the motion of Aeschylean form, a preview of the anarchivic electromagnetic loop.

At the beginning of *Prometheus Bound*, tragic form fashions "the inexplicable mass of rock"[56] not just as the iconic object and place of Promethean torture—the Scythian mountains—but also as a marker of deep time, still solid, if not unworn. After the first couplet, where the setting is bookended by *chthôn* ("earth"), the first word, and *a-broton . . . erêmian* ("the deserted place with no mortals"), which closes the second line in a formal circling back, Prometheus appears as a two-syllable deictic direct object, *tonde* "this man" (4–6):

> ... *tonde pros petrais*
> *hupsêlokrêmnois ton leôrgon ochmasai*
> *adamantinôn desmôn en ar-rêktois pedais*

> *Kratos* ... [it's your job] to nail this man to rocks, high-craggy ones, the criminal, in unbreakable chains of adamantine fetters.

In this exhortation, which the personified Kratos ("Might") addresses to Hephaestus, Prometheus's presence in language barely registers within the overdetermined thicket of nouns and adjectives clustered around the rock and the chains, the quasi-homophonic *petrais* ("rocks")/*pedais* ("fetters") at the end of almost consecutive lines. One gains the impression of metallic and stony matter seeking to connect with, or press upon, the human body—an impression that persists when Hephaestus announces Prometheus's eternal punishment: "You [Prometheus] will guard *this rock* (*tênde ... petran*), *standing* (*orthostadên*), sleepless, without bending your knee" (31–32). The immobility of Prometheus— "sleepless," always "standing" (*orthostadên*), never flexing his limbs—assimilates him to the rock, as does the resonance in endings between the adverb *orthostadên*, effectively a modifier for Prometheus, the subject of the sentence, and *tên-de ... petran* ("this rock"), the objectifying object in the accusative. Although the clamorously metallic punishment of shackling—a spectacular re-enactment of Athenian practices of torture—inflicts upon Prometheus a perennial insomnia, denies him any respite, exposing him to the petrifying frenzy of thanatopower,[57] the formal texture of poetic form conjures a different condition—not the bare life imposed by colonial biopolitics, but a fantasy of deep, achronic time that arises in the undoing of poetic form. Fanon asserted that "the colonized are denied their freedom and thus relegated ontologically to the status of things—things like stones. They are denied their dynamism; they are forced violently into an unfree and inhuman 'zone of nonbeing.'"[58] Prometheus's rocky quasi-assimilation, transmuted into Khan's becoming soil, suggests the constant circulation, the persistent beyondness of colonized flesh, the very object of the extractivism that ultimately exposes the vulnerable self-dispersion of colonization. Denise Ferreira da Silva's words are important in this regard:

> Flesh is no more and no less than what has been (which nourishes us as animal, vegetable, or mineral) and of what has yet to become, that which returns to the soil to be broken down into the nano elements, the particles that emerged at the beginning and remain in the composition of everything that happens and exists in the universe. . . . If the flesh holds, as a mark/sign, colonial violence, the Dead's rotting flesh returns this marking to the soil, and the Dead then remain in the very compositions of anything, yes, as matter, raw material, that nourishes the instruments of production, labor, and capital itself. That is how the dead slave/Native lives in/as capital.[59]

As I will suggest, in the symbolism of ancient and modern Prometheus, we can also discern a kind of de-petrifying rupture, a break that opens a breathing channel.[60] As Moten and Stefano Harney put it, "Blackness operates as the modality of life's constant escape and takes the form of flight"; it is located "in the invention of escape, stealing away in the confines, in the form, of a break."[61] We can say that Prometheus stands for tragic form (verbal, kinaesthetic, digital) in the sense that he embodies the break of form—the potential insurrectionary break that form always is.[62] In the Aeschylean play, deep time is felt in the stretched-out length of adjectival compounds, aggregates of letters, which threaten the discreteness of language, the avatar of digital discontinuity. For example, in line 109 (*narthêko-plêrôton de thêrômai puros*), where Prometheus describes the theft of fire that enabled humans to continue breathing ("And I hunt for the fennel-stalk-filling [fountain] of fire"), half of the line is occupied by the sesquipedalian compound *narthêko-plêrôton* ("fennel-stalk-filling"), whose length is further prolonged by the postpositive *de*. There is the effect of phonemic matter liable to disorganize itself into an undifferentiated sequence, resistant to word breaks and to articulation into distinct semantic units, eager to be *just* aerial vibration.[63]

If we see meaning constructed by syntax as an archival consignation, a series of orderly graphemic aggregates, whereby order consists of multiple regular intervals, the compounds that appear to prolong the sprawling of letters resemble an uncontrolled gathering of signs that, by banning discontinuity, explodes meaning, turning it into what may seem to be continuous gibberish. We can think of possible violations of the principle of discrete information in the digital realm as well: randomly overextended, tilted coding, hypertrophic accretions of symbols corresponding to the "wrong" succession of electromagnetic signals. In line 20 (*pros-passaleusô tôid' ap-anthrôpôi pagôi* "I will nail [you] to this crag far from men"), in which Hephaestus executes Zeus's command, verbally affixing Prometheus to the rock, the drawn-out verb *pros-passaleusô* ("I will nail [you]") is followed by the tetrasyllabic compound *ap-anthrôpôi* ("far from men"), modifying "crag." While separating Prometheus from the human realm, de-deifying him and, in a sense, dehumanizing him, the prefix *ap(o)*, which works as a kind of alpha privative, is also the glimmer of the rebellious manifestation of a counter-ontopower—mineral, verbal, or digital—that refuses to be colonized, to be contained in bound, controlled units. The juxtaposition of *pros-passaleusô* and *ap-anthrôpôi* furthers the formal impression of matter stubbornly opposing its own fragmentation, its division into units of meaning, just like the heap of dirt which Khan comes out of.

The discontinuity enforced by verbal and digital language corresponds to the breach that is the beginning of life, the rupture of the Symbolic. This rupture, which may deny the colonized even the bond of Symbolic belonging,[64] launches the continuous, raging loop that we see in the breathlessness of Aeschylean form and Khan's spinning kinaesthetics. When in line 799, as part of the prophecy he discloses to Io, one of his commiserating visitors, Prometheus deploys three bulky words (pentasyllabic, trisyllabic, and tetrasyllabic) to refer to the "snake-fleeced, mortal-hating Gorgons," the petrifying creatures the sight of whom will leave every mortal without "breath" (*pnoas*), we are primed to think of the two word breaks in the first line as short inhalations (799–800):[65]

drakonto-malloi Gorgones broto-stugeis
has thnêtos oudeis eisidôn hexei pnoas.

Prometheus ... snake-fleeced mortal-hating Gorgons, seeing whom no mortal man will keep his breath.

While rupturing the potential apnea of a petrifying burial with injections of *élan vital*, these inhalations simply prolong the breathlessness induced by the continual growth of Promethean form, its de-individuating conation.[66] Besides the imperative of a continued versification, of an orderly repetition of structures of meaning, there is a different compulsion, a competing drive, which combats the breathlessness of verse-making, the endless reproduction of language (patriarchally driven just as much as reproduction tout court and, of course, the archive and war). In *Prometheus Bound*, the long speeches of Prometheus and the characters who come to console (or threaten) him, are what keep the play going, while simultaneously making it static, petrifying it, that is, mimicking the calcifying, suffocating force of Zeus's paternal *logos*, the ancestor of the colonial power invisibly torturing Khan's performer. In a sense, the dramaturgical conceit of the play, which forces the same, protagonistic actor to remain onstage (in some kind of subaltern posture) and deliver lines from the beginning to the end, enacts the phallologocentrism of the sovereign, who always "enlists" its victim, paining his throat, potentially reducing him to silence through sadistic mimesis. But the emerging possibility of graphemes not entrapped in words, of characters spreading and spilling, going nowhere, refusing the destination of meaningful consignation creates the sense of what, following Moten, I call the break of form. This break, which fractures the verbal distribution of the sensible, is the unruly continuity, Fanon's Real "infinitude," the expanding rage that energizes the looping kinetics of Khan's solo Prometheus, his sensuously vertiginous, persistent siege of a system petrifying through partitions, distinctions, cutting intervals, through the very rupture that brings about life.[67]

While reading the long Promethean compounds in our post-digital, pandemic world, we cannot but imagine the possibility that, acquiring radical autonomy, they may turn into gibberish characters stubbornly glued together, into out-of-control accumulations of motley symbols—impossible to parse— into viscous bundles of electromagnetic sensation. Transforming the viscous ongoingness of Aeschylean form, the movements of Khan's body figure the "anomie" or the looping drive of the digital archive, the flux of continuous sensation that is repressed by its discrete logic, the very support of representation. In a sense, this continuous kinetics does not just figure, but it also activates the digital anarchivic, destabilizing the electromagnetic medium—in itself a colonizing structure—that brings the soldier to life, makes him visible, albeit contained and short of breath.

The Aeschylean play itself suggests synchronies and synergies of unstoppable bodily and formal kinetics, which foreshadow the digital anarchivic. In the parodos, the Chorus of Ocean's daughters, an assemblage of waves, of liquid motions as well as actorial bodies,[68] enter flowing through the air,[69] singing in iambic and choriambics, to console Prometheus, who has already been chained to the rock, petrified into his status of colonial pseudo- or non-subjectivity— "hang[ing] before us, immobile ... his face masked, his hands unable to gesture."[70] While in kinaesthetic agitation, aerial and aqueous, the Chorus seems to stall verbal form, its contortions convey the sense of a sprawling expansion in danger of paralyzing or petrifying *logos*, annihilating words into a viscous blob. In these lines, sung by the Chorus, compounds appear to visualize the eternity of Prometheus's punishment, his assimilation to the rock to which he has been affixed (146–48):

> ... *son demas eisidousa*
> *petrai pros-auainomenon*
> *taisd' a-damanto-detoisi lumais*

Chorus ... I saw your body drying up by the rock, with the wounds of these adamantine bonds.

The apparent lithification described here is precisely what makes graphic matter spin around, disorganize itself into a frenetic unboundness, with fading markers of semiotic distinction, with no intervals. While mimicking the oppressive immobility of the punishment, that is, the "untameable" materiality of Zeus's chains, the triple compound (*a-damanto-detoisi* "adamantine," that is, "untameably bound"), parallel to *pros-auainomenon* ("drying up"), arrests the logocentric flow. It releases the energy of a negative resistance—carried by the single letter *a* (the alpha privative)—which has the power to break, to "tame," the enslaving chains of the signifier and of signification through anarchivic indistinction. This indistinction can be viewed, in fact, as the self-sabotaging consequence of colonial power's all-encompassing grip, of its archival manic greed, intolerant, as it were, of its own partitions, of the logic of discontinuity that enforces it, in all its forms (digital or not). Modifying the word *demas*—the imprisoned body of Prometheus—the participle *pros-auainomenon* does not simply convey his eternal torture, but it also links recalcitrant poetic form with Promethean physicality, previewing Khan's spasmodic choreographic movements, their insurrectionary rebellion against the festering of colonial time.[71] This syntactical agreement also creates a connection between Prometheus's apparently immobile body and the marine Chorus, the moving (in)corporeal assemblage that is the most conspicuous *demas* in this lyric section. The formal expanse of *pros-auainomenon*, which comes to qualify or define this *demas*, codes kinaesthetics as a crazed accumulation, a looping swathe of material impulses (see the chiastic structure *petrai pros-auainomenon ... a-damanto-detoisi lumais* 147–48), an endlessly circulating stretch of unruly desire, just like the continuous undulation of the waves, on the verge of filling intervals. We could even compare the temporal register of this de-individuation to the "Oceanic lifespan," or the time of "undifferentiated identity" that, following Hortense Spillers's meditation on the Middle Passage, Habiba Ibrahim has proposed as a "theoretical condition of possibility for reimagining black age" as a "fluid time," like that of the waves, "comprised not of 'natural' development, but of being made and remade."[72] There is a sense in which the graphic expansion conveying Prometheus's petrification paradoxically mobilizes him, diffusing the Chorus's kinetic breathlessness, bringing forth an interruptive insistence, or an interruption through feverish continuation that is the aesthetico-political marker of this experimental play, a genuinely Promethean break of form.

When in his response, Prometheus voices the desire to be hauled down into Tartarus, he is not simply verbalizing a suicidal fantasy, or the wish to rejoin the *archê* of the Titanic world or of chaos itself—the shapeless mass that we may see reflected in the pile of detritus from which Khan's soldier emerges (152–55):

ei gar m' hupo gên nerthen th' Haidou
tou nekro-degmonos eis a-peranton
Tartaron hêken
desmois a-lutois

Prometheus If only he [Zeus] had sent me down the earth, underneath dead-accepting Hades, into the boundless Tartarus, with unloosened bonds ...

In the juxtaposition—only interrupted by the short preposition *eis* ("into")—between *nekro-degmonos* ("dead-accepting") and *a-peranton* ("boundless") we feel the force of an expressive form that longs to extend itself, to cover the whole graphic space with its own expansive convulsion.[73] This is a desire pressing against "bounds" (the *perata* negatively present in the word *a-peranton*)—not just the chains hurting Prometheus's feet, or the signifiers entrapping his tongue in the play's suffocating verbal cascade. These "bounds" are also the apparent breaks, the inhalations, that prevent a word such as *nekro-degmonos* from spilling over, from being precisely *a-peranton*. When later on Prometheus includes writing in the catalog of his technological benefactions to humankind—*grammatôn te suntheseis / mnêmên hapantôn, mousomêtor' erganên* ("combinations of letters, memory of everything, the Muses' mother, effective" 460–61)—he presents it as a *sun-thesis* of letters, but, followed by the maternal compound *mousomêtor'* ("the Muses' mother"), this "*com*bination" or "*con*signation" seems to jeopardize a priori any principle of mnemic distinction, of (paternal) semiotic cutting, conjuring an image of pre-linguistic maternal de-individuation, of phonemes affectively cemented together.[74] The compound forms *sidêro-mêtora . . . aian* ("iron-mother earth" 301) and *pam-mêtor . . . gê* ("all-maternal earth" 90) suggest a resistance to the cut, to the imposed separation of extractivist violence, metallurgical as well as somatic.[75] The formal lack of breath, a kind of strained breath in itself, or a *thumos*, that is generated in the somatics of the Chorus, Khan, and of tragic form can be reclaimed as an emancipatory and anticolonial gesture, which bring us back to Fanon's idea of "in-finitude" (almost a translation of *a-peranton*). The fantasy of occupying an undifferentiated, chaosmic space may thus implicate not non-being, but a kind of persistent being, the continued intensity of a *thumos* ("breath" as well as "rage") not confined to the moment, but pressing with no relief against the divisory cutting of every distribution of the sensible. The digital space that allows Khan to move before our eyes exemplifies this hierarchical partition, but it is also a potential chaotic or chaosmic formation permeated by a material desire that flows through all interstices, subjecting every division to a loop of appearance and disappearance.

When Io, the only mortal character in the play, arrives onstage launching frenzied balletic convulsions that make her seem the most direct ancestor of

Khan's performer, tragic form seems to be shaken, just like a digital surface, by electric, or electromagnetic, jolts. The word breaks that, in the play, pierce the sprawling formal matter are like the sting of the gadfly on Io, the girl turned into a cow—another victim of Zeus's colonial violence—whose appearance "as a wild and tormented dancer"[76] unsettles the static non-plot of the play. In this line delivered by Io in the midst of her dizzying lyric fit, bodily spasms ripple through rhythmic and formal contortions, just like seismic rifts or electric waves (580):

he he,
oistr-êlatôi de deimati deilaian

Io Ah ah, [me] wretched with fear driven by the gadfly . . .

As Sarah Nooter puts it, "The grating persistence of the [bug's] music is temporally limitless."[77] The interjection *he he*, which vocalizes the pain of the insect's sting, turns into sound the breaks in Io's skin/hide, rending the expanse of formal matter like the breach in the earth's entombment of Khan. But as though in response, the *e* sound stretches into the triple alliterative sequence *de deimati deilaian* ("wretched with fear") that ends the line as matter strives to reconstitute its punctured protective shell, its violated impermeability. The push-and-pull between the vivifying puncture and the sprawling recalcitrance of formal matter manifests a loop of formal contraction and expansion. There is a dissensual dimension to the verbal fragmentation provoked by Io's frenzy—a "queer" repudiation of "speech, song, and language"[78] or a cyborgic becoming.[79] Caused by a sadistic power deceptively taking on a minoritarian disguise, this fragmentation brings to mind the words of Fanon on his condition as colonized (pseudo-)subject, "I am being *dissected* under white eyes, the only real eyes . . . they . . . *cut away slices* of my reality."[80] The dissection undergone by Io as she swirls—a quasi-electrocution that "cuts away" pieces of her body—is, after all, an extreme version of the discrete, individuating logic of verbal, and digital, language, another manifestation, in spite of her apparently ex-cessive, deterritorialized appearance, of what Fanon calls colonial contraction. The phonemic continuity engendered by the triple alliterative sequence *de deimati deilaian* thus marks a rebellion against a marking, a formal and somatic breaching—not through reparation, but through a faint yet relentless motion toward the full being and duration of "infinitude," the onset of a sprawling wave that stretches out the body, yielding an unyielding, electromagnetic *orgê*, an expansive *thumos*, a raging breathlessness as a demand for a deep, unbroken breath.

The gadfly's sting looks ahead to the eagle's poking of Prometheus's liver— an image of the dissection that life is for the colonial subject, like Khan's performer, who is exposed to discrete electric shocks every time he is digitally brought to life and light breaches out from within the screen's metallic darkness. The eagle transforms Zeus's punishment into torture,[81] but, along with a breaking of *bios* or *zôê*, there is a breaking out of colonized life, which, like the rapacious bird, never stops poking, prodding, awakening, "enlisting." In his prophecy of Prometheus's future destiny, Hermes announces that, after having been enveloped and held tight in a kind of embrace by a rock,[82] Prometheus, "after a long stretch of time (*makron . . . mêkos . . . chronou* 1020)," will come back to life, that is, will be reborn into a painful loop, launched by a cruel dissection of flesh at the behest of Zeus's animal emissary (1023–25):

di-artamêsei sômatos mega rhakos
aklêtos herpôn daitaleus pan-êmeros
kelaino-brôton d' hêpar ek-thoinêsetai

Hermes [Zeus's eagle] will render your body a big rag, the uninvited banqueter, crawling all day long; your blackened-from-gnawing liver he will eat away.

Line 1025 comprises two other pentasyllabic compounds, the adjective *kelaino-brôton* ("blackened-from-gnawing") and the verb *ek-thoinêsetai* ("[he] will eat away"), which besiege *hêpar*, the word for "liver."[83] The two intervals that prevent these three words from forming a thick, de-individuated mass of letters correspond to the bodily tear inflicted by the eagle's beak—what, two lines earlier, is called *rhakos*, a "rag," literally a "rupture." The gap eaten out of Prometheus's body is homologous to the brief gap between the dual punishments of growth and consumption, the space where we find near-contiguity between the two rhythms in the loop between, on the one hand, a deadening or inanimating filling-in of tissue tending toward matter's closed-off impermeability and, on the other, the enlivening or animating carving-out of tissue tending toward life's gaping vulnerability.

For Bernard Stiegler, "Prometheus's liver, consumed by day and restored by night, is the Titan's clock ... It is the ceaseless process of différance in which time is constituted with that one coup of technicity that is the mark of mortality."[84] Prometheus's liver is the organ, physical and formal, of his mortality because it is what produces Symbolic life, what, in other words, separates the words *kelaino-brôton* and *ek-thoinêsetai*, causing the fundamental dissection, *distinctio verborum*, or individuation, that obstructs a phonemic infinitude, an atmospheric *différance* liberated from the enslavement of signifying chains. A digital Prometheus, the body of Khan's soldier is enlisted to experience the technologies of colonial-as-virtual life—not just the gadfly's sting morphed into electric shocks, but also the kingly eagle's sadistic play of expansion and contraction turned into the loop of "on" and "off," a digital lifedeath. Yet in the unruly temporal expansion, in the impression of sprawling duration that is created by the all-encompassing force of his *kinêsis* we can feel the claim of infinitude, the possibility that the word for "liver" in line 1025 may no longer separate or be separated, but become part of an anarchivic phonemic aggregate, or a non-finite expressivity.

I want to compare the aesthetico-political force of Khan's digital Prometheus to the use that Puerto Rican queer artist Ryan Rivera makes of video performance to conceptualize the relation between time and the colonized subject's condition through breathlessness. In a series of experimental videos, shorter than one minute each, which were shown at NYC El Museo del Barrio in 2002, "the spectator assumes the bodily effects" of Rivera's self-inflicted violence "through editorial techniques that speed up, overexpose, and loop the video frames."[85] As Rivera puts it, "Each video becomes a concentrated moment played on a relentless loop; a hyper-reality that I like to compare to the replaying of moments in our lives over and over again." For Sandra Ruiz, this technique "creates a sort of eternal immanence,"[86] which is exemplified especially in the so-called *Breath Piece*, where Rivera films himself holding breath in a close-up, staging and self-inflicting colonial violence, but simultaneously breaking it by expanding and contracting its temporality, emptying it out by turning it into a quasi-campy hyper-reality. "As [this] piece progresses," Ruiz observes, "his head and neck move at an increasingly frantic pace" and "the way in which Rivera holds his breath and moves his head/neck rapidly simultaneously stops and speeds up time, and doubly dirupts the viewer's sense of temporality."

For the Prometheus of *Xen*, the infinitude reclaimed by Fanon for colonized subjectivity amounts to an "eternal immanence," an attempt to turn somatic and technological looping into the intense insistence of a dilated and diluted temporality—just as the exhausting continuity of grammatical infinitives in the background of the "WE. DANCE." video casts the *colonisé*'s raging infinity as a spiraling overexposure, a self-expansion beyond time or an hyper-presence, which dislodges spectators from their safe position, making them breathless too, assimilating the colonizer to the colonized.

Akram Khan's digital and dancing Prometheus does not only show the dissensual potential of the Aeschylean play's apparently static aesthetics, but it invites us to rethink current theorizations of *dissensus*. Allowing us to draw out possible connections with anti-cathartic modes of tragic affect, it brings us back to BLM protests at a time—the summer of 2022—when the pandemic and colonization, synergically polluting the atmosphere, converge in the impossibility of an aftermath.[87] Jacques Rancière has seen dance as a primary expression of dissensual aesthetics, of how sensation can open lines of flight within the maintenance of the political status quo that is enforced by representation, with its constitutive division between subject and object, those who have part and those who have no part. In his discussion of the spectacular balletic performance of Loïe Fuller at the Folies Bergère of 1893, he observes:

> This new art comes from a new body, relieved of the weight of its flesh, reduced to a play of lines and tones, whirling in space.... The serpentine dance ... illustrates a certain idea of the body and what makes for its aesthetic potential: the curved line.... The novelty of Loïe Fuller's art ... is the invention of a new body: this body is a "dead center" in the midst of movement; it engenders forms by placing itself outside itself.... The veil is music because it is the artifice through which a body extends itself to engender forms into which it disappears.[88]

The bodily *ex-cess*, the self-extension into forms of disappearance that, for Rancière, marks the performance of Loïe Fuller—"whirling in space," turning the body into a line—exemplifies the notion of *dis-sensus* as *dis*-incorporation, *dis*-identification, the moment in which a system exits from itself. But the idea of disappearance also evokes the distinctive temporality of *dissensus*, which, for Rancière, "is always of the moment and provisional."[89] Seeking to combat the discontinuity of digital semiosis and unleash the unruly continuum of virtual sensation, Khan's convulsions translate the dissensual force of Aeschylean form, a *dis*-identification that occurs through the constant threat of linguistic de-individuation, non-distribution of the verbal sensible. But tending toward an unbroken infinitude in time, an uninterrupted right to breathe through, paradoxically, breathless, continuous *kinêsis*, the body of the colonized soldier also contests the temporality of Rancierean *dissensus*—a constant starting over, at different times, of rupturing moments.[90] Speaking about the surge of demonstrations, of peaceful *dissensus* on the streets provoked by the assassination of George Floyd, Angela Davis has voiced the need for prolonging the intensity of the moment, for thinking of "how we act in the aftermath," and how we respond to the "lost intensity of the moment."[91] With a "fluidity of role switching and the intensity and continuity of character portrayal," and "no 'gaps' for the spectator," the tradition of Kathak choreography alters the distribution of the sensible—"leading spectators to experience the heights of that which is neither actually seen not is directly seeable."[92] Yet it goes beyond the temporal limits of Rancierean *dissensus*—generating multiple points of disruption folded into ongoingness. Khan's digital choreography offers an apparently contradictory model of intensive temporality that does not get lost in the moment—it is a kind of durational punctuality, which expands a spasm of *dis*-identification through a frantically gesturing body prospectively swarming around the aftermath, about which we cannot stop fantasizing, and encircling the promise of the future (the end of colonization, of the pandemic) with its looping energy. This colonized Prometheus is "a swelling wave"—another phrase used by Rancière for Fuller—which makes an iconic tragic urge for never contracted *thumos*, lingering yet mobile, percolate through the narrow, electrified interstices of Aeschylean form.

9

Hecuba

In September 2015, several years before the pandemic, the conscience of the world was shaken by an image of Syrian toddler Alan Kurdi, who had washed up on the Turkish shore: "a solitary body deprived of life, movement, speech, indeed of a future ... the 'ideal' figure of the refugee."[1] The picture of Kurdi brings to mind Hecuba's son from the Euripides play that bears her name: Polydorus, who is also found on the shore, having escaped war but not the transhistorical neglect and greed of an inhospitable world. At a time when the reflexive motion of respiration has been confiscated from many—by the virus of the pandemic, wildfire smoke, or inveterate social afflictions—we may find ourselves clinging to the air itself, an insurrectionary gesture of possession in dispossession. Polydorus and Kurdi themselves lie on, but also cling to, the shore that has brought their dead bodies back to the world of the living and bestowed upon them some vicarious postmortem care after they were swallowed in the maw of a tempestuous sea unwittingly allied with necropolitical powers, ancient and modern.[2] In this chapter, I am concerned with the convergence between insurrectionary attachments to the environment and *survivance*, a non-normative survival through poetic form.[3]

There is a connection, even a morphological affinity, between, on the one hand, Polydorus and Kurdi as figures of the dead *xenos* and, on the other, the sea. Both the exile or refugee and the sea embody a horizontal extension that disrupts sameness, the familiarity of the *oikos*. A guest, a ghost, and, within the compass of his name, a gift, Polydorus is the event—unexpected, unbound, recalcitrant, "an-economic" (in the sense of disrupting the *oikos*):[4] he is the rupture brought on by the sea. To lay the groundwork for my reading of *Hecuba* and other contemporary texts in light of atmospheric attachment, I touch upon the encounter in the play between the sea and Polydorus and Hecuba—the displaced person (exile, refugee, slave)—suggesting ways in which tragedy circulates a posthuman, non-historical, non-hierarchical survivance through intensive formal surges. In heeding the surge of survivance, I am also thinking of the "surplus emotion" of in*sur*rection,[5] where insurrection entails not just "rising up against" or "standing up against," but also a springing forth, a coming into existence.[6] Imperiled by the pandemic and global ecological catastrophe, air as such becomes the focus of insurrectionary effort, of insurgent form, while providing the precarious medium for the transmission and precarious residuality of insurrectionary voices and a potential space for survivance.

As we have seen throughout this book, tragic form, with its destructive plasticity, its aesthetico-political impact, offers an opportunity to locate an expressive, quasi-impersonal agency, beyond the human subject, that resists or rebels. In this chapter, looking at the tragic as an affective category stretching from antiquity to the contemporary, a capacious carrier of micropolitical force that, through the phenomenology of poetic form, in its minute components, moves across genres and beyond programmatic adaptations, I will consider *Hecuba* in light of two contemporary works: Toni Morrison's *Beloved*, which is permeated by what she herself saw as tragic affect, expressed in lyric modulations that mingle the Greek Chorus with blues and jazz,[7] and Valeria Luiselli's *Lost Children Archive*, a recent experiment in autofiction—compared by a reviewer to a Greek tragedy[8]—that connects the traumas at the American border with the genocide of Native Americans. I will start with *Hecuba* and the Middle Passage, casting the sea as a space where past atrocities and their effects survive spectrally, anarchivally through present and future ones. I will use Luiselli's work to illustrate how atmospheric survivance pushes against archival survival and what has been called melancholic historicism. I will then propose a new reading of the finale of *Beloved*, pointing to formal intensities expressive of a surging survivance. I will conclude by retrieving this formal survivance at the end of Euripides' play, where Hecuba gradually disappears, then appears anew through an intensive surging into language, which diffuses the sensation of a clinging to the air.

Like Morrison's *Beloved*, Euripides' play concerns motherhood, slavery, and a murdered child who returns as a ghost—in a thematization of sea and ships that brings to mind the Middle Passage. At the end of the play, Polymestor, the killer of Hecuba's son, prophesies that she will ascend to the masthead of the ship transporting her to slavery in Greece, become a dog, and throw herself into the sea (1259–65).[9] For a contemporary reader, this suicidal plunge conjures the trauma of the Middle Passage, during which many newly enslaved Africans hanged, starved, or "drown[ed] themselves to end their living apocalypse, [held] their breath or swallow[ed] their tongues in attempts at self-strangulation."[10] In the same prophecy Hecuba is promised a kind of memorialization: the Greek victors will build an empty sepulcher named "the Sign of the Dog" that will benefit her enemies, Greek sailors, by guiding them as a beacon, helping them navigate a tempestuous sea (1271–73). The hoarse murmur and even barking of the sea, which are not mentioned in the text of the play but which we can glean from Ovid's account in *Metamorphoses*, are markers of Hecuba's further transformation into water, the sounds of self-undoing as resistance not just against slavery itself but against memorialization, the semiosis imposed on her.[11] Hecuba's monument has the same containing function as the ship—a function that Christina Sharpe, in her searing account of the Middle Passage, has captured with the phrase "slave ship hold."[12] But Sharpe has also drawn attention to what she calls "an insistent Black visualsonic resistance to … non/being"[13]—that is, a non/being semiotically imposed by the ship hold. This "visualsonic resistance" is supplied by the wake, by the "transverse waves … that run through the back … perpendicular to the direction of the motion of the ship."[14] A similar motion, by means of which "every instant that the boat is moving through water it has the potential to generate a new wave,"[15] can be imaginatively located in the aftermath of Hecuba's becoming imperceptible, her prophesied deterritorialization as a nonperson, as water. As T. J. Demos has observed in reference to John Akomfrah's 2015 video installation *Vertigo Sea*, the waters are the venue of "a spectropoetics" (a spectral poetics) "of colonial violence, slavery, and multispecies death," but also "a field of endless discovery."[16] The space of an "ecology-as-intersectionality," as Demos calls it, water is "an element that 'remembers the dead,' even though its abstract visibility suggests … a blank continuous surface."[17] The specters that constitute marine hauntology refuse to rest amid the ongoing tragedies of the now, as the violence of slavery reverberates through coerced migration and racialized capitalism. A counterpart to the final prophecy, the prologue delivered by the ghostly Polydorus brings onstage the "dead child" jettisoned into the sea who while setting the plot in motion immobilizes it in the out-of-joint temporalities of a beginning-as-ending and an ending-as-beginning.[18] Polydorus does not simply relay his own tragic death but pours forth the expressive waves of a marine and aerial "spectropoetics" (25–30):

> *kteinei me chrusou ton talaipôron charin*   25
> *xenos patrôios kai ktanôn es oidm' halos*
> *methêch', hin' autos chruson en domois echêi.*
> *keimai d'ep'aktais, allot'en pontou salôi,*
> *pollois diaulois kumatôn phoroumenos,*
> *a-klautos a-taphos . . .*   30

Polydorus The guest of my father killed me, wretched, for the gold and after having killed me he threw me into *the waves of the sea* (*oidm' halos*) so that he himself might keep the gold in his house. I lie sometimes on the shore, *sometimes* (*allot'*) *in the rolling swell of the sea* (*en pontou salôi*), transported in the *multiplying* (*pollois*) *to and fro* (*diaulois*) of the waves, unwept (*a-klautos*), unburied.

The endings of lines 26 and 28—closed by two words for the sea that are anagrammatically interchangeable (*halos/salôi*)—turn versification into a figurative rendition of the ebb and flow of the wave. The result is not just a mimetic game. With abundant liquidity, the phonemic sequence that constitutes the acoustic texture of lines 26–30 (*halos . . . allot' . . . salôi pollois diaulois . . . a-klautos*) dissolves the breath into the watery substance of a seascape, into an oceanic rhythm. At the same time, these aural waves are marked with traces of Polydorus's name (*pollois* "many") and of his wounded body—and, perhaps, in an uncanny anamorphic premonition, of Hecuba too, with her many filial losses, her ghostly presence signaled by *di-aulois*, an adjective evoking a "double course, as in a race in a Greek stadium, from one point to another and back"[19] It is as though, in a synchronic, spectropoietic conflation of the boundaries between present, past, and future, dramatic beginning and ending, the ebb and flow of the waves brought together the seaborne traces of Polydorus and those of Hecuba, already "in the air" but yet to come. Residues of Polydorus's and Hecuba's (in)corporealities stick to the waves rippling through the breath, attaching themselves to and becoming (dis)integral parts of the insurrectionary sonorities of the sea.[20]

Published in 2018, Valeria Luiselli's *Lost Children Archive* addresses the question of air as an anarchivic medium. In this novel, a married couple, both documentarists albeit with irreconcilable visions, set off on a journey from New York City to Arizona to rescue the children of a family friend, two of the many undocumented children forced, at the border, to inhabit a debilitating, if not lethal, liminality. Setting itself up as a quasi-novel or an "impossible" novel, as A. C. Alvarez calls it,[21] Luiselli's book is a narrative enterprise that stages an archival failure from which it draws anarchivic energy.[22] The marital failure that unfolds in Luiselli's metaleptic novel is precipitated by the unnamed wife's rejection of her husband's project: an "archive of echoes," as he calls it, an effort to record the vocal residues of lost Apache children, which he believes he can retrieve from the thick, parched air of a canyon. This effort is in keeping with the recovery imperative that sustains melancholy historicism, the view that, as Stephen Best puts it, "history consists in the taking possession of . . . grievous experience and archival loss."[23] This "taking possession," as though in a melancholic introjection, informs the husband's enterprise, but also the procedure that underlies, in the current practices of Western countries, the transition from *undocumented* to *documented*, which while removing the otherized foreigner from the traumatic condition of utter exclusion, throws them into the predicament of an alienating (non-)belonging—hierarchical incorporation and surveillance,[24] the metaphorization, or matterphorization of precarious lives, past and present.[25] The collapse of the marriage in Luiselli's novel coincides with the self-exile and the self-loss of the couple's own documented children, who, evading parental surveillance, pursue a fantasy of undocumented denizenship through a disappearance or an undoing that the undocumentable archive of the Apache children mimetically generates.[26] The Apache children, who keep their echoes buried, are echoed, in a sense, by their latter-day counterparts in the refusal to be possessed or repossessed, a refusal that constitutes a non-connective connection, a negative relation, a tragic rupture. This refusal to be possessed is at the center of Michel Foucault's "Lives of Infamous Men," originally conceived as a preface to an edition of private petitions to the king buried in the archives of the Bastille, each one requesting the state's intervention in managing a troublesome family member.[27] Here we find quasi-novelistic sketches, including many stories of marital conflict, which survive thanks to, and in spite of, the political power that sought to suppress, in Foucault's phrase, the "guttural cry" of the institutionalized.[28] As Giorgio Agamben observes, in his commentary on the essay, these lives appear like flashes of lightning, "exceed[ing] the subjectivation that condemns them to opprobrium": they are encountered as "laconic statements," "brief moment[s]."[29] Although Agamben does not dwell on his use of the adjective "brief" (*breve* in Italian), which etymologically expresses a break, almost a shaking sensation, as can be felt in the rough aspiration of the Greek cognate *brachus*, the rupture implied by *breve* can be understood not just as a space for the "cry" that tears apart the smooth surface of power or as the loss to which melancholic criticism cathectically attaches itself, but as a space of self-erasure refusing to be repaired, fixed, or filled in the gap between appearance and disappearance. This recoil, this desire for self-dispossession, manifests itself as something approximating the coarse vibration of *brachus*, which disarrays the voice, leaving an anarchivic impression *in* or *on* the air.

A performance of survivance, *Lost Children Archive* is a novel that, like the archival records of the Bastille, comes together by refusing to come together, showcasing its material basis: lists of objects that are, in turn, grouped in boxes, at once containers of the characters' belongings and places where the fragments of the narrative are (un)gathered. Both within and outside the story, the boxes are as metaleptic as the narrator—as we are invited to believe, Luiselli herself, who, in 2017, published an essay on her experience of helping undocumented people facing deportation fill out a forty-question form written only in English.[30] However, rather than bringing us close to the author, reinforcing our intimacy with her, the novel's metalepsis—i.e., the sense that the character *is* and *is not* Luiselli—mimetically produces a possibility of self-dispossession whereby we both *are* and *are not* ourselves.[31] In this state of self-dispossession, we can perceive the intensity of what lingers yet refuses to be possessed, the unrecoverable traces of the Apache children, the noise rupturing the air that refuses to be documented and is indifferent to borders. This almost imperceptible intensity exemplifies survivance, the Derridean concept that has been used in Native American studies to suggest the repudiation of survival understood as the endlessly recolonizing practice of memorialization, the so-called recognition politics.[32] Survivance registers as an overload that lingers, a kind of sensory surplus, not continuous but surreptitious, then surging in the moment, like a wave, an insurrection, as it were, the disorienting rasp of the guttural cry.[33] In the second half of the novel, the children of the couple seem to descend into a kind of Underworld, embarking on a journey between reality and imagination, accessing a world inhabited by the ghosts of Apache tribes. Here, as we read, "a woman ... appeared before them ... foretelling ... bits of stories that they could not afford to hear complete": she throws an orange at them, which "remained there, round, untouched" for many days and weeks, eventually "fermenting first sweet and bitter inside, then gradually blackening, shrinking, shriveling until it disappeared into the gravel."[34] Survivance emerges here in the formal surplus produced by the difference in repetition of "shrinking" and "shriveling," two synonyms of disappearance that generate a perceptive insistence, an intensive surge through their overlapping phonemes, an insurrectionary fermentation, a surging negativity, on the threshold between sound and smell, which does not simply circulate in the air, but bursts and, like a virus, lingers in the air. In a discussion of Max Scheler's "On the Phenomenon of the Tragic," Judith Butler has demonstrated that, for this phenomenologist, "the tragic depends on aerobic emanations," "has viral character," resembles "a heavy breath that gives off something."[35] In Valeria Luiselli's novel, survivance, the tragic form of its political aesthetics, is the "heavy breath" of an arid biome, which frustrates colonization, paralyzing its documenting imperative, its impulse toward cannibalizing inclusion.

I wish to use Luiselli's instantiation of aerial survivance to reconsider a similar formal phenomenology in the finale of Toni Morrison's *Beloved*. Despite the final exorcism, the ghost of Beloved, the protagonist's dead daughter, cannot be forgotten, and the refrain "this is not a story to pass on" suggests, among various possible meanings, that her story keeps going and cannot die.[36] The community that the ghost haunted cannot ever heal; it is not cleansed in the "Clearing," the communal quasi-baptismal ritual organized by one of the characters. The anti-catharsis in *Beloved* arises, at a basic level, from the impossibility of extricating the community from the ghost, whom we in turn seek to hold onto in our cathexis to the past trauma she symbolizes. In other words, what the community cannot extricate itself from is precisely the object of our melancholic desire; from the perspective of melancholic historicism, we experience this non-catharsis as healing.[37] But a more radical anti-catharsis may result from the impossibility of this historicist healing, an impossibility arising from the unbound nature of what we melancholically seek to "recover" and safeguard, from the ghost's resistance to containment or storage such as the "ship hold" of the Middle Passage. In the last page of the novel the ghost of Beloved manifests herself as "the rustle of a skirt" that "hushes" when the members of the community awake:

> So they forgot her. Like an unpleasant dream during a troubling sleep. Occasionally, however, the rustle of a skirt hushes when they wake, and the knuckles brushing a cheek in sleep seem to belong to the sleeper.[38]

Roland Barthes has observed that, in general terms, "the rustle denotes . . . an impossible noise, the noise of what . . . has no noise" and "makes audible the very evaporation of noise."[39] Taking a further step, we could say that the rustle communicates a push toward dissolution that defies the possibility of recovery, of recuperation. Eluding the containment of historical knowledge, of comprehension in its etymological meaning (that is, of "holding"), this "impossible noise" is enacted in the very dissolution of language. Meaning—what history seeks to dig up, re-assemble, and treasure—is undone in the flow of "rustle," "skirt," "hushes," "wake," "knuckles," "brushing," "cheek," and "sleep," and in the formal surge engendered by their proximity, by the surplus of "hushes" reconfigured as "knuckles" or "rustle," of "cheek" attracted in "sleep."[40] As words disintegrate into the liquid, sibilant, and guttural, one feels the *sur* (the overload) of the never fully comprehensible, never fully reparable history of slavery. In Morrison's coda the ghost's persistence cannot be separated from an unboundedness that preempts melancholy's storage operation, its surrogate possession.[41] The spectral persistence also runs counter to the possibility of an impression, the marking of a surface, of a *hypomnêma*, its own form of storage. The knuckles against a cheek are an aerial impression that leaves no impression, that pushes away before disappearing. The ghost of Beloved, in her final epiphany, may figure a haunting that, as it crisps the air, refuses to be more than a rustle or a passing touch yet provokes a surge of feeling.

The aerial insurrection that springs forth in the tragic finales of *Lost Children Archive* and *Beloved* also shakes the texture of a 2013 poem by Deborah Paredez entitled "Hecuba on the Shores of Da Nang, 1965," which will offer a point of entry into the ending of Euripides' play:[42]

> Again the sea-machines creep from the east,
> their Cronus jaws unlatched and pups expelled.
> The scene the same. Again. Again. The sand
> now boot-lace muck, the rutted shore resigned.
> No words will do. Laments will not withstand
> this thrashing tide. It's time for snarling beast-
> speak. Gnash-rattle. Fracas-snap. Unmuzzled
> hell-hound chorus unbound from roughened tongues.
> *Kynos-sema* keen-keen lash-kaak *nein* grind
> then ground and rot and reek and teeth and grief
> and gabble ratchet growl: custodian
> of woe. It doesn't end. Fleets on the reef,
> horizon buckling. To meet what comes
> the body cleaves from all that is human.

Accompanied by the clamorous motions of threatening war engines, of animal-sounding machinic contraptions, of robotic technologies of invasion and death, the landing of American troops in the coastal city of Da Nang in Central Vietnam evokes the arrival of the Greeks in Troy, as well as their invasion of the city through the cyborgic wooden horse, a container that imagistically looks ahead to Hecuba's first experience of slavery, her confinement in the Greek ship's hold. Her canine metamorphosis is anticipated and multiplied by canine soldiers birthed out of the hulls of the enslavers' machines. Hecuba's coerced entrance into a space of violent dispossession is retold as the attackers' occupation of the land, the sea, and the air—an ecocide announcing and supplementing, as it were, an impending genocide.[43] The invasion is, for the moment, primarily of the ears (of victims, perpetrators, and readers), subjugated by a deafening noise (human, animal, machinic), which takes possession of bodies, souls, environments, and the page. Not a monument, complicitous in surveillance over the sea, but a "custodian of woe," an anarchivic defender of loss through melancholic repetition, Hecuba is herself a noise machine. The hostile contraptions filling the air with and making their way through the sonic concentration of "sand," "withstand," "snarling," and "snap" wreak havoc—a "growling," "snarling," and "gabbling" barely distinguishable from Hecuba's rebellious barking, which, while objectifying her and making her abject, spread a wild *patho-logy*, a confusion of loud mimeticism and nonsensical excess.[44] Here a striking effect of formal *surplus*, enraged survivance, and posthuman insurrection runs through a tragic-lyric texture that overflows the page and the aerial space: "*Kynos-sema* keen-keen lash-kaak *nein* grind / then ground and rot and reek and teeth and grief / and gabble ratchet growl." The formal uprising of grief and rage fearlessly overturns or dismantles verbal boundaries, as showcased by the juxtaposition of "kaak" and "*nein*," which evokes *canine*, a becoming animal encompassing the harsh negativity of *nein*. The force of this negativity, a noisy response to ecocidal noise, is felt in the final, sententious statement "to meet what comes the body cleaves from all that is human," where the double meaning of "cleave" suggests clinging as well as separating, a separation that affectively clings, or a clinging to language that cuts through the air.

It is this convergence of clinging to language and air that I wish to locate in the final lines of Euripides' play. At the end of *Hecuba*, we witness a gradual self-eclipse of Hecuba through a continuous reduction of her speech: from a long monologue (1187–1237) to a stichomythic dialogue with Polydorus's killer, whose children she has, in turn, just slaughtered in revenge (1254–78), to a complete silence, after Polymestor has prophesied to Agamemnon his murder at home (1279–95). The prophecy of Hecuba's canine metamorphosis, her plunge into the sea, and her becoming a beacon for sailors occurs during the stychomythic exchange with Polymestor, which contains her last line, a response to the foreshadowing of Clytemnestra's revenge on her husband: "May the daughter of Tyndareus never act so crazily" (*mêpô maneiê Tundaris tosonde pais* 1278). The last word uttered by the character, who, in the play, loses a son and a daughter, Polydorus and Polyxena, is "child" (*pais*), while the line opens with a striking maternal intensity (*mêpô maneiê*). After hearing about his death at the hands of his wife, Agamemnon commands Hecuba to bury her *paides*, Polyxena and Polydorus, and sends the other Trojan women to the ships, to their enslavement (1288–92):

> *despotôn d'humas chreôn*
> *skênais pelazein, Trôiades; kai gar pnoas*
> *pros oikon êdê tasde pompimous horô.*
> *eu d'es patran pleusaimen, eu de tan domois*
> *echont' idoimen tônd' apheimenoi ponôn*

Agamemnon You should *approach* (*pelazein*) the tents of your masters (*despotôn*), Trojan women; for I see these breezes (*pnoas*) *favorable to sail* (*pompimous*) home. *May we set sail* (*pleusaimen*) to the fatherland (*patran*) with success, and may we see the affairs at home in good shape, liberated from this pain (*ponôn*).

While the abundant labial *p* sounds in this passage evoke maternal attachment—the same feeling that marks Hecuba's last line—there is "an incredible plurality of breaths,"[45] a striking formal blur between *potôn* in *despotôn*, *pompimous*, and *ponôn*. "Masters" (*des-potôn*) collapse into the pain (*ponôn*) they inflict—and the surplus of labial phonemes in *pom-pim-ous*, conjuring the sailing expedition, engenders a maternal impetus against the movement of the ship.[46] This trio of overlapping words (*despotôn, pompimous, ponôn*), a phonetic surge, a concentration of nurturing breaths, of caring vibrations, stages a re-encounter of Hecuba with her two children, the spectral, aerial *Po*lydorus and *Po*lyxena, whose names, starting in *po*, recirculate in mutilated disguise. The deterritorialization between *potôn* in *despotôn* and *ponôn* cryptically materializes *pontos*, a sea traversed by the micro-disturbances of over-signifying phonemes. Hecuba, we could say, redivides the words in the space where they move, invisibly, impersonally performing a maternal redistribution of the sensible. It is as though the dispossessed, now silent Hecuba were able to appropriate not just language but also its environment: the air denied to her by the prospect of suffocating slavery. Through the breath of Agamemnon, Hecuba's intermittent, surreptitious intensity creates a space of tragic posthuman resistance. Clinging to the air, even becoming the air, she seeps into Agamemnon—as well as us.

After exploring survivance in the modern tragedies of Morrison and Luiselli, we can view Hecuba's relationship with the environment—the sea or the air—as transcending the continuing spectropoietic movement of past, present, and future traumas and resonating with the ecocides of our time, with experiments in aeropolitics that cannot be separated from the planetary virological crisis we (will) continue to experience. Joseph Pugliese has discussed the "epidemiological effects" of the air pollution caused by IDF bombardment of Gaza.[47] In one account reported by Pugliese, 2014's Operation Protective Edge left behind "clouds ... loaded with large quantities of toxic gases and fine particles ... that spread into the air and ... led to many serious respiratory diseases."[48] In his description of the plague of Athens, Thucydides reports that the Spartans were accused by some of having poisoned the Athenian wells.[49] The Russian invasion of Ukraine has revived the ghost of Chernobyl, as we read in the blog post of a Ukrainian mother:

> The detonation of missiles and artillery shells is unleashing a great number of toxic substances, which accumulate in the surrounding soil, wood, turf, and other structures. Explosions in the air release chemicals that may cause acid rain, which changes the acidity of the soil and can cause burns to people, plants, mammals, and birds. ... During the intense fighting around Kyiv, the city was periodically covered in smog. ... As a person who vividly remembers the Chernobyl disaster ... I was scared by the news of missiles flying over the Chernobyl New Safe Confinement. ... Fear of an impending environmental disaster has forced many of us to leave Ukraine and become environmental migrants. We can assume that the ongoing destruction of industrial facilities and infrastructure, leading to the pollution of land, water, and air, will result in an increased flow of refugees from Ukraine if the war drags out.[50]

Hecuba's apparently voluntary silence at the end of Euripides' play foreshadows her impending enslavement, an act of aerial ecocide in its own right, for in inducing her to become water through suicide and entrapping her in a monumental rock, it deprives her of breath—the "vibration that touches, simultaneously, the living being and the world that surrounds it."[51] Yet by impersonally, imperceptibly haunting Agamemnon's *phônê*, Hecuba becomes breath itself, which affirms its force of admixture in the very moment that the law of master and slave seems to be laid down once again. Not yet killed, but already reduced to silence, Hecuba's body anarchivally "breathes itself into words, and finds some provisional survival there"[52] through the very enactment of respiratory admixture, of maternal de-individuation.[53] While Agamemnon naively records the favor of the winds (*pnoas*), Hecuba's own *pnoê* infects him both as a fugitive exhalation—entering, mixing with Agamemnon's imperious voice—and an anticolonial insurgency, a demand for collective justice that continues, occupying the narrowest, invisible but not inaudible, spaces of expressivity, even when ecocide seems to restore the illusory idea that breath is an individual privilege, a bounded right, a circumscribed possession, the dividing line between master and slave. Detectable in tragic form, Hecuba's survivance—like that of the Apache children or Beloved—is not simply a negative survival, or a call to repair or reconstruct, but a surplus, a surging, an inchoate insurrection, or "a glimmering of insurgency,"[54] that spurs us, too, to cling to the necessities of human and non-human life that are being taken away, to cry out for ourselves and others, to fill the air—never possessed but always possessing us—with our barking and murmurs, to surge and sway like a wave of the sea.

10

The Trojan Women

Visualized as "an ancient emaciated sled dog of filth and wrath," Hecuba became one of the faces of Greek tragedy in the second year of the pandemic, thanks to Rosanna Bruno and Anne Carson's *The Trojan Women: A Comic*.[1] In this graphic experiment, Euripides' most formally unconventional and thus, arguably, his most tragic tragedy—with adaptations ranging from Sartre's *Les Troyennes* (1965) to a 2016 London production by Syrian refugees[2]—is converted "into a comic populated not by persons, but by animals, plants, and things, each iconically commenting on the singularity" of the characters (Cassandra, Andromache, and Helen, besides Hecuba).[3] In the comic, the notorious episodicity of Euripides' play—a dissensual refusal of the constraining power of *muthos*, a display of form-as-crisis at a harrowing moment of Athenian imperialism[4]—is heightened by the decomposition of structure into precariously assembled tableaux, sketches, vignettes, in which the letters of tragic text, in voice bubbles, blend into the lines of drawings on the threshold between figure and abstraction, representation and non-representation. As Carla Freccero observes:[5]

> The graphic-linguistic form of the comic offers a literalization of irony's disaggregating interruptive effect on narrative cohesion, with its spatialized blocks of sometimes non-sequential text surrounded and at times overwhelmed by images.... The figural undoes meaning-making in a particularly ironic way, insofar as the text/image stages the disconnect between tragic narrative and comic juxtaposition at every turn.

One of the disaggregating, interruptive, juxtapositional features of this version of *Trojan Women*, a marker of the disconnect between text and image, tragic and comic aesthetics, is the *noir* atmosphere, the choice of gray tonalities, the literal chiaroscuro (a page layout constituted by the adjacency of black and white), and the resulting layering and generative confusion of elemental and animal shapes. I wish to dwell on this atmosphere, to understand how Bruno and Carson's *Trojan Women* interprets, instills, and gives urgent currency to tragic feeling.

It is through immersion, almost a drowning, in an overdetermined chiaroscuro that the reader experiences the prologue, a revelation beyond the play that is traumatically brought within, an apparent projection forward leading to the anti-futural backwardness of the Greek winners' destruction, their "unreturning return" (*dus-noston ... noston* 75).[6] The chiaroscuro embraced by *Trojan Women* is encapsulated in Poseidon's first intervention, on the first page, including a quotation from the beginning of Frederick Seidel's poem "James Baldwin in Paris" (1999), inspired by Baldwin's essay "Equal in Paris" (1955), which describes, in tragic form, his absurd arrest in the French capital:[7]

> The leopard attacks the trainer it
> Loves, over and over, on every
> Page, loves and devours the only one it allows to feed
> It.

A formalistic intimacy between words makes them fold into, almost eat, each other—"love" turns into an iterated "over," "devour," and "allow"—until "It," the compound of two black vertical markers, emerges as an objectified substitution for "I," engulfed in the blank expanse of white homogeneity, making a claim for objectivity against the inherently exclusionary logic of subjectivity. This intimate effect is the counterpart of the graphic chiaroscuro, a play of distinction and indistinction, a rendition of the freighted encounter of Blackness and whiteness, which confounds "trainer" and leopard, just as, in the comic, Greeks are confounded with Trojans, the colonizer with the colonized, the atmosphere with the surface of the sea.

As we leaf through Bruno and Carson's *Trojan Women*, we are struck by the overlap[8] between, on one side, a stormy sky folded into the sea, oblique lines filling the page with a thick flurry of spiky raindrops, or scattered ocean water, and, on the other side, a strait, shaped like a promontory, which breaks the white page, disseminating a proliferation of negative silhouettes, gray in various gradations, bodies lost in the tide, as the Trojan captives, along with the Greeks, will be after the war, like latter-day refugees and immigrants re-enacting (and anticipating) other traumas of the sea. The images of the punishment of the hubristic Greeks cast its executors, Zeus, Poseidon, and Athena, as graphic artists who will convert the sea and the atmosphere into blank pages to "blacken," "cram," and "explode," in Carson's words, just like "the very salt of the Aegean."[9] Visualizing the "dark breaths of the sky" (*dnophôdê ... aitheros phusêmata* 79), which symbolize the Greeks' impossible return in the Euripidean Poseidon's threatening prophecy, the blackened atmospheric (or marine) page enveloping a multitude of anonymous silhouettes also evokes the victims of the polluted air of the pandemic—and of the environmental catastrophe of which it is just one symptom. Another page and the stormy sea become interchangeable spaces, in which we encounter the precarious contours of expanding heaps of Trojan dogs mixed with, or morphing into, cows (and vice versa), which connect with (and, to an extent, already are) the dead bodies we see at the bottom of the page, but also rendered elsewhere in thin, angular, and round lines, or thick strokes.[10] The black and white page flattens out the depth of the marine abyss while transforming it into the bounded space of a mass grave, of a pit of white bones and pale skulls darkened by emptied eye sockets[11]—images that have been made too familiar by the atrocities of the twentieth-century and that are conjured by the mass graves of the pandemic and the Ukrainian war.[12] These are never fully ending catastrophes alluded to, on another page, by the barbed wire fences—instruments of necropolitical security and surveillance at the border—which force the human animals allegorized by dogs and cattle to experience their animality through the brutal treatment routinely reserved for non-human animals.[13] Immersed in the sea, the dots that constitute the vulpine figure of Helen amount to the points, or puncta, of ships carrying both enslavers and enslaved, which, according to a para-etymology of her name, she was destined to destroy.[14] Likewise, a portion of the face of dog-like Hecuba becomes a topography of lethal depths, her eyes pits where *no*'s resembling minuscule bodies are swallowed yet disrupt the smoothness of homogenizing destruction, of the all-encompassing sea.[15] The *no*'s that swim in Hecuba's eyeballs also phonically unsettle the threatening announcement "Odysseus owns you now," disintegrating "owns" and "now" into an iterated refusal virally amplified, circulating through a blackened page, a darkened atmosphere.[16]

The view of war and post-war victims as an animal pack or a heap (an undifferentiated plurality) is replaced, on many pages, by a network of animal portraits, individuals encompassed by Jacques Derrida's *animot*, the neologism he used to signal the vast heterogeneity within the homogenizing word *animal*.[17] In a choral play in which only the most prominent Trojan women are named while the Chorus's affirmatively de-individualizing force and collective opacity veers into a hierarchical division between the few and the "rest," these pages rupture the pack of the Chorus of Trojan-women-turned-animals into a lattice of mugshots, similar to the windows of a Zoom screen.[18] These windows are the miniature stages and (im)material cases of actors' face masks (or, more precisely, mask faces) in current online performances of Greek tragedy, which, despite the electronic abyss, strive to circulate the impression of a close-knit community, of intimate face-to-face encounters with their invisible audiences, an unseen beyond, and, conversely, with untimeliness (notwithstanding their spatial and temporal situatedness).[19] More darkly, the grids of faces in Bruno and Carson's comic bring to mind archives like the Tuol Sleng Museum of Genocide in Cambodia, where the photographic display is arguably animated by an effort to overcome the reiterative function of the picture and to "recuperate the individuality and humanity of the subjects through transforming those mugshots into portraits,"[20] that is, through transforming matterphorization into the face as a site of an intersubjective or interobjective encounter.[21] On page 16—and on many others that are framed by these pictures—we see the face as bearing an affirmative indexicality ("Here I am, I exist"), which problematizes Aristotle's and Agamben's opposition of *zôê* and *bios*.[22] The face invites us to construe *zôê* not simply as a thanatopolitical degradation of *bios*, but perhaps as the disavowed animality that grounds human existence in vulnerable flesh,[23] as a claim for presence that exceeds representation, that manifests itself even in an archival trace, as in the Cambodian Museum, in an impression that constitutes survivance. On the facing page, the announcement and depiction of the arrival of the

Messenger-as-raven, an ominous guardian of the Law of the winners, a keeper of death—"Oh! Here's the herald from the Greek camp with information about each one's specific destination"—turns around this indexicality, presenting pale, gray, spectral replicas of the same faces, which recall the defacing, racializing technologies of biometrical digitalization at the border.[24]

As a raven, Talthybius diffuses into the air the traumatic message of a non-futural future, or of a future of slavery that delays the moment of liberation from life. The announcements of the particular enslavements awaiting the Trojan women has the power of a bomb, blasting the environment, burdening the air with a thicket of lines that previews bodies confused with ripples.[25] The aerial violence of Talthybius's voice is also visualized by the assault of two trumpets tearing, whitening a black background, emitting futurepasts, while reactions in the Chorus's voice bubbles partially cover the animals' faces, defacing them.[26] Andromache, a tree holding Astyanax as a restful shoot, urges Talthybius-as-raven to "spit out" the truth about her child's destiny; his response—"He [Odysseus] told them [the Greeks], throw the boy off the city wall of Troy"[27]—precipitates "a blizzard of broken branches, twigs, and leaves,"[28] as the narrator puts it, a spiral of white curved lines, a vortex shattering a blackened atmospheric surface, the conflagration after a bomb has been dropped. Astyanax himself is like a bomb, destroying the ground where it lands and the continuity of the lives of those who deludedly trust they will safely be able to tread on it.[29] The conflagration is a shattering of life, but also of breath itself if we read this page alongside the Euripidean Andromache's farewell speech to Astyanax, in which the lyrical address "O sweet breath (*pneuma*) of your skin" (758) is preceded by a graphic depiction of his impending death, "falling a gloomy fall from a height onto your neck *you will* pitilessly *break* (*apo-rrhêxeis*) your breath (*pneum'*)" (755–56).[30] The disjoining and dissolution of life is materialized on the page as a spinning, hallucinatory fragmentation of unbound breath into toxic particles of a broken future.

When I enter the noir world of Bruno and Carson's *The Trojan Women*, I am reminded of the work that Pablo Picasso painted in the aftermath of the Nazi bombardment of the Basque town in 1937, *Guernica*, which has become the

tragic scene par excellence, circulating in multifarious forms—"placards on
sticks, elaborate facsimiles, tapestries, banners"—"carried in anger or agony ...
in Ramallah, Oaxaca, Calgary ... Kurdistan ... Cape Town, Belfast, Calcutta ...
in marches against the Iraq invasion, in struggles of all kinds against state
repression, as a rallying point for *los indignados.*"[31] Addressing the Spanish
parliament, Ukrainian president Volodymyr Zelenskyy evoked the Picasso
painting, "It's April 2022, and the reality in Ukraine is the same as in April 1937
when the whole world learned the name of one of your cities: Guernica."[32] The
Mexican artist Roberto Marquez painted his version of the image in Irpin,
Ukraine, on the site of a bridge destroyed during the invasion of Russian
troops.[33] In a 1939 poem on his painting—whose subject, for T. J. Clark, is
"death from the air"[34]—Picasso centered his thoughts around the image of an
eagle-bomber:

> in a corner at the bottom of the drawer
> the eagle vomits its wings
>
> on the skin torn from the house
> snaps at the window forgotten at the center of the infinite void
> the black honey of the sheet torn by icy flames
> from the sky the eagle vomits its wings[35]

"Spitting out" the bomb-like news of Astyanax's imminent execution as a bomb
dropped from the walls, as death coming from the sky, Talthybius the raven is
a revenant of Picasso's bomb-vomiting eagle. In *Guernica*, where women and
animals in *noir* seem to be facing, that is, staring at detonation and destruction,[36]
the scene is bookended by two screaming maternal figures, one holding a dead
infant,[37] both caught in a striking verticality, an upward motion that rigidifies
them, suggesting an arboreal transformation. For the mother on the right, her
mouth immobilized in a gaping scream, like that of the horse in the middle,
weeping is a form of persistent, perverse lactation, something similar to the
tree-like Andromache's weeping of sap,[38] which immediately follows the image
of the Trojan horse dripping blood, set against a black background framed by
choral animal mugshots.[39] The horse himself is weeping, his wood becoming
flesh, reversing Andromache's metamorphosis, modeling a liquid solidarity of

animality and vegetality.

In Astyanax's funeral, one of the final moments of this tragic "comic"—an experiment on the threshold between Euripides' *Trojan Women*, *Guernica*, and Art Spiegelman's *Maus*—Hecuba the dog seems to be defaced, or to deface herself, as the other Trojan women do by turning around.[40] Her defacement is a becoming Andromache, that is, a becoming tree, with the animal body now a trunk, and Astyanax's shield-shaped urn joined to it like foliage, a quasi-face and at the same time something that exceeds the face. The indexicality of the face is replaced, for a moment, by a more radical indexical *zôê*, by a zoo-power or a phyto-power, both visible and invisible, both transparent and opaque. This *zôê* is a form of tragic refusal seated in the chthonic—noir—spectrality of the root, the nocturnal flesh of the plant body, in the excessive, inhuman or more-than-human aesthetics of black and white.[41] What survives the child's lethal plunge into the abyss, the detonation—or the fallout of a virus's explosion in the atmosphere—is a *zôê* that is not defaced but denies its face, asking to be seen even as it refuses to make itself visible, gathering itself into a pananimistic commons.[42] We see in Hecuba an organism that reads variously as a woman, a bug, or a tree, springing before an aggregation of animal bodies, of heterogeneous parts maintaining yet stretching their contours into each other. The animals forming a vegetal assemblage turn their backs to us, invisible if insistent viewers, masking themselves with the backs of their faces and, thus, reclaiming a space for the obstructing force of the past, the opaque, the ungraspable, the repressed, in the face of pressing demands for a rushed return to an (impossible) future. The funeral of Astyanax, visible not as a human but rather as an urn, a pod or a cocoon, shielded from sight, places us before a surging viral pananimism fed by the breaths of plants and animals, by a phytoanimal congestion, which obstructs the human eye, confronting us with the clinging hindrance, but also the potentiality, of our animality and even our vegetality; our inhuman *zôê*; a different, inter- and trans-species sense of belonging.

Epilogue

How might we read Greek tragedy not just in pandemic times, but "moving forward," as many would put it? To offer a tentative response, I will direct my attention first to a novel released in the United States in August 2022 (three weeks before I submitted this book to the press) and then to a pair of moments in Aeschylus's *Suppliant Women*, which was performed on Zoom in July by Theater of War Productions with a chorus of Ukrainians.

An experimental novel between fiction and autofiction, *Delphi* by Clare Pollard traces the experiences of a classics lecturer through the various phases of the pandemic: outbreak, lockdown, and the lingering post-lockdown present, which we are too eager to characterize as post-pandemic. As announced by the title and the book structure, a mise en abyme of a projected monograph on ancient prophecy—in which each chapter is named after a different mode of divination, historically accurate or purely fanciful—the central preoccupation of the ego narrator is a desire for beyondness, for a world (or a non-world) beyond this one, fully beyond the pandemic, or for an otherworldly time. A "bleakly funny lockdown tale"[1] and a "domestic dark comedy" whose characters include the narrator's depressed, neurodiverse son and her disengaged, alcoholic husband, Jason, the novel synthesizes what a *Guardian* reviewer calls "narratives of the future": "What do we want to know, what do we not want to know, what do we have to believe to keep going and how much do we want to know the truth of what we have to believe?"[2] The reason for the titular fascination with the priestess of Delphi, the ventriloquist par excellence, whom, ironically, the narrator seeks to ventriloquize, is encapsulated by statements such as "I just really need some kind of . . . future. I just want to know there's a future," which are complemented and problematized by a clear identification with an anti-futural prophetess, Cassandra.[3] Epistemically grasping or feeling the sense of a possible "beyondness"— whether survival or destruction—is the escapist pathway chosen by the narrator, as though thinking an outside could remove us from our predicament. This outward projection, a quest for an elsewhere, is allegorized by the existential condition of the Pythia, able to air her prognostications only when she is ecstatically possessed by the god and is consequently "out of her mind"— "out of herself." Digging into the mythological archive, the narrator seizes on an image of the Delphic priestess as a bee buzzingly occupying the atmosphere, breaking pandemic paralysis with its winged motion, like "a tiny drone." The "bleakly funny lockdown tale," "the domestic dark comedy," is a version of Greek tragedy. Reflecting on the first months of the pandemic, the narrator speaks of "thousands of tragic deaths ... occurring beyond the *skênê* of our curtains," brought to public attention by the constantly rolling machine of news and social media, a kind of *ek-kuklêma*, as she eruditely adds, though one that does not display the corpses of those killed offstage. (The daily digital bulletins of deaths during the lockdown folded the container into the content, transforming the media into a mass grave.)[4] The future longed for by the narrator is also associated with the Aristotelian idea of *anagnôrisis* ("recognition"), reinterpreted, in the pandemic era, as a transition from denial and self-delusion to the realization of an atmospheric catastrophe.[5] At the same time, the domestic drama is shaped according to the distinct contours of Euripides' *Medea*, a play that is not just about familial tension, but also, in a sense, about the end of the world, a violent interruption of biological reproduction, the end of the human species (which I have read into *Antigone* and Aeschylus's *Niobe*).[6] It is not just that Jason is the name of the narrator's husband, whom she, following the ritualistic theory of the origins of tragedy, imagines as a sacrificial goat to lead "up to the altar."[7] Her self-assimilation to Medea continues, in explicit terms, as she exculpates the heroine as an accidental infanticide[8] and stigmatizes Jason's "dragon's breath," a phrase transferring Medea's iconic chariot drivers (who enable her getaway at the end of Euripides' play) to her husband's body. Domestic toxicity, an obvious equivalent of the pandemic, as I discussed in relation to *Alcestis*, causes a

"crazed thirst for fresh air," as snakes, which she claims to feel in her hair—
rem(a)inders of Medea's hissing rebukes of Jasons—turn her into an Erinys or
a Medusa.⁹ The narrator also depicts herself as carrying, at a women's protest,
a sign with the most explicitly feminist statement in Greek tragedy, Medea's cry
in all caps, a possible motto of a feminist commons—like the pluralized,
supplemented maternal *poli-as* (instead of *polis*) that I located in Euripides'
Suppliant Women—OF ALL CREATURES THAT CAN FEEL AND THINK, WE
WOMEN ARE THE WORST TREATED THINGS ALIVE.¹⁰

The Medea inhabited by the narrator of *Delphi* is one who manages to save
her child: in one of the last moments of the novel, she relays the conclusion of
her efforts to rescue her son, who had suddenly disappeared (and, as we
discover, had tried to take his life). After the narrator's many vain attempts to
reach her son, when his image eventually appears on her device, we read:

> I can hardly see him in that somewhere, which is dark and grainy. The realm
> of Hades. And Xander, my son, laughs a deadpan laugh when he sees who I
> am and then reaches to switch me off again and I can see his wrists, streaked
> in the dark with blood, and I hate that screen so much, that thief. I want to
> shatter the iPad howling and crawl through the smashed screen into that
> place where he is, but he's gone. . . . Tragedy is all about Unity of Place. He's
> not there, there's nowhere he's allowed to go—nowhere that wants him. He's
> here, I realize, in the house . . . where he always is. . . . And I'm bounding up
> the stairs like some maenad, crazed, screeching his name. . . . Until I open
> the door of the cupboard and look at him, then, Xander is neither alive nor
> dead.¹¹

The narrator's obsession (mythological, as well as epistemological and
existential) with the beyondness that we call future immediately induces her to
assume, erroneously, that her son has already entered Hades, the Underworld,
the quintessential space of "beyondness." Wishing to metamorphose into
Antigone, this Medea is tempted to smash the screen, enter the abyss behind it,
reconnect with her son through self-annihilation, and, thus, merge both with
the "content"—the news that, during the lockdown, materialized a stifling,
perpetual continuity—and the "container," the dark, mysterious, virtual, empty
storer of the news, the iPad. However, entering Hades is no longer an

option when it dawns upon her that her son may be somewhere inside the house, having withdrawn into an immanent Hades, a domestic Underworld. As she says, echoing but also subverting an Aristotelian principle, "Tragedy is all about Unity of Place." There is thus a sense in which Aristotle's normative thinking epitomized precisely by the hierarchical idea of "unity" can be reconceptualized as a refusal of an elsewhere—if there is a sense in which tragedy can save us, it may reside, paradoxically, in raising the possibility of staying in the same place, not pursuing the illusion, "cruelly optimistic," of a place outside.[12] The escapist movement behind the narrator's infatuation with the Pythia is turned inward, as it were, internalized as a psycho-physical dynamic, through her maenadic kinesis, an ecstatic behavior from within, a domestic ascent—instead of the Bacchants' departure from their home to climb up Cithaeron, and exchange the present of toxic domesticity for the beyondness of Dionysian intoxication. This inward maenadism—a middle ground between *mania* and the *monia* that I emphasized in my reading of *Bacchae*—is also reflected in the narrator's "breathing into him [her son]," as though she were exiting herself only to relocate into a version of herself. The tragic machinery of the *ek-kuklêma* exemplifies this self-contradictory dynamic: the outside becomes nothing but the inside of the *skênê*, which is itself the inside of the inside that is the bounded, closed space of the theatrical fiction (though we might imagine it as situated in the open space of an ancient theater). What I am suggesting is that, at the end of the novel, an escapist orientation toward the pandemic that leans into the future and the Pythian capability for predictive otherworldliness, that nurtures the fantasy of overcoming the borders of an eternal present by imagining, by linguistically externalizing, an elsewhere, gives way to domestic dispossession, to the paradox of turning maenadic in our homes, of inhabiting an ecstatic mood while remaining cloistered inside. This is a Medea who does not escape to Athens, but remains—not in the sky but in her house in Corinth.[13] The "remaining" that I am thinking of is not the equivalent of "resilience" or "endurance," notions difficult to separate from familiar if evolving neoliberal manifestations of hierarchical normativity. It is not simply the polemical recognition that the future is inevitably the projection and self-perpetuation of the present's sameness, nor is it only a commitment to messianicity, that is, to the refusal of identifying the future with any future present. It is, rather, a valorization of forms of sensing, feeling, knowing differently—what we can call a personal or political neurodiversity[14]—that derive from fully inhabiting the intensity of lingering, from modes of hyper-attention, or intensified apprehension, where the excess conveyed by the prefix *hyper* disrupts conventional, "productive" models of attention and reinvents care (a notion etymologically contained in the word *at-tention*) by developing a kind of hyper-focus that is also non-goal-centered, or even unfocused. This neurodiverse attunement can help us "loosen the object," as Lauren Berlant has put it. Berlant speaks of "us[ing] the contradictions the object prompts to . . . reconfigure it, exploiting the elasticity of its contradictions, the incoherence of the forces that overdetermine it."[15] I conceive of this loosening of the object as a way of loosening oneself while remaining cathected to the object—a practice reflected, in my intentions, in re-reading Greek tragedy for hyper-formalistic effects.

The kind of maenadic remaining I am proposing is a rebellious staying that unsettles the status quo from within, that views *insistence in* or *on* as a necessary step for reaching or provoking a breaking point; it is a gathering, a conflation of persistent breaths that causes condensation, the saturation before the storm. In keeping with themes and imagery emerging from my readings of *Prometheus Bound* and *Iphigenia in Aulis*, I am suggesting a non-escapist infinitude bringing about an explosion of the systemic inequalities that the pandemic has epitomized and aggravated. The suffocating no-sense that I explored in the first chapter, on *Oedipus the King*, can perhaps be thought of as an unsustainable, unbearable oversaturation containing its own immanent rupture. This rupture is comparable to the Pythia's prophecies, conceivable as outbursts ensuing from and blended with exhalations, vapors at Delphi, where the breath of the Pythia persists in the environment even after her death (a kind of survivance, as I discussed in the *Hecuba* chapter).[16]

A few days before the release of *Delphi*, the Theater of War Zoom production of Aeschylus's *Suppliant Women*—the quintessential refugee play[17]—with a chorus of Ukrainians, at home and dispersed around the globe, brought me back to the parodos, in which the Danaids pray (33–36) for their predatory cousins to be blocked by a storm and dispersed in the sea:

pempsate pontond'; entha de lailapi
cheimôno-tupôi brontêi steropêi t'
ombro-phoroisin t'anemois agrias
halos antêsantes olointo.

Chorus [O gods,] send them to the sea; and having met there the storm-beaten whirlwind, thunder and lightning, and the rain-carrying winds of the wild sea, may they perish.

The atmospheric density delivering death in the sea is displayed, in these lines, by the accumulation of exhalation effected by the compounds *cheimôno-tupôi* ("storm-beaten") and *ombro-phoroisin* ("rain-carrying"). The Chorus's voice enacts oversaturation: the compounds' formal extension reflects the gathering of air that morphs into a storm. The Danaids—who, in a later play of the trilogy, conspired to kill their bridegrooms, the Egyptian cousins[18]—are said, in the mythological tradition, to have brought water to the waterless Argos and to resemble ominous, wild fluvial or marine nymphs, creatures who manifest themselves through environmental disruption.[19] The refugees (ancient or modern, on the screen, onstage, in the text) mobilize a rupture through the continuity, the densifying of their breaths. When Danaus reports that the city of Argos has voted in favor of offering hospitality to his daughters, he depicts air roughened by an assembly or an assemblage of hands, which is, significantly, called *pan-dêmia* (607–8):

pandêmiai gar chersi dexi-ônumois
ephrixen aithêr . . .

Danaus The air bristled *with the people all assembled* (*pan-dêmiai*), with their right hands fittingly named.

Roughening or shattering the air—making it vibrate or shiver—figures shaking up homogeneity, breaking through the status quo with breaths allied to, pressing on each other, forming not a whole, but an effect of extreme congestion—social and political—which constitutes its own form of *pandemic.*[20] Through the voice of Danaus, the breath of singular pluralities—he is the advocate of the suppliant women and, in a sense, the spokesman of the Argive community—the air shaken by the laments and prayers of his daughters contagiously spreads into the all-male assembly of the Argives. In the context of the performance of the play in the current Ukrainian crisis—in which people stay and breathe together while being in the same virtual (non-) space—this *pan-dêmia* rupturing the atmosphere is not just the consensual assemblage of citizens' hands, but the plurality of exhalations emitted by a kind of diasporic, feminist commons, by Ukrainian women building transnational, transpolitical bonds.[21] As observed by Tim Ingold, citing Stanley Cavell, "Winding up on the inbreath, and unwinding on the outbreath, the soul as vortex is a place not of rest but of tumult, adrift on the current of air that it temporarily pulls aside, into the 'whirl of organism,' prior to its re-release."[22] To reimmerse oneself, affectively and interpretively, in the contagious oversaturation of Greek tragedy is to breathe the sensation of this pandemic— a curdled, clinging aggravation that, densifying the atmosphere, portends not a singular "storm-beaten whirlwind," but a proliferating, unbound agitation, a force of de-individuation that confounds the homogenization of time, never ceasing to bristle the air.

Notes

Introduction

1   Higgins 2021, 128.

2   Here and throughout the book, I am aware of the inherent risks and the fundamental impossibility of ever positing a *we*—especially in these pandemic times, which have only heightened socio-economic differences. Like Tremblay (2022, 138), following Singh (2017), I believe that "the pronoun *we* is inescapable in critical theoretical projects committed to social justice." Singh (2017, 173) says: "My own 'we' . . . is a question as much as it is a hopeful summons to the (always imagined) future readers who might be or might become invested in collective reorientations in the world."

3   On the "heroic" role imposed on "essential workers," see Osmundson 2022 (ch. 6). See also chapter 3.

4   The words "tragedy" and "tragic," in the more familiar sense, occur frequently in reference to Covid-19. See, e.g., Schultz 2021, 10 and 12: "The social reactions to the novel coronavirus [are] related to the helplessness societies are experiencing in the face of another civilizational tragedy: climate change."

5   Osmundson 2022, 47.

6   Danowski and Viveiros de Castro 2017, 15: "Humankind . . . is a catastrophe: a sudden, devastating event in the planet's biological and geophysical history." Sharma (2020) observes: "While Covid-19 is figured as an 'invader,' an outsider determined to destroy 'us,' it is evident that it has arisen from inside the globally operative system of nation states and capital. . . . It is . . . a pathogen whose basis of existence is in the global systems of capital accumulation and governance." See also Povinelli 2020 on the virus as a manifestation of the destructively extractivist power of "late liberal capitalism."

7   Osmundson 2022, 42.

8   Osmundson 2022, 114.

9   On the concept of *lifedeath*, see Derrida 2020; on the applicability of this concept for a theorization of Greek tragedy's anti-cathartic, anti-reparative aesthetics, see Telò 2020b.

10 See Telò 2020b, 23–24 and 279–82.

11 See Telò 2020b; see also Telò 2016 (on contagious aesthetics in comedy's relation to tragedy). Plague and contagion are, of course, essential to the imagistic universe of tragedy: see, e.g., Sophocles' *Oedipus the King, Women of Trachis,* and *Philoctetes.* See Honig, forthcoming, on *Hippolytus* and what she calls "a democratic theory of contagion," a "contagion of rights" (in the phrase of Patricia Williams). In this book, I do not pursue any sustained connections between tragic plays and plagues that afflicted classical Greece, in particular the Athenian one in the second year of the Peloponnesian war: for such an approach, see Mitchell-Boyask 2007.

12 Baudrillard 1989, 33–34.

13 See, e.g., Sanyal 2020, Young 2020, and Osmundson 2022.

14 While I am sympathetic with Jennifer Wallace's attempt to problematize the conventional divide between tragic "events" and tragic texts/performances—in a book that was produced before the pandemic (2020)—my focus is not primarily on the pandemic *as* a tragic event, or a (Greek) tragedy, but on possibilities of re-reading tragedy *through* the pandemic, and vice versa.

15 Sontag 2001 (the 1978 book *Illness as Metaphor* was supplemented in 1989 by *AIDS and Its Metaphors*) and Wallace 2020, 19.

16 Among these productions, one should mention the Zoom performances of scenes from various Greek tragedies organized by Theater of War Productions and Out of Chaos since the beginning of the pandemic; Wayne Shorter and esperanza spalding's *. . . (Iphigenia)*, an opera performed in Boston, New York, Washington, Berkeley, and Los Angeles in spring 2022: see Morales and Telò 2023; and Loukia Alavanou's virtual reality version of *Oedipus at Colonus* at the fifty-ninth Venice Biennale, which reimagines Sophocles' play in a Roma community in the region of Nea Zoi, west of Athens: see Sanyal, forthcoming.

17 See Osmundson 2022, 22: "Viruses were discovered as an invisibility: a deadly force we couldn't explain. Born from failure, how queer." On the queerness of tragic feeling, see Telò 2020b, 23–25, 279–82, and passim; Armstrong et al. 2022; and Telò and Olsen 2022. On "reading into," see Doyle and Getsy 2013.

18 On anachronism and practices of reading antiquity, see esp. Bassi and Euben 2010, ix; The Postclassicisms Collective 2020 (ch. 2.8); Telò and Olsen 2022; and Telò 2023a (Introduction). I agree with Eccleston and Padilla Peralta (2022) that the philological ideal of a textual analysis "disembedded from the world around it, untainted by contemporary feelings, biases, and agendas" reinscribes well-established practices of race-based disciplinary exclusion in classical studies. See also Rankine (2019, 353), who observes that "pure philology, unmixed with contemporary realities, is and always has been a pretense, and pernicious lie."

19 My privileged position—as a white, tenured cis-man—makes my experience of dispossession incommensurable with that of people of color and the so-called essential workers facing the pandemic in inveterate, systemic conditions of inequality and oppression.

20 On literary/poetic form as a crisis, see, with various inflections, de Man 1983, 8; Mallarmé 2001 (on which see, esp., Felman 1992, 19); Moten 2018b, 17, 36, and 51; Spillers 2020, 683; and Telò 2023a (Introduction).

21 On form as care, see Colon 2016; on interobjectivity as a posthumanist reconceptualization of intersubjectivity, see Chen 2011.

22 Moten 2017, 266.

23 I agree with Kornbluh (2021, 265) that close reading asks "of literature not literalism but mediacy, and giving in return not extracted direct messages of immediate saliency, but affirmative regard for the constructions of alternative conceptuality."

24 As Batuman (2020) observes, Greek tragedy subjects viewers and readers to a "cognitive overdrive, toggling between the text and the performance, between the historical context, the current context, and the 'universal' themes."

25 J. Butler 2021a.

26 Osmundson 2022, 18.

27 Queer unhistoricism entails conceiving of the experience of reading as an encounter with a "shifting web in which proximity and distance, similarity and difference are constantly (re-)negotiated and in which changing desires give rise to moments of communion" (Matzner 2016, 192). On Greek tragedy and reperformance, see Telò 2017 and Uhlig 2019.

28 Batuman 2020. In 2022, Theater of War Productions staged Aeschylus's *Suppliant Women* with Ukrainian performers: https://theaterofwar.com/schedule/the-suppliants-ukraine. See Epilogue.

29 On tragedy and the digital, see chapter 8. I intend "Real" in the Lacanian sense, "as what is located before and beyond symbolization, that is, before the entrance into language that constitutes the subject after birth and defines it as inescapably alienated" (Telò 2020b, 20–21); according to Johnston (2018), the Real "becomes . . . a transcendence troubling and thwarting Imaginary–Symbolic reality . . . from without as well as an immanence perturbing reality/language from within." Crockett (2018, 86–87) suggests a connection between this Real and Timothy Morton's notion of the hyperobject, such as "the Solar system, a black hole, an oil field . . . the biosphere . . . global warming" (83) and Covid-19, as we will see in chapter 1.

30 "Can Greek Tragedy Get Us through the Pandemic? A Theater Company Has Spent Years Bringing Catharsis to the Traumatized. In the Coronavirus Era, That's All of Us."

31 With reference to H. White (1978, 8), David Scott (2004, 134–35) says that "where the Romantic mode of historical emplotment rides a rhythm of progressive overcoming and ultimate victory over the world's misfortunes, the tragic mode offers an agonic confrontation that holds out no necessary promise of rescue or reconciliation." On anti-catharsis, see Telò 2020b; see also Armstrong et al. 2022 and Weiberg 2022. In light of the pandemic, Taplin (2022, 39) critiques Aristotle's catharsis, but valorizing Schiller's idea of "inoculation," he proposes the moralistic idea that "nobody can be exempted from trouble and grief, but through tragedy people may be strengthened to face up to them."

32 As J. Butler (2022, 2) observes, "We cannot register a global phenomenon such as the pandemic without at once registering . . . inequalities and, in this current case, seeing those inequalities intensify."

33 Chen 2020. See also Livingston 2022 on comorbidities.

34 See chapters 8 and 9.

35 J. Butler 2022, 64. Differently from classical phenomenology, critical phenomenology provides a "rigorous account of how contingent historical and social structures . . . play a constitutive role in shaping the meaning and manner of our experience" (Guenther 2020, 12).

36 J. Butler 2022, 112.

37 J. Butler 2022, 22; Scheler 1954.

38 From a Lacanian perspective, Fradenburg (2013, 170) suggests that "respiration marks our constitutive permeability, our embeddedness in the Øther." In his theorization of breathing aesthetics, Tremblay (2022, 14) states that "we become ourselves . . . by incorporating a milieu into which we are also pouring ourselves." Heine (2021, 3) says that "in ongoing excessive exhalations, the subject continually outbreathes itself."

39 J. Butler 2022, 25.

40 Marx 1978, 577. Taplin (2022, 40) says that Greek tragedy "is most effectively experienced by being shared in the live, *breathing*, intangibly tangible theatre" (my italics). While I am less ready to accept that only performance in an open space (as opposed to "closed" performances, including reading) can give us the most effective experience of Greek tragedy, I am intrigued by the implicit suggestion that this experience may encompass a pregnant feeling of *breathing* or *not breathing*.

41 Derrida defines "hauntology" as that which "begins by coming back" (1994, 11): see chapter 1.

42 Here and elsewhere, by "pandemic times" and similar expressions, I refer to the acute phase (lockdowns, closures, high mortality rates, uncertainty) without excluding the present moment, as of summer 2022 (readily available vaccines, at least in the United States, and few restrictions on behavior, reduced mortality, together with persistently high rates of transmission and no end in sight).

43 Szendy 2021, 63–64.

44 Ward 2020.

45 J. W. Scott 2022, 54.

46 Passavant 2021, 187.

47 Gossett and Hayward (2020, 533) remark that although for some "the time of AIDS is
... either an obliterated past tense or an HIV+ pharmacological futurity, still 'AIDS
remains. AIDS continues.'" See also Gill-Peterson and Lavery 2020, 638.

1 Oedipus

1 Commenting on Albert Camus's *The Plague*, Sanyal (2020) observes, "We are all
carriers of the plague, condemned to the exposure and aggression of relationality
itself." On relational ontology in a feminist perspective, see esp. J. Butler 2001 and
2015a; see also Cavarero 2016. For critical-phenomenological perspectives, see Landes
2020, Marratto 2020, and Sullivan 2020. One could also say that the pandemic gives us
a tragic sense of "how the world touches us," as Merleau-Ponty (1964, 19) remarked.
For an engagement with Merleau-Ponty in an expansive theorization of our pandemic
times, see J. Butler 2022.

2 Nancy 2020, 79.

3 See https://theaterofwar.com/projects/the-oedipus-project.

4 In Timothy Morton's definition (2013, 27–29), hyperobjects are things—like a black
hole, the biosphere, or the solar system—that are "massively distributed in time and
space relative to humans." "More than a little demonic," they "leer at [us], menacingly,"
disrupting the hierarchy between subject and object, giving us a sense of our own
objecthood.

5 For this definition, see Irigaray (1999, 14), discussing Heidegger's exclusion of air from
philosophical attention; see also 2004, 166, and 2016 (in Irigaray and Marder 2016,
24–25), on breath as the quintessential principle of relationality. Coccia (2019, 47) says
that "the air we breathe is not a purely geological or mineral reality ... but rather the
breath of other living beings. It is a byproduct of 'the lives of others.'" On air as a
sensory means of relationality in Henry James, see Zhang 2020, 75–76; Zhang (2018,
127) suggests that the atmosphere "is a matter of finding one's body not only affected
by its surroundings but also not easily demarcated from them." In this sense, one can
say that atmosphere overlaps with the concept of affect: see, e.g., Anderson 2009 and
Stewart 2011.

6 Menely 2009, 95.

7 Buser 2017, 5. See Derrida 1994. Hauntology is a form of relational ontology in its own
right. As Hägglund (2008, 82) notes, while the idea of ontology presupposes "being in
terms of self-identical presence," the specter "has no being in itself but marks a relation
to what is *no longer* or *not yet.*"

8 In chapter 3, we will see how forms of intense, haptic lingering in the atmosphere of
reduced affective bonding caused by the lockdown can offer a sense of overanalyzed
time that conveys a different if equivalent feeling of achrony.

9 See Pallasmaa 2017, 25: "Atmosphere emphasizes a sustained being in a situation rather than a singular moment of perception." On anaesthetic time, see Heyes 2021. See also chapter 3.

10 See, differently, Taylor 2016, 79: "Atmospheric phenomenology blends the faculties of perception, interfusing the registers of sensuous experience artificially divided by the idea of multiple discrete senses."

11 An exploration of Victorian and modernist "atmospherics" has been at the center of recent discussions of Conrad, Dickens, James, and Woolf: see Abramson 2018, Pizzo 2014, and Zhang 2018 and 2020.

12 On Thucydides, see esp. S. Butler 2011, 53–56. On Lucretius's description, see esp. Porter 2003 and Greenblatt 2020.

13 See Mitchell-Boyask 2007, 56–66, and Meinel 2015, 46–73; see also Michelakis 2019 (on the lexicon of the plague in Sophocles' play). Knox (1956) famously used the Theban plague and its apparent resonances with Thucydides' account of the Athenian plague as an argument for dating *Oedipus the King*; against this suggestion, Taplin (2022, 34) avers that the premise of "a city suffering from widespread and devastating illness" would have been "too close to . . . immediate experience to work as tragedy."

14 See Berlant 2011, 80, on trauma circulating in the air.

15 See lines 220 *aetheris puri* and 650–51 *spiritus puros dabit / vitalis aura* ("life-giving air will provide pure breaths").

16 Alfaro 2021, 137, 144, 176, and 178.

17 Alfaro 2021, 176. On old and new colonialisms as pollution, see Liboiron 2021.

18 Culler 1988.

19 Goldhill 1996, 157. For deconstructive and psychoanalytic readings of *Oedipus the King*, see esp. Goodkin 1982, Ahl 1991, Pucci 1992, Segal 1996, as well as Goldhill 1984 and 1996; see also Telò 2020b, 250–60.

20 Goldhill 1984, 184.

21 See esp. Vernant 1978, 483–84; Edmunds 1988; and Pucci 1992 (ch. 5).

22 On *oidêma* in the treatise *On the Sublime*, see below.

23 Culler (1988, 3) observes that "puns present the disquieting spectacle of a functioning of language where boundaries—between sounds, between sound and letter, between meanings—count for less than one might imagine and where supposedly discrete meanings threaten to sink into fluid subterranean signifieds too undefinable to call concepts." One could say that one of my goals is to refashion Culler's liquid image as an aerial one.

24 Peponi 2018, 167. Peponi refers to Gumbrecht's theorization of *Stimmung* as an affective atmosphere: see Gumbrecht 2012.

25 Porter 1986. See Vitruvius, *On Architecture* 5.3.1–2: "At the play citizens with their wives and children remain seated in their enjoyment; their bodies motionless with pleasure have the pores (*venas*) opened (*patentes*). On these *the breath of the wind* (*aurarum flatus*) falls, and if it comes from marshy districts or other infected quarters, it will pour (*infundent*) *harmful breaths* (*nocentes spiritus*). If therefore special care is taken in choosing a site, *infection will be avoided* (*vitabuntur vitia*)." In the same passage an air-based concern with the spatial orientation of the theater emerges: "When the sun fills the circuit of the theatre, the *air being enclosed within the curved space* (*aer conclusus curvatura*) and not having the opportunity of circulating, revolves and becomes heated; hence it blazes, burns up, draws out and reduces the moisture of the body" (trans. F. Granger, adapted). Porter sees traces of atomistic, especially Democritean, and Hippocratic traditions in this account.

26 Irigaray (2004, 169) advocated a "return to an awareness and to a cultivation of the breath before and beyond any representation and discourse." On *peri-echon*, see Spitzer (1942), who borrows the term from the Hippocratic corpus and pre-Socratic philosophy to establish an equivalence between "ambience" and style.

27 I borrow this formulation from Ngai (2015), who uses it to interpret phrases in Marx's *Capital* and Rob Halpern's *Music for Porn* (2012) such as "aura hardening" and "nature hardens," which attribute a visceral concreteness to "conspicuously *intangible*" entities. I am sympathetic with the deconstructive materialism of Terada (2007, 177), who, in the wake of Paul de Man, observes that every writing "machinery resubscribes to systems of mind that understate the complexity, not only of reading, but of the very idea of sensory perception."

28 The quotation repurposes Foucault's account of the eighteenth-century rhetoric of infection (1965, 203). On this Foucauldian passage, see Sarasin 2008, 271–72. On Foucault's Oedipal (and Deleuzian) virality, see Telò 2023b.

29 Swift (2010, 75) observes that "from the beginning of the play, we find an ambiguity in the way the *paian* is deployed, and a sense that its normal associations with divine beneficence have somehow become *tainted*" (my italics).

30 See R. Parker 1983, 218, on the Hippocratic notion that plagues are provoked by aerial infection; on this theme in the Hippocratic and post-Hippocratic medical traditions, see esp. Pinault 1986 and Pappas et al. 2008. See also Mitchell 2011, 536–38, and Jouanna 2012.

31 Fretwell 2020, 159.

32 Derrida defines auto-immunity as a process that "consists for a living organism . . . of protecting its self-protection by destroying its immune system" (2002a, 80n27).

33 Morton 2012. Connolly (2019, 44) observes that "Freud's reduction of the Oedipus story to an Oedipus complex has been infected by plagues and droughts—elemental features of existence already appreciated by the wise Sophocles."

34 "Both prayers to Apollo and lamentation," as observed by Finglass (2018, 168).

35 See Dickens on London: "The streets were so full of dense brown smoke that scarcely anything was to be seen" (*Bleak House* [1853]).

36 See Levinas 1998, 3; for discussion, see Coe 2014.

37 Hornby 2018.

38 Meinel (2015, 60) suggests that in this line τεθραμμένον χθονί (*tethrammenon chthoni*) points to Oedipus himself.

39 *Pa-* . . . *pa-* . . . *po-* . . . *pô-* . . . *po-* . . . *pô-* . . . *po-* . . . *pa-* . . .

40 *Phoberan phrena* is the direct object of *pallôn* ("shaking"), which appears after *deimati*. In omitting this participle, I aim to convey the quasi-autonomy—or alternative syntax—of the chiasmus.

41 See Telò 2020b, esp. 250–60.

42 Conrad 2002, 105.

43 See lines 28–29 "the most hateful plague . . . by which the house of Cadmus is emptied out."

44 For a different analysis of this passage, see Telò 2020b, 258–59.

45 See Telò 2020b, 251–52, on line 786.

46 *To pneuma athroon* and *athroon asthma* are, in fact, Hippocratic technical terms for difficulty in breathing: see, e.g., Thivel 2005.

47 See Ahl 1991, 67 and 255–56, on the "laity" of Cadmus in line 144.

48 *Etymologicum Magnum* 199.24–31, discussed by Karakantza (2020, 24).

49 On the punning resonance between *Laios, palai*, and *palaios*, see Ahl 1991, 254–57.

50 See Derrida 1988 and 1991 on the interchangeability of sensory orifices.

51 The distribution of the sensible is the system of perceptual taxonomy that shapes the social order as a hierarchical *consensus*: see Rancière 1999.

52 Finglass 2018 ad loc.

53 See Morton 2013.

54 Bennett 2020, 63.

55 I borrow this term from Tanner (2016), who uses it in reference to forms of musical hauntology typical of late capitalism: "Usually focusing on one fragment of an entire song, a vaporwave producer will then loop that fragment *ad nauseam*" (7).

56 Segal (1996, 163), referring to Freud (my italics).

57 On the notion of the right to opacity, see Glissant 1990.

58 Mackey 1993, 235.

59 For a theorization of the wild, see Halberstam 2020.

60 I am repurposing a formulation of Lenssen (2020, 73).

61 As a prefix, *ana* can connote "delay," as in *ana-ballô*.

62 Pseudo-Longinus, *On the Sublime* 1–3. Porter (2016, 440n166) suggests that "pomposity and turgidity . . . are for Longinus a natural hazard of sublimity, but a mere shade away from laudable *onkos*"; however, the critique appears to concern "inopportunity" (*to para melos oidein*).

63 Pseudo-Longinus, *On the Sublime* 3.

64 On the aerial implications of *meteôros* ("hanging in the air"), see Porter 2016, 440–41. On medical and "scientific" language in Pseudo-Longinus's theorization, see Arthur-Montagne 2017.

65 I am here paraphrasing Berlant (2022, 101), commenting on the poetry of Juliana Spahr: "Verses scale up, moving across mesosphere, stratosphere."

66 Segal (1999, 211) observes: "On the verge of discovering the truth concealed in his name, Oedipus is preoccupied with naming. . . . His own name is a kind of antiname: it is a 'reproach' or 'insult' (*oneidos*). It is the 'insult' of his name which, as he laments at the end, he will pass on to his daughters (1494, 1500)." See also Pucci 1979, 130, and Ahl 1991, 180–81.

67 On *hodous*, see Goldhill (1984, 185), who observes that "the king's name multiplies and divides into punning etymologies."

68 At the end of line 1303, *all'oud' esidein* feels like a crypt of *oidein*, a "swelling" that materializes in the triple repetition of "many" (*polla*)—analyzable as palindromic quasi-anagram of *allos*—in the following lines: . . . *poll' aneresthai,* / *polla puthesthai, polla d'athrêsai* ("many things to ask, many things to learn, many things to see"). On lyric cryptography, see Shoptaw 2001.

69 See Pucci 1992, 156: "Through a chiasmus that graphically opposes his physical and spiritual pains, Oedipus . . . combines them as parallel woes . . . that together pierce himself."

70 On *punctum*, see Barthes 1981; on Oedipus's goads, see Telò 2020b, 72–77.

71 DeLillo 2020.

72 Moten 2017, 268.

2 Teiresias Cadmus Dionysus

1 Žižek 2021b, 4–5.

2 On this view of democracy, see esp. Derrida 2005, 28–41; W. Brown 2009; and Rancière 2010, 61.

3 Alloa 2021, 76.

4 Szendy 2021, 63–64.

5 On the eco-decontructionist use of the Derridean term "an-economic" (in the sense of "disruptive of the *oikos*, of the everyday"), see esp. Marder 2018.

6 On the misogynistic and transphobic accretions of the word "estrogen," see Hayward 2014. Honig, forthcoming, observes that the Bacchants are "'honeyed,' which is Merleau-Ponty's term for a certain sticky contagion that transforms subject/object relations."

7 As Toscano (2020, 5–6) puts it, in these pandemic times "we witness a widespread *desire for the state*," but "waging war on a 'virus' is ultimately no more cogent than waging war on a noun."

8 Robinson 2022, 42–43.

9 Toscano 2020, 9: "Can we avoid the seemingly intractable tendency to treat crises as opportunities for a further widening and deepening of state powers?"

10 See https://www.washingtonpost.com/health/2022/05/14/pandemic-decision-fatigue/; https://www.latimes.com/science/story/2022-02-07/decision-fatigue-is-another-pandemic-malady; https://www.smithsonianmag.com/science-nature/why-its-so-hard-to-make-risk-decisions-in-the-pandemic-180980037.

11 Derrida's *à venir* captures the notion of a future that never materializes as present. As J.-L. Nancy puts it, the Derridean "*à venir* is always strictly opposed to the future, to l'*avenir*, that is, to the present-future that is projected, represented, given in advance as an aim and a possible occurrence" (in Fabbri 2007, 431).

12 Baudrillard (1989, 30) observes that "a lack is never dramatic; it is satiation that is disastrous, for it simultaneously leads to lockjaw and inertia."

13 Prevented from sharing time with other people (coevalness), refugees experience waiting as a condition of protracted displacement, a perennially, cruelly deferred recognition of basic rights. On the deprivation of coevalness, see Ramsay 2019. My reading is not, of course, meant to ignore or deny the draining physical and emotional pain engendered in those waiting to be acknowledged or listened to by the state during the Covid and the AIDS crises, as discussed by Caron (2021); see also Hass 2021, 6, on "waiting for no more waiting."

14 Khosravi (2021, 206) observes that "navigation through the spatio-temporal contexts of waiting might create openings for new political orientations." See also Al-Saji 2022, 189 (on Fanon).

15 Blanchot 1986, 1 and 5.

16 Blanchot 1986, 2.

17 See Blanchot 1986, 1–2 ("The disaster is its imminence, but since the future ... belongs to the disaster, the disaster has always already withdrawn"), 4 ("The disaster has already passed"), and 40 ("'Already' or 'always already' marks the disaster, which is outside history").

18 Derrida 2021, 92.

19 Blanchot 1986, 41. In the introduction to *Glas* (2021, xviii), Bennington and Wills say that *déjà* is "used repeatedly by Derrida as a signet or signature through play on, and inversion of, his own initials."

20 In *Specters of Marx* (1994, 45), Derrida famously describes "the future-to-come" as an "always imminently eschatological coming." On the idea of imminence integral to the Derridean *à venir*, see Cheah and Guerlac 2009, 14: "It is an advent or coming that is structurally *imminent* to every present reality insofar as it is the pure event that interrupts present reality but without which reality could not maintain or renew itself as a presence" (my italics). See also above.

21 Derrida 2011a, 43.

22 Derrida 2000a, 97. See Blanchot 1986, 33: "The passive is the torment of the time which has always already passed and which comes ... as a return without any present."

23 Blanchot 1986, 3: "We are passive with respect to the disaster, but the disaster is perhaps passivity, and thus past, even in the past, out of date."

24 Derrida 2000a, 64. See Barad 2017, 58.

25 Derrida 2000a, 65. Compare Blanchot 1986, 7: "The disaster, unexperienced. It is what escapes the very possibility of experience."

26 Blanchot 1986, 11: "The disaster is what one cannot welcome except as the imminence that gratifies." In re-interpreting the *a* in Derrida's *à venir* as a lack instead of the simultaneity that the *a* stands for in *différance*, I am, to an extent, deliberately reading Derrida against himself.

27 For the various takes on this "problem," see most recently Seidensticker 2016, 276nn5–6. Taplin (1996, 190–91) detects "a strange uncertainty of tone." My approach converges with Honig's invitation (2022) to "decenter" the play's plot. Rather than defining Teiresias and Cadmus's preparation as transvestitism, I prefer to think in terms of the all-encompassing, non-teleological, disidentificatory notion of trans*: see Halberstam 2018 and Bey 2022 (on trans* as a non-category pointing toward gender abolition); on Teiresias's transgenderism, see Corfman 2020.

28 On the polyvalence of *thalamos* in this passage, see Segal 1997, 84–85. For a range of rationalistic interpretations of lines 94–95, see Seaford 1996, 160.

29 See Sophocles, *Oedipus the King* 1268–69; for Euripides' play with the confusion between Laius's goad and Jocasta's pins, see Telò 2020b, 75–76, on *Phoenician Women* 805. On the elements of anti-Oedipal sexuality in *Bacchae*, see Wohl 2005.

30 Thus Davidson (2012, 126 and 128), on the figure of the pregnant male in modernism.

31 Soyinka 1974, 60.

32 Dionysus exemplifies the Derridean foreigner/guest, who ought to be received unconditionally, the absolute Other, both a promise and a threat: see Derrida 2000b, esp. 25.

33 Regarding this passage, Goldhill (1988, 143) notes that "the common idiom of polyptoton may be thought to have a specific rhetorical point."

34 Fragments 27.4 and 28.2 Diels and Kranz. For the connection of *moniê* with *menô*, see O'Brien 2010.

35 On Cadmus and Teiresias as a singular plurality, see esp. Goldhill 1988, 143–44.

36 In her analysis of "kinship trouble," J. Butler (2017) observes that "Dionysus has two mothers," and Zeus is more a mother than a father; he can be called "a pregnant father" and, in that sense, almost resembles a trans* man. On *Bacchae* and the transgenderism of Pentheus, see Gabriel 2018 and Ruffell 2022. On somatotechnics and the notion of the transgender body as "flesh torn apart and sewn together again," see esp. Stryker 1994, 238, and 2015. In lines 243–44 and 286–87, the verbs *rhaptô* ("sew") and *en-rhaptô* ("to sew in") describe the conditions of the birth of Dionysus, "sewn" in Zeus's thigh.

37 See esp. Bey 2017, 276 and 284: "*Trans** and *black* . . . denote para-ontological forces. . . . They move in and through the abyss underlying ontology, rubbing up alongside it and causing it to fissure"; see Telò 2023a (ch. 4).

38 Hill 2016, 193.

39 Hill 2016, 193.

40 Ngai 2020, 2.

41 Ngai 2020, 64.

42 Jameson 2015, 113.

43 Ngai 2020, 68.

44 Ngai 2020, 68.

45 J. Butler (2020a, 688) speaks of "the sometimes manic effort to restart the market economy" during the Covid pandemic. See Toscano 2020 on the militarization of the pandemic in some European countries.

46 Here I am influenced by critical phenomenologist Al-Saji's reading (2022) of Fanon (1967a, 120): "If I had to define myself, I would say that I wait; I interrogate the surroundings, I interpret everything in terms of what I discover, I become sensitive." Waiting, for Al-Saji, is a way "not to be brought back to life" as we have always known it, but "to permit the leap to another dimension of possibility as yet unrealizable and unforeseen" (189).

47 "We, cowherds and shepherds, *gathered* (*xun-êlthomen*) to offer each other *a contest* (*erin*) of *shared speech* (*koinôn logôn*)" (714–15).

48 In making the case for the identification of "decision/*de-cision*" with *mania*, I am reacting against the structuralist reading that sees "a striking contrast between . . . bacchantic hunting . . . and the men's 'strife of words'" (Segal 1997, 284).

49 Seaford (1996, 235) says that "the threefold repetition . . . reflects the slow pulling down of the branch." The following lines give an overdetermined sense of Pentheus's death-driven circling around: *kuklouto d' hôste toxon ê kurtos trochos / tornôi graphomenos peri-phoran helkedromon* ("like a bow or a curved wheel, he circled around, tracing a course-dragging perimeter with a compass" 1066–67).

50 See, e.g., Derrida 1978, 31; 1992, 26; and 1995, 59. See esp. Bennington 2011, 110–11.

51 As Derrida (2002a, 252) puts it, "The undecidable . . . is not merely the oscillation between two significations or two contradictory and very determinate rules. . . . A decision that would not go through the test and ordeal of the undecidable would not be a free decision; it would only be the programmable application or the continuous unfolding of a calculable process."

52 See esp. Sokoloff 2005.

53 Cacciari 2009a and b; see Lampert 2018, 240–41.

54 Warren 2018, 94. For Warren, "The undecidable . . . is situated in a temporality beyond time, a primordial time in which the present, future, and past are all thrown into crisis," while the law, which expresses the force of decision, "attempts to provide a retreat from the heaviness of the undecidable by compressing the legal subject into the present" (95).

55 Derrida 2014, 259 (my italics).

56 Derrida 2014, 256–57.

57 Derrida 2014, 256.

58 Here I cite Jack Halberstam's introduction to Moten and Harney 2013, 7 and 9.

59 Moten and Harney 2013, 19.

60 See Honig 2021a. For responses to Honig's book, see Bassi 2022b, Battezzato 2022, Conybeare 2022, Morales 2022, and Shirazi 2022.

61 In this respect, the emancipatory Agambian "inoperativity" that Honig reads into the life of leisure offered to the Theban women by Dionysus on the mountains may be complicated a priori by their incorporation into the Dionysian world. J. Butler (2017) observes that *Bacchae* "is not a story about women's liberation" and "women are not really liberated but submit deliriously to another man's command"; see also Morales (2022), who observes that "maddened by Dionysus," the women of Thebes "have no, or far less, agency." Honig (2022) responds that, in her reading, "Dionysus cannot force people to do things they do not desire. He can only . . . uninhibit them, and free them to do what they desire." While the murder of Pentheus may be seen as a dismantling of patriarchy, the women's violence against animals makes them enforcers of what has been called "inanimal" biopolitics, on which see Pugliese 2020, 36.

62 The phrase is from Hohti and Osgood 2020. Honig (2021a, 22–23) focuses on the Maenads' breastfeeding of animals as a form of non-heteronormative reproduction. Dell'Aversano (2010, 103) sees the inherent queerness of the animal as the embodiment of "no future": "Unlike the parent-child bond, which is defined by teleology, the human-animal bond . . . does not sagely postpone gratification, it does not project anything into, or onto, the future."

63 On the idea of animacy, see Chen 2012a.

64 On the "feral child," see Halberstam (2020, 145), who observes that "in the implicit ties between the unscripted nature of the infant/wild child's desires, we can begin to understand the wildness of the child and the queerness of the animal."

65 Differently, Honig (2021a, 79) reads Agave's re-entry into sanity and the city as the beginning of "a radical repartitioning of the city's arrangements of gender, sexuality, and power." On the "closure" of *Bacchae* as *pathei mathos*, see Segal 1999–2000. For other aspects of the play's finale, see Telò 2020b, 261–74.

66 See Honig 2021a, 79: "Cadmus . . . reinterpellates [Agave] into the world. . . . Cadmus carefully shifts Agave from a proud revolutionary to a mourning mother."

67 See also chapter 3.

68 Esposito 2019, 207.

69 See Butler and Athanasiou 2013, 156.

70 Bissell 2007, 279.

71 Sheldon 2019, 127.

72 As one of my anonymous referees points out, the "war on Covid" can be easily paired with the "war on drugs," "war on terror," and even the "war on wokeness."

73 See Osmundson 2022, 145–46, on Trump's comment, in spring 2020, describing health care workers as "running into death just like soldiers run into bullets" (Trump added: "It's incredible to see. It's a beautiful thing to see"). As Osmundson adds, "In this 'war' against Covid-19, we can . . . see how society suspends the agency of exposed 'essential workers.' . . . Doctors, baristas, grocery store clerks are all transformed into a 'they' whose self-sacrifice saves 'us.'" See also Povinelli 2020. Thucydides' account of the plague is strongly shaped by the language of war, as demonstrated by Parry (1969); see also Kallet 1999.

74 Osmundson 2022, 148.

75 Osmundson 2022, 157: "When we wage 'war' against unseen, personified concepts . . . we are forced to imagine a perpetrator."

76 Osmundson 2022, 152.

77 Osmundson 2022, 166 (my italics).

78 On *durée* as bearing "the affective weight of the past," see the critically phenomenological account of Al-Saji (2020). Barthes (2005, 133) says that "oscillation,

hesitation, alternation accomplish (on the existential plane of the subject, of his life as existence) a time that vibrates" (my italics).

79 The quotation is from Osmundson 2022, 161.

3 Iphigenia

1 This is one of the many messages that we can extrapolate from Wayne Shorter and esperanza spalding's version of Euripides' play, ... *(Iphigenia)*, which was produced in spring 2022: see the papers gathered in Morales and Telò 2023.

2 Žižek 2021a, 79. See Ibrahim and Ahad 2022, 3: "The recent Covid-19 pandemic has taught us [that] living in a crisis-state over a prolonged and indefinite period of time ceases to *feel* like a crisis."

3 Ibrahim and Ahad 2022, 9.

4 Ibrahim and Ahad 2022, 3: "To persist in an ongoing state of crisis is to be made vulnerable by time's indefatigability."

5 On thematic and dramaturgical links between the two plays, see Michelakis 2006b, 85–87. On indecision in *Iphigenia in Aulis*, see esp. Wohl 2022.

6 On the thematics of *aporia* in the play, see esp. Luschnig 1988; on the politics of *aporia*, see Wohl 2022.

7 Thanks to one of my anonymous readers for this observation.

8 On the assimilation of Iphigenia to the tablet, see esp. Rabinowitz 1993, 42.

9 Wohl 2022, 67.

10 Collard and Morwood (2017, 331) remark that "line 332 could surely serve as a motto for the play."

11 Said (2007, 12) calls late style "a bristling, difficult, and unyielding, perhaps inhuman, challenge".

12 On the influence of the so-called new music on Euripides' play, see the judicious assessment offered by N. Weiss (2018, ch. 5).

13 On the parodos's catalogic orientation, see Torrance 2013, 82–93; on the ecphrastic dimension, see Zeitlin 1995.

14 *Pessôn* patently evokes *peos*, the word for penis.

15 See *chruso-daidaltois* ("gold-decorated," modifying horses' bits at 219); *leuko-stiktôi* ("white-dappled," modifying equine hair at 222); *seiro-phorous* ("trace-horses" at 223); *purso-trichas* ("red-haired," modifying trace-horses at 225–26); and *poikilo-dermonas* ("dappled-skinned," modifying horses at 227–28).

16 Achilles becomes part of an interobjective space. On interobjectivity, see esp. Chen 2011, 280–81.

17 In the Iliadic catalog of ships (2.685–94), the mention of Achilles is inserted where we cut away to his men entertaining themselves on the shore, no longer fighting, but (again, still) waiting.

18 On the "comic" tradition of the guessing game and its tragic incursions, see Fantuzzi and Konstan 2013. The exercise of "guessing" is explicitly evoked at line 845 (*eikaze*).

19 Here and elsewhere I sidestep the debate concerning authenticity and interpolations, which have been central to the history of the play's interpretation: see esp. Gurd 2005, Michelakis 2006a, and Haselswerdt 2022. I heuristically treat the play as a textual whole, the synchronic product of authorial/actorial strata that, despite their apparent heterogeneity, are integrated into the script's composite yet unified structure.

20 On wind as a self-reflexive force of oral poetry and narrative in the post-Aulis world of the *Iliad*, see Purves 2010.

21 See, e.g., Lashua et al. 2021. On the problem of free or unfillable time during the Covid lockdown, see esp. Smith 2020, 19–28. See also Tina Campt in Nash 2022, 7, on the pandemic's generation of "an intense field of micro-perceptions"; Nash views the slowness mandated by Covid-19 as "a call . . . for attending to detail, and for sitting with an intense array of feelings and connections that the buzz of capitalism and its temporality of rush makes impossible."

22 On the translation of line 1147, see Collard and Morwood 2017, 527–28.

23 On this unconventional Euripidean invention, see esp. Gibert 2005; see also Michelini 1999–2000.

24 W. Benjamin 1969, 261.

25 Barad 2017, 59. Fraenkel (1950 ad loc.) clarifies the meaning of the Aeschylean compound *palim-mêkê*: "When they have waited a long time and think it must all be over now and they can set out, they are thrown 'back' again and the trouble begins afresh."

26 According to the translation of *tribôi* offered by Fraenkel (1950 ad loc.).

27 See McEleney 2021, 11 and 17, on "overanalysis." McEleney suggests that "to overanalyze a situation or text . . . is to be *stuck*: stuck in a ruck, wandering in place, trapped in a labyrinth with no center or exit in sight" (9); he also points out that "the dismissal of any form of analysis as overanalysis—as unproductive, masturbatory, endless, and overly divisive or complicating—may constitute one of the anti-intellectual weapons by which the Right achieves and preserves its power" (24).

28 On slowness and slow life, see esp. Berlant 2007 and Nash 2022; cf. Puar 2021. On slowness and the pandemic, see Telò 2023a (ch. 2).

29 The way I visualize this formal and affective breaking of unfillable or drawn-out time is comparable to Muybridge's photographic and cinematic splitting of the singular kinetic gesture into a sequence of individual cuts. See Doane 2002, 46–48; Gunning

2003; and Purves 2019. Unfilled or unfillable time starkly isolates and dilates the individual instant; it makes it exhaustingly perceptible, as it were—oppressively distinct and yet shapelessly extended. I am also inspired by Manning's reference to Arthur Jafa's films' "capacity to make felt the infrathin of time in the making" (2020, 26).

30 I borrow the phrase "supremely tiny acts" from the title of Huber 2021, a memoir whose style resembles a stream of consciousness with no syntax, no punctuation, and thoughts seamlessly folded into each other. In this book, life is broken up into "plans and to-do lists . . . essential to pulling [the author] out of depression and fear" (27). The act of dressing up and getting ready to leave home is, for example, fractured into myriad mini-acts that occupy whole pages (31–32).

31 Like many commentators, Michelakis (2006b, 95–96) underscores the grandiosity of the entrance.

32 Lines 616 (*ochêmatôn*); 618 (*eklipô kalôs* [a clear anagram of *pôlikous*]); 619 (*pôlikôn zugôn*); 620 (*omma pôlikon*).

33 This is the effect of the use of the participle *dameis* ("tamed") in line 623, which evokes the complex Iliadic dynamics of human and non-human domestication, as demonstrated by Press (2022) in his reading of the last word of the poem (*hippo-damoio*).

34 On *menô*, see chapter 2.

35 Steiner and Veel 2021, 89.

36 On this concept, see the papers gathered in Gurd and Telò 2024.

37 On "touch hunger," see Durkin et al. 2020.

38 Kaimio 1988, 87–89.

39 See Feldman 2010, 143: "The *prosopon* fuses the sense of face, facing, and person; *pros* is to be toward, in front of; *opon* derives from *opsis* as vision, so *pros-ops* can be glossed as that which faces the eyes of another."

40 Agamben 2000, 58.

41 Merleau-Ponty 1968, 185: "The flesh is an ultimate notion . . . it is not the union or compound of two substances, but thinkable by itself, if there is a relation of the visible with itself that traverses me and constitutes me as a seer, this circle which I do not form, which forms me, this coiling over of the visible upon the visible, can traverse, animate other bodies as well as my own."

42 J. Butler 2015a, 54; see also J. Butler 2022.

43 On the tragic mask, see esp. Wiles 2007 and Meineck 2011.

44 J. Butler 2015a, 54.

45 See Sigley 2020: "The taboo against the sense of touch, vital to reduce risk of contagion, has been easily weaponized to reinforce inequalities and to suit the relative comfort of the privileged." See also Starks 2021.

46 See Worman 2020b, 203–5.

47 Levinas 1986, 23–24. For a discussion of this passage, see J. Butler 2004, 131.

48 I owe this term to Riva Lehrer in Holdsworth 2021.

49 Steiner and Veel 2021, 45.

50 On this point as a corrective to Levinas's valorization of the face, see esp. Serpell 2020. See also Chen 2012b.

51 Riva Lehrer in Holdsworth 2021. Differently, in the same article (Holdsworth 2021), Namwali Serpell observes that "we have placed a greater burden on the face than we need" and that the pandemic is offering the opportunity to imagine relational possibilities beyond the face-to-face encounter; see also Serpell 2020.

52 See, emblematically, line 648, where Iphigenia asks Agamemnon: "Now release your eyebrow and relax your face, which is dear to me." Commentators use references like this to build positivistic arguments about the modes of acting in the fifth century BCE; Michelakis (2006b, 90–91) infers, for example, that Achilles' and Agamemnon's masks must be bearded.

53 The fact that, according to canonical reconstructions, the fifth-century Greek mask left the actor's eyes visible does not diminish the impression of a face hiding its expressions, hiding itself, as it were.

54 See the Introduction and chapter 8.

55 Sanyal 2023.

56 See Barnett 2020, 14, and Osmundson 2022 (ch. 6); see also chapter 2, on the rhetoric of "heroic" health care workers. See Bradol 2004 on the logic of sacrifice in wars waged for the "sacred liberal international order that aspires to defend humanity and advance moral progress" (Barnett 2020, 13).

57 I owe this phrase to Anker (2022), who uses it to discuss the American abuse of the concept of "freedom" to justify imperialistic and neocolonial enterprises in the global South.

58 J. Butler 2020b, 75.

59 On the corpse, see esp. chapter 5.

60 On this complicity, see, e.g., Lush 2012.

61 Roy (2021, 176), discussing the radical non-harm practiced by Bodhisattvas in Buddhist texts.

62 Roy 2021, 176.

63 J. Butler 2023.

64 I am citing here from Mackey 2021, 12.

65 Mbembe 2021.

66 On the sources for this version of the story, see most recently Nelson 2022, 60–61.

67 Osmundson (2022, 12 and 18) observes that "to be human is to have herpesviruses inside our cells replicating alongside us, to be a human/virus hybrid almost from the year we're born." One can thus say that "the bodies we inhabit are made of the invisible," that "our thoughts and feelings originate from our body's invisibility."

68 The text repeatedly marks the common gender noun for deer, *elaphos*, with feminine articles and pronouns.

69 J. Butler 2020b, 76: "And what about insects, animals, and other living organisms—are these not all forms of living that deserve to be safeguarded against destruction? Are they distinct kinds of being, or are we referring to living processes or relations? What of lakes, glaciers, or trees? Surely they can be mourned and they can, as material realities, conduct the work of mourning as well."

70 The very word "zoonosis" is anthropocentric. See Dardenne 2021 on the words "anthropozoonotic" and "zooanthroponotic." Kirksey (2020) refers to Covid as "a multispecies assemblage."

71 I borrow this language from Chen (2021). As Dardenne (2021) observes, "A new environmental ethics is needed, so is a new ethics of care and respect for sentient life, at the nexus of human health, animal welfare and ecological equilibrium, to foster the harmonisation of the warring elements of this planet in crisis."

72 "Who is to blame for the deep, unprecedented modification of natural spaces that has caused such intensification of interaction? In the last fifty years hunting, farming, and urbanization have led to massive declines in biodiversity and increased the risk of dangerous viruses spilling over from nonhuman to human animals" (https://www.nytimes.com/2020/04/13/opinion/animal-cruelty-coronavirus.html). See also, among others, Robinson 2022, 38.

73 According to Choy (2011, 152), "The coproductive engagements between people and air" constitute "air's poesis" or "the tactility of the atmosphere." As Tremblay (2022, 1) puts it, "As long as we breathe, and as long as we're porous, we cannot fully shield ourselves from airborne toxins and toxicants as well as other ambient threats."

74 Chen 2021, 282.

75 Chen 2021, 281. See also Mbembe 2021, 62: "Humankind and biosphere are one. Alone, humanity has no future. Are we capable of rediscovering that each of us belongs to the same species, that we have an indivisible bond with all life?"

76 On this *nostos*, see chapter 10.

77 See chapter 1.

78 Jue and Ruiz (2021, 3 and 5) define "saturation" as "the co-presence of multiple phenomena within the complexity of our symbiogenic world" or as an elementality that "exceeds the solidity of earth, the fluidity of water, the temperature-sensitivity of fire, and the mobility of air."

79 *Elaphos*, the Greek word for deer, has a masculine ending, even though here it is applied to a female animal. See Haselswerdt 2022.

80 There is also a dynamic comparable to trans species, a concept that "highlights the ways in which trans formations are connected to and made possible by relationships among humans and nonhuman animals that disrupt . . . kinship formations" (Weaver 2014, 253). The overturning of subject/object and gazer/gazed dichotomies is central to the revolutionary valorization of animals' subjectivity in Derrida 2002b. If we think of a god as the quintessential sovereign, Derrida's observation that "the beast and the sovereign resemble each other in that they both seem to be outside the law, above or alongside the law" (2011b, 45), seems relevant here.

81 For examples of the historicist tendency to see the trilogy to which both *Bacchae* and *Iphigenia in Aulis* belonged as a dramatization of the impending defeat of Athens in the Peloponnesian War, see Duclos 1980 and Scanlon 2018.

82 On the citizen body as a fetish, see Saha 2019, 101–5.

83 Aeschylus, *Agamemnon* 119 and 134–36. Peradotto (1969, 245) defines the Aeschylean hare as "fecund, timid, and innocent in appearance and wild." Halberstam (2020, 155–59) connects the "wild" with animal revolution against the domesticating human, with the animal as "plotting its escape, its revenge."

4 Alcestis

1 https://www.vanityfair.com/news/2020/03/dan-patrick-coronavirus-grandparents. See also a similar statement attributed to Dominic Cummings, Boris Johnson's chief political adviser: Aumercier, Homs, et al. 2020, 62.

2 As Žižek (2021b, 4–5) reminds us, in 2020 "Italy [had] already announced that, if things get worse, difficult decisions about life and death will have to be made for those over eighty or with underlying conditions."

3 Gullette (2022) coined this term.

4 See Sicking 1998, 52, and Jakob 1999, 281.

5 On this oscillation, see esp. Sontag 2001. See Young 2020 on Todd Haynes's film *Safe* (1995): "Just as the film dissolves the distinction between literal and metaphorical toxicity, it also declines to arbitrate between 'real' and 'hysterical' illness."

6 Issacharoff 2022, 150. Similarly, Young (2020) considers *Safe*, where the environmental toxicity afflicting the main female character, played by Julianne Moore, cannot be distinguished from her domestic asphyxiation: "From the beginning of the film, she is imprisoned within the interior spaces that shape the habitus of her social class. . . . Moore is framed against these interiors as if caught in a still life, an incongruous, human element in what the French more aptly call *nature morte*." For Tremblay (2022,

17), "*Safe* stages the HIV/AIDS moral panic's worst nightmare: the infiltration and dissolution of white heterosexual domesticity by an overpowering threat."

7   See below.

8   An important precedent for the thesis of Ward's book is Halberstam 2012.

9   https://www.insider.com/why-straight-relationships-are-doomed-according-to-sex-researcher-2020-12. On heteronormativity and race, see Levina 2020, 199; see also Castillo 2021, 250, on femicide in Nicaragua during the pandemic. Lewis (2020) discusses the problems of domesticity that the lockdown may have aggravated: "the mystification of the couple form"; "the romanticization of kinship"; "the sanitization of the fundamentally unsafe space that is private property."

10   Kurr 2020, 151.

11   See Berlant 2008 on Hollywood sentimentality as an instrument for constructing the intrinsic desirability of what Ward (2020, 128) calls "heteroromantic love." At the time of writing (June 2022), I am, like many, perhaps most Americans, shaken by the Supreme Court's decision to revoke federal abortion rights and by Clarence Thomas's opinion that the court "should reconsider" past rulings concerning contraception, same-sex relations, and gay marriage.

12   O'Higgins 1993, 90.

13   On this point, see esp. Rabinowitz 1993, 70–73, and Wohl 1998 (chs. 7–9).

14   My queer reading is, in a sense, a form of "irresponsible" reading. Saint-Amour (2022, 231) wonders: "Are there cases in which . . . responsible reading might be understood to entail irresponsible reading rather than simply to avoid or negate it? Does a theory of the responsible need to include and preserve some notion of responsible irresponsibility?" See also Blanshard 2022.

15   "What a beautiful character you have given Alcestis—she is my perfect idea of what a wife should be," cited in Woolford 2012, 564.

16   "Your description of Leighton's picture [is] . . . much more beautiful than the picture which never half satisfied me." This letter is cited in Woolford 2012, 565. See *Balaustion's Adventure*, lines 2672–97.

17   Maxwell 1993.

18   Browning 1981, i.816.

19   On this tradition, see, e.g., Ingleheart 2015.

20   See Young 2020 on the Grim Reaper in a 1987 Australian AIDS awareness TV ad.

21   In Euripides' play, Heracles' (subliminally erotic) attraction to Death is suggested by the resonance, noted by Ahl (1997, 11), between Heracles' statement in line 847 ("I will place the circle of my arms around him") and Admetus's fantasy, as Ahl puts it, of "enfolding a statue of Alcestis in his arms after she has died" (on which see below).

22 See Callimachus, *Hymns* 2.49: "[Apollo] burning with love for the young Admetus." Rabinowitz (1993, 97) remarks: "Apollo and Admetos exchange the reciprocal roles of lover and beloved characteristic of some initiation cults. . . . That homoerotic phase is not over for Admetos, however, but is sublimated into his homosocial ties with Heracles. Pelias and Admetos, Apollo and Admetos, Herakles and Admetos: all are related through the exchange of Alcestis."

23 Sedgwick 1985.

24 On this castration anxiety, see Rabinowitz 1993, 69.

25 "This poem absolutely owes its existence to you—who not only suggested but imposed it on me as a task" (Browning 1895, 602).

26 As Wohl (1998, 128) puts it, "Admetus is forced to choose between Heracles and Alcestis: he cannot both mourn Alcestis and entertain Heracles . . . so Heracles replaces Alcestis in Admetus's house—this quite literally, as the same actor would have played both parts."

27 Derrida 1986, xvi and xix.

28 On the comic/satyric Heracles in *Alcestis*, see esp. Shaw 2014, 78–105, and Jendza 2020, 60–66.

29 See also line 801, where Admetus says, "I envy those among mortals who are unmarried (*agamous*) and childless (*ateknous*)."

30 Ward 2020, 114 and 125: "Heterosexuality is *intended* to be boring, its very design aimed at control and predictability."

31 "Why do you look so *serious* (*semnon*) and *concerned* (*pephrontikos*)?" (773); "the current *gloominess* (*skuthrôpou*) and *clottedness* (*xun-estôtos*) of your mind" (797); "for those who are serious and have their brows knitted together" (*tois ge semnois kai sun-ôphruômenois* 800).

32 J. Butler 1990, 70, and Ward 2020, 116.

33 On "safe," as an adjective and a noun in Haynes's *Safe*, see Young 2020.

34 On tragicomedy and *Alcestis*, see esp. Mastronarde 1999–2000, 35–38.

35 Rabinowitz (1993, 82) observes that Admetus's "dream of going to bed with the statue . . . fulfills his homo-erotic desires." On Admetus's cold embrace, see also Bassi 2018, 46–47.

36 Paschalis (2015, 394–406) sees Euripides' *Alcestis* as the model of Ovid's Eurydice; see also Liveley 2017, 292.

37 Nielsen (1976, 97) asks the question: "Do Euripides and Admetos forget that Orpheus's gaze kills Eurydike?"

38 Admetus's Orpheus is perhaps not altogether different from the young man absorbed in the contemplation of his own beauty that Pheres, Admetus's father, invokes with the

phrase, "you the beautiful young man (*tou kalou sou . . . neaniou* 698)," while reviling his son's cold cowardice, which Pheres says makes him inferior to a woman.

39 See Wohl 1998, 139: "So superlative is Alcestis that equivalencies become impossible. . . . Beaten by a woman, Admetus is feminized; Alcestis, the victor, is correspondingly masculinized. . . . She is compared at several points in the play to Homeric heroes, an association reinforced by the repeated epithet *aristê*."

40 Rabinowitz 1993, 71: "The text constructs female power as liminal, therefore threatening, but it is controlled by gestures that claim to celebrate it." Rabinowitz adds that "the adoration of Alcestis as the 'best of women' itself inscribes her mutilation by rewarding her for passivity and the repression of all desire."

41 The boredom emanating from the very notion of "bestness" is homologous to the originary use of "straight" in the 1960s and 1970s as a synonym of "stifling and uninspired" (Ward 2020, 117). On "standing"—"staying in one's place" as opposed to "moving"—in the power relation between Penelope and patriarchy in the *Odyssey*, see Wohl 1993 and Purves 2019, 136–52 (with emphasis on epic repetition); see also Telò 2023a (on *Lysistrata*).

42 Bringing out the queerness in Adriana Cavarero's feminist valorization of "inclination" (2016), J. Butler (2021b, 50–51) connects "rectitude" with "rectum": "If the upright posture requires or implies the rectum, then a certain form of inclination is presupposed by a form of rectitude built upon its denial."

43 The demand for rectitude, of course, afflicts both sexes. To an extent, the overdetermined "orthomorphic" demand put on wives is an extension of expectations put on men, which are, in turn, embraced in the bodily normativity of gay male culture. There is thus an implicit homoeroticism in the hierarchical foundation of heterosexuality. See again J. Butler 2021b, 50–51.

44 In conceptualizing heterosexist habituation as an atmosphere, I am inspired by Ahmed's queer phenomenology (2006). On "compulsory heterosexuality," see Rich 1986a.

45 Lines 250–51: "Raise yourself (*ep-aire sautên*), wretched woman, don't abandon me; beg (*lissou*) the gods who are in charge to take pity on you." See also line 277: "Rise up (*ana*), have courage," in which *ana* very possibly stands for *ana-stathi*.

46 Ward 2020, 59: "Straight culture was . . . marked by men's . . . pervasive sense of *burden*" (my italics).

47 On this translation of *pronôpês*, see L. P. E. Parker 2007, 83.

48 Commenting on Podolsky 1991, Ward (2020, 130) observes that "queerness . . . is an affront to the celebration of heteroromantic hardship."

49 See Worman 2020b, 230: "[Heracles] never names [Alcestis]; both he and Admetus after him only refer to her as the object of giving and taking, most often using either . . . 'woman' (*gunaika*) or the demonstrative 'this one here.' Her status as thing thus reinforces the sense that she is barely or not really human, 'slip-sliding' between the 'us' and the 'it.'"

50 See Wohl 1998, 166–67 and 169. See also Rabinowitz 1993, 84.

51 See, e.g., Dyson 1988. Ahl (1997) assumes that Euripides' *Alcestis* is a two-actor play—a possibility that does not affect my reading. I use the three-actor rule informing fifth-century Athenian theatrical practice as an interpretive heuristic, not as a privileged mode of envisioning the staging of the scene.

52 For Stieber (1998, 85), "The woman is spoken of as if she were a statue because she *is* a statue." More subtly, Bassi (2018, 47) observes that "the anatomization of Alcestis into a face and a body draws attention to what is visible on stage while it simultaneously expresses ambiguity about whether the audience is looking at a character who is dead or alive."

53 Foley (2001, 330) says that "the returning Alcestis, as a fictional concubine and prize of Heracles given to Admetus with strong hints of wedding ritual, literally embodies the fantasized combination of concubine and spouse otherwise absent from tragedy."

54 See the equivalent use of *echeis* in Euripides, *Helen* 652, where Helen is reconnected with Menelaus.

55 Commenting on the iconography of the Gorgon, Vernant (2003, 212) notes that "the enlarged rounded head recalls the face of a lion."

56 Wohl (1998, 170), referring to Kristeva.

57 Differently, de Jáuregui (2016, 218) suggests that Euripides' finale aims to repair the broken romance between Orpheus and Eurydice.

58 On the assimilation of the Gorgon to the mask, see Vernant 2003; see also Calame 1986.

59 See Edelman and Litvak 2019, 302, on "the plural that makes the essence of the couple an oscillation between one and two while always also opening onto the necessary presence of a third"; see Youd 2022 for a reading of the political aesthetics of the throuple in Euripides' *Orestes*.

60 On Orpheus's backward glance, see S. Butler 2009; on feeling backward as a queer affect, see Love 2007.

61 See Luschnig 1992, 24: "The staging has made this a new beginning. . . . It is the same place, but transfigured in the interim into a simulacrum of what it had been and transformed again in the final scene back to itself."

62 Nyong'o 2010, 247.

63 M. M. Bailey 2020, 178.

64 Even if Covid, together with monkeypox, has brought back some of the limits to free queer intimacy familiar from the AIDS experience (see https://sexandthepandemic.com), it could become an opportunity for "more queerly" imagining "the politics of belonging," as Bradway and Freeman (2022, 10) observe, following d'Emilio (1983). For a valorization of anonymous friendship ("Is it friendship when two strangers nod at each other on the street . . . when a smile [or an eye roll] moves through a crowd watching the same scene?"), see Allen and Garrison 2022.

5 The Suppliant Women

1 Ticktin 2021. On the feminist commons, see also, in particular, Federici 2018. See also Rifkin 2022, 149 and 156–57, on queer kinship as a possibility for "index[ing] zones of privatized intimacy, . . . care, and interdependence distinct from public processes of political decision making," that is, as "an alternative way of envisioning governance in which enfamilyment is not the racializing means of (pre)qualifying for personhood and political subjectivity."

2 On the undercommons, see Moten and Harney 2013; as McLeod (2019, 255) remarks, "In the undercommons it is . . . through critique—through a project of critical collective study—that new social forms, new forms of truly democratic collective governance, and a new society may take shape."

3 For J. Butler (2022, 3), the "commons" refers to the "sense of belonging to a world, or a sense of the world itself as a site of belonging." One facet of the notion of a feminist commons is offered by the internationalism of Ukrainian feminists as they work to build solidarity across borders in a time of war: https://transformingsolidarities.net/de/activities/transnational-feminist-solidarity-with-ukrainian-feminists. Concerning abolition feminism, another expression of the commons, see the recent intervention of Davis, Dent, Meiners, and Richie (2022), who remind us that "gender violence"—what they call "the pandemic of gender violence"—"produces and reinforces state violence" (120 and 165). In the view of Berlant (2022, 85), the commons is "not annihilative, as it involves care for the world . . . but its potential focus on specific undoing loosens up, disrupts, and reshapes registers and planes of existence."

4 On this phrase, see esp. Orozco Mendoza 2016. This maternal activism can be connected with the reconfiguration of maternity as a revolutionary "mothering" that, in the wake of Adrienne Rich (1986b), has been revitalized by Gumbs, Martens, and Williams (2016) and, within a context of family abolition, by Lewis (2022).

5 https://www.lastampa.it/cuneo/2020/03/14/news/l-addio-in-solitudine-ai-tempi-del-coronavirus-e-dei-tanti-divieti-che-cosa-cambia-in-questa-emergenza-1.38592205.

6 Thucydides 2.52: "The dead and dying lay on top of one another. . . . All the funeral customs . . . were thrown into confusion. . . . Some put a corpse of their own on the pyres of others and set fire to them before those who had built them could, while others put the body they were carrying on top of another that was being burned and went away" (trans. S. Lattimore).

7 Braunstein 2021, 67 and 71.

8 Orozco Mendoza 2019, 214; cf. Orozco Mendoza 2017. See also Nash 2021, 196, on the Mothers of the Movement as "a political affiliation forged through shared trauma," trauma that is "born both from the death—or murder—of a child and from the *state inaction* that marked many of these cases" (my italics).

9 Theseus says that the women's accoutrements are not *theôrika*, do not befit a *theôria*, an officially approved pilgrimage to a sanctuary: see Morwood 2007 ad loc.

10 See Orozco Mendoza 2017, 358: "The funeralization of the city is not only the activists' effort to make feminicide and enforced disappearance visible, but also a shared commitment to unveiling the criminal nature of the state ... [its] failure to mobilize its protective apparatus on behalf of poor women as well as its readiness to deploy the instruments of violence—policing, detention, prison, torture, and even murder— against the victims' families and ... anti-feminicide activists."

11 Bargu (2016, 3) includes among the various practices of necropolitical violence "suspension of the conduct of funerary rituals, the imposition of mass or anonymous interment, the pressure for clandestine interment, and the repression and dispersion of funeral processions for the newly dead"; cf. Bargu 2019. See also Martel (2018), who devotes particular attention to *Antigone*; see also Karakantza 2022.

12 Bargu (2014, 27) defines necroresistance as "a form of *refusal* ... that acts by wrenching the power of life and death away from the apparatuses of the ... state in which the power is conventionally vested."

13 On contagion as a central metaphor of affect, see Deleuze and Guattari 1987, 28; Brennan 2004, 68–69; Gibbs 2010, 186; and Chen 2012a.

14 As suggested by the punning overlap between *êchô* ("echo") and *achos* ("pain"): see Telò 2020b, 142–43.

15 "Work of mourning": Derrida 2001. Tragic mourning, according to Loraux (2002), introduces the anti-political into the realm of the political (on tragedy's valorization of mourning, see also Taxidou 2004); but on the politics of mourning, see esp. J. Butler 2000, 2004, and 2009. Following the critique of "mortalist humanism" espoused by Honig (2013), Wohl (2015, 161n19) suggests that *Suppliant Women* "locates the political force of tragedy" in the "interval" between "civic politics and universal lament." She observes that "unable to sublimate their grief in the exquisite aesthetics of pathos, all [the] mothers can do is name it over and over again" (100).

16 The neuter plural *melê/melea* appears at the beginning of the parodos: "Lawless are ... those who leave *limbs* (*melê*) to *limb-loosening* (*lusi-melei*) death" (45–46).

17 Martel 2018, 35.

18 On (in)animation, see Wills 2016; on the tragic corpse and new materialism, see Bassi 2018.

19 On grievability, see J. Butler 2020b; see J. Butler 2022, 102, on BLM's "assertion of grievability" before and during the pandemic.

20 On the interpretation of *desmon ... a-desmon*, see Morwood 2007 ad loc.

21 On "strange intimacies" as "relations between mothers and fathers, mothers and sons, mothers and daughters, and black mothers" that contest "paradigms of normative white middle-class motherhood and its inverse, pathological representations of black motherhood," see Nash and Pinto 2020.

22 Sabsay (2016, 286) observes that "permeability indicates the relational character of vulnerability in a way that highlights the impossibility of establishing a clear origin and destiny for the circulation of affect . . . and by this move it also reminds us of the unstable . . . boundaries of the vulnerable 'I.'"

23 See J. Butler 2022, 39 and passim.

24 This pandemic "implicates each of us in an interconnected world," says J. Butler (2022, 2), who re-etymologizes "implication" and "implicate" while theorizing "intertwining as ethics and politics" during the pandemic.

25 See above.

26 Baudrillard 1993, 129.

27 For allegorical or (new-)historicist readings of *Suppliant Women*—which has traditionally been seen as participating in anti-Spartan propaganda—see, e.g., Goff 1995, Bowie 1997, Mendelsohn 2002, and Tzanetou 2011; for a discussion of these readings, see Wohl 2015, 89–93.

28 The word *poleis* occurs at the end of line 191, establishing a liaison with *ponos* at the end of line 323 ("your fatherland [*patris*] grows with labors [*ponoisi*]"); see also 393–94 (Theseus's words): "Gladly, *the city* has accepted this *labor* (*polis ponon*)." In Theseus's response to Aethra, once again, *ponos* closes lines 342 ("It is not possible for me to refuse *labors*") and 345 ("You, Aethra, are the first one to command me to take on this *labor*"). "Labor" is the city's auto-immunitarian impulse: for this valence of *ponos* in Aeschylus's *Eumenides*, see Telò 2020b, 222–23.

29 *Drastêrios* is a Euripidean adjective: see, e.g., *Ion* 1185 and *Orestes* 1554. In lines 951–52, when Adrastus, grandiosely addressing the whole race of "mortals," proclaims, "Stop and, ceasing labors (*lêxantes ponôn*), guard your cities, being quiet with quiet people," he re-etymologizes his name.

30 On the queer politics of the useless, see Ahmed 2019; see also Telò 2023a (ch. 2).

31 See chapter 2.

32 As Schwartz (2015, 3) puts it, corpses are conventionally regarded as "bodies *without* agency or subjectivity" (my italics).

33 On the state's fetishization of the baby, see esp. Berlant 1994 and Lewis 2019.

34 On these polarities raised by the literary representation of supplication, see esp. Gould 1973; Kaimio 1988, passim; and Telò 2002.

35 Agamben 2016, 278.

36 On the alleged "inoperativity" of the corpse, see Martel 2018, 30–36.

37 In Telò 2022, I use Roland Barthes's notion of the male lesbian to characterize Adrastus.

38 Mendelsohn (2002, 150–51) characterizes Adrastus as "feminized" or "womanish," conforming to an influential structuralist model of gender binarism that I push against in Telò 2022.

39 On this "pantomimic" sensuousness of mourning, see J. Butler (2003), referring to Walter Benjamin.

40 Worman 2020a, 770.

41 On "animacy" as a queer, affective interaction of human and non-human, see Chen 2012a.

42 See Loraux 1981.

43 The quotation is from Edelman 2004, 9. J. Butler (2022, 41–42) observes that during the pandemic, "all individuation is haunted by a dependency that is imagined as if it could be overcome or has already been vanquished." Berlant (2022) sees individuation as threatened by what they call "inconvenience," "the phenomenality of self-disturbance in the space of coexistence."

44 Moten 2017, 268, and 2018a.

45 The queer kinship I am theorizing exemplifies what Bradway and Freeman (2022, 4) call "kin-aesthetics," predicated on formalism and figuration as sites "for the creation or recreation of relationality." Kin-aesthetics "foregroun[d] how form is a technology that a social body uses to replicate, remake, and extend itself through time." On relational formalism, see also Bradway 2021. See also Lewis 2022, 83, for a critique of kinship as a bond that denies contingency.

46 On breath and feminist politics, see Allen 2020, 86.

47 I borrow this language from Pugliese 2004, a contribution in the field of law theory and refugee studies.

48 J. Butler 2022, 10. See also Povinelli 2020 on the virus's designation as a "terrorist"—"a disavowal of the terror of the history of colonial capitalism." On queerness and maternity, see, e.g., Musser 2018, 176: "In their estrangement from a phallocentric economy, the mother, the lesbian, and the woman-loving woman *sit alongside each other*" (my italics).

49 See Derrida 2000b. Hannah (2010, 184) observes that Derrida's idea "of an absolute, unconditional hospitality—of an openness that resists . . . the hostile fixing of language's demands on the stranger, the guest, the other—is . . . queer in its antinormative . . . structure."

50 See lines 940, 1125, and 1129. See also the occurrence of the *baros* ("weight") of supplication in *Heracles* 1205: see Telò 2020b, 125.

51 On this concept, see esp. Dean 2019. See also Lewis 2022, 21, on "comradeship" or "kith" as an alternative to kinship and the institution of the family.

52 See Ticktin 2020: "If we think of the specificity of a masked mob, we might say it enables an even more flexible solidarity. In being medically cautious, it enables a form of political contagion." J. Butler (2022, 102) remarks that "the Movement for Black Lives is at once a form of public mourning ... that crosses borders" and could be called "a counter-contagion." Speaking of the 2020 protests, Choy (2020, 586) notes that "a transpersonal gestural enactment of momentarily shared pandemic respiratory thickening paired incommensurably yet viscerally with linguistic and textual repetitions of racialized respiratory violence."

53 On this point, see esp. Cavarero 2024.

54 Nash 2021, 151.

55 Bargu 2016.

56 Ticktin 2021. See also The Care Collective 2020, 93: "More porous borders between nation states are ... vital to achieve a more caring world." Making a case for "ethical relationality as interlacing," J. Butler (2022, 83) suggests that in these times "our task is to establish, as if for the first time, a reciprocal relation that dissolves into neither self-interest nor communitarianism ... nor national identity."

57 On "becoming-with" as a corrective to Deleuzian–Guattarian becoming, see Haraway 2009.

6 Antigone

1 Gibney 2020.

2 Chakrabarty 2021, 7.

3 I am here relying on Chakrabarty 2021, 7. In the view of Povinelli (2021, 142), "Covid-19 emerged from extractive capitalism and was disseminated by transportation capitalism." As Colebrook (2020) puts it, "The Anthropocene as the intrusion of geological forces into the experience of being human was only possible because some humans—slaves—were regarded as energy to be extracted, torn from the ground of existence, and rendered into nothing more than matter for the sake of human progress." Crary (2022, 35) speaks of "scorched earth capitalism."

4 Latour (2017) suggests a return to the use of the term and prefix *Gaia* instead of *geo* to save the earth from geology.

5 See Yusoff 2018, 5 and 80: "The biopolitical category of nonbeing is established through slaves being exchanged for and as gold. ... The context of slavery and the practices of geology as an extractive science provide a co-constituting fabric to colonial enterprise and the projects of description of both the earth and the 'place' of different humans within it." For overarching analyses that place slavery at the center of the interpretation of *Antigone* while striving to decolonize critical-theoretical approaches to it, see Chanter 2011 and Henao Castro 2021.

6 Doyle 1929, 17 (my italics). This idea of a breathing earth found in various indigenous cultures is denied by settler colonialism: see esp. H. Davis 2021; see also chapter 8. On

the necropolitical violence generated by the denial of burial, see Bargu 2016 and chapter 5.

7   Mameni (2021) proposes replacing the term *Anthropocene* with *Terracene*: "While the words 'terror' and 'terra' do not share an etymological root, the alliterative intersection of the two allows us to think through the processes of desertification and wastelanding that the War on Terror has enabled, while holding space for multiple *terrans* (those inhabiting 'terra') to conceptualize the geosphere" (100).

8   This is the distinction behind the concept of *geontopower*—as opposed to *geopower* (on which, see below)—theorized by Povinelli (2016) and (2021). As she puts it, "Biopower (the governance through life and death) has long depended on a subtending geontopower (the difference between the lively and the inert)." On Creon's instrumentalization of the cave, see esp. Gsoels-Lorensen (2014, 114), who observes that for Creon the cave is "a site not merely for just or unjust punishment . . . but a legal and political figuration underpinning sovereignty's putatively 'blameless' . . . rupturing of a person's juridico-political existence."

9   J. Butler 2016, 14–15 (my italics), and 19 ("All action requires support and . . . even the most punctual and seemingly spontaneous act implicitly depends on an infrastructural condition that quite literally supports the acting body"); see also J. Butler 2015b (ch. 4).

10   Writing before the pandemic, Neyrat (2016, 58–59) advocates for "planetary Antigones" who would say that "instead of excavating the bottom of Earth . . . we need to leave fossil fuels in the ground. The dead must remain in the realm of the dead, so that the living can breathe."

11   Grosz in Grosz et al. 2017, 135 (my italics). See also Toadvine 2020, 150: "*Earth* names the phenomenological experience of materiality as what grounds, supports, and shelters the emergence of meaning while simultaneously receding from its own disclosure."

12   The cited description is from Sanyal, Telò, and Young 2022, 12, in the introduction of the special issue of *Representations*, in which Hartman's experimental narrative appears. Elsewhere, Hartman has observed that "for every year between 1906 and 1920, black folks in cities experienced a rate of death that equaled the white rate of death at the peak of the pandemic" (2020). See Feigenbaum et al. 2019. On the disproportionately higher impact of Covid on communities of color—what has been called the "pandemic divide"—see Wright, Hubbard, and Darity Jr. 2022.

13   Du Bois 1999, 149–60.

14   Hartman (2020), adapting Du Bois 1999, 160.

15   Hartman 2020.

16   Holloway 2022, 2: "In this era of ecological disaster, attempts at a new frontier are ubiquitous—flights and departures that . . . promise to catapult us *out of this world*."

17   Here I repurpose language from Holloway (2022, 6).

18 Hartman 2022, 43 (my italics).

19 As Stengers (2015, 46) observes, Gaia "is *intruding* on us whether we like it or not." The ecocritical tack of my reading here encompasses but is not primarily concerned with the psychoanalytic idea of the matrix correlated with maternity; cf. Ettinger 2010 on the relationship between Antigone and Jocasta and what she calls "matrixial subjectivity."

20 Chakrabarty 2021, 15. As Ginn, Bastian, et al. 2018 put it, "The enchantment of deep time is an uncanny and unsettling reminder of vast forces beyond one's control." On the karstic, hydrogeological imaginary of Graeco-Roman literatures, see Connors and Clendenon 2016. Appel (2010) seeks to connect Antigone with a self-undermining, self-ironizing notion of autochthony in which legitimacy comes from nothing and nowhere; differently, Heidegger's connection of Antigone with autochthony and "enrootedness" has colonialist and nationalistic implications: see Nichols 2009 and Telò 2020b, 71n18.

21 Hartman 2022, 41.

22 See chapter 5.

23 Honig 2013. On the comma as stillness, see Carson 2021.

24 For a critique of vertical ontology, see esp. Cavarero 2016; see Honig 2021b on the clash between the vertical (i.e., the hierarchical) and the inclinational (i.e., the dissensual) as "personified . . . by Creon and Antigone," but also exemplified by traditional readings of the respective positions of Ismene and Antigone.

25 See Benardete 1999, 45: "The play . . . seems to give an exhaustive list of the ways in which the earth can be understood. . . . Somewhere between the earth . . . and the earth's hard and unyielding surface, which either the goddess Earth or the earth in itself comprehends, lies the city."

26 This is the phrase that Harney and Moten (2015, 83) use in relation to the body of Michael Brown, killed by a policeman in Ferguson, Missouri, on August 9, 2014—a body "left lying unburied (and uncovered) because he was black" (Martel 2018, 99). On the *Antigone in Ferguson* initiative, see esp. Morales 2020, x.

27 Mueller (2011, 421) suggests that Antigone's gesture of bowing her head underscores a political opposition in the play between *chthôn* and *polis*: "Creon's failure to recognize that *chthôn* does not come under the legislative purview of the *polis* is symptomatic of his tyrannical frame of mind and of his autocratic leadership style."

28 Griffith (1999 ad loc.) observes that "the unusual double repetition in 73 . . . emphasizes both the bond of φιλία . . . and the physical closeness of the two bodies." On the intense incestuous overtones of the combination of *keisomai* and the repeated *philos*, see esp. Benardete 1999, 13; Wohl 2009a, 128–29; and Worman 2020b, 22.

29 Jebb (1900 ad loc.) says that ἀφ-αγιστεύω and ἐφ-αγιστεύω are equally possible.

30 In the translation of Griffith (1999 ad loc.).

31 Jacobs (1996, 902) observes that there is "no way to distinguish Nature and Antigone, both arriving, it seems, coincidentally and performing the same rite of scattering the dust that neither buries nor leaves unburied the decomposing figure of the male."

32 See lines 821–22: "Of your own initiative (*auto-nomos*), alone (*monê*) among mortals, you will descend into Hades." On *monos* and *monia*, see chapter 2.

33 See lines 409–10: "After *having swept away* (*sêrantes*) *all the dust* (*pasan konin*) that was holding the corpse . . ."

34 On *Oedipus at Colonus*, see Telò 2020b, esp. 48–52.

35 According to Toadvine (2020, 152), "The abyssal character of deep time, whether the prehistorical span of the geological or the earth's far future, is our experience of its anachronous interruption of lived temporality from within."

36 Yusoff 2013, 779.

37 Yusoff 2013, 792.

38 On the interpretation of these lines, where, differently from the OCT, I presuppose, like most recent commentators, the reading *konis* ("dust"), see esp. Ferrari 2010; see also Cairns 2014.

39 Yusoff 2013.

40 I owe the term "geosociality" to Palsson and Swanson (2016), who conceptualize it as a set of "embodied" and "down to earth" "entangled relations of the earth and biological beings."

41 Griffith 1999 ad loc. On the symbolic topography of Antigone's cave, see esp. Fantuzzi 1989.

42 See J. Butler 2000, 23: "Antigone's death is always double throughout the play: she claims that she has not lived, that she has not loved, and that she has not borne children, and so that she has been under the curse that Oedipus laid upon his children, 'serving death' for the length of her life."

43 Griffith (1999, 275) remarks that *peri-ptussô* is "used especially of human 'embraces.'" Benardete (1999, 107) observes that Creon "tells his servants to imprison Antigone in her grave as if they were to wrap her in a garment." Worman (2020b, 4) notes that "Antigone's bodily inhabitation . . . shares features with her rocky tomb." For Worman, the cave is an image of Antigone's body—part of a "gendered topography of bodily containment"; in other words, "the emphasis on interior cavities, clefts, entrances, passageways, and their breaching and penetration . . . encourage chorus and audience to view her as a violated container" (155). Worman also urges "more attention to her inhuman qualities, her proximity to not only the gods . . . and the dead, but also creatures and things (e.g., birds, rocks)."

44 Cant 2003, 73.

45 See, e.g, de la Cadena 2015, esp. 83–85 and 94–95.

46 As Hawkins (2019, 3–4) puts it, "The ground immerses us into a world of intimate geologies," a world of "projections and imaginations of being within the ground," or "an invitation to bodies to be in contact with the Earth, to be, even if so shallowly, within it, beneath the surface," to experience "the radically incommensurate time of the geologic." See also Yusoff 2015, 383.

47 The description of the topography of the Underworld in Plato, *Phaedo* 111d–113c is permeated by a concentration of similar harsh sounds, which all together create a phonesthetic atmosphere suggestive of karstic asperities. For examples of meta-descriptive iconism in the textual representation of landscape, see esp. Schiesaro 1993; Martin 2002; S. Butler 2011, ch. 2 (on Thucydides' description of the plague of Athens); Purves 2013; and Telò 2019.

48 In these lines, textual and topographical uncertainties proliferate: for a discussion, see Griffith 1999, 332–33.

49 Yusoff 2018, 84.

50 The interpretive link between Antigone and the earth-as-ground that I am positing differs from—yet complements—structuralist symbolic readings of Antigone as "the grieving figure of the Great Mother . . . the Earth Mother who grieves over her children" (Segal 1999, 180).

51 Du Bois 1999, 149–50.

52 Hartman 2020. As observed by Gómez-Barris (2017, xvii), the various manifestations of global *extractivismo* "enable and normalize resource exploitation that ends up perpetuating anti-Indigenous and anti-Black racism."

53 In her rendition of the play, Carson (2012, 43) has Creon arrive onstage and exclaim: "O laugh of Death / you crack me / you crack me open / you crack me open again." The use of the verb "crack" conveys the sense of a fractured earth, a fissured ground, about to collapse.

54 See Griffith 2005, 121: "At the end [Antigone's] body is not brought back on stage with the others to be mourned and memorialized; she is just left lying (or hanging?) in the cave, as if this is where she must finally reside. No lamentation and recrimination, no presentation of her body, no burial is even mentioned for her."

55 As Elizabeth Povinelli in Povinelli et al. 2017 puts it, "The Anthropocene might be usefully considered a geontological drama not for its disclosure of the intimacy of bios to geos but by virtue of its re-dramatization of this interface in terms of the looming threat of human extinction, and the triumph of a planet devoid of life."

56 In *Glas*, Derrida (2021, 187) observes that "nothing should be able to survive the death of Antigone." For Derrida, "she is the figure of the fall, of decline" (196), but, "present at every catastrophe, every fall, every carnage, [she] remains invulnerable to them" (210). If Antigone embodies what remains, which is integral to the idea of *Sittlichkeit*, her disappearance must amount to "the absolute end of history."

57 Hartman 2020.

58 Martel 2018, 62. From a Lacanian perspective, Braunstein (2021, 72) observes in "The Return of Antigone: Burial Rites in Pandemic Times": "The corpse does not *jouit* ... but is the object of the desire of the Other. . . . The disposition and arrangement of the burial rites . . . belong to the jouissance of the Other, including the power of the state, the power of present-day Creons to *jouir* the bodies of the Labdacids, extinguished because they had no offspring."

59 See Mameni 2021, 106: "Thinking with the vibrancy of materials . . . anchor[s] us within the interconnectedness of all terrans, where life/non-life distinctions no longer hold; as it is precisely such divisions that cast racialized bodies outside of the category of Human."

60 Garcia 2022, 35. See also the feeling of an (im)possible emergence described by Georges Bataille (2005) in his account of his visit to the Lascaux caves with their prehistoric paintings—"the deepest point in the bowels of the earth that it was . . . possible to reach" (49).

61 Yusoff 2015, 383. See Morton 2010; Nyong'o 2018, 111–12; and H. Davis 2022.

62 On the notion of a Terracene instead of an Anthropocene era, see Mameni 2021.

63 See Hartman 2020.

64 Harney and Moten 2015, 82.

65 And, in this, way, actualizing forms of decolonized ecology, heeding "Indigenous cosmologies" that—before the so-called New Materialisms—"offer ecological wisdom about localized and sustainable forms of life based on synergies with biodiverse . . . environments" (Demos 2016, 23). See Horton and Berlo 2013.

66 H. Davis (2022, 101–2) advocates for a queer future defined by "finding a way to live with toxicity and extinction." The pandemic can perhaps help us understand that the very idea of the Anthropocene, as Szeman (2020, 147) puts it, "returns us to questions of ends—to whether we see the present as ecological fate about which we can do nothing, or as a revolutionary opportunity to redefine the kinds of individuals and societies we are and want to become." Padwe (2020, 158) observes that "from a human perspective, the Anthropocene is a way of speaking about the end of the world"; it is a "figure of the Eschaton."

7 Niobe

1 Murakami 2002.

2 "Niobe in Distress for her Children slain by Apollo, from Ovid's Metamorphoses, Book 6 and from a view of the Painting of Mr. Richard Wilson," lines 213–16 (Wheatley 1988, 112). The last line translates Ovid's *nullos movet aura capillos* (6.303). On Wheatley's Niobe, see esp. Spigner 2021, drea brown 2024, Cavarero 2024, and Umachandran 2024.

3   See, e.g., fig. 15 in Taplin 2007. On Aeschylus's *Niobe* (fragments 154–62 Radt) and its visual representations, see Taplin 1972, 60–62, and 2007, 74–79; Seaford 2005; Pennesi 2008; and Sevieri 2010. See also Telò 2023a (ch. 2).

4   For Rimell (2024), "Aristophanes' sketch uses humor to expose—and displace—the notion that Niobe's trauma is contagious."

5   As Rimell (2015, 285) puts it.

6   These are the only two passages in the Ovidian corpus where *con-gelo* occurs. On the *Tristia* as a hauntological play with origins and lost futures, see Martelli 2021, 73–75.

7   Rimell 2015, 280.

8   See *Letters from the Black Sea* 1.2.29–30 ("Happy Niobe who, even though she saw so many deaths, cast off the perception of the misfortune by becoming stone") and *Tristia* 5.1.57–58 ("Even if the offspring of Latona made Niobe childless, nevertheless they did not demand that she also have dry cheeks"). On Ovid's play with the etymology of Tomis from Greek *temnô* ("to cut"), see Nawotka 1994.

9   On this meaning of *gl-* see the introduction of Bennington and Wills to *Glas* (Derrida 2021).

10 Stevens (2009) argues that Ovid's journey to Tomis has a regressive dimension—it brings him back to *in-fancy* (etymologically, "not speaking"), that is, "a sort of second linguistic infancy" or "the prelinguistic state traditionally attributed to human prehistory."

11 I owe this observation to David Youd.

12 Lines 822–25: see esp. line 822 *phrixas d'auto-komou lophias lasi-auchena chaitan* ("bristling the shaggy-necked shock of his hirsute ridge," trans. Henderson), which itself bristles with aspirated consonants. On bristliness and coldness, see Telò 2019.

13 In this characterization there is a convergence of a number of theoretical orientations: Levinasian ethics, the Blanchotian disaster, the Adornian "recalcitrance of the object," and the object of object-oriented ontology. See also chapter 2.

14 Deleuze 1991 (see esp. chs. 2, 4, and 6).

15 See Zeavin (2021), who observes that the binary of hot and cool "is not a coincidence or a neutral media theory of parenting, but a misogynistic and racist media theory of parenting that depends on reducing the mother to a mechanized stimulus transmission" (68).

16 Deleuze 1991, 70 and 71.

17 Deleuze 1967, 46–47.

18 Deleuze 1991, 55.

19 Rimell (2020, 558) suggests that "Ovidian exile is staged as an oedipal drama of separation from the *patria* and from parricidal poetry which results in the fictional loss of his mother-tongue." On the Oedipal dramas of Ovid's exile poetry, see Walker 1997.

20 Deleuze 1991, 51.

21 Feldherr 2010, 300.

22 Feldherr 2010, 301.

23 Feldherr (2010, 301), referring to *Metamorphoses* 6.195–96.

24 Deleuze 1991, 32. On Augustus's Rome as "a city of marble," see esp. Lamp 2013.

25 Discussing the reference to Medea's dismemberment of her brother in *Tristia* 3.9 (the poem before the description of Tomis), Oliensis (1997, 189) observes that "Ovid is at pains to depict his place of exile as the negation and antithesis of his former home," but the evocation of the mutilation of Cicero's corpse through Medea's fratricide "reveal[s] Tomis to be the very image of Rome."

26 On the raging *tristitia* of Ovid in *Tristia*, see Oliensis (2004), who suggests that poetry of the exile constantly implicates Augustus even with Ovid at the center. For the *Tristia*'s built-in invitation to "read more" and perform "paranoid readings," see Barchiesi 1997, 28–30, and Casali 1997.

27 Deleuze 1991, 53.

28 In these lines, Ovid compares his poems to Athena/Minerva, assimilating himself to Zeus/Jupiter and borrowing from the father of the gods his reproductive envy, as it were. These lines can perhaps be seen as a mockery of Augustus's own reproductive aspirations—paternal but also, in a sense, maternal.

29 The Ara Pacis is a marmoreal receptacle conceived as a celebration of fertility and reproduction: on the monument's connection with the mother Ceres, see, e.g., Spaeth 1994. Deleuze (1991, 70) observes that "the novels of Masoch display the most intense preoccupation with arrested development."

30 Deleuze 1991, 52.

31 On the connection between Niobe's petrification and erectile hardness, see Morales 2004, 171, on Achilles Tatius.

32 Deleuze 1991, 53 and 54.

33 Fox 2009, 37.

34 Morton 2007, 196.

35 Morton 2007, 125.

36 Alaimo 2000, 88, and 2008, 252.

37 This is one of the major take-aways of Judith Butler's theoretical intervention on the pandemic (2022). As they put it, "The world is not just out there as the backdrop for human action or the field for human intervention. . . . Bits of the world are incorporated into the body itself" (11). The *pan*demic has also increased our levels of *pan*ic, thus bringing the Greek god Pan, a pervasively (im)material inhabitant and embodiment of Nature, into our lives: see Giordano 2020, 61–63.

38 Toadvine 2018, 53.

39 Toadvine 2018, 54.

40 Toadvine 2018, 75. See also Nancy 1993, 92.

41 Lynes 2018, 117. See also Neyrat (2017, 9), who following Merleau-Ponty's point that "Nature is the primordial—that is, the nonconstructed, the noninstituted" (2003), conceives of "the earth-withdrawn, non-objective and irreducible to a body . . . the nocturnal side of nature." From a Marxist perspective, Toscano (2018, 140) defines nature as a "historical limit of society, and of capital."

42 See Danowski and Viveiros de Castro 2017, 19: "Every thought of the end of the world . . . poses the question of the beginning of the world and that of the time before the beginning."

43 Meillassoux 2006 and 2014. McLean (2021, 296) observes that the very idea of the Anthropocene carries with itself "the prospect of humanity's own becoming-mineral—one more stratum, one more trace in the fossil record that may or may not be legible to the paleontological curiosity of a hypothetical posthuman observer."

44 Meillassoux 2014, 13.

45 Huffer (2017, 81 and 82), commenting on "Monsters and Fossils" in Foucault's *Order of Things* (2002).

46 Farbman 2012. See also Toscano (2018) on Engels's identification of the demise of humanity with a nature no longer warmed by the sun.

47 Freud 1920.

48 Lacan 1992, 346.

49 See lines 827 (*petraia blasta damasen*) and 830 (*chiôn t' oudama leipei*), which present the same syntactical structure. According to O. Harris (2013, 255), Lacan's Niobe is Ovid's Niobe, whom Lacan would connect with another Ovidian character, Narcissus: "In so far as we are created in fascination before the mirror, the self emerges 'petrified,' frozen as an image, and so already bound to the 'inanimate condition' of death."

50 See, e.g., Lacan 1981, 178 and 182.

51 I owe this phrase to Berlant (2022, 124). For Berlant, the tragic is precisely "the desire to stay in life but not in the world, an affect made unbearable by an incessantly pressuring structural continuity."

52 It is significant that in Todd Haynes's *Safe* (1995), a film that, as we saw in chapter 4, can be read as an allegory of the HIV pandemic (as well as the current one), the "safe" where the protagonist's immunitarian anxieties are sheltered looks like an icy solitary pod.

53 See McNulty 2015, 117: "The 'glacial epoch' . . . that masochistic suspension seeks to isolate appears as a depiction or construction of the phallic mother."

54 Mulvey (1995) offers a feminist Freudian reading of the film, emphasizing its fetishistic elements.

55 On Dionysus's denied mortality in *Bacchae*, see Telò 2020b, 261–74.

56 On these compounds, see Telò 2023a (ch. 2).

57 Deleuze 1989, 111.

58 On female white masks in Greek tragedy, see, e.g., Marshall 1999, 190–91. On the identification of Niobe with a white *lekythos* (an oil-bearing ritual vessel), see Comay 2024. The possibility of a white mask for Niobe is enhanced if her lithic transformation was dramatized in the Aeschylean play. In any case, the association of white makeup with mourning is culturally well-established in classical Athens: see Neils 2008; on women's white masks as a (misogynistic) marker of death in Aristophanes' *Assemblywomen*, see Slater 1989.

59 Mbembe 2003 and 2019 and Nixon 2011. See also Puar 2017. For a different take on necropolitics, see Bargu 2016, discussed in chapter 5.

60 Puar 2017, 139.

61 On the auto-immunitarian consequences of this distinction and of an unequal recognition of shared "grievability," see J. Butler 2020b; regarding the Israeli-Palestinian conflict, J. Butler (2013, 21) remarks that "grievability is . . . a precondition of value, and there can be no equal treatment without a prior understanding that all lives have an equal right to be protected from violence and destruction."

62 On this concept, see W. Brown 1993.

63 See Kotef 2020, 162: "What we see in this attachment [to ruins] is the possibility that political identity is constructed, not despite destruction, beside it, through overcoming it, or ignoring it, but through and by means of destruction itself."

64 On Fanon's idea of petrification in relation to the *colonisé*, see chapter 8.

65 Kotef 2020, 161.

66 See Cao 2017, 49, on the "assertive materiality of ice." Kotef (2020, 196) says that "the ruin . . . freezes time."

67 For this distinction between life and living, see Thacker 2011, 129. A. Benjamin (2024) considers Niobe in light of the relation between life and the artwork's afterlife. In a book that aims to provide "solutions" for a "better future" *after* the pandemic, Schwab and Malleret (2022, 171) affirm the "need for greater resilience"—a rhetoric that smacks of neoliberal normativity: for a critique, see Umachandran (2022), who suggests ways in which the rupture of Covid could become an opportunity for much-needed academic disciplinary reorientations, for example anti-racist classics.

68 On the distinction between pandemic and endemic, see Foucault 1976, 273–74. In using the term "pan-endemy," I deconstruct this opposition, which has the serious drawback of naturalizing and normalizing racism (customarily presented as "endemic").

69 Aeschylus, fragment 161.1 Radt.

70 Deleuze 1989, 68–69, 71, 81, and 103. Regarding the "crystal image," Deleuze's film descriptions bring to mind Niobe: "The two protagonists stay in the middle of their fight, *frozen* and covered in mud"; "wanderings, *immobilizings, petrifications* . . . are constant evidence of a general dissolution of the action image" (my italics).

71 As Musser (2021, 102) puts it, in her analysis of sweat, liquidity "challenges epistemologies of containment by gesturing toward flesh's expressive possibilities."

72 See https://abyasun.medium.com/frozen-to-death-afghan-mother-dies-to-protect-her-kids-during-blizzard-on-turkish-border-7743a92d9f93.

73 See W. Benjamin 2021, 55–57. On this passage, see Comay 2024 and Umachandran 2024.

74 Moten 2017, 259: "What it is to refuse the limits of the body is to refuse the limit as regulation in and for possessive individuation and to embrace the proliferation of limits' irregular devotion to difference and blur." On the nexus of maternity (or "matrical ecology") and de-individuation, see Moten 2003, 214–16, and esp. 2017, 276 and 278. See also J. Butler 2022, 41–42: "All individuation is haunted by a dependency that is imagined as if it could be overcome or has already been vanquished."

75 In *Antigone* 88, Ismene says to Antigone: "You have a warm (*thermên*) heart for cold (*psuchroisi*) things." As we have seen, Antigone compares herself to Niobe later in the play. See Rimell 2024 on Niobe's warmth in *Iliad* 24.617.

76 Berlant 2022, 18 and 26.

8 Prometheus

1 On the protests with the signs "We Can't Breathe" that followed the murder of Eric Garner in 2014, see Passavant 2021, 192–204. Discussing Eric Garner's "I can't breathe," Sharpe (2016, 112) observes that "slavery . . . simultaneously exhausted the lungs and bodies of the enslaved even as it was imagined and operationalized as that which kept breath in and vitalized the Black body."

2 Crawford 2021, 120.

3 Warren 2021, 30–31. As he puts it, "What is at stake is the *function* of the black object to facilitate enjoyment (as victim of violence) and not the enjoyment of black subjects" (31).

4 Crawley 2016, 42.

5 Crawley 2016, 48.

6 For Górska (2018, 253), "Breath in its trans-corporeal and lively and deadly operations becomes not only a symbolic but also a literal enactment of the struggle for breathable life—a struggle that . . . is inherently intersectional and posthumanist."

7 Regarding "matterphorics," Gandorfer and Ayub (2020, 4) pose the question: "What would it mean . . . to slide between language and materiality . . . to not limit life's 'speech' to communication but . . . to acknowledge . . . that concepts matter-forth, that some concepts are lethal?"

8 See, e.g., Crawford 2021, 119, and Hesse and Thompson (2022), who observe that "*pandemic* describes what has been symptomized by both the spread of Covid-19 and antiblackness in their respective transmissions from person to person, city to city, nation to nation, namely, a sudden or long-term eruption or outbreak of microbiological violence . . . or colonial racial violence (anti-blackness) within a social gathering, or in an attack on a single person" (452). On the idea of a *pan-endemic*, see chapter 7.

9 See Colebrook 2020: "Like the 1918 pandemic to which it is so often compared, the spread of Covid-19 was highly racialized." As Hartman (2020) observes in reference to the 1918 pandemic, "For every year between 1906 and 1920, black folks in cities experienced a rate of death that equaled the white rate of death at the peak of the pandemic." As Bradway and Freeman (2022, 9) put it, Covid "indexes the genocidal sovereignty of anti-Blackness." See also Wright, Hubbard, and Darity Jr. 2022 on the so-called "pandemic divide."

10 Nancy 2020, xii.

11 Levina 2020, 199.

12 Bowman 2020, 312.

13 https://www.youtube.com/watch?v=ORyvXqdBtvs.

14 Bennett 2020, 63.

15 Mackey 2021, 11.

16 Moten 2017, 183.

17 Colebrook 2020.

18 Darnella Frazier filmed the death of George Floyd because, as she said, "I knew if I didn't, no one would believe me": see Hesse and Thompson 2022, 450. On slow death, see esp. Berlant 2007; see Colebrook 2020: "Slow violence . . . led to a series of catastrophes, including the spectacle of the 2020 pandemic, the racial injustice intensified by that pandemic, and then a sense that this unravelling world might be the occasion for a destruction of a system of policing inextricably intertwined with centuries of Black death."

19 Fanon 1967a, 114–15. Marriott (2021, 20) observes that "faced with the *irréalisable* the *colonisé*, insofar as he wills himself white, can only recognize himself as less than nothing, caught between nothingness and *infinity*" (my italics).

20 Mbembe 2021, 60. Crary (2022) connects the digital with what he calls "scorched earth capitalism."

21 As Hristova and Howard (2021, 484) observe, "Reliance [on] technology and the pervasiveness of social media as a component of our living world . . . creates a level of

power for platforms," by which "they are . . . implicitly empowered to globally impact knowledge [and] opportunities, and ultimately, biopolitically influence life and the ability to breathe."

22 On this tradition, see the seminal study by Hickman (2017), who observes that "the black Prometheus embodies both a critique of racial slavery as the product of a blasphemous religion of whiteness . . . and a call for and often a calling into being of gods whose responsiveness to global humanity would make it impossible to justify in their name anything like racial history" (23). See also Hall 2011. Rankine (2021) connects Prometheus with the murder of George Floyd and the lynching of Emmett Till in James Baldwin's 1964 play *Blues for Mister Charlie*.

23 See Fanon 1965b, 65, on breathing in the colonial state: "The individual's breathing is an observed, an occupied breathing. It is a combat breathing." See Perera and Pugliese 2011, 1: "Combat breathing names the mobilization of the target subject's life energies merely in order to continue to live, to breathe, and to survive the exercise of state violence"; see also Hesse and Thompson (2022, 459), who suggest that "George Floyd was murdered in a state of the shifting nexus between occupied breathing and combat breathing for all the world to see." Fanon's notion of colonization as atmospheric goes along with his emphasis on racialization as "en-fleshment" and "epidermalization" (1967a, 11). See also below.

24 Fazi 2019, 4.

25 Deleuze 1992.

26 Fazi 2019, 9. See also Munster 2006.

27 Ibrus and Ojamaa 2020, 66.

28 Povinelli 2016, 150 and 163.

29 On (in)animation, see Wills 2016. On the muscular tension of the colonized, according to Fanon, see esp. Dariek Scott 2010, 71–77.

30 The terms "anarchivic," "anarchival," "archiviolithic," date back to Derrida 1996; see also, among others, Best 2018.

31 Burke 2018.

32 See esp. Shah 1998.

33 See chapter 5.

34 https://www.politico.com/news/2022/04/03/blinken-stoltenberg-russia-genocide-00022567.

35 Wojnarowicz 1991, 75–77. Félix Guattari in Wojnarowicz 1989 observes that his "revolt against death and the deadly passivity" of society "gives a deeply emotional character to his life work, which . . . transcends the style of passivity . . . which characterizes this present period."

36 Smithson 1996, 100.

37 On metalworking in Scythia as the cultural background of *Prometheus Bound*, see Bakola (2019, 232–33), who, writing in 2018–19, observed that "our evidence for iron production and extraction in areas north of the Black Sea is very limited," adding, almost presciently, that "the question has been debated among Russian and Ukrainian scholars." On extractivism and rebordering between Russia and Ukraine, see Rogatchevski 2021. In Sergey Kamshylin's *Prometheus: Monument in Memory of Chernobyl Disaster* (Kiev 2018), a bronze Prometheus affixed to a gray vertical background resembles a "precious" commodity emerging, or extracted, from stone.

38 Fanon 1965a, 61. See Marriott 2018, 68 (on Fanon's imagery of petrification): "The truth of personification . . . refers to the work of imposition within us, the sense of wanting to flee or speak but remaining frozen, under the weight of a certain *style* of embodiment (petrified, rigidified, inanimate . . .), by which the body mimes or acts out the signs of its own subjugation and its own petrified perversion as a subject."

39 Britto 2009, 149.

40 See Marriott 2018, 242: "The *colonisé* cannot think or speak or even breathe without being reminded that the forms of their allegiance are under constant surveillance."

41 J. Butler 2015a, 189.

42 Marriott 2021, 108.

43 Barthes 1981, 92.

44 Curtis 2004, 241.

45 See Fanon 1967a, 109 and 114.

46 Prabhu 2006, 202.

47 As Marriott (2021, 4 and 10) puts it, in his revisitation of Lacanian theory through Fanon and Afropessimism, "We are all irredeemably enslaved *as* speaking subjects"; for Marriott, "What meaning offers us . . . is neither truth nor consolation, but a desire for a certain mastery in which blackness is once again figured as something enslaved, dominated by its appearance." Differently from Marriott, Calvin Warren sees Blackness as a denial of inclusion within the Symbolic. See Warren 2021, 32: "The black object is 'barred from participation' in the Symbolic as a *subject*. . . . In this sense, the black does not assume a subject position but is *situated* as an object—crushed by the foreclosure of the fantasy of Being and, concomitantly, an illicit access to *jouissance*."

48 Sedgwick 2011, 71.

49 Moten 2003, 12.

50 Fanon 1967a, 109.

51 Vicuña 2009, 27, and Bryan-Wilson 2017, 116.

52 Hudson 2013, 267. See Marriott 2021, 95: "Blackness is neither imaginary nor symbolic but a certain symbolic regression by which the real reappears, not as a lost thing, but as an object that is magically conjured into being."

53 On the breath of the earth, see chapter 6.

54 See Marriott 2018, 275.

55 On relational vibrations, see esp. D. Harris 2022, 13. See Warren 2021, 37: "Police brutality exposes the way the Law perverts itself.... Society 'gifts' *jouissance* as a necessary feature of enforcement; perhaps, policing is *impossible* without a valve, or avenue, for direct surplus-pleasure."

56 Kafka 1971, 432.

57 See Ruffell 2012, 85: "Criminals were strapped to a board, with throat rather than chest bands." Bakola (2019, 228) notes that "the repeated sequences of metal pounding on metal would have filled the scene with elemental power." The best treatment of torture in *Prometheus Bound* is offered by Bassi (2010).

58 Fanon 1967a, 8.

59 Ferreira da Silva 2020, 43. Ferreira da Silva builds upon Hortense Spillers's discussion of slavery and the flesh (1987): see also Weheliye 2014, 38–45 and 121–32.

60 See Moten 2003.

61 Moten and Harney 2011, 355.

62 On form and insurrection, see Telò 2023a (Introduction).

63 Tremblay (2022, 3 and 4) observes that "phonemes, these units of sound that distinguish one word from another, reside in the air" and "breathing exceeds the utterances whose sonority it modulates."

64 See Warren 2021.

65 The mention of the Gorgons is part of an "orientalizing" speech, in which, as S. White (2001, 118) observes, "unlike the European mortals [Io] encounters, which are savage but recognizably human, the denizens of Asia are deformed and monstrous hybrids."

66 On individuation, see Moten 2017, 259 and 278 ("black life . . . is anti- and ante-foundational . . . is neither the subject of nor subject to individuation and (ac)count").

67 See Marriott 2018, 72: "An analysis of Fanon's writings on decolonial war reveals this [decolonial] violence to induce a kind of vertigo or anguish.... an almost ecstatic transformation or annihilation, preserving the rupture and movement of the tabula rasa." See also Dariek Scott 2010, 79, on Fanon's vertigo as "an affliction of disorientation" corresponding to the "muscular tension" that is the "interarticulated temporality" of a past "fully determin[ing] and occupy[ing] the present" (75).

68 Uhlig (2020, 122) observes that as a result of the Oceanids' arrival onstage, in *Prometheus Bound*, the orchestra was "simultaneously rendered liquid and uncertain by their presence."

69 Regardless of the staging practicalities (see, e.g., Taplin 1977, 252–60; Griffith 1983, 109; Sienkewicz 1984; and Kokkiou 2014), the Chorus's own self-presentation strongly suggests, at least imaginatively, an aerial entrance (see esp. lines 132 and 135). Hitting the cave, where the Chorus of Ocean's daughters resides, the sound of the iron that tortures Prometheus's flesh is equipped with penetrative violence: "The echo of the iron's tumult *pierced (di-êixen) the depth of the cave (antrôn muchon)* and struck my grave *modesty (aidô)*" (133–34). The aerial/liquid ontology of their (im)material bodies is, in itself, a challenge to penetrative heteronormativity, which also breaks through the stale colonial air.

70 Griffith 1983, 22.

71 See Fanon 1967a, 122, on ankylosis as the condition of colonial or white affectivity, which translates into a desire to impose on the colonized flesh "a past that coalesces and adheres, repeatedly over time, but may also . . . become gangrenous" (Al-Saji 2022, 187). Fanon (1967b) famously said, "We revolt simply because . . . we can no longer breathe." On the spasm as a form of resistant activity against ankylosis, see Al-Saji 2022, 189; see also Dariek Scott 2010 and Moten 2018b (esp. ch. 1).

72 Ibrahim 2021, 10. The phrase "undifferentiated identity" is from Spillers (1987, 72), referring to Freud's notion of the "oceanic" in *Civilization and Its Discontents* (1930): "Those African persons in 'Middle Passage' were literally suspended in the 'oceanic,' if we think of the latter in its Freudian orientation as an analogy for undifferentiated identity: removed from the indigenous land and culture, and not yet 'American' either, these captive persons . . . were in movement across the Atlantic, but they were also *nowhere* at all."

73 See Moten 2003, 12, on "the generative force of a . . . phonic propulsion, the ontological and historical priority of resistance to power and objection to subjection."

74 Moten (2017, 278) speaks of "a recrudescence of the brutal forces of individuation that refused to *black matrical ecology* the capacity for those terrible incapacities of personality that *black matrical ecology* refused" (my italics). Moten posits a nexus between maternity (or "matrical ecology"), de-individuation, and Blackness. See Moten 2003, 16: "Enslavement—and the resistance to enslavement that is the performative essence of blackness . . . is a *being maternal* that is indistinguishable from a *being material*."

75 Bakola (2019, 232) remarks that *sidêro-mêtora . . . aian* "is perhaps intended to invoke a reputation for the land's natural production of iron."

76 Olsen 2020, 61.

77 Nooter 2017, 62. On the imagistic complex in these lines, see Mossman 1996, 63. Worman (2020b, 35) remarks that Io "is essentially a rape victim in waiting, undergoing the gadfly's constant jabbing as a kind of precursor to the ultimate violation of the virgin's bodily surfaces."

78 Olsen 2020, 69.

79 See Provenza 2019.

80 Fanon 1967a, 116 (my italics).

81 See Bassi 2010.

82 See Griffith 1983, 266.

83 See Telò 2020a, 118–19.

84 Stiegler 1998, 203.

85 Ruiz 2019, 143.

86 Ruiz 2019, 143.

87 After nearly two and a half years of evading Covid, I now find myself, at the end of July, in bed with a fever, having tested positive.

88 Rancière 2013, 94–97.

89 Rancière 2010, 51.

90 Speaking of the phenomenon of "circular breathing in jazz," Mackey (2021, 21) defines it as "an uninterrupted hyper-abundance of breath whose continuous flow intimates eternal ongoingness, unending abidance, everlasting life."

91 A. Davis 2020.

92 Shah 1998, 7 and 12.

9 Hecuba

1 Sanyal 2019, 435. Wallace (2020, 145) observes that "there was a new wave of compassion for refugees, prompted by the sentimental photo of a little child" and this photo "marked the beginning of an era of *aidôs*," which, however, did not last; Sanyal rightly warns that "the moral outrage and compassion" this photo and similar ones "provoke can foreclose an inquiry into the political conditions that produce the crisis in the first place."

2 Even though, in the prologue of Euripides' play, Polydorus's ghost presents himself as "suspended in the air" (*aiôroumenos* 32), leading one to surmise that "he probably appears on the *skênê* roof, also known as *theologeion*" (Battezzato 2018, 71), he shows a particular attachment to the shore in lines 28–30, analyzed below.

3 *Survivance*, albeit as a posthumous condition, resonates with *collective continuance*, which critical phenomenologist Kyle Whyte has defined as "an understanding of existence as living through diverse, constantly changing relationships with different species, ancestors, future generations, and spiritual and ecological beings (e.g., water)" (2020, 56).

4 The characterization of Polydorus that I am proposing here is similar to the one I offered for Dionysus in my reading of *Bacchae* in chapter 2. On Polydorus as a figuration of Derridean hauntology through the mediation of the ghost of Shakespeare's *Hamlet*, see Bassi 2017.

5   For the phrase "surplus emotion," see Clover 2016, 1.

6   I owe this point about "surging" to Cavarero (2021, 12), analyzing Hannah Arendt's political thought.

7   See, e.g., Morrison 1994, 176, and 2008, 38–39; on Morrison's novels and Greek tragedy, see, among others, Jones 1985; Haley 1995; Otten 1998; Emmett 2010; Roynon 2013, 11–14 and (ch. 3); McConnell 2016; Quayson 2021 (ch. 6); and Cullhed 2022.

8   See Ellen Prentiss Campbell: "In riveting passages, the migrant children's voices mingle with" that of the ego narrator's son, "building to a conclusion powerful and pre-ordained as a passion play or Greek tragedy" (https://www.nyjournalofbooks.com/book-review/lost-children).

9   For a reading of this prophecy, see Telò 2020b, 174–78.

10 Here I quote Best (2018), 94. On the Middle Passage, see, among others, the foundational works of Gilroy (1993), Baucom (2005), Hartman (2007), and V. Brown (2008).

11 See Telò 2020b, 174–80.

12 Sharpe 2016, 21.

13 Sharpe 2016, 21.

14 Sharpe 2016, 40.

15 Sharpe 2016, 40.

16 Demos (2020, 23) observes that the installation "investigates the ocean as a multivalent site of geopolitical conflict, liquid nationality, and postnational uprooting, all set within still-unfolding histories of colonialism, migration, slavery, and environmental transformation." As Demos continues, "The sea . . . becomes a vast sea of dissolving bodies . . . an abstract space of abstract liquidity" (32).

17 Demos 2020, 36.

18 The Shakespearean phrase "out of joint," central to Derridean hauntology and queer theory, was first applied to the play by Luschnig (1976); see Telò 2020b, 161–80. On Polydorus as the queer figure of "the dead child," see Bassi 2022a.

19 Battezzato 2018 ad loc. The prefix *di-* in *di-aulois* is the numeral *duo* ("two"), etymologically connected with the preposition *dia* ("through"), which indicates a passage, a cutting through. The ending of the play—with Hecuba prospectively becoming Polydorus—is a movement backward, which mimics this "double course."

20 As Ingersoll (2016, 6) puts it, considering Indigenous seascape epistemology, "The ocean . . . is the point from which we have always leapt off, physically and philosophically, into our pasts and our futures."

21 Alvarez 2019.

22 Enríquez (2021, 81) calls the novel "an archive of what is missing, has been disregarded, or cannot be apprehended."

23 Best 2018, 15. While the husband embodies a conventional notion of documentarism as a kind of (re)collection, acquisition, and possession, we could say that the vision embraced by the wife/ego narrator is perhaps closer to the one laid out by Demos (2013, 208), who thinks of the documentarian mode not "as the truthful depiction of an already existing subject, but the construction of a system of possibility that remains open, realizable in a multiplicity of views" by various audiences. This model is also perhaps close to Saidiya Hartman's idea of "fabulation," predicated on "enacting the impossibility of representing the lives of the captives precisely through the process of narration" (2008, 11).

24 Incorporation and surveillance are expressions of what De Genova (2013) has called "the obscene of inclusion," the flip side of "the scene of exclusion," in the so-called humanitarian (un)welcoming of immigrants and refugees at the border.

25 Archival "documentation" can replicate the practices of "legalization" at the border, which turn the immigrants into a number, a biometric datum, or a commodity, in a process where "metaphorization" slips into "matterphorization" in line with the *longue durée* of colonialism: see, esp., Sanyal 2021, 325–26. On the term *matterphorical*, see Gandorfer 2020 and Gandorfer and Ayub 2020. See also chapter 8.

26 Klaas (2021, 88) observes that Luiselli's novel gives expression to "fugitive literacies" that "work to explore the lives and the spaces that have been rendered illegible in the process of drafting sovereign territories and citizens." For Klaas, *Lost Children Archive* "develops an epistemology of insecurity that works to keep the children 'safe' by thwarting their capture within reliable and familiar representational patterns" (89).

27 Foucault 2000 and 2019.

28 See Best 2018, 17–19, and Telò 2020b, 177.

29 Agamben 2007, 65.

30 Luiselli 2017.

31 On metalepsis as a trope of disappearance, see Best 2018, 103–6.

32 "Recognition politics" refers to the state's self-exculpatory gesture of recognizing Indigenous genocides while relegating them to an inert notion of the past, incorporating them into official, hierarchical forms of remembrance, and failing to take full responsibility for them. Commenting on the foundational work of Vizenor (1998), Madsen (2008, 66) observes that "survivance ... is not passive survival but an active resistance as well: it is the refusal of the 'manifest manners' of dominance, which posits insistently Native people as 'Vanished,' or as tragic victims, or as ig/noble savages frozen in a mythical past, or even as ecowarriors in an idealised New Age future."

33 See Derrida 2011a, 119: "If from *life* we appeal to *light*, from *vie* to *vision*, we can speak here of *sur-vie*, of living on in a life-after-life or a life-after-death, as *sur-vision*, 'seeing on' in a vision-beyond-vision." As Derrida continues, "*More-than-life* (*sur-vie*) marks ... a temporal extension of life, in the form of a reprieve (*sursis*)" (147). Derrida's theorization operates explicitly with marine imagery and the idea of the "shore." Saghafi (2020, 102) explains that "living 'beyond' one's death, *sur-vivre* is not life *after* death (a state of life or a continuation of life) but rather sur-viving, *more* life still."

34 Luiselli 2019, 170.

35 J. Butler (2022, 22), commenting on Scheler 1954. See also the Introduction.

36 Morrison 2000, 260. As Best (2018, 69) observes, "Paralepsis is called on to gentle the reader's experience of the terror of slavery, and, as in the Bible, the novel's koan-like phrase ('This is not a story to pass on') emphasizes the recovered story by appearing to pass over it."

37 For readings of the healing power of the "Clearing," see Henderson 2006 and Reed 2007; but see J. Bailey (2017, 31), who points out that "Baby Suggs's desire for a purely safe and communal black space . . . protected and extracted from white space is a romanticized vision that fails to capture just how pervasive and unspeakable the trauma of slavery is." See also Wyatt 1993, 484, and George 2012.

38 Morrison 2000, 275 (my italics).

39 Barthes 1989, 76–77.

40 Though not in reference to this passage, J. Bailey (2017) discusses the subversive force of sound in *Beloved*.

41 Erickson (2009, 54) suggests that in the novel's coda, which "conflates erasure and denial," "a trace of Beloved remains as a feeling of unease." Quayson (2021, 202) observes that "Sethe's account of time is . . . of the persistent recalcitrance of past moments to being subsumed within any simple framework of temporality. It is an active constitutive principle of time that is independent of the interpreter's intentionality or viewpoint . . . something that waits in its chronotopic singularity to be reencountered rather than simply reinterpreted."

42 Paredez 2013. The poem is part of Paredez's archival reflection on her Latinx father's service in Vietnam and "the full impact" of such service, an enterprise made difficult by the fact that "the military categorized Latinxs racially as white" (Paredez in Ben-Oni 2020). Hecuba, her canine abjection, and her rough sonorities are central to Paredez's poetic imaginary: see the beginning of "Self-Portrait with Weeping Woman" in her collection *Year of the Dog* (2020): "I know why I feel hard for Hecuba— / shins skinned and lips split to blooming lupine / on her throat's rough coat, *hurled down the whole length / of disaster.*"

43 On the herbicidal warfare that the U.S. government deployed in Vietnam from 1961 to 1971, see Zierler (2011), who shows that the very concept of "ecocide" emerged in response to the ecological catastrophe of the war. See also Nguyen 2009.

44 I am using "patho-logy" in the sense of affective unsettledness as theorized by Barthes (2005, 77), who also uses the notion of "queasiness" in connection with anger.

45 I owe the phrase to A. S. Weiss (2002, 35–36), who refers to Bachelard 1943. For A. S. Weiss, "poetic exuberance" is a quality that allows the interpreter to perceive the texture of poetry as "an incredible plurality of … breaths."

46 Moten (2003, 16) observes that "the resistance to enslavement that is the performative essence of blackness … is a *being maternal* that is indistinguishable from a *being material*."

47 Pugliese 2020, 96. Pugliese shows how what he calls "more-than-human entities"—that is, "trees, water, soil, and so on"—"are exposed to practices of destruction due to … various biopolitical campaigns" (8). He coins the terms *aquapolitics*, *phytopolitics*, *pedonpolitics*, and *aeropolitics* to describe the "biopolitical destruction, expropriation, and control" of Palestine's water resources, vegetal life, soil, air, and atmosphere.

48 Pugliese 2020, 97–98.

49 Thucydides 2.48.2. Hornblower (1991 ad loc.) notes that "allegations of well-poisoning were made against minority groups (Jews, Arabs, pilgrims, lepers) at the time of the Black Death."

50 Perga 2022.

51 Coccia (2019, 55), who adds that "only breath can touch and feel the world, giving it existence."

52 Here I repurpose a sentence of J. Butler (2009, 61), commenting on the poetry of Guantanamo prisoners.

53 Crawley (2016, 75) observes that "the air, the breath, allows in admixture, produces the violent force of violence's own dissolution."

54 I borrow this phrase from Hartman (1997, 48).

10 The Trojan Women

1 Bruno and Carson 2021, 14.

2 In this production, entitled *Queens of Syria*, the "horizon of an inarticulable future" and "intensity of … grief" define its "expressive power" and the "urgency of its hope," as Eberwine (2018) remarks.

3 Freccero 2022, 48.

4 The production of Euripides' *Trojan Women* in 415 BCE, on the eve of the Sicilian expedition and after the Athenian assault on the neutral island of Melos, in which all male citizens were killed and women and children were enslaved, has made the play the target of the most sustained historicist approaches: see, most recently, Kovacs 2018, 2–16. (The necropolitical realpolitik that emerges from Thucydides' account of Athens'

ultimatum to Melos before the massacre was regarded as inspirational by Steve Bannon and the Trump administration: see https://www.theatlantic.com/international/archive/2017/07/the-summer-of-misreading-thucydides/533859/). The critique of the formal "anomaly" of *Trojan Women* was formulated, in 1905, by one of the play's greatest fans, Gilbert Murray: "Judged by common standards, the *Troades* is far from a perfect play; it is scarcely even a good play. It is an intense study of one great situation, with little plot, little construction, little or no *relief* or variety" (2005, 3 [my italics]). While for Murray this lack of "relief" makes the play "[pass] beyond the due limits of tragic art," it is precisely the rejection of relief and the episodic disruption of the *muthos* that make this play deeply tragic: see Telò 2020b, esp. 156–61 and 178–82, and 2023a, ch. 1 (on the political aesthetics of episodicity in the light of J. Rancière). The author of the most recent commentary on the play, Kovacs (2018, 51–52) maintains that the play "lacks the kind of unity that allows one to see actions earlier in the play leading to the dénouement at the end." After the dialogue between Poseidon and Athena, when we see Hecuba unable (or unwilling) to stand up, we experience the metapoetic feeling of a play not wanting to begin, refusing to take shape: see Shirazi 2022 on Hecuba's refusal ("Her performance questions the possibility of any action, movement or dance that one would expect from a Greek tragedy").

5   Freccero 2022, 48.

6   On the anti-futural orientation of Euripides' *Trojan Women*, see Freccero 2022; see also Wohl 2018, 31–33.

7   Bruno and Carson 2021, 6; Seidel 1999. That Carson alludes to Baldwin's essay through Seidel's poem is shown by the image of Troy as a run-down hotel, which evokes "the ludicrously grim hotel," where, in Baldwin's account, an alleged theft of linen led to his arrest.

8   Bruno and Carson 2021, 12–13.

9   Bruno and Carson 2021, 12–13.

10 I am referring to the thicket of lines that surrounds—and almost enwraps—the raven Talthybius when he addresses Agamemnon as "king of all Greeks" and warns him of the disastrous consequences of his infatuation with Cassandra (Bruno and Carson 2021, 27).

11 Bruno and Carson 2021, 14 and 25, where the text accompanying the drawing of the mass grave says: "Shall I list all they lost? Ten thousand men for the sake of Helen … Lost to them all their lives at home. The wife, the child, the hearth, the winding sheet. The proper grave site and someone to call out their name. Their tomb is homelessness. Their name is *nothing*. Air."

12 See chapters 5 and 8. In relation to mass graves on Hart Island in New York City, which "[drove] home both the dehumanization and the structural inequalities underlying Covid illness, treatment, and death," Blair (2021, 54) observes, "No Covid victims can be seen, only the bulldozed earth waiting to enclose them."

13 Bruno and Carson 2021, 18.

14 Bruno and Carson 2021, 32.

15 Bruno and Carson 2021, 19.

16 Bruno and Carson 2021, 19–20. On page 19, "Odysseus owns you now" is followed by a voice bubble with this text, "NO. NO. NO. That Toad. That plague. That double-tongued twister of love into hate, *that vapour of every thing poisoned. No*" (my italics). On the following page, the metaphor of the "vapor" is literalized by the appearance of a proliferation of NO's projected onto a black surface.

17 See Derrida 2002b. Derrida connects the plurality of *animot* with what can be called frontal indexicality: "The animal is there before me, there close to me, there in front of me" (380).

18 Bruno and Carson 2021, 16–17.

19 See King 2022, 40: "Everything on Zoom appears to take place in a timeless vacuum."

20 Willis 2014, 137. Blair (2021, 53) notes that "the display of portrait photos has been a shared practice of protest across pandemic contexts, in demonstrations against police killings of Black Americans like Breonna Taylor."

21 On the face and Levinas, see chapter 3. On matterphorization, see chapters 8 and 9. Discussing the circulation of photo portraits of health care workers in the midst of the pandemic's first year, Blair (2021, 48) wonders: "How long does recognition of the ethical power and courage, the 'beauty', of frontline workers, medical or otherwise, obstruct a view of the structural conditions that underlie their efforts? Can the humanism of the portrait be separable from neoliberal and corporate contexts of its invocation?"

22 See, e.g., Campbell 2006, 17, on Roberto Esposito's affirmative biopolitics: "When the immunitary apparatus attacks *bios* by producing *zôê*, a space opens in which it becomes possible to posit *bios* but as its ultimate horizon. There can be no *zôê* that isn't already *bios*."

23 Feldman (2010, 123 and 128) theoretically advocates for a "a zoo-anarchism that trespasses against the interior, thresholds, and edges of the political enclosures of qualified life" or, in other terms, an "animality . . . preceding the political and . . . insulated as a founding transhistorical apolitical *arkhé*."

24 On the connection of these technologies of racializing surveillance with practices of epidermalization and "branding," see Browne 2015, ch. 3. See also, among others, van der Ploeg 2005, Currah and Mulqueen 2011, Sanyal 2021, and Blair 2021, 43.

25 Bruno and Carson 2021, 27.

26 Bruno and Carson 2021, 28–29.

27 Bruno and Carson 2021, 44.

28 Bruno and Carson 2021, 45.

29 The root attached to the child's body is barely distinguishable from a fuse. Astyanax's quasi-mechanization is perhaps a mimetic response to Menelaus, transformed by

Bruno and Carson into "some sort of gearbox, clutch or coupling mechanism" (2021, 52).

30 Bersani (1976, 3–14) chooses a scene from Racine's *Andromaque* (where Astyanax figures only as a marginal character) to theorize how "the activity of desiring may include a pleasure intense enough to *shatter* the desiring self" (my italics [14]). The Euripidean line "you will shatter your breath" seems to look ahead to Bersani's later embrace of Laplanche's "self-shattering" in his reflection on the HIV epidemic: see esp. Bersani 2010 (ch. 1).

31 Clark 2017, 20.

32 https://www.reuters.com/world/europe/invoking-guernica-bombing-ukraines-zelenskiy-urges-spain-force-russia-out-2022-04-05/.

33 https://www.latimes.com/world-nation/story/2022-06-01/an-artist-confronts-the-anguish-and-hope-of-ukraine.

34 Clark 2017, 44. In an interview cited by Clark, Picasso spoke of death that "could fall from heaven on so many."

35 I borrow the translation of the original French of the poem from Clark (2017, 47–48).

36 Clark (2017, 49) reads this "stare" as an impossible search for Aristotelian *anagnōrisis* ("recognition").

37 On this figure, see Wagner 2017.

38 Bruno and Carson 2021, 38–41.

39 Bruno and Carson 2021, 34–35.

40 Bruno and Carson 2021, 71.

41 Toadvine 2020, 150: "The self-emergence of *phusis* is inseparable from its withdrawal or self-concealment, which is not a hiddenness but rather a source of sheltering and reserve: to emerge and extend itself into the air, the plant must be rooted in the dense opacity of the soil."

42 On breathing and Indigenous pananimisms, see Rahman and Brabec de Mori 2020.

Epilogue

1 https://www.theguardian.com/books/2022/jul/30/delphi-by-clare-pollard-review-bleakly-funny-lockdown-tale.

2 Ibid.

3 See the epigraph of the book: "Kassandra: [scream] [scream] [scream] [scream]—Anne Carson." Elsewhere the narrator says: "Apollo speaks through me in a surge. I feel him

clack my jaw and writhe my tongue in my mouth as Ancient Greek words pour pour pour" (118). As I write, I am reading about Helen Eastman's production of *Cassandra*, the 1908 poetic drama of pioneer Ukrainian feminist Lesya Ukrainka, at the Omnibus Theatre in London in October 2022.

4 "And news just keeps coming, the endless news. News is our lives now. It gives our lives a narrative, in place of individual action—news has rushed in to fill the void" (145).

5 "Aristotle's *Poetics* tells us that in tragedy the tragic hero always has a *hamartia*—a tragic flaw; a mistake. It comes from the term *hamartanein*, for an archer missing his target. At the end the tragic hero has a moment of *anagnorisis*. A change from ignorance to awareness" (116).

6 See Telò 2020b, 90–113.

7 "I kind of push Jason up the first steep step and then he trips up the set of them like a sacrificial goat up to the altar" (69).

8 "Medea's filicide revolts us because it is impossible. We can't believe she kills her children deliberately: it goes against our every instinct. . . . Many women kill their children by accident, don't they? I sometimes wonder if I'll be one of them" (103–4).

9 "His [Jason's] breath like a dragon's breath; a rotting body in a fissure . . . and the snakes in my hair hiss at him to fuck off. . . . I feel this crazed thirst for fresh air, like I'll die without it" (152).

10 Pollard 2022, 183. Euripides, *Medea* 230–31.

11 Pollard 2022, 187–89.

12 Berlant 2011.

13 For a different reading of Medea's escape, see Telò 2020b, 108–13, and Nooter 2022.

14 On politics and neurodiversity as "overfeeling," an intense "feeling-with-the world," see Manning (2020, 256), who observes that the aim of recognizing neurodiversity is "a commitment to the singular ways difference expresses itself and the qualities of desire, knowledge, and creation it produces" (291).

15 Berlant 2022, 28.

16 See Plutarch, *On the Oracles at Delphi* 398c–d. On the Pythia's prophecies as an "air-borne vapor" (*pneuma*), a meteorological/geological phenomenon, see Green 2009; see also Littleton 1986, 77–84.

17 See esp. Bakewell 2013 and Derbew 2022 (ch. 3). Wohl (2009b, 409) reads Aeschylus's play as an exemplification of how "the Western state undertakes to represent the foreign woman politically . . . slotting her into a narrative that evacuates her political agency and replaces her indigenous voice with its own righteous action."

18 On the trajectory of the trilogy, see, e.g., Zeitlin 1996 (ch. 4).

19 Hesiod, fragment 128 Merkelbach-West. See Keuls 1974 and, esp., Bachvarova 2009. By becoming nymphs, the Danaids express their refusal to become *numphai* ("wives"). The Danaids will be condemned to fetch water in leaking pots forever.

20 See the abundance of *sun* compounds (*su-strephô* and *sun-istêmi*) in the description of condensed air causing rain in Hippocrates, *Airs Waters Places* 8.

21 In her pioneering reading of the play, Zeitlin (1996, 162) observes that "the Danaids . . . are called a band, swarm, or flock in implicit contrast to the masculine community (*koinon*) of the polis, whose members, persuaded by *logos*, act unanimously in the political arena of the assembly." However, the very word *pan-dêmia* in an explicitly atmospheric, vibrating context disrupts the opposition by turning the assembly into a "swarm" itself: on the rhetoric of the swarm in refugee discourse, see Telò 2023a (ch. 3).

22 Ingold (2020, 165), who sees "to breathe" as "not to run with the current, but to deviate from it." See Cavell 1969, 52.

Bibliography

Abramson, A. J. 2018. "Joseph Conrad's Atmospheric Modernism: Enveloping Fog, Narrative Frames, and Affective Attunement." *Studies in the Novel* 50.3: 336–58.

Agamben, G. 2000. *Means without End*. Minneapolis.

Agamben, G. 2007. *Profanations*. New York.

Agamben, G. 2016. *The Use of Bodies*. Stanford, CA.

Ahl, F. 1991. *Sophocles' Oedipus: Evidence and Self-Conviction*. Ithaca, NY.

Ahl, F. 1997. "Admetus Deuteragonistes." *Colby Quarterly* 33.1: 9–25.

Ahmed, S. 2006. *Queer Phenomenology: Orientations, Objects, Others*. Durham, NC.

Ahmed, S. 2019. *What's the Use?* Durham, NC.

Alaimo, S. 2000. *Undomesticated Ground: Recasting Nature as Feminist Space*. Ithaca, NY.

Alaimo, S. 2008. "Trans-Corporeal Feminisms and the Ethical Space of Nature." In *Material Feminisms*, edited by S. Alaimo and S. Hekman, 237–64. Bloomington, IN.

Alfaro, L. 2021. *The Greek Trilogy of Luis Alfaro: Electricidad/Oedipus El Rey/Mojada*. London.

Allen, I. K. 2020. "Thinking with a Feminist Political Ecology of Air-and-breathing-bodies." *Body and Society* 26.2: 79–105.

Allen, L. C., and J. S. Garrison. 2022. "Against Friendship." In *Queer Kinship: Race, Sex, Belonging, Form*, edited by T. Bradway and E. Freeman, 227–47. Durham, NC.

Alloa, E. 2021. "Coronavirus: A Contingency That Eliminates Contingency." *Critical Inquiry* 47.2: 73–76.

Al-Saji, A. 2020. "*Durée*." In *50 Concepts for a Critical Phenomenology*, edited by G. Weiss, A. V. Murphy, and G. Salamon, 99–106. Evanston, IL.

Al-Saji, A. 2022. "Too Late: Fanon, the Dismembered Past, and a Phenomenology of Racialized Time." In *Fanon, Phenomenology, and Psychology*, edited by L. Laubscher, D. Hook, and M. U. Desai, 177–93. New York.

Alvarez, A. C. 2019. "Valeria Luiselli's Impossible Novel". *The New Republic* (April 4, 2019). https://newrepublic.com/article/153460/valeria-luisellis-impossible-novel.

Anderson, B. 2009. "Affective Atmospheres." *Emotion, Space, and Society* 2.2: 77–81.

Anker, E. 2022. *Ugly Freedoms*. Durham, NC.

Appel, L. 2010. "Autochthonous Antigone: Breaking Ground." In *Interrogating Antigone in Postmodern Philosophy and Criticism*, edited by S. E. Wilmer and A. Zukauskaite, 229–39. Oxford.

Armstrong, R., et al. 2022. "Symposium on M. Telò, *Archive Feelings: A Theory of Greek Tragedy*." https://syndicate.network/symposia/literature/archive-feelings.

Arthur-Montagne, J. 2017. "Symptoms of the Sublime: Longinus and the Hippocratic Method of Criticism." *GRBS* 57: 325–55.

Aumercier, S., C. Homs, et al. 2020. *De virus* [sic] *illustribus: Crise du coronavirus et épuisement structurel du capitalisme*. Albi.

Bachelard, G. 1943. *L' air et les songes: essai sur l'imagination du mouvement*. Paris.

Bachvarova, M. R. 2009. "Suppliant Danaids and Argive Nymphs in Aeschylus." *CJ* 104.4: 289–310.

Bailey, J. 2017. "Breaking the Back of Words: Sound and Subversion in Toni Morrison's *Beloved*." *Palimpsest* 6.1: 28–43.

Bailey, M. M. 2020. "Black Queerness and the Cruel Irony of the Covid-19 Pandemic." *QED* 7.3: 174–78.

Bakewell, G. 2013. *Aeschylus' Suppliant Women: The Tragedy of Immigration*. Madison, WI.

Bakola, E. 2019. "Space, Place, and the Metallurgical Imagination of the *Prometheus* Trilogy." In *Ancient Theatre and Performance Culture around the Black Sea*, edited by D. Braund, E. Hall, R. Wyles, 225–51. Cambridge.

Barad, K. 2017. "Troubling Time/s and Ecologies of Nothingness: Re-turning, Re-membering, and Facing the Incalculable." *New Formations* 92.1: 56–86.

Barchiesi, A. 1997. *The Poet and the Prince*. Berkeley.

Bargu, B. 2014. *Starve and Immolate: The Politics of Human Weapons*. New York.

Bargu, B. 2016. "Another Necropolitics." *Theory & Event* 19.1 (Supplement) [No pages].

Bargu, B., ed. 2019. *Turkey's Necropolitical Laboratory: Democracy, Violence, and Resistance*. Edinburgh.

Barnett, M. 2020. "Covid-19 and the Sacrificial International Order." *International Organization* 74 (Supplement): 1–20.

Barthes, R. 1981. *Camera Lucida: Reflections on Photography*. New York.

Barthes, R. 1989. *The Rustle of Language*. Berkeley.

Barthes, R. 2005. *The Neutral*. New York.

Bassi, K. 2010. "Making Prometheus Speak: Dialogue, Torture, and the Power of Secrets in *Prometheus Bound*." In *When Worlds Elide: Classics, Politics, Culture*, edited by K. Bassi and P. Euben, 77–109. Lanham, MD.

Bassi, K. 2017. "Mimesis and Mortality: Reperformance and the Dead among the Living in *Hecuba* and *Hamlet*." In *Imagining Reperformance in Ancient Culture*, edited by R. Hunter and A. Uhlig, 138–59. Cambridge.

Bassi, K. 2018. "Morbid Materialism: The Matter of the Corpse in Euripides' *Alcestis*." In *The Materialities of Greek Tragedy: Objects and Affect in Aeschylus, Sophocles, and Euripides*, edited by M. Telò and M. Mueller, 35–48. London.

Bassi, K. 2022a. "*Hecuba*—The Dead Child, or Queer for a Day." In *Queer Euripides: Re-readings in Greek Tragedy*, edited by S. Olsen and M. Telò, 167–75. London.

Bassi, K. 2022b. Review of B. Honig, *A Feminist Theory of Refusal*. *Political Theory* 50.6: 980–85.

Bassi, K., and J. P. Euben. 2010. "Introduction." In *When Worlds Elide: Classics, Politics, Culture*, edited by K. Bassi and J. P. Euben, ix–xxi. Lanham, MD.

Bataille, G. 2005. *The Cradle of Humanity: Prehistoric Art and Culture*. New York.

Battezzato, L., ed. 2018. *Euripides: Hecuba*. Cambridge.

Battezzato, L. 2022. "Migrant Refusals: the Inoperativity of the Asian Bacchae in Euripides." *CA* 41.2: 4–15.

Batuman, E. 2020. "Can Greek Tragedy Get Us through the Pandemic?" *The New Yorker*. https://www.newyorker.com/culture/culture-desk/can-greek-tragedy-get-us-through-the-pandemic.

Baucom, I. 2005. *Specters of the Atlantic: Finance Capital, Slavery, and the Philosophy of History*. Durham, NC.

Baudrillard, J. 1989. "Anorexic Ruins." In *Looking Back on the End of the World*, edited by D. Kamper and C. Wulf, 29–45. Los Angeles.

Baudrillard, J. 1993. *Symbolic Exchange and Death*. New York.

Benardete, S. 1999. *Sacred Transgressions: A Reading of Sophocles'* Antigone. South Bend, IN.

Benjamin, A. 2024. "Countering Injury: On the Deaths of the Niobids." In *Niobes: Antiquity Modernity Critical Theory*, edited by M. Telò and A. Benjamin. Columbus, OH.

Benjamin, W. 1969. *Illuminations: Essays and Reflections*. New York.

Benjamin, W. 2021. *Toward the Critique of Violence*. Stanford, CA.

Bennett, J. 2020. *Influx and Efflux: Writing Up with Walt Whitman*. Durham, NC.

Bennington, G. 2011. "A Moment of Madness: Derrida's Kierkegaard." *Oxford Literary Review* 33.1: 103–27.

Ben-Oni, R. 2020. "Verve {in} Verse: Deborah Paredez." *Kenyon Review* https://kenyonreview.org/2020/10/verve-in-verse-deborah-paredez/

Berlant, L. 1994. "America, 'Fat,' the Fetus." *boundary 2* 21.3: 145–95.

Berlant, L. 2007. "Slow Death (Sovereignty, Obesity, Lateral Agency)." *Critical Inquiry* 33.4: 754–80.

Berlant, L. 2008. *The Female Complaint: The Unfinished Business of Sentimentality in American Culture*. Durham, NC.

Berlant, L. 2011. *Cruel Optimism*. Durham, NC.

Berlant, L. 2022. *On the Inconvenience of Other People*. Durham, NC.

Bersani, L. 1976. *A Future for Astyanax: Character and Desire in Literature*. Boston.

Bersani, L. 2010. *Is the Rectum a Grave? And Other Essays*. Chicago.

Best, S. 2018. *None Like Us*. Durham, NC.

Bey, M. 2017. "The Trans*-ness of Blackness, the Blackness of Trans*-ness." *TSQ* 4.2: 275–95.

Bey, M. 2022. *Cistem Failure: Essays on Blackness and Cisgender*. Durham, NC.

Bissell, D. 2007. "Animating Suspension: Waiting for Mobilities." *Mobilities* 2.2: 277–98.

Blair, S. 2021. "Facing Our Pandemic." In *Being Human during Covid*, edited by K. A. Hass, 43–63. Ann Arbor, MI.

Blanchot, M. 1986. *The Writing of Disaster*. Lincoln, NE.

Blanshard, A. 2022. "*Heracles*—Homosexual Panic and Irresponsible Reading." In *Queer Euripides: Re-Readings in Greek Tragedy*, edited by S. Olsen and M. Telò, 133–44. London.

Bowie, A. M. 1997. "Tragic Filters for History: Euripides' *Supplices* and Sophocles' *Philoctetes*." In *Greek Tragedy and the Historian*, edited by C. B. R. Pelling, 39–62. Oxford.

Bowman, B. 2020. "On the Biopolitics of Breathing: Race, Protests, and State Violence under the Global Threat of Covid-19." *South African Journal of Psychology*: 1–4.

Bradol, J.-H. 2004. "Introduction: The Sacrificial International Order and Humanitarian Action." In *The Shadow of "Just Wars": Violence, Politics, and Humanitarian Action*, edited by F. Weissman, 1–22. Ithaca, NY.

Bradway, T. 2021. "Queer Narrative Theory and the Relationality of Form." *PMLA* 136.5: 711–27.

Bradway, T., and E. Freeman. 2022. "Introduction: Kincoherence/Kin-aesthetics/Kinematics." In *Queer Kinship: Race, Sex, Belonging, Form,* edited by T. Bradway and E. Freeman, 1–22. Durham, NC.

Braunstein, N. 2021. "The Return of Antigone: Burial Rites in Pandemic Times." In *Coronavirus, Psychoanalysis, and Philosophy: Conversations on Pandemics, Politics, and Society,* edited by F. Castrillón and T. Marchevsky, 66–75. London.

Brennan, T. 2004. *The Transmission of Affect.* Ithaca, NY.

Britto, K. A. 2009. "*L'esprit de corps*: French Civilization and the Death of the Colonized Soldier." In *Empire Lost: France and Its Other Worlds,* edited by E. Mudimbe-Boyi, 145–61. Lanham, MD.

brown, drea. 2024. "'How Strangely Changed.' Phillis Wheatley in Niobean Myth and Memory: An Essay in Verse." In *Niobes: Antiquity Modernity Critical Theory,* edited by M. Telò and A. Benjamin. Columbus, OH.

Brown, V. 2008. *The Reaper's Garden: Death and Power in the World of Atlantic Slavery.* Cambridge, MA.

Brown, W. 1993. "Wounded Attachments." *Political Theory* 21.3: 390–410.

Brown, W. 2009. "Sovereign Hesitations." In *Derrida and the Time of the Political,* edited by P. Cheah and S. Guerlac, 114–32. Durham, NC.

Browne, S. 2015. *Dark Matters: On the Surveillance of Blackness.* Durham, NC.

Browning, R. 1895. *The Complete Poetic and Dramatic Works.* Cambridge.

Browning, R. 1981. *The Poems,* edited by J. Pettigrew and T. Collins. Harmondsworth.

Bruno, R., and A. Carson. 2021. *Euripides: The Trojan Women. A Comic.* New York.

Bryan-Wilson, J. 2017. *Fray: Art and Textile Politics.* Chicago.

Burke, S. 2018. "In *XENOS*, a Dancer Turns Troubled Warrior." *New York Times,* November 1. https://www.nytimes.com/2018/11/01/arts/dance/review-xenos-akram-khan-white-light.html.

Buser, M. 2017. "The Time Is Out of Joint: Atmosphere and Hauntology at Bodiam Castle." *Emotion, Space and Society* 25: 5–13.

Butler, J. 1990. *Gender Trouble: Feminism and the Subversion of Identity.* New York.

Butler, J. 2000. *Antigone's Claim: Kinship between Life and Death.* New York.

Butler, J. 2001. "Giving an Account of Oneself." *Diacritics* 31.4: 22–40.

Butler, J. 2003. "Afterword: After Loss, What Then?" In *Loss: The Politics of Mourning,* edited by D. L. Eng and D. Kazanjian, 467–73. Berkeley.

Butler, J. 2004. *Precarious Life: The Powers of Mourning and Violence.* London.

Butler, J. 2009. *Frames of War: When Is Life Grievable?* London.

Butler, J. 2013. *Parting Ways: Jewishness and the Critique of Zionism.* New York.

Butler, J. 2015a. *Senses of the Subject.* New York.

Butler, J. 2015b. *Notes toward a Performative Theory of Assembly.* Cambridge, MA.

Butler, J. 2016. "Rethinking Vulnerability and Resistance." In *Vulnerability in Resistance,* edited by J. Butler, Z. Gambetti, and L. Sabsay, 12–27. Durham, NC.

Butler, J. 2017. "Kinship Trouble in the *Bacchae*." Housman Lecture, UCL. https://www.youtube.com/watch?v=ixwrw0PMC8I.

Butler, J. 2020a. "Companion Thinking: A Response." *NLH* 51.4: 687–94.

Butler, J. 2020b. *The Force of Nonviolence*. London.

Butler, J. 2021a. "Fury and Justice in the Humanities." Danziger Lecture, University of Chicago, November 11.

Butler, J. 2021b. "Leaning Out, Caught in the Fall: Interdependency and Ethics in Cavarero." In *Toward a Feminist Ethics of Nonviolence: Adriana Cavarero with Judith Butler, Bonnie Honig, and Other Voices*, edited by T. J. Huzar and C. Woodford, 46–62. New York.

Butler, J. 2022. *What World Is This? A Pandemic Phenomenology*. New York.

Butler, J. 2023. "Improvisational Solidarity: A Conversation with Judith Butler." In *Shorter and spalding's . . . (Iphigenia)*, edited by H. Morales and M. Telò. *Ramus*.

Butler, J., and A. Athanasiou. 2013. *Dispossession: The Performative in the Political*. Cambridge.

Butler, S. 2009. "The Backward Glance." *Arion* (ser. 3) 17.2: 59–78.

Butler, S. 2011. *The Matter of the Page*. Madison, WI.

Cacciari, M. 2009a. *Hamletica*. Milan.

Cacciari, M. 2009b. *The Unpolitical: On the Radical Critique of Political Reason*. New York.

Cairns, D. 2014. "The Bloody Dust of the Nether Gods: Sophocles, *Antigone* 599–603." In *Paradeigmata: Studies in Honor of Ø. Andersen*, edited by E. K. Emilsson et al., 39–51. Athens.

Calame, C. 1986. "Facing Otherness: The Tragic Mask in Ancient Greece." *History of Religions* 26.2: 125–42.

Campbell, T. 2006. "*Bios*, Immunity, Life: The Thought of Roberto Esposito." *Diacritics* 36.2: 2–22.

Cant, S. G. 2003. "'The Tug of Danger with the Magnetism of Mystery': Descents into 'the Comprehensive, Poetic-Sensuous Appeal of Caves.'" *Tourist Studies* 3.1: 67–81.

Cao, M. 2017. "Icescapes." *American Art* 31.2: 48–50.

Caron, D. 2021. "Waiting=Death: Covid-19, the Struggle for Racial Justice, and the AIDS Pandemic." In *Being Human during Covid*, edited by K. A. Hass, 93–116. Ann Arbor, MI.

Carson, A. 2012. *Antigo Nick*. New York.

Carson, A. 2021. "Stillness." *Critical Inquiry* 48.1: 1–22.

Casali, S. 1997. "*Quaerenti Plura Legendum*: On the Necessity of 'Reading More' in Ovid's Exile Poetry." *Ramus* 26.1: 80–112.

Castillo, E. 2021. "The Virus That Kills Twice: Covid-19 and Domestic Violence under Governmental Impunity in Nicaragua." In *Being Human during Covid*, edited by K. A. Hass, 250–55. Ann Arbor, MI.

Cavarero, A. 2016. *Inclinations: A Critique of Rectitude*. Stanford, CA.

Cavarero, A. 2021. *Surging Democracy: Notes on Hannah Arendt's Political Thought*. Stanford, CA.

Cavarero, A. 2024. "Niobe's Hypermaternity." In *Niobes: Antiquity Modernity Critical Theory*, edited by M. Telò and A. Benjamin. Columbus, OH.

Cavell, S. 1969. *Must We Mean What We Say? A Book of Essays*. Cambridge.

Chakrabarty, D. 2021. *The Climate of History in a Planetary Age*. Chicago.

Chanter, T. 2011. *Whose Antigone? The Tragic Marginalization of Slavery*. Albany, NY.

Cheah, P., and S. Guerlac. 2009. "Introduction: Derrida and the Time of the Political." In

Derrida and the Time of the Political, edited by P. Cheah and S. Guerlac, 1–37. Durham, NC.

Chen, M. Y. 2011. "Toxic Animacies, Inanimate Affections." *GLQ* 17.2–3: 265–86.

Chen, M. Y. 2012a. *Animacies: Biopolitics, Racial Mattering, and Queer Affect*. Durham, NC.

Chen, M. Y. 2012b. "Masked States and the 'Screen' between Security and Disability." *WSQ* 40.1–2: 76–96.

Chen, M. Y. 2020. "Feminisms in the Air." *Signs* 47.1. http://signsjournal.org/covid/chen/oogle_vignette.

Chen, M. Y. 2021. "Fire and Ash." In *Meat! A Transnational Analysis*, edited by S. Chatterjee and B. Subramaniam, 279–87. Durham, NC.

Choy, T. 2011. *Ecologies of Comparison: An Ethnography of Endangerment in Hong Kong*. Durham, NC.

Choy, T. 2020. "A Commentary: Breathing Together Now." *Engaging Science, Technology, and Society* 6: 586–90.

Clark, T. J. 2017. "Picasso and Tragedy." In *Pity and Terror: Picasso's Path to* Guernica, 19–64. Madrid.

Clover, J. 2016. *Riot. Strike. Riot: The New Era of Uprisings*. London.

Coccia, E. 2019. *The Life of Plants*. Cambridge.

Coe, C. D. 2014. "The Sobering Up of Oedipus: Levinas and the Trauma of Responsibility." *Angelaki* 18.4: 5–21.

Colebrook, C. 2020. "Fast Violence, Revolutionary Violence: Black Lives Matter and the 2020 Pandemic." *Journal of Bioethical Inquiry* 17.4: 495–99.

Collard, C., and J. Morwood, eds. 2017. *Euripides: Iphigenia in Aulis*. Liverpool.

Colon, E. 2016. "Securing Form in Times of In/Security: Strategies of Formal Care in Antoine Volodine's Post-Exotic Literature." *English Language Notes* 54.2: 141–57.

Comay, R. 2024. "*Nihil Est in Imagine Vivum*." In *Niobes: Antiquity Modernity Critical Theory*, edited by M. Telò and A. Benjamin. Columbus, OH.

Connolly, W. E. 2019. *Climate Machines, Fascist Drives, and Truth*. Durham, NC.

Connors, C., and C. Clendenon. 2016. "Mapping Tartaros: Observation, Inference, and Belief in Ancient Greek and Roman Accounts of Karst Terrain." *CA* 35.2: 147–88.

Conrad, J. 2002. *Heart of Darkness and Other Tales*. Oxford.

Conybeare, C. 2022. "Honig's *Bacchae*/Euripides' Theory of Refusal." *CA* 41.2: 1–3.

Corfman, S. B. 2020. "Melting Muscles: Cassils's *Tiresias* at the Intersection of Affect and Gendered Embodiment." *TSQ* 7.1: 5–19.

Crary, J. 2022. *Scorched Earth: Beyond the Digital Age to a Post-Capitalist World*. London.

Crawford, R. 2021. "Connecting Breaths." *Critical Inquiry* 47.2: 119–20.

Crawley, A. T. 2016. *Blackpentecostal Breath: The Aesthetics of Possibility*. New York.

Crockett, C. 2018. *Derrida after the End of Writing: Political Theology and New Materialism*. New York.

Culler, J. 1988. "The Call of the Phoneme: Introduction." In *On Puns: The Foundation of Letters*, edited by J. Culler, 1–16. Oxford.

Cullhed, S. S. 2022. "Procne in Toni Morrison's *Beloved*." *Classical Receptions Journal* 14.1: 89–103.

Currah, P., and T. Mulqueen. 2011. "Securitizing Gender: Identity, Biometrics, and Transgender Bodies at the Airport." *Social Research* 78.2: 557–82.

Curtis, S. 2004. "Still/Moving: Digital Imaging and Medical Hermeneutics." In *Memory Bytes: History, Technology, and Digital Culture*, edited by L. Rabinovitz and A. Geil, 218–54. Durham, NC.

Danowski, D., and E. Viveiros de Castro. 2017. *The Ends of the World*. Cambridge.

Dardenne, É. 2021. "The Tipping Point? The Covid-19 Crisis, Critical Animal Studies and Academic Responsibility." *E-Rea* 18.2. https://journals.openedition.org/erea/12283.

Davidson, M. 2012. "Pregnant Men: Modernism, Disability, and Biofuturity." In *Sex and Disability*, edited by R. McRuer and A. Mollow, 123–44. Durham, NC.

Davis, A. 2020. "Race at a Boiling Time: The Fire This Time." https://www.youtube.com/watch?v=3I22E2Sezi8.

Davis, A., G. Dent, E. R. Meiners, and B. E. Richie. 2022. *Abolition. Feminism. Now*. Chicago.

Davis, H. 2021. "The Breathing Land: On Questions of Climate Change and Settler Colonialism." In *Routledge Companion to Contemporary Art, Visual Culture, and Climate Change*, edited by T. J. Demos, E. E. Scott, and S. Banerjee, 204–13. London.

Davis, H. 2022. *Plastic Matter*. Durham, NC.

Dean, J. 2019. *Comrade: An Essay on Political Belonging*. London.

De Genova, N. 2013. "Spectacles of Migrant 'Illegality': The Scene of Exclusion, the Obscene of Inclusion." *Ethnic and Racial Studies* 36.7: 1180–98.

de Jáuregui, M. H. 2016. "The Meanings of σῴζειν in *Alcestis*'s Final Scene." *Trends in Classics* 8.2: 205–25.

de la Cadena, M. 2015. *Earth Beings: Ecologies of Practice across Andean Worlds*. Durham, NC.

Deleuze, G. 1967. *Présentation de Sacher Masoch: le froid et le cruel*. Paris.

Deleuze, G. 1989. *Cinema 2: The Time-Image*. Minneapolis.

Deleuze, G. 1991. *Masochism: Coldness and Cruelty*. New York.

Deleuze, G. 1992. "Postscript on the Societies of Control." *October* 59 (Winter): 3–7.

Deleuze, G., and F. Guattari. 1987. *A Thousand Plateaus: Capitalism and Schizophrenia*. Minneapolis.

DeLillo, D. 2020. *The Silence: A Novel*. New York.

Dell'Aversano, C. 2010. "The Love Whose Name Cannot Be Spoken: Queering the Human-Animal Bond." *Journal for Critical Animal Studies* 8.1–2: 73–125.

de Man, P. 1983. "Criticism and Crisis." In *Blindness and Insight: Essays in the Rhetoric of Contemporary Criticism*, 3–19. Minneapolis.

D'Emilio, J. 1983. "Capitalism and Gay Identity." In *Powers of Desire: The Politics of Sexuality*, edited by A. Snitow, C. Stansell, and S. Thompson, 100–13. New York.

Demos, T. J. 2013. *The Migrant Image: The Art and Politics of Documentary during Global Crisis*. Durham, NC.

Demos, T. J. 2016. *Decolonizing Nature: Contemporary Art and the Politics of Ecology*. Cambridge, MA.

Demos, T. J. 2020. *Beyond the World's End: Arts of Living at the Crossing*. Durham, NC.

Derbew, S. F. 2022. *Untangling Blackness in Greek Antiquity*. Cambridge.

Derrida, J. 1978. *Writing and Difference*. Chicago.

Derrida, J. 1986. "*Fors*: The Anglish Words of Nicolas Abraham and Maria Torok." Translated by B. Johnson. Foreword to N. Abraham and M. Torok, *The Wolf Man's Magic Word: A Cryptonymy*, xi–xlviii. Minneapolis.

Derrida, J. 1988. *The Ear of the Other: Otobiography Transference Translation*. Lincoln, NE.

Derrida, J. 1991. "'Eating Well,' or the Calculations of the Subject: An Interview with Jacques Derrida." In *Who Comes after the Subject?*, edited by E. Cadava, P. Connor, and J.-L. Nancy, 96–119. New York.

Derrida, J. 1992. "Force of Law: The 'Mystical Foundation of Authority.'" In *Deconstruction and the Possibility of Justice*, edited by D. Cornell, M. Rosenfeld, and D. G. Carlson, 3–67. New York.

Derrida, J. 1994. *Specters of Marx*. London.

Derrida, J. 1996. *Archive Fever: A Freudian Impression*. Chicago.

Derrida, J. 2000a. *Demeure: Fiction and Testimony*. Stanford, CA.

Derrida, J. 2000b. *Of Hospitality*. Stanford, CA.

Derrida, J. 2001. *The Work of Mourning*. Chicago.

Derrida, J. 2002a. *Acts of Religion*. London.

Derrida, J. 2002b. "The Animal That Therefore I Am (More to Follow)." *Critical Inquiry* 28.2: 369–418.

Derrida, J. 2005. *Rogues: Two Essays on Reason*. Stanford, CA.

Derrida, J. 2011a. *Parages*. Stanford, CA.

Derrida, J. 2011b. *The Beast and the Sovereign*. Vol. 2. Chicago.

Derrida, J. 2014. *Death Penalty*. Vol. 1. Chicago.

Derrida, J. 2020. *Life Death*. Chicago.

Derrida, J. 2021. *Clang*. Minneapolis.

Doane, M. A. 2002. *The Emergence of Cinematic Time: Modernity, Contingency, the Archive*. Cambridge, MA.

Doyle, A. C. 1929. *When the World Screamed*. http://www.forgottenfutures.com/game/ff3/wscream.htm.

Doyle, J., and D. J. Getsy. 2013. "Queer Formalisms." *Art Journal* 72.4: 58–71.

Du Bois, W. E. B. 1999. *Darkwater: Voices from within the Veil*. Minneola, NY.

Duclos, G. S. 1980. "Aeschylus' *Eumenides* and Euripides' *Bacchae* in the Context of Fifth-Century Athens." *The Classical Outlook* 58.4: 100–102.

Durkin, J., et al. 2020. "Touch in Times of Covid-19: Touch Hunger Hurts." *Journal of Clinical Nursing* 30.1–2: 1–2.

Dyson, M. 1988. "Alcestis' Children and the Character of Admetus." *JHS* 108: 13–23.

Eberwine, P. 2018. "Hope through Tragedy: Euripides' *Trojan Women* as Refugee Theater." *Eidolon*, September 20. https://eidolon.pub/hope-through-tragedy-5608605009cc.

Eccleston, S.-M., and D. Padilla Peralta. 2022. "Racing the Classics: Ethos and Praxis." *AJP* 143.2: 199–218.

Edelman, L. 2004. *No Future: Queer Theory and the Death Drive*. Durham, NC.

Edelman, L., and J. Litvak. 2019. "TWO MUCH: Excess, Enjoyment, and Estrangement in Hitchcock's *Strangers on a Train*." *GLQ* 25.2: 297–314.

Edmunds, L. 1988. "The Body of Oedipus." *Psychoanalytic Review* 75.1: 51–66.

Emmett, H. 2010. "The Maternal Contract in *Beloved* and *Medea*." In *Unbinding Medea*, edited by H. Bartel and A. Simon, 250–62. Oxford.

Enríquez, E. V. 2021. "The Sounds of the Desert: *Lost Children Archive* by Valeria Luiselli." *Latin American Literary Review* 48: 75–84.

Erickson, D. 2009. *Ghost, Metaphor, and History in Toni Morrison's* Beloved *and Gabriel Garcia Márquez's* One Hundred Years of Solitude. New York.

Esposito, R. 2019. *Politics and Negation: For an Affirmative Philosophy.* Cambridge.

Ettinger, B. L. 2010. "Antigone with(out) Jocaste." In *Interrogating Antigone in Postmodern Philosophy and Criticism*, edited by S. E. Wilmer and A. Zukauskaite, 212–28. Oxford.

Fabbri, L. 2007. "Philosophy as Chance: An Interview with Jean-Luc Nancy." *Critical Inquiry* 33.2: 427–40.

Fanon, F. 1965a. *The Wretched of the Earth.* New York.

Fanon, F. 1965b. *A Dying Colonialism.* New York.

Fanon, F. 1967a. *Black Skin, White Masks.* New York.

Fanon, F. 1967b. *Toward the African Revolution.* New York.

Fantuzzi, M. 1989. "L'ambigua prigione di Antigone." In *Scena e spettacolo nell'antichità*, edited by L. de Finis, 193–203. Florence.

Fantuzzi, M., and D. Konstan. 2013. "From Achilles' Horses to a Cheese-Seller's Shop: On the History of the Guessing Game in Greek Drama." In *Greek Comedy and the Discourse of Genres*, edited by E. Bakola, L. Prauscello, and M. Telò, 256–74. Cambridge.

Farbman, H. 2012. "From the Cold Earth: BP's Broken Well, Streaming Live." *Postmodern Culture* 23.1.

Fazi, M. B. 2019. "Digital Aesthetics: The Discrete and the Continuous." *Theory, Culture & Society* 36.1: 3–26.

Federici, S. 2018. *Feminism and the Politics of the Commons.* Oakland.

Feigenbaum, J., et al. 2019. "Regional and Racial Inequality in Infectious Disease Mortality in US Cities, 1900–1948." *Demography* 56.4: 1371–88.

Feldherr, A. 2010. *Playing Gods: Ovid's* Metamorphoses *and the Politics of Fiction.* Princeton.

Feldman, A. 2010. "Inhumanitas: Political Speciation, Animality, Natality, Defacement." In *In the Name of Humanity: The Government of Threat and Care*, edited by I. Feldman and M. Ticktin, 115–50. Durham, NC.

Felman, S. 1992. "Education and Crisis, or the Vicissitudes of Teaching." In *Testimony: Crises of Witnessing in Literature, Psychoanalysis, and History*, edited by S. Felman and D. Laub, 1–56. New York.

Ferrari, F. 2010. "La luce soffocata: Soph. *Ant.* 583–603." In *Antigone e le Antigoni*, edited by A. M. Belardinelli and G. Greco, 50–58. Milan.

Ferreira da Silva, D. 2020. "Reading the Dead: A Black Feminist Poethical Reading of Global Capital." In *Otherwise Worlds: Against Settler Colonialism and Anti-Blackness*, edited by T. L. King, J. Navarro, and A. Smith, 38–51. Durham, NC.

Finglass, P., ed. 2018. *Sophocles: Oedipus the King.* Cambridge.

Foley, H. P. 2001. *Female Acts in Greek Tragedy.* Princeton.

Foucault, M. 1965. *Madness and Civilization: A History of Insanity in the Age of Reason.* New York.

Foucault, M. 1976. *"Society Must Be Defended": Lectures at the Collège de France, 1975–1976.* New York.

Foucault, M. 2000. "Lives of Infamous Men." In *Power: Essential Works of Foucault, 1954–84*, 1–89. New York.

Foucault, M. 2002. *The Order of Things.* London.

Foucault, M. 2019. "All about the *Lettres de Cachet.*" In *Archives of Infamy: Foucault on State Power in the Lives of Ordinary Citizens*, edited by N. Luxon, 85–126. Minneapolis.

Fox, D. 2009. *Cold World: The Aesthetics of Dejection and the Politics of Militant Dysphoria.* Winchester, UK.

Fradenburg, L. O. A. 2013. "Breathing with Lacan's Seminar X: Expression and Emergence." In *Staying Alive: A Survival Manual for the Liberal Arts*, edited by L. O. A. Fradenburg et al., 163–91. New York.

Fraenkel, E., ed. 1950. *Aeschylus: Agamemnon.* Oxford.

Freccero, C. 2022. "*Trojan Women*—No Futures." In *Queer Euripides: Re-Readings in Greek Tragedy*, edited by S. Olsen and M. Telò, 43–50. London.

Fretwell, E. 2020. *Sensory Experiments: Psychophysics, Race, and the Aesthetics of Feeling.* Durham, NC.

Freud, S. 1920. *Beyond the Pleasure Principle. SE* 18: 1–64.

Freud, S. 1930. *Civilization and Its Discontents. SE* 21: 64–145.

Gabriel, K. 2018. "Specters of Dying Empire: The Case of Carson's *Bacchae.*" *Tripwire* 14: 315–23.

Gandorfer, D. 2020. *Matterphorics: On the Laws of Theory.* Princeton, Ph.D. Dissertation.

Gandorfer, D., and Z. Ayub. 2020. "Introduction: Matterphorical." *Theory & Event* 24.1: 2–13.

Garcia, E. 2022. *Emergency: Reading the Popol Vuh in a Time of Crisis.* Chicago.

George, S. 2012. "Approaching the *Thing* of Slavery: A Lacanian Analysis of Toni Morrison's *Beloved.*" *African American Review* 45.1–2: 115–30.

Gibbs, L. 2010. "After Affect: Sympathy, Synchrony, and Mimetic Communication." In *The Affect Theory Reader*, edited by M. Gregg and G. J. Seigworth, 186–205. Durham, NC.

Gibert, J. 2005. "Clytemnestra's First Marriage: Euripides' *Iphigenia in Aulis.*" In *The Soul of Tragedy: Essays on Athenian Drama*, edited by V. Pedrick and S. M. Oberhelman, 227–48. Chicago.

Gibney, E. 2020. "Coronavirus Lockdowns Have Changed the Way Earth Moves." *Nature* 580: 176–77.

Gill-Peterson, J., and G. Lavery. 2020. "Strategic Inessentialism." *TSQ* 7.4: 638–45.

Gilroy, P. 1993. *The Black Atlantic: Modernity and Double Consciousness.* Cambridge, MA.

Ginn, F., Bastian, M., et al. 2018. "Unexpected Encounters with Deep Time." *Environmental Humanities* 10.1: 213–25.

Giordano, P. 2020. *How Contagion Works.* London.

Glissant, E. 1990. *Poetics of Relation.* Ann Arbor, MI.

Goff, B. 1995. "Aithra at Eleusis." *Helios* 22.1: 65–78.

Goldhill, S. 1984. "Exegesis: Oedipus (R)ex." *Arethusa* 17.2: 177–200.

Goldhill, S. 1988. "Doubling and Recognition in the *Bacchae.*" *Metis* 3.1–2: 137–56.

Goldhill, S. 1996. "East Coast Oedipus: Suspicious Readings." *Arion* (ser. 3) 4.2: 155–71.

Gómez-Barris, M. 2017. *The Extractive Zone: Social Ecologies and Decolonial Perspectives.* Durham, NC.

Goodkin, R. 1982. "Tracing the Trace: Oedipus and Derrida." *Helios* 9.1: 15–27.

Górska, M. 2018. "Feminist Politics of Breathing." In *Atmospheres of Breathing*, edited by L. Skof and P. Berndtson, 247–59. Albany, NY.

Gossett, C., and E. Hayward. 2020. "Trans in a Time of HIV/AIDS." *TSQ* 7.4: 527–53.

Gould, J. 1973. "Hiketeia." *JHS* 93: 74–103.

Green, P. 2009. "Possession and Pneuma: The Essential Nature of the Delphic Oracles." *Arion* (ser. 3) 17.2: 27–47.

Greenblatt, S. 2020. "Invisible Bullets: What Lucretius Taught Us About Pandemics." *The New Yorker*, March 16. https://www.newyorker.com/culture/culture-desk/invisible-bullets-what-lucretius-taught-us-about-pandemics.

Griffith, M., ed. 1983. *Aeschylus: Prometheus Bound*. Cambridge.

Griffith, M., ed. 1999. *Sophocles: Antigone*. Cambridge.

Griffith, M. 2005. "The Subject of Desire in Sophocles' *Antigone*." In *The Soul of Tragedy: Essays on Athenian Drama*, edited by V. Pedrick and S. M. Oberhelman, 91–135. Chicago.

Grosz, E. et al. 2017. "An Interview with Elizabeth Grosz: Geopower, Inhumanism, and the Biopolitical." *Theory, Culture & Society* 34.2–3: 129–46.

Gsoels-Lorensen, J. 2014. "Antigone, Deportee." *Arethusa* 47.2: 111–44.

Guenther, L. 2020. "Critical Phenomenology." In *50 Concepts for a Critical Phenomenology*, edited by G. Weiss, A. V. Murphy, and G. Salamon, 11–16. Evanston, IL.

Gullette, M. M. 2022. "American Eldercide." In *The Long Year: 2020 Reader*, edited by T. J. Sugrue and C. Zaloom, 237–44. New York.

Gumbrecht, H. U. 2012. *Atmosphere, Mood, Stimmung: On a Hidden Potential of Literature*. Stanford, CA.

Gumbs, A. P., C. Martens, and M. Williams, eds. 2016. *Revolutionary Mothering: Love on the Front Lines*. Oakland.

Gunning, T. 2003. "Never Seen This Picture Before: Muybridge in Multiplicity." In *Time Stands Still: Muybridge and the Instantaneous Photography Movement*, edited by P. Prodger, 222–72. Oxford.

Gurd, S. A. 2005. *Iphigenias at Aulis: Textual Multiplicity, Radical Philology*. Ithaca, NY.

Gurd, S. A., and M. Telò, eds. 2024. *The Before and the After: Critical Asynchrony Now*. Goleta, CA.

Hägglund, M. 2008. *Radical Atheism: Derrida and the Time of Life*. Stanford, CA.

Halberstam, J. 2012. *Gaga Feminism*. Boston.

Halberstam, J. 2018. *Trans*: A Quick and Quirky Account of Gender Variability*. Oakland.

Halberstam, J. 2020. *Wild Things: The Disorder of the Desire*. Durham, NC.

Haley, S. P. 1995. "Self-Definition, Community, and Resistance: Euripides' *Medea* and Toni Morrison's *Beloved*." *Thamyris* 2.2: 177–206.

Hall, E. 2011. "The Problem with Prometheus: Myth, Abolition, and Radicalism." In *Ancient Slavery and Abolition: From Hobbes to Hollywood*, edited by E. Hall, R. Alston, and J. McConnell, 209–46. New York.

Hannah, D. 2010. "Queer Hospitality in Herman Melville's 'Benito Cereno'." *Studies in American Fiction* 37.2: 181–201.

Haraway, D. 2009. *When Species Meet*. Minneapolis.

Harney, S., and F. Moten. 2015. "Michael Brown." *boundary 2* 42.4: 81–87.

Harris, D. 2022. "The Smear: Vibrational Flesh and the Calculus of Black Queer Becoming in Barry Jenkins's *Moonlight*." *differences* 33.1: 1–27.

Harris, O. 2013. "The Ethics of Metamorphosis or a Poet Between Two Deaths." In *Classical Myth and Psychoanalysis: Ancient and Modern Stories of the Self*, edited by V. Zajko and E. O' Gorman, 251–66. Oxford.

Hartman, S. 1997. *Scenes of Subjection: Terror, Slavery, and Self-Making in Nineteenth-Century America*. Oxford.

Hartman, S. 2007. *Lose Your Mother: A Journey along the Atlantic Slave Route*. New York.

Hartman, S. 2008. "Venus in Two Acts." *Small Axe* 26: 1–14.

Hartman, S. 2020. "The End of White Supremacy, an American Romance." *Bomb* 152 https://bombmagazine.org/articles/the-end-of-white-supremacy-an-american-romance.

Hartman, S. 2022. "Litany for Grieving Sisters." In *Proximities: Reading with Judith Butler*, edited by D. Sanyal, M. Telò, and D. R. Young, *Representations* 158.1: 39–44.

Haselswerdt, E. 2022. "*Iphigenia in Aulis*—Perhaps (Not)." In *Queer Euripides: Re-Readings in Greek Tragedy*, edited by S. Olsen and M. Telò, 53–64. London.

Hass, K. A. 2021. "Introduction: Living with the Virus That Knows How We See Each Other." In *Being Human during Covid*, edited by K. A. Hass, 1–19. Ann Arbor, MI.

Hawkins, H. 2019. "(W)holes—Volume, Horizon, Surface—Three Intimate Geologies." *Emotion, Space and Society* 32: 1–9.

Hayward, E. 2014. "Transxenoestrogenesis." *TSQ* 1.1–2: 255–58.

Heine, S. 2021. *Poetics of Breathing: Modern Literature's Syncope*. Albany, NY.

Henao Castro, A. F. 2021. *Antigone in the Americas: Democracy, Sexuality, and Death in the Settler Colonial Present*. Albany, NY.

Henderson, C. E. 2006. "Refiguring the Flesh: The Word, the Body, and the Rituals of Being in *Beloved* and *Go Tell It on the Mountain*." In *James Baldwin and Toni Morrison: Comparative Critical and Theoretical Essays*, edited by L. King and L. O. Scott, 149–65. New York.

Hesse, B., and D. Thompson. 2022. "Introduction: Antiblackness—Dispatches from Black Political Thought." *SAQ* 121.3: 447–75.

Heyes, C. J. 2020. *Anaesthetics of Existence: Essays on Experience at the Edge*. Durham, NC.

Hickman, J. 2017. *Black Prometheus: Race and Radicalism in the Age of Atlantic Slavery*. Oxford.

Higgins, H. B. 2021. "Sonic Images of the Coronavirus." *Critical Inquiry* 47.2: 128–31.

Hill, L. 2016. "From Deconstruction to Disaster (Derrida, Blanchot, Hegel)." *Paragraph* 39.2: 187–201.

Hohti, R., and J. Osgood. 2020. "Pets That Have 'Something Inside': The Material Politics of in/Animacy and Queer Kin within the Childhood Menagerie." *Genealogy* 4.2 https://www.mdpi.com/2313-5778/4/2/38/htm.

Holdsworth, P. 2021. "Reimagining the Face-to-Face Encounter in the Time of Covid." https://www.cbc.ca/radio/ideas/reimagining-the-face-to-face-encounter-in-the-time-of-covid-1.6163077.

Holloway, T. 2022. *How to Live at the End of the World: Theory, Art, and Politics for the Anthropocene*. Stanford, CA.

Honig, B. 2013. *Antigone, Interrupted*. Cambridge.

Honig, B. 2021a. *A Feminist Theory of Refusal*. Cambridge, MA.

Honig, B. 2021b. "How to Do Things with Inclinations: *Antigones, with Cavarero*." In *Toward a Feminist Ethics of Nonviolence: Adriana Cavarero, with Judith Butler, Bonnie Honig, and Other Voices*, edited by T. J. Huzar and C. Woodford, 63–90. New York.

Honig, B. 2022. "A Method in the Madness: After *A Feminist Theory of Refusal*, in Grateful Reply." *CA* 141.2: 34–49.

Honig, B. forthcoming. "Toward a Democratic Theory of Contagion (or: the 1990s Revisited)."

Hornblower, S. ed. 1991. *A Commentary on Thucydides, Books 1–3*. Oxford.

Hornby, L. 2018. "Film's Atmospheric Setting." *Modernism/modernity*. https://modernismmodernity.org/forums/posts/films-atmospheric-setting.

Horton, J. L., and J. C. Berlo. 2013. "Beyond the Mirror: Indigenous Ecologies and 'New Materialisms' in Contemporary Art." *Third Text* 27.1: 17–28.

Hristova, S., and A. L. Howard. 2021. "'I Can't Breathe': The Biopolitics and Necropolitics of Breath during 2020." *Mortality* 26.4: 471–86.

Hubbard, L., G. L. Wright, and W. A. Darity Jr. 2022. "Introduction. Six Feet and Miles Apart: Structural Racism in the United States and Racially Disparate Outcomes during the Covid-19 Pandemic." In *The Pandemic Divide: How Covid Increased Inequality in America*, edited by G. L. Wright, L. Hubbard, and W. A. Darity Jr., 1–28. Durham, NC.

Huber, S. 2021. *Supremely Tiny Acts: A Memory of a Day*. Columbus, OH.

Hudson, P. 2013. "The State and the Colonial Unconscious." *Social Dynamics* 39.2: 263–77.

Huffer, L. 2017. "Foucault's Fossils: Life Itself and the Return to Nature in Feminist Philosophy." In *Anthropocene Feminism*, edited by R. Grusin, 65–88. Minneapolis.

Ibrahim, H. 2021. *Black Age: Oceanic Lifespans and the Time of Black Life*. New York.

Ibrahim, H., and B. Ahad. 2022. "Introduction: Black Temporality in Times of Crisis." *SAQ* 121.1: 1–10.

Ibrus, I., and M. Ojamaa. 2020. "The Creativity of Digital (Audiovisual) Archives: A Dialogue between Media Archaeology and Cultural Semiotics." *Theory, Culture & Society* 37.3: 49–70.

Ingersoll, K. A. 2016. *Waves of Knowing: A Seascape Epistemology*. Durham, NC.

Ingleheart, J. 2015. "The Invention of (Thracian) Homosexuality: The Ovidian Orpheus in the English Renaissance." In *Ancient Rome and the Construction of Modern Homosexual Identities*, edited by J. Ingleheart, 56–73. Oxford.

Ingold, T. 2020. "On Breath and Breathing: A Concluding Comment." *Body & Society* 26.2: 158–67.

Irigaray, L. 1999. *The Forgetting of Air in Martin Heidegger*. Austin, TX.

Irigaray, L. 2004. *Key Writings*. London.

Irigaray, L., and M. Marder. 2016. *Through Vegetal Being: Two Philosophical Perspectives*. New York.

Issacharoff, J. 2022. "'Toxins in the Atmosphere': Reanimating the Feminist *Poison*." In *Reframing Todd Haynes: Feminism's Indelible Mark*, edited by T. L. Geller and J. Leyda, 137–57. Durham, NC.

Jacobs, C. 1996. "Dusting Antigone." *MLN* 111.5: 889–917.

Jakob, D. J. 1999. "Der Redenstreit in Euripides' *Alkestis* und der Charakter des Stückes." *Hermes* 127.3: 274–85.

Jameson, F. 2015. "The Aesthetics of Singularity." *New Left Review* 92: 102–32.

Jebb, R. C., ed. 1900. *Sophocles: Antigone*. Cambridge.

Jendza, C. 2020. *Paracomedy: Appropriations of Comedy in Greek Tragedy*. Oxford.

Johnston, A. 2018. "Jacques Lacan." In *Stanford Encyclopedia of Philosophy*. Stanford University, 1997–. Article published April 2, 2013; substantive revision July 10, 2018. http://plato.stanford.edu/archives/fall2018/entries/lacan.

Jones, B. W. 1985. "Greek Tragic Motifs in *Songs of Salomon*." In *The World of Toni Morrison: Explorations in Literary Criticism*, edited by B. W. Jones and A. L. Vinson, 103–14. Dubuque, IA.

Jouanna, J. 2012. "Air, Miasma, and Contagion in the Time of Hippocrates and the Survival of Miasmas in Post-Hippocratic Medicine (Rufus of Ephesus, Galen, and Palladius)." In *Greek Medicine from Hippocrates to Galen*, 119–36. Leiden.

Jue, M., and R. Ruiz. 2021. "Thinking with Saturation beyond Water: Thresholds, Phase Change, and the Precipitate." In *Saturation: An Elemental Politics*, edited by M. Jue and R. Ruiz, 1–28. Durham, NC.

Kafka, F. 1971. *The Complete Stories*. New York.

Kaimio, M. 1988. *Physical Contact in Greek Tragedy: A Study of Stage Conventions*. Helsinki.

Kallet, L. 1999. "The Diseased Body Politic, Athenian Public Finance, and the Massacre at Mycalessos (Thucydides 7.27–29)." *AJP* 120.2: 223–44.

Karakantza, E. D. 2020. *Who Am I? (Mis)identity and the Polis in* Oedipus Tyrannus. Cambridge, MA.

Karakantza, E. D. 2022. "'To Be Buried or Not to Be Buried?' Necropolitics in Athenian History and Sophocles' *Antigone*." In *Myth and History: Close Encounters*, edited by M. Christopoulos et al., 207–20. Berlin.

Keuls, E. 1974. *The Water-Carriers in Hades: A Study of Catharsis through Toil in Classical Antiquity*. Amsterdam.

Khosravi, S. 2021. "Afterword: Waiting, a State of Consciousness." In *Waiting and the Temporalities of Irregular Migration*, edited by C. M. Jacobsen, M.-A. Karlsen, and S. Khosravi, 202–8. London.

King, H. 2022. "The Brown Commons in the Time of Pandemic: Reflections on Zoom and Livestreamed Performance." *Afterimage* 49.1: 39–44.

Kirksey, E. 2020. "The Emergence of Covid-19: A Multispecies Story." *Anthropology Now* 12.1: 11–16.

Klaas, S. 2021. "Changing Scales, Changing Hands: Fugitive Literacies and Reading beyond Citizenship in Valeria Luiselli's *Lost Children Archive*." In *Citizenship, Law, and Literature*, edited by C. Koegler, J. Reddig, and K. Stierstorfer, 85–104. Berlin.

Knox, B. M. W. 1956. "The Date of the *Oedipus Tyrannus* of Sophocles." *AJP* 77: 133–47.

Kokkiou, C. 2014. "Choral Self-Referentiality in the *Prometheus Bound*: Song, Dance, and the Emotions." *Logeion* 4: 127–43.

Kornbluh, A. 2021. "Ecocide and Objectivity: Literary Thinking in *How the Dead Dream*." In *The Work of Reading: Literary Criticism in the 21st Century*, edited by A. Sridhar, M. A. Hosseini, and D. Attridge, 261–78. New York.

Kotef, H. 2020. *The Colonizing Self: Or, Home and Homelessness in Israel/Palestine*. Durham, NC.

Kovacs, D., ed. 2018. *Euripides: Troades*. Oxford.

Kurr, J. A. 2020. "The Homonormative Economic Frame and Covid-19 Relief Debates." *QED* 7.3: 151–56.

Lacan, J. 1981. *The Four Fundamental Concepts of Psychoanalysis: The Seminar of Jacques Lacan, Book 11*. Edited by J. A. Miller. Translated by A. Sheridan. New York.

Lacan, J. 1992. *The Ethics of Psychoanalysis: The Seminar of Jacques Lacan, Book 7*. Edited by J. A. Miller. Translated by B. Fink. New York.

Lamp, K. S. 2013. *A City of Marble: The Rhetoric of Augustan Rome*. Columbia, SC.

Lampert, J. 2018. *The Many Futures of a Decision*. London.

Landes, D. A. 2020. "The Flesh of the World." In *50 Concepts for a Critical Phenomenology*, edited by G. Weiss, A. V. Murphy, and G. Salamon, 141–48. Evanston, IL.

Lashua, B., et al. 2021. "Leisure in the Time of Coronavirus: A Rapid Response." *Leisure Sciences* 43.1–2: 6–11.

Latour, B. 2017. "Why Gaia Is Not a God of Totality." *Theory, Culture & Society* 34.2–3: 61–81.

Lenssen, A. 2020. *Beautiful Agitation: Modern Painting and Politics in Syria*. Oakland, CA.

Levina, M. 2020. "Queering Intimacy, Six Feet Apart." *QED* 7.3: 195–200.

Levinas, E. 1986. *Face to Face with Levinas*, edited by R. A. Cohen. Albany, NY.

Levinas, E. 1998. *Entre Nous: Thinking-of-the-Other*. New York.

Lewis, S. 2019. *Full Surrogacy Now: Feminism against Family*. New York.

Lewis, S. 2020. "The Virus and the Home." April 1. https://bullybloggers.wordpress. com/2020/04/01/the-virus-vs-the-home-what-does-the-pandemic-reveal-about-the-private-nuclear-household-by-sophie-lewis-for-bunkerbloggers-originally-published-on-patreon-reblogged-by-permission-of-the-author.

Lewis, S. 2022. *Abolish the Family: A Manifesto for Care and Liberation*. London.

Liboiron, M. 2021. *Pollution Is Colonialism*. Durham, NC.

Littleton, C. S. 1986. "The *Pneuma Enthusiastikon*: On the Possibility of Hallucinogenic 'Vapors' at Delphi and Dodona." *Ethos* 14.1: 76–91.

Lively, G. 2017. "Orpheus and Eurydice." In *A Handbook to the Reception of Classical Mythology*, edited by V. Zajko and H. Hoyle, 287–98. Malden, MA.

Livingston, J. 2022. "To Heal the Body, Heal the Body Politic." In *The Long Year: A 2020 Reader*, edited by T. J. Sugrue and C. Zaloom, 229–36. New York.

Loraux, N. 1981. "Le lit, la guerre." *L'Homme* 21.1: 37–67.

Loraux, N. 2002. *The Mourning Voice: An Essay on Greek Tragedy*. Ithaca, NY.

Love, H. 2007. *Feeling Backward: Loss and the Politics of Queer History*. Cambridge, MA.

Luiselli, V. 2017. *Tell Me How It Ends: An Essay in 40 Questions*. Minneapolis.

Luiselli, V. 2019. *Lost Children Archive*. New York.

Luschnig, C. A. E. 1976. "Euripides' Hecabe: The Time Is Out of Joint." *CJ* 71.3: 227–34.

Luschnig, C. A. E. 1988. *Tragic Aporia: A Study of Euripides'* Iphigenia in Aulis. Berwick, Victoria.

Luschnig, C. A. E. 1992. "Interiors: Imaginary Spaces in *Alcestis* and *Medea*." *Mnemosyne* n.s. 45.1: 19–44.

Lush, B. 2012. "Popular Authority in Euripides' *Iphigenia at Aulis*." *AJP* 136.2: 207–42.

Lynes, P. 2018. "The Posthuman Promise of the Earth." In *Eco-Deconstruction: Derrida and Environmental Philosophy*, edited by M. Fritsch, P. Lynes, and D. Wood, 101–20. New York.

Mackey, N. 1993. *Discrepant Engagement: Dissonance, Cross-Culturality, and Experimental Writing*. Cambridge.

Mackey, N. 2021. *Breath and Precarity*. Chicago.

Madsen, D. L. 2008. "On Subjectivity and Survivance: Re-reading Trauma through *The Heirs of Columbus* and *The Crown of Columbus*." In *Survivance: Narratives of Native Presence*, edited by G. Vizenor, 61–88. Lincoln, NE.

Mallarmé, S. 2001. "Crisis of Verse." In *The Norton Anthology of Theory and Criticism*, edited by V. Leitch, 841–51. New York.

Mameni, S. 2021. "View from the Terracene." In *The Routledge Companion to Contemporary Art, Visual Culture, and Climate Change*, edited by T. J. Demos, E. E. Scott, and S. Banerjee, 100–7. London.

Manning, E. 2020. *For a Pragmatics of the Useless*. Durham, NC.

Marder, M. 2018. "Ecology as Event." In *Eco-Deconstruction: Derrida and Environmental Philosophy*, edited by M. Fritsch, P. Lynes, and D. Wood, 141–64. New York.

Marratto, S. 2020. "Intercorporeality." In *50 Concepts for a Critical Phenomenology*, edited by G. Weiss, A. V. Murphy, and G. Salamon, 197–202. Evanston, IL.

Marriott, D. S. 2018. *Whither Fanon? Studies in the Blackness of Being*. Stanford, CA.

Marriott, D. S. 2021. *Lacan Noir: Lacan and Afro-pessimism*. London.

Marshall, C. W. 1999. "Some Fifth-Century Masking Conventions." *G&R* 46.2: 188–202.

Martel, J. 2018. *Unburied Bodies*. Amherst, MA.

Martelli, F. K. A. 2021. *Ovid*. Leiden.

Martin, R. 2002. "A Good Place to Talk: Discourse and Topos in Achilles Tatius and Philostratus." *Ancient Narrative* (Supplementum 1): 143–60.

Marx, K. 1978. "Speech at the Anniversary of the People's Paper." In *The Marx-Engels Reader*, edited by R. C. Tucker, 577–78. London.

Mastronarde, D. J. 1999–2000. "Euripidean Tragedy and Genre: The Terminology and Its Problems." *ICS* 24–25: 23–39.

Matzner, S. 2016. "Queer Unhistoricism." In *Deep Classics*, edited by S. Butler, 179–201. London.

Maxwell, C. 1993. "Robert Browning and Frederic Leighton: 'Che Farò Senza Euridice?'" *The Review of English Studies* 44: 362–72.

Mbembe, A. 2003. "Necropolitics." *Public Culture* 15.1: 11–40.

Mbembe, A. 2019. *Necropolitics*. Durham, NC.

Mbembe, A. 2021. "The Universal Right to Breathe." *Critical Inquiry* 47.2: 58–62.

McConnell, J. 2016. "Postcolonial *Sparagmos*: Toni Morrison's *Sula* and Wole Soyinka's *The Bacchae of Euripides*: A Communion Rite." *Classical Receptions Journal* 8.2: 133–54.

McEleney, C. 2021. "The Resistance to Overanalysis." *differences* 32.2: 1–38.

McLean, S. 2021. "Nature." In *Anthropocene Unseen: A Lexicon*, edited by C. Howe and A. Pandian, 295–99. Goleta, CA.

McLeod, A. M. 2019. "Law, Critique, and the Undercommons." In *A Time for Critique*, edited by D. Fassin and B. E. Harcourt, 252–70. New York.

McNulty, T. 2015. "Speculative Fetishism." *Konturen* 8: 99–132.

Meillassoux, Q. 2006. *After Finitude: An Essay on the Necessity of Contingency*. London.

Meillassoux, Q. 2014. *Time without Becoming*. Milan.

Meineck, P. 2011. "The Neuroscience of the Tragic Mask." *Arion* (ser. 3) 19.1: 113–58.

Meinel, F. 2015. *Pollution and Crisis in Greek Tragedy*. Cambridge.

Mendelsohn, D. 2002. *Gender and the City in Euripides' Political Plays*. Oxford.

Merleau-Ponty, M. 1964. *Sense and Non-Sense*. Evanston, IL.

Merleau-Ponty, M. 1968. *The Visible and the Invisible*. Evanston, IL.

Merleau-Ponty, M. 2003. *Nature: Course Notes from the Collège de France*. Evanston, IL.

Michelakis, P. 2006a. "Reception, Performance, and the Sacrifice of Iphigenia." In *Classics and the Uses of Reception*, edited by C. Martindale and R. F. Thomas, 216–26. Malden, MA.

Michelakis, P. 2006b. *Euripides: Iphigenia in Aulis*. London.

Michelakis, P. 2019. "Naming the Plague in Homer, Sophocles, and Thucydides." *AJP* 140.3: 381–414.

Michelini, A. N. 1999–2000. "The Expansion of Myth in Late Euripides: *Iphigenia at Aulis*." *ICS* 24–25: 41–57.

Mitchell, P. 2011. "Geographies/Aerographies of Contagion." *Environment and Planning D: Society and Space* 29.3: 533–50.

Mitchell-Boyask, R. 2007. *Plague and the Athenian Imagination: Drama, History, and the Cult of Asclepius*. Cambridge.

Morales, H. 2004. *Vision and Narrative in Achilles Tatius' Leucippe and Clitophon*. Cambridge.

Morales, H. 2020. *Antigone Rising: The Subversive Power of the Ancient Myths*. New York.

Morales, H. 2022. "Bonnie Honig's *A Feminist Theory of Refusal* with Kehinde Wiley's *After John Raphael Smith's 'A Bacchante after Sir Joshua Reynolds'*." *CA* 41.2: 25–33.

Morales, H., and M. Telò, eds. 2023. *Shorter and spalding's . . . (Iphigenia). Ramus*.

Morrison, T. 1994. *Conversations with Toni Morrison*, edited by D. Taylor-Guthrie. Jackson, MS.

Morrison, T. 2000. *Beloved*. New York.

Morrison, T. 2008. *Toni Morrison: Conversations*, edited by C. C. Denard. Jackson, MS.

Morton, T. 2007. *Ecology without Nature: Rethinking Environmental Aesthetics*. Cambridge, MA.

Morton, T. 2010. "Queer Ecology." *PMLA* 125.2: 273–82.

Morton, T. 2012. "The Oedipal Logic of Ecological Awareness." *Environmental Humanities* 1.1: 7–21.

Morton, T. 2013. *Hyperobjects: Philosophy and Ecology after the End of the World*. Minneapolis.

Morwood, J., ed. 2007. *Euripides: Suppliant Women*. Liverpool.

Mossman, J. 1996. "Chains of Imagery in *Prometheus Bound*." *CQ* 46.1: 58–67.

Moten, F. 2003. *In the Break: The Aesthetics of the Black Radical Tradition*. Minneapolis.

Moten, F. 2017. *Black and Blur: Consent Not to Be a Single Being*. Durham, NC.

Moten, F. 2018a. "Ensemble: An Interview with Fred Moten." https://micemagazine.ca/issue-four/ensemble-interview-dr-fred-moten.

Moten, F. 2018b. *The Universal Machine*. Durham, NC.

Moten, F., and S. Harney. 2011. "Blackness and Governance." In *Beyond Biopolitics: Essays on the Governance of Life and Death*, edited by P. T. Clough and C. Willse, 351–61. Durham, NC.

Moten, F., and S. Harney. 2013. *The Undercommons: Fugitive Planning and Black Study*. New York.

Mueller, M. 2011. "The Politics of Gesture in Sophocles' *Antigone*." *CQ* 61.2: 412–25.

Mulvey, L. 1995. "*Citizen Kane*: From Log Cabin to Xanadou." In *Perspectives on Orson Welles*, edited by M. Beja, 281–303. New York.

Munster, A. 2006. *Materializing New Media: Embodiment in Information Aesthetics*. Dartmouth, NH.

Murakami, H. 2002. *After the Shake: Stories*. New York.

Murray, G. 2005. *Gilbert Murray's Euripides:* The Trojan Women *and Other Plays*. Bristol.

Musser, A. J. 2018. *Sensual Excess: Queer Femininity and Brown Jouissance.* New York.

Musser, A. J. 2021. "Sweat, Display, and Blackness: The Promises of Liquidity." *Feminist Media Histories* 7.2: 92–109.

Nancy, J.-L. 1993. *The Sense of the World.* Minneapolis.

Nancy, J.-L. 2020. *An All-Too-Human Virus.* Cambridge.

Nash, J. 2021. *Birthing Black Mothers.* Durham, NC.

Nash, J. 2022. "Slow Loss: Black Feminism and Endurance." *Social Text* 40.2: 1–20.

Nash, J., and S. Pinto. 2020. "Strange Intimacies: Reading Black Mothering Memoirs." *Public Culture* 32.3: 491–512.

Nawotka, K. 1994. "Tomos, Ovid, and the Name Tomis." *Studies in Latin Literature and Roman History,* edited by C. Deroux, 406–15. Brussels.

Neils, J. 2008. "Women Are White: White Ground and the Attic Funeral." In *Papers on Special Techniques in Athenian Vases,* edited by K. Lapatin, 61–72. Los Angeles.

Nelson, T. J. 2022. "Iphigenia in the *Iliad* and the Architecture of Homeric Allusion." *TAPA* 152.1: 55–101.

Neyrat, F. 2016. "Planetary Antigones: The Environmental Situation and the Wandering Condition." *Qui Parle* 25.1–2: 35–64.

Neyrat, F. 2017. "Eccentric Earth." *Diacritics* 45.3: 4–21.

Ngai, S. 2015. "Visceral Abstractions." *GLQ* 21.1: 33–63.

Ngai, S. 2020. *Theory of the Gimmick: Aesthetic Judgment and Capitalist Form.* Cambridge, MA.

Nguyen, T. T. 2009. "Environmental Consequences of Dioxin from the War in Vietnam: What Has Been Done and What Else Could Be Done?" *International Journal of Environmental Studies* 66.1: 9–26.

Nichols, D. 2009. "Antigone's Autochthonous Voice: Echoes in Sophocles, Hölderlin, and Heidegger." In *Time, Memory, and Cultural Change,* edited by S. Dempsey and D. Nichols. Vienna. https://files.iwm.at/jvfc/25_3_Nichols.pdf.

Nielsen, R. M. 1976. "Alcestis: A Paradox in Dying." *Ramus* 5.2: 92–102.

Nixon, R. 2011. *Slow Violence and the Environmentalism of the Poor.* New York.

Nooter, S. 2017. *The Mortal Voice in the Tragedies of Aeschylus.* Cambridge.

Nooter, S. 2022. "*Medea*—Failure and the Queer Escape." In *Queer Euripides: Re-Readings in Greek Tragedy,* edited by S. Olsen and M. Telò, 99–109. London.

Nyong'o, T. 2010. "Trapped in the Closet with Eve." *Criticism* 52.2: 243–51.

Nyong'o, T. 2018. *Afro-Fabulations: The Queer Drama of Black Life.* New York.

O'Brien, D. 2010. "Μοvίη in Empedocles: Slings' 'Iron Rule.'" *Mnemosyne* n.s. 63: 268–71.

O' Higgins, D. 1993. "Above Rubies: Admetus' Perfect Wife." *Arethusa* 26: 77–97.

Oliensis, E. 1997. "Return to Sender: The Rhetoric of *Nomina* in Ovid's *Tristia.*" *Ramus* 26.2: 172–93.

Oliensis, E. 2004. "The Power of Image-Makers: Representation and Revenge in Ovid *Metamorphoses* 6 and *Tristia* 4." *CA* 23.2: 285–321.

Olsen, S. 2020. *Solo Dance in Archaic and Classical Greek Literature: Representing the Unruly Body.* Cambridge.

Orozco Mendoza, E. F. 2016. "Maternal Activism." In *The Wiley Blackwell Encyclopedia of Gender and Sexuality Studies,* edited by N. Naples, 1–6. Malden, MA.

Orozco Mendoza, E. F. 2017. "Feminicide and the Funeralization of the City: On Thing Agency and Protest Politics in Ciudad Juárez." *Theory & Event* 20.2: 351–80.

Orozco Mendoza, E. F. 2019. "*Las Madres De Chihuahua*: Maternal Activism, Public Disclosure, and the Politics of Visibility." *New Political Science* 41.2: 211–33.

Osmundson, J. 2022. *Virology: Essays for the Living, the Dead, and the Small Things in Between*. New York.

Otten, T. 1998. "Transfiguring the Narrative: *Beloved* from Melodrama to Tragedy." In *Critical Essays on Toni Morrison's* Beloved, edited by B. Solomon, 284–99. Boston.

Padwe, J. 2020. "Eschaton." In *Anthropocene Unseen: A Lexicon*, edited by C. Howe and A. Pandian, 157–61. Goleta, CA.

Pallasmaa, J. 2017. "Touching the World: Vision, Hearing, Hapticity and Atmospheric Perception." *Invisible Places* 7–9 April: 15–28.

Palsson, G., and H. A. Swanson. 2016. "Down to Earth: Geosocialities and Geopolitics." *Environmental Humanities* 8.2: 149–71.

Pappas, G., et al. 2008. "Insights into Infectious Disease in the Era of Hippocrates." *International Journal of Infectious Diseases* 12.4: 347–50.

Paredez, D. 2013. "Hecuba on the Shores of Da Nang." *Adanna Literary Journal*.

Paredez, D. 2020. *Year of the Dog: Poems*. Rochester, NY.

Parker, L. P. E., ed. 2007. *Euripides: Alcestis*. Oxford.

Parker, R. 1983. *Miasma*. Oxford.

Parry, A. 1969. "The Language of Thucydides' Description of the Plague." *BICS* 16: 106–18.

Paschalis, S. 2015. *Tragic Palimpsests*, Harvard University, Ph.D. Dissertation.

Passavant, P. A. 2021. *Policing Protest: The Post-Democratic State and the Figure of Black Insurrection*. Durham, NC.

Pennesi, A. 2008. *I frammenti della* Niobe *di Eschilo*. Amsterdam.

Peponi, A.-E. 2018. "Lyric Atmospheres: Plato and Mimetic Evanescence." In *Music, Text, and Culture in Ancient Greece*, edited by T. Phillips and A. D'Angour, 163–82. Oxford.

Peradotto, J. J. 1969. "The Omen of the Eagles and the HΘΟΣ of *Agamemnon*." *Phoenix* 23.3: 237–63.

Perera, S., and J. Pugliese. 2011. "Introduction: Combat Breathing: State Violence and the Body in Question." *Somatechnics* 1.1: 1–14.

Perga, T. 2022. "Ecocide in Ukraine: How Russia's War Will Poison the Country (and Europe) for Decades to Come." https://blog.degruyter.com/ecocide-in-ukraine-how-russias-war-will-poison-the-country-and-europe-for-decades-to-come.

Pinault, J. R. 1986. "How Hippocrates Cured the Plague." *Journal of the History of Medicine and Allied Sciences* 41.1: 52–75.

Pizzo, J. 2014. "Esther's Ether: Atmospheric Character in Charles Dickens's *Bleak House*." *Victorian Literature and Culture* 42.1: 81–98.

Podolsky, R. 1991. "Sacrificing Queer and Other 'Proletarian' Artifacts." *Radical America* 25.1: 53–60.

Pollard, C. 2022. *Delphi: A Novel*. New York.

Porter, J. I. 1986. *The Material Sublime: Towards a Reconstruction of a Materialist Critical Discourse and Aesthetics in Antiquity*. UC Berkeley, Comparative Literature Ph.D. Dissertation.

Porter, J. I. 2003. "Lucretius and the Poetics of Void." In *Le jardin romain: Épicurisme et poésie à Rome. Mélanges offerts à Mayotte Bollack*, edited by A. Monet, 197–226. Villeneuve d'Ascq.

Porter, J. I. 2016. *The Sublime in Antiquity*. Cambridge.

Povinelli, E. 2016. *Geontologies: A Requiem to Late Capitalism*. Durham, NC.

Povinelli, E. 2020. "Virus: Figure and Infrastructure." *e-flux* https://www.e-flux.com/architecture/sick-architecture/352870/the-virus-figure-and-infrastructure/

Povinelli, E. 2021. *Between Gaia and Ground: Four Axioms of Existence and the Ancestral Catastrophe of Late Liberalism*. Durham, NC.

Povinelli, E., et al. 2017. "An Interview with Elizabeth Povinelli: Geontopower, Biopolitics, and the Anthropocene." *Theory, Culture & Society* 34.2–3: 169–85.

Prabhu, A. 2006. "Narration in Frantz Fanon's *Peau noire, masques blancs*: Some Reconsiderations." *Research in African Literatures* 37.4: 189–210.

Press, A. 2022. "Broken Horses and Broken Heroes: The Last Word of the *Iliad*." *CW* 115.3: 213–23.

Provenza, A. 2019. "The Myth of Io and Female Cyborgic Identity." In *Classical Literature and Posthumanism*, edited by G. M. Chiesi and F. Spiegel, 211–16. London.

Puar, J. K. 2017. *The Right to Maim: Debility/Capacity/Disability*. Durham, NC.

Puar, J. K. 2021. "Spatial Debilities: Slow Life and Carceral Capitalism in Palestine." *SAQ* 120.2: 393–414.

Pucci, P. 1979. "On the 'Eye' and the 'Phallos' and Other Permutabilities in *Oedipus Rex*." In *Arktouros: Hellenic Studies Presented to B. M. W. Knox*, edited by G. W. Bowersock, W. Burkert, and M. C. J. Putnam, 130–33. Berlin.

Pucci, P. 1992. *Oedipus and the Fabrication of the Father*. Baltimore.

Pugliese, J. 2004. "The Incommensurability of Law to Justice: Refugees and Australia's Temporary Protection Visa." *Law and Literature* 16.3: 285–311.

Pugliese, J. 2020. *Biopolitics of the More-Than-Human: Forensic Ecologies of Violence*. Durham, NC.

Purves, A. 2010. "Wind and Time in Homeric Epic." *TAPA* 140.2: 323–50.

Purves, A. 2013. "Thick Description: From Auerbach to the Boar's Lair (*Od.* 19.388–475)." In *Geography, Topography, Landscape: Configurations of Space in Greek and Roman Epic*, edited by M. Skempis and I. Ziogas, 37–62. Berlin.

Purves, A. 2019. *Homer and the Poetics of Gesture*. Oxford.

Quayson, A. 2021. *Tragedy and Postcolonial Literature*. Cambridge.

Rabinowitz, N. S. 1993. *Anxiety Veiled: Euripides and the Traffic in Women*. Ithaca, NY.

Rahman, E., and B. Brabec de Mori. 2020. "Breathing Song and Smoke: Ritual Intentionality and the Sustenance of an Interaffective Realm." *Body & Society* 26.2: 130–57.

Ramsay, G. 2019. "Time and the Other in Crisis: How Anthropology Makes Its Displaced Object." *Anthropological Theory* 20.4: 385–413.

Rancière, J. 1999. *Disagreement*. Minneapolis.

Rancière, J. 2010. *Dissensus: On Politics and Aesthetics*. London.

Rancière, J. 2013. *Aisthesis: Scenes from the Aesthetic Regime of Art*. London.

Rankine, P. 2019. "The Classics, Race, and Community-Engaged or Public Scholarship." *AJP* 140.2: 345–59.

Rankine, P. 2021. "Touching the Body: Some Observations on Rights, Punishment, and Justice, with Reference to Prometheus, Emmett Till, and George Floyd." https://visitbristol.co.uk/whats-on/the-2021-morse-lecture-with-prof-patrice-rankine-p2928983.

Reed, R. R. 2007. "The Restorative Power of Sound: A Case for Communal Catharsis in Toni Morrison's *Beloved*." *Journal of Feminist Studies in Religion* 23.1: 55–71.

Rich, A. 1986a. "Compulsory Heterosexuality and Lesbian Existence." *Signs* 5.4: 631–60.

Rich, A. 1986b. *Of Woman Born: Motherhood as Experience and Institution*. New York.

Rifkin, M. 2022. "Beyond Family: Kinship's Past, Queer World Making, and the Question of Governance." In *Queer Kinship: Race, Sex, Belonging, Form*, edited by T. Bradway and E. Freeman, 138–58. Durham, NC.

Rimell, V. 2015. *Closure of Space in Roman Poetics: Empire's Inward Turn*. Cambridge.

Rimell, V. 2020. "The Intimacy of Wounds: Care of the Other in Seneca's *Consolatio ad Helviam*." *AJP* 141.4: 537–74.

Rimell, V. 2024. "Philosophers' Stone: Enduring Niobe." In *Niobes: Antiquity Modernity Critical Theory*, edited by M. Telò and A. Benjamin. Columbus, OH.

Robinson, W. I. 2022. *Global Civil War: Capitalism Post-Pandemic*. Oakland.

Rogatchevski, A. 2021. "Extractivism as Rebordering: Dmitrii Savochkin's *Mark Sheider*, Russo-Ukrainian Mining Literature, and the Fragmentation of Post-Soviet Ukraine." *Textual Practice* 35.3: 467–84.

Roy, P. 2021. "On Being Meat." In *Meat! A Transnational Analysis*, edited by S. Chatterjee and B. Subramaniam, 162–93. Durham, NC.

Roynon, T. 2013. *Toni Morrison and the Classical Tradition: Transforming American Culture*. Oxford.

Ruffell, I. 2012. *Aeschylus: Prometheus Bound*. London.

Ruffell, I. 2022. "*Bacchae*—'An Excessively High Price to Pay for Being Reluctant to Emerge from the Closet?': A Trans Reading." In *Queer Euripides: Re-Readings in Greek Tragedy*, edited by S. Olsen and M. Telò, 239–48. London.

Ruiz, S. 2019. *Ricanness: Enduring Time in Anticolonial Performance*. New York.

Sabsay, L. 2016. "Permeable Bodies: Vulnerability, Affective Powers, Hegemony." In *Vulnerability in Resistance*, edited by J. Butler, Z. Gambetti, and L. Sabsay, 278–303. Durham, NC.

Saghafi, K. 2020. *The World after the End of the World: A Spectro-Poetics*. Albany, NY.

Saha, P. 2019. *An Empire of Touch: Women's Political Labor and the Fabrication of East Bengal*. New York.

Said, E. 2007. *On Late Style: Music and Literature against the Grain*. New York.

Saint-Amour, P. K. 2022. "Afterword: Necessary–Impossible and Responsible–Irresponsible Reading." In *Modernism, Theory, and Responsible Reading: A Critical Conversation*, edited by S. Ross, 225–33. London.

Sanyal, D. 2019. "Humanitarian Detention and Figures of Persistence at the Border." *Critical Times* 2.3: 435–65.

Sanyal, D. 2020. "The Virus and the Plague: Albert Camus on Covid-19." https://bullybloggers.wordpress.com/2020/03/27/the-virus-and-the-plague-albert-camus-on-covid-19.

Sanyal, D. 2021. "Race, Migration, and Security at the Euro-African Border." *Theory & Event* 24.1: 324–55.

Sanyal, D. 2023. "Wayward Voices: Chorus, Improvisation, and Upheaval in . . . (Iphigenia)." In *Shorter and spalding's . . . (Iphigenia)*, edited by H. Morales and M. Telò. *Ramus*.

Sanyal, D. forthcoming. *Arts of the Border: Displacement at the Edges of Europe*. Durham, NC.

Sanyal, D., M. Telò, and D. R. Young. 2022. "Proximities." In *Proximities: Reading with Judith Butler*, edited by D. Sanyal, M. Telò, and D. R. Young, *Representations* 158.1: 1–16.

Sarasin, P. 2008. "Vapors, Viruses, Resistance(s): The Trace of Infection in the Work of Michel Foucault." In *Networked Disease: Emerging Infections in the Global City*, edited by H. S. Ali and R. Keil, 267–80. Malden, MA.

Scanlon, T. 2018. "Achilles and the Apobates Race in Euripides' *Iphigenia in Aulis*." *Classics@* https://classical-inquiries.chs.harvard.edu/achilles-and-the-apobates-race-in-euripides-iphigeneia-in-aulis/

Scheler, M. 1954. "On the Tragic." Translated by B. Stambler. *Cross Currents* 4.2: 178–91.

Schiesaro, A. 1993. "Il *locus horridus* nelle *Metamorfosi* di Apuleio." *Maia* 37: 211–23.

Schultz, N. 2021. "The Climactic Virus in an Age of Paralysis." *Critical Inquiry* 47.2: 9–12.

Schwab, K., and T. Malleret. 2022. *The Great Narrative for a Better Future*. Cologny.

Schwartz, M. 2015. *Dead Matter: The Meaning of Iconic Corpses*. Minneapolis.

Scott, Dariek. 2010. *Extravagant Abjection: Blackness, Power, and Sexuality in African American Literary Imagination*. New York.

Scott, David. 2004. *Conscripts of Modernity: The Tragedy of Colonial Enlightenment*. Durham, NC.

Scott, J. W. 2022. "The Job of Critical Thinking Now." In *The Long Year: A 2020 Reader*, edited by T. J. Sugrue and C. Zaloom, 53–58. New York.

Seaford, R., ed. 1996. *Euripides: Bacchae*. Warminster.

Seaford, R. 2005. "Death and Wedding in Aeschylus' *Niobe*." In *Lost Dramas of Classical Athens: Greek Tragic Fragments*, edited by F. McHardy, J. Robson, and D. Harvey, 113–27. Exeter.

Sedgwick, E. K. 1985. *Between Men: English Literature and Male Homosocial Desire*. New York.

Sedgwick, E. K. 2011. *The Weather in Proust*. Durham, NC.

Segal, C. 1996. *Sophocles' Tragic World: Divinity, Nature, Society*. Cambridge, MA.

Segal, C. 1997. *Dionysiac Poetics and Euripides'* Bacchae. Princeton, NJ.

Segal, C. 1999. *Tragedy and Civilization: An Interpretation of Sophocles*. Norman, OK.

Segal, C. 1999–2000. "Lament and Recognition: A Reconsideration of the Ending of the *Bacchae*." *ICS* 24–25: 273–91.

Seidel, F. 1999. "James Baldwin in Paris." *The Paris Review* 150: 66.

Seidensticker, B. 2016. "The Figure of Teiresias in Euripides' *Bacchae*." In *Wisdom and Folly in Euripides*, edited by P. Kyriakou and A. Rengakos, 275–83. Berlin.

Serpell, N. 2020. *Stranger Faces*. Oakland.

Sevieri, R. 2010. "La forma del dolore: le immagini vascolari apule relative al mito di Niobe." In *Le immagini nel testo, il testo nelle immagini: rapporti fra parola e visualità nella tradizione greco-latina*, edited by L. Belloni et al., 197–240. Trento.

Shah, P. 1998. "Transcending Gender in the Performance of Kathak." *Dance Research Journal* 30.2: 2–17.

Sharma, N. 2020. "The Global Covid-19 Pandemic and the Need to Change Who We Think 'We' Are." *Theory & Event* 23.4: 19–29.

Sharpe, C. 2016. *In the Wake: On Blackness and Being*. Durham, NC.

Shaw, C. 2014. *Satyric Play: The Evolution of Greek Comedy and Satyr Drama*. Oxford.

Sheldon, R. 2019. "Accelerationism's Queer Occulture." *Angelaki* 24.1: 118–29.

Shirazi, A. 2022. "Glimpses of Gesture: Refusing and Recovering Loss in Honig and Euripides." *CA* 141.2: 16–24.

Shoptaw, J. 2000. "Lyric Cryptography." *Poetics Today* 21.1: 221–62.

Sicking, C. M. J. 1998. "Admetus's Case." In *Distant Companions: Selected Papers*, 48–62. Leiden.

Sienkewicz, T. J. 1984. "The Chorus of *Prometheus Bound*: Harmony of Suffering." *Ramus* 13.1: 60–73.

Sigley, I. 2020. "It Has Touched Us All: Commentary on the Social Implications of Touch during the Covid-19 Pandemic." *Social Sciences and Humanities Open* 2. https://www.ncbi.nlm.nih.gov/pmc/articles/PMC7380212.

Singh, J. 2017. *Unthinking Mastery: Dehumanism and Decolonial Entanglements*. Durham, NC.

Slater, N. W. 1989. "*Lekythoi* in Aristophanes' *Ecclesiazusae*." *Lexis* 3: 43–51.

Smith, Z. 2020. *Intimations*. London.

Smithson, R. 1996. *The Collected Writings*. Berkeley.

Sokoloff, W. W. 2005. "Between Justice and Legality: Derrida on Decision." *Political Research Quarterly* 58.2: 341–52.

Sontag, S. 2001. *Illness as Metaphor and AIDS and Its Metaphors*. New York.

Soyinka, W. 1974. *The Bacchae of Euripides: A Communion Rite*. New York.

Spaeth, B. S. 1994. "The Goddess Ceres in the Ara Pacis Augustae and the Carthage Relief." *AJA* 98.1: 65–100.

Spigner, N. A. 2021. "Phillis Wheatley's Niobean Poetics." In *Brill's Companion to Classics in the Early Americas*, edited by M. Feile Tomes, A. J. Goldwyn, and M. E. Duquès, 320–42. Leiden.

Spillers, H. 1987. "Mama's Baby, Papa's Maybe: An American Grammar Book." *Diacritics* 17.2: 64–81.

Spillers, H. 2020. "Critical Theory in Times of Crisis." *SAQ* 119.4: 681–83.

Spitzer, L. 1942. "Milieu and Ambiance." *Philosophy and Phenomenological Research* 3.2: 1–42, 169–218.

Starks, B. 2021. "The Double Pandemic: Covid-19 and White Supremacy." *Qualitative Social Work* 20.1–2: 222–24.

Steiner, H., and K. Veel. 2021. *Touch in the Time of Corona: Reflections on Love, Care, and Vulnerability in the Pandemic*. Berlin.

Stengers, I. 2015. *In Catastrophic Times: Resisting the Coming Barbarism*. London.

Stevens, B. 2009. "*Per Gestum Res Est Significanda Mihi*: Ovid and Language in Exile." *CP* 104.2: 162–83.

Stewart, K. 2011. "Atmospheric Attunements." *Environment and Planning D: Society and Space* 29.3: 445–53.

Stieber, M. 1998. "Statuary in Euripides' *Alcestis*." *Arion* (ser. 3) 5.3: 69–97.

Stiegler, B. 1998. *Technics and Time, 1: The Fault of Epimetheus*. Stanford, CA.

Stryker, S. 1994. "My Words to Victor Frankenstein above the Village of Chamounix: Performing Transgender Rage." *GLQ* 1.3: 237–54.

Stryker, S. 2015. "Transing the Queer (In)Human." *GLQ* 21.2–3: 227–30.

Sullivan, S. 2020. "Ontological Expansiveness." In *50 Concepts for a Critical Phenomenology*, edited by G. Weiss, A. V. Murphy, and G. Salamon, 249–54. Evanston, IL.

Swift, L. 2010. *The Hidden Chorus: Echoes of Genre in Tragic Lyric*. Oxford.

Szeman, I. 2020. "Ends." In *Anthropocene Unseen: A Lexicon*, edited by C. Howe and A. Pandian, 145–49. Goleta, CA.

Szendy, P. 2021. "Viral Times." *Critical Inquiry* 47.2: 63–67.

Tanner, G. 2016. *Babbling Corpse: Vaporwave and the Commodification of Ghosts*. Winchester, UK.

Taplin, O. 1972. "Aeschylean Silences and Silences in Aeschylus." *HSCP* 76: 57–97.

Taplin, O. 1977. *The Stagecraft of Aeschylus*. Oxford.

Taplin, O. 1996. "Comedy and the Tragic." In *Tragedy and the Tragic: Greek Theatre and Beyond*, edited by M. S. Silk, 188–202. Oxford.

Taplin, O. 2007. *Pots & Plays: Interactions between Tragedy and Greek Vase-Painting of the Fourth Century B. C*. Los Angeles.

Taplin, O. 2022. "Tragedy in the Time of Plague." *Arion* (ser. 3) 30.1: 31–40.

Taylor, J. O. 2016. *The Sky of Our Manufacture: The London Fog in British Fiction from Dickens to Woolf*. Charlottesville.

Taxidou, O. 2004. *Tragedy, Modernity, and Mourning*. Edinburgh.

Telò, M. 2002. "Per una grammatica dei gesti nella tragedia greca (II): la supplica." *MD* 49: 9–51.

Telò, M. 2016. *Aristophanes and the Cloak of Comedy: Affect, Aesthetics, and the Canon*. Chicago.

Telò, M. 2017. "Reperformance, Exile, and Archive Feelings: Rereading Aristophanes' *Acharnians* and Sophocles' *Oedipus at Colonus*." In *Imagining Reperformance in Ancient Culture*, edited by R. Hunter and A. Uhlig, 87–110. Cambridge.

Telò, M. 2019. "Iambic Horror: Shivers and Brokenness in Archilochus and Hipponax." In *The Genres of Archaic and Classical Greek Poetry: Theories and Models*, edited by M. Forster, L. Kurke, and N. Weiss, 271–96. Leiden.

Telò, M. 2020a. "Between Emotion and the Emetic: Francis Bacon and the Tragic Body at the Margins of the *Oresteia*." *Literary Imagination* 22.2: 109–20.

Telò, M. 2020b. *Archive Feelings: A Theory of Greek Tragedy*. Columbus, OH.

Telò, M. 2022. "*Suppliant Women*—Adrastus' Cute Lesbianism: Labor Irony Adhesion." In *Queer Euripides: Re-Readings in Greek Tragedy*, edited by S. Olsen and M. Telò, 86–98. London.

Telò, M. 2023a. *Resistant Form: Aristophanes and the Comedy of Crisis*. Goleta, CA.

Telò, M. 2023b. "Foucault, Oedipus, and Virality." *symplokê* 30.1–2.

Telò, M., and S. Olsen. 2022. "Queer Euripides: An Introduction." In *Queer Euripides: Re-Readings in Greek Tragedy*, edited by S. Olsen and M. Telò, 1–18. London.

Terada, R. 2007. "Seeing Is Reading." In *Legacies of Paul de Man*, edited by M. Redfield, 162–78. New York.

Thacker, E. 2011. *In the Dust of this Planet*. Winchester, UK.

The Care Collective. 2020. *The Care Manifesto*. London.

The Postclassicisms Collective. 2020. *Postclassicisms*. Chicago.

Thivel, A. 2005. "Air, Pneuma, and Breathing from Homer to Hippocrates." In *Hippocrates in Context*, edited by P. J. Van der Eijk, 239–50. Leiden.

Ticktin, M. 2021. "Building a Feminist Commons in the Time of Covid-19." *Signs* 47.1.
    https://www.journals.uchicago.edu/doi/abs/10.1086/715445?journalCode=signs.
Toadvine, T. 2018. "Thinking after the World: Deconstruction and Last Things." In
    Eco-Deconstruction: Derrida and Environmental Philosophy, edited by M. Fritsch,
    P. Lynes, and D. Wood, 50–80. New York.
Toadvine, T. 2020. "Geomateriality." In *50 Concepts for a Critical Phenomenology*, edited by
    G. Weiss, A. V. Murphy, and G. Salamon, 149–54. Evanston, IL.
Torrance, I. 2013. *Metapoetry in Euripides*. Oxford.
Toscano, A. 2018. "Antiphysis/Antipraxis: Universal Exhaustion and the Tragedy of
    Materiality." *Mediations* 31.2: 125–44.
Toscano, A. 2020. "The State of the Pandemic." *Historical Materialism* 28.4: 3–23.
Tremblay, J.-T. 2022. *Breathing Aesthetics*. Durham, NC.
Tzanetou, A. 2011. "Supplication and Empire in Athenian Empire." In *Why Athens?
    A Reappraisal of Tragic Politics*, edited by D. M. Carter, 305–24. Oxford.
Uhlig, A. 2019. *Theatrical Reenactment in Pindar and Aeschylus*. Cambridge.
Uhlig, A. 2020. "Dancing on the Plain of the Sea: Gender and Theatrical Space in
    Aeschylus' Achilleis Trilogy." In *Female Characters in Fragmentary Greek Tragedy*,
    edited by P. J. Finglass and L. Coo, 105–24. Cambridge.
Umachandran, M. 2022. "Disciplinecraft: Toward an Anti-Racist Classics." *TAPA* 152.1: 25–31.
Umachandran, M. 2024. "Niobe between Benjamin and Arendt—and Beyond." In *Niobes:
    Antiquity Modernity Critical Theory*, edited by M. Telò and A. Benjamin. Columbus, OH.
van der Ploeg, I. 2005. *The Machine-Readable Body: Essays on Biometrics and the
    Informatization of the Body*. Maastricht.
Vernant, J.-P. 1978. "Ambiguity and Reversal: On the Enigmatic Structure of *Oedipus Rex*."
    NLH 9.3: 475–501.
Vernant, J.-P. 2003. "Frontality and Monstrosity." In *The Medusa Reader*, edited by
    M. B. Garber and N. J. Vickers, 210–31. New York.
Vicuña, C. 2009. *The Precarious*. Hanover, NH.
Vizenor, G. 1998. *Fugitive Poses: Native American Indian Scenes of Absence and Presence*.
    Lincoln, NE.
Wagner, A. M. 2017. "*Mater dolorosa*: The Women of *Guernica*." In *Pity and Terror: Picasso's
    Path to* Guernica, 107–44. Madrid.
Walker, A. 1997. "Oedipal Narratives and the Exilic Ovid." *Ramus* 26.2: 194–204.
Wallace, J. 2020. *Tragedy Since 9/11*. London.
Ward, J. 2020. *The Tragedy of Heterosexuality*. New York.
Warren, C. 2018. *Ontological Terror: Blackness, Nihilism, and Emancipation*. Durham, NC.
Warren, C. 2021. "Barred Objects (Θ): Police Brutality, Black Fetishes, and Perverse
    Demonstrations." *The Comparatist* 45: 29–40.
Weaver, H. 2014. "Trans Species." *TSQ* 1.1–2: 253–54.
Weheliye, A. G. 2014. *Habeas Viscus: Racializing Assemblages, Biopolitics, and Black
    Feminist Theories of the Human*. Durham, NC.
Weiberg, E. 2022. Review of M. Telò, *Archive Feelings: A Theory of Greek Tragedy*
    (Columbus, OH 2020). *CP* 117.4: 753–58.
Weiss, A. S. 2002. *Breathless: Sound Recording, Disembodiment, and the Transformation of
    Lyrical Nostalgia*. Middletown, CT.

Weiss, N. 2017. *The Music of Tragedy: Performance and Imagination in Euripidean Theater.* Oakland.

Wheatley, P. 1988. *The Collected Works,* edited by J. Shields. Oxford.

White, H. 1978. *Metahistory: The Historical Imagination in Nineteenth-Century Europe.* Baltimore.

White, S. 2001. "Io's World: Intimations of Theodicy in *Prometheus Bound." JHS* 121: 107–40.

Whyte, K. 2020. "Collective Continuance." In *50 Concepts for a Critical Phenomenology,* edited by G. Weiss, A. V. Murphy, and G. Salamon, 53–60. Evanston, IL.

Wiles, D. 2007. *Mask and Performance in Greek Tragedy: From Ancient Festival to Modern Experimentation.* Cambridge.

Willis, E. 2014. *Theatricality, Dark Tourism and Ethical Spectatorship.* Basingstoke.

Wills, D. 2016. *Inanimation: Theories of Inorganic Life.* Minneapolis.

Wohl, V. 1993. "Standing by the Stathmos: The Creation of Sexual Ideology in the *Odyssey." Arethusa* 26.1: 19–50.

Wohl, V. 1998. *Intimate Commerce: Exchange, Gender, and Subjectivity in Greek Tragedy.* Austin, TX.

Wohl, V. 2005. "Beyond Sexual Difference: Becoming-Woman in Euripides' *Bacchae."* In *The Soul of Tragedy: Essays on Athenian Drama,* edited by V. Pedrick and S. M. Oberhelman, 137–54. Chicago.

Wohl, V. 2009a. "Sexual Difference and the Aporia of Justice in Sophocles' *Antigone."* In *Bound by the City: Greek Tragedy, Sexual Difference, and the Formation of the Polis,* edited by D. E. McCoskey and E. Zakin, 119–48. Albany, NY.

Wohl, V. 2009b. "*Suppliant Women* and the Democratic State: White Men Saving Brown Women from Brown Men." In *When Worlds Elide: Classics, Politics, Culture,* edited by K. Bassi and P. Euben, 409–35. Lanham, MD.

Wohl, V. 2015. *Euripides and the Politics of Form.* Princeton.

Wohl, V. 2018. "Stone into Smoke: Metaphor and Materiality in Euripides' *Troades."* In *The Materialities of Greek Tragedy: Objects and Affect in Aeschylus, Sophocles, and Euripides,* edited by M. Telò and M. Mueller, 17–34. London.

Wohl, V. 2022. "The Aporia of Action and the Agency of Form in Euripides' *Iphigeneia in Aulis."* In *The Politics of Form in Greek Literature,* edited by P. Vasunia, 65–82. London.

Wojnarowicz, D. 1989. *In the Shadow of Forward Motion, Notes by Félix Guattari.* Paris.

Wojnarowicz, D. 1991. *Close to the Knives: A Memoir of Disintegration.* New York.

Woolford, J. 2012. "The Genesis of *Balaustion's Adventure." Victorian Poetry* 50.4: 563–81.

Worman, N. 2020a. "Euripides and the Aesthetics of Embodiment." In *Brill's Companion to Euripides,* edited by A. Markantonatos, 749–74. Leiden.

Worman, N. 2020b. *Tragic Bodies: Edges of the Human in Greek Drama.* London.

Wyatt, J. 1993. "Giving Body to the Word: The Maternal Symbolic in Toni Morrison's *Beloved." PMLA* 108.3: 474–88.

Youd, D. 2022. "*Orestes*—Polymorphously Per-verse: On Queer Metrology." In *Queer Euripides: Re-readings in Greek Tragedy,* edited by S. Olsen and M. Telò, 155–64. London.

Young, D. R. 2020. "Safe Spaces." https://bullybloggers.wordpress.com/2020/03/25/safe-spaces.

Yusoff, K. 2013. "Geologic Life: Prehistory, Climate, Futures in the Anthropocene."
    Environment and Planning D: Society and Space 31.5: 779–95.
Yusoff, K. 2015. "Geologic Subjects: Nonhuman Origins, Geomorphic Aesthetics, and the
    Art of Becoming *Inhuman*." *Cultural Geographies* 22.3: 383–407.
Yusoff, K. 2018. *A Billion Black Anthropocenes or None*. Minneapolis.
Zeavin, H. 2021. "Hot and Cool Mothers." *differences* 32.3: 53–84.
Zeitlin, F. I. 1995. "Art, Memory, and *Kleos* in Euripides' *Iphigenia in Aulis*." In *History,
    Tragedy, Theory: Dialogues on Athenian Drama*, edited by B. E. Goff, 174–201. Austin,
    TX.
Zeitlin, F. I. 1996. *Playing the Other: Gender and Society in Classical Greek Literature*.
    Chicago.
Zhang, D. 2018. "Notes on Atmosphere." *Qui Parle* 27.1: 121–55.
Zhang, D. 2020. *Strange Likeness: Description and the Modernist Novel*. Chicago.
Zierler, D. 2011. *Invention of Ecocide: Agent Orange, Vietnam, and the Scientists Who
    Changed the Way We Think about the Environment*. Athens, GA.
Žižek, S. 2021a. *Pandemic! 2: Chronicles of a Time Lost*. Cambridge.
Žižek, S. 2021b. "Is Barbarism with a Human Face Our Fate?" *Critical Inquiry* 47.2: 4–8.

Index

Page numbers in **bold** refer to figures